Hartmann
von Aue

SUSAN L. CLARK

Hartmann von Aue

Landscapes of Mind

RICE UNIVERSITY PRESS

Houston, Texas

Copyright © 1989 by Rice University Press
All rights reserved
First Edition, 1989
Printed in the United States of America
Requests for permission to reproduce material
from this work should be addressed to
Rice University Press
P. O. Box 1892
Houston, Texas 77251

Library of Congress Catalog Card Number 89-43285
ISBN 0-89263-270-4

For Charles Lovekin and Miriam and R. W. Clark

CONTENTS

Introduction / 1

1. *Die Klage*: A Mind in Conflict / 8

2. *Erec*: Language, Perception, and Mind / 46

3. "ir wizzet wol": Knowledge in *Gregorius* / 90

4. *Der arme Heinrich*: Admonition and Expectation / 121

5. *Iwein*: Strife and Landscape of the Mind / 166

Summary / 199

Editions and Translations / 201

Notes / 216

ACKNOWLEDGMENTS

Sincere thanks go to the people who have fostered my love for medieval studies over the years and have supported me emotionally: the late Fred Oppermann of Mount Union College; Marlene Ciklamini of Rutgers University; my dissertation director, the late W. T. H. Jackson of Columbia University; Hugo Bekker of The Ohio State University; Hubert Heinen of the University of Texas at Austin; Rice colleagues Jane Chance, Graciela Daichman, Linn Konrad, Elizabeth Long, and Deborah Nelson; former colleagues Beverly Harris-Schenz, Deborah Modrak, Elizabeth Sanders, and Mary Rawlinson; former students Vincent Uher, Ian Hersey, Jeanne Cooper, Dennis Clark, Robert Ritner, Matthew Noall, Carolyn Dahl Reese, and Candace Barrington Waldrop; my Chairperson, Ewa Thompson; Dean Allen Matusow; and especially the staff of Rice University Press, who kindly and firmly worked to hone my manuscript.

INTRODUCTION

Hartmann von Aue wrote Middle High German lyric and epic poetry around the year 1200. From what can be extrapolated from his verses and taken for granted by his titular status, he was a landless knight—that is, a *ministerialis*—but who nevertheless had other, less tangible but more lasting intellectual goods in his possession: considerable book-learning, command of several languages, a strong and quirkish sense of humor, and tremendous insight into how people of all ages—and within different historical ages—function. He tells the reader/listener family legends, tales of the Age of Arthur and of past popes, and makes them live by employing an understanding of how people both seek out new and different experiences and respond to crises of joy as well as pain.

This study treats the works of a man who lived in a time far removed from our own, and I must state at the outset that it bears my individual imprint: in it are the observations of a modern woman writer from the Northeast—transplanted to Texas—who reads older languages, critiques books for literary journals, and moonlights by reviewing mystery novels and women's literature. I am that writer and that reader, and my small bit of biography is necessary to this introduction. I have always loved older languages, works that feature strong women and male/female relationships, and mysteries. Further, I understand the "stranger in a strange land" *topos* that informs medieval romance, where each turn in the path offers danger and opportunity, as well as the "what's missing?" premise that underlies much feminist interpretation and mystery fiction criticism. Hartmann offers me texts that strike personal resonances as well as provide an occasional dead body.

Writers of literary criticism, whether they focus on medieval or modern literature, admit that they find reasons for choosing to write about *this* as opposed to *that* author or for examining one facet of an author's works. Critics accordingly can give seemingly objective but ultimately idiosyncratic justifications for elevating one writer or theme, while disregarding other equally important authors or topics.

I believe that when one decides to be a critic, one enters a profession in which one literally picks and chooses but in which one must know a great deal of background in order to make sense of detail. I further believe that this is a profession in which attention to detail can illuminate an entire literary-historical picture, where the recognition and identification of one theme can make sense of a writer's entire work.

My own history as a critic and reviewer has given and continues to give me a background against which to view how the Western literary canon evolved and continues to expand, a perspective that ever widens, just as I see how opportunities have been limited for women writers. Moreover, given the way in which academic endeavors function, choice *is* limited by those who have access to the pen and who have the tools to read what has been put down by the pen. Clearly patronage, dissemination, and reception have functioned as "given" authorities, in the guise of the Church Fathers, a medieval *scriptorium* clerk, a Renaissance printing press owner, a modern publisher, or a book reviewer. The media decide what receives publicity, and the canon is ever being re-formed. Not only writing but also teaching change the shape of the canon, for the chance to teach older literature, to discuss it with students and colleagues, offers a window into past and present literature and an opportunity to reflect on how people think about what they think. In my own case, subjects for investigation come from books or articles suggested by colleagues, references to interesting authors, conference papers, off-prints, and reading proclivities sustained over the years by friends.

And inspiration may come from chance encounters, as it certainly has in writing this book. No one "introduced" me to Hartmann von Aue (as I was "introduced" to my dissertation topic, or as one reference in scholarly literature necessarily leads to another), and no one recommended Hartmann to me as one of the "don't miss" authors of the German Middle Ages, giants such as Gottfried von Straßburg, Wolfram von Eschenbach, or Walther von der Vogelweide. Nor did I seek Hartmann out for pleasure reading, as I have sought out other writers in the field. But in teaching Hartmann in an introductory Middle High German course, I found him not only disarming—he *seems* so straightforward—but also unusually intriguing, because he imbeds meaning, employs irony, and treats the relationships between the sexes in a complex and fully realized way. Medieval audiences clearly valued him for his subject matter and technique—witness Gottfried von Straßburg's praise of him in the literary excursus in *Tristan*—but modern audiences can easily appreciate his analyses of courtship and marriage, work and home-life, indecision and decision, sickness and wellness, and life and death. Since Hartmann speaks with such an astonishing directness, with a mixture of complexity and simplicity, his voice is such that a modern and generalist audience can appreciate and learn from him initially without extensive study and subsequently with training that gives full access to the language of his well-crafted verse. In my case, teaching his texts set the hook—and I was caught. The result is this book, which is directed not just to the specialist in Hartmann studies, but also to the medievalist interested in comparative literature, and, finally, to modern readers.

Individual but interrelated close readings of Hartmann von Aue's five longer poems—*Die Klage, Erec, Grêgôrius, Der arme Heinrich*, and *Iwein*—can best do justice to Hartmann's wisdom about relationships; in a sense, the relationships between the poems speaks to the individual relationships presented in them. I build my readings from the poems outward, whereas a number of critics have superimposed ideas and ideologies on the poems. Scholarly interest in Hartmann has quickened recently, but broad-based interpretative studies written in English are few. To be sure, comparisons between *Iwein* and *Erec* abound, and studies of sins of omission and commission in *Grêgôrius* and *Der arme Heinrich* are not lacking. Even *Die Klage* has a number of secondary works devoted to it or ones that treat it in passing. Yet few studies consider his entire work—and then chronology and antecedents are generally the focus—rather than themes and narrative technique.

Unlike Wolfram von Eschenbach and Gottfried von Straßburg, Hartmann has not received the attention he well deserves from critics writing lengthier studies in English and has not benefited until lately from the exposure that good English translations bring. With the recent publication of English translations of *Erec, Iwein*, and *Der arme Heinrich*, as with an earlier verse rendition of *Grêgôrius*,[1] students—and medievalists in different disciplines who lack fluency in Middle High German—have access to Hartmann's insights into the disparate ways of God and man, the convoluted and often volatile relationship between the sexes, and the literary interaction among the poetic *personae*, characters, and audience that goes on when a work of literature receives response from a reading/listening public.

The gap between Hartmann's "religious" and "courtly" works[2] is a distinction that critics have emphasized, but it is one, I contend, that the poet himself would not have noted. The poems' interrelated thematic sophistication has long been masked by Hartmann's surface lucidity and seemingly ready accessibility of meaning.[3] I argue that the workings of the human and divine minds create the singleness of purpose of which the poems' individual themes are manifestations, that concern to which Hartmann repeatedly returns. His fascination with the mind, in short, forms the glue that binds his longer poems together.[4]

Hartmann takes as his abiding and overriding concern the workings of the *mind*—and by mind shall be understood cerebral functions as well as the emotive and perceptual functions tied to mind—and translates mind into terms individual to each of his poems. Hartmann, more so than Gottfried or Wolfram, is occupied constantly with how characters think, how their minds and therefore their lives change, and how what they think they know is continually called into question. This occupation with mind expresses itself variously: for example, in the relationship among interior monologues, speech, and dialogues (*Erec*), in the loss and regaining of mind (*Iwein*), in the recurrent reference to what a character does or does not know (*Grêgôrius*), in the playing upon what the reader[5] "knows" and therefore has come to expect (*Der arme Heinrich*), and in the interior debates that are couched in terms of body ("lîp") and heart ("herze") (*Die Klage*). Each work is structured to reflect those various aspects of mind so that no scene is superfluous. Each scene works to restate the central issue, to reflect it in true or inverted fashion, or, through augmentation or modification, to show the mind in the very process of change. Hartmann is drawn to the idea of transformation, to the mechanics of change; and the mind in the process of imagination, willfulness, reflection, evaluation, memory, and penitence receives his repeated scrutiny.

Because the interior world of mind is tied in that particularly and delightfully medieval way to the exterior world of landscape, the journey each of Hartmann's protagonists willingly or unwillingly undertakes reflects the congruence of mental condition and physical geography.[6] Like Chrétien de Troyes, Hartmann imbues the turnings in the forest path and the obstacles (human and otherwise) encountered with a spiritual dimension: the rocky track in the woods, the ship's windy passage over the waves, and even the key-bearing fish's movements in the depths all reflect the journey the mind makes toward or away from God. It has long been recognized, and particularly since Auerbach's landmark study,[7] that directions obtain a spiritual significance for medieval writers (so that a turn to the left bodes moral ill, for example) and speak to the worth of an undertaking, yet Hartmann's understanding of the employment of psychic landscape goes much farther than mere compass directions. It extends not only to edifices, so that a castle serves as a metaphor of a mind assailed, but also to individuals, so that an opponent exhibits the characteristics of the unregenerate hero.

Orientation in Hartmann's complex physical landscape becomes the task of the hero, yet the reader, too, must find his/her bearings.[8] For the hero, understanding and progress become a matter of reflection upon his encounters and *âventiuren*, while, for the reader, the task is somewhat more complicated, because the reader participates, as no character in a literary work can, in the detached unfolding of the poet's argument. The hero can speculate about his fate and perhaps fathom the meaning of the way he has come once he has reached the end of his journey, but he cannot abstractly view the work's grand design, precisely because he is an integral part of that pattern. The reader, however, readies intellectual and emotional responses to each challenge posed by Hartmann through turns of plot, and he/she scrutinizes the work as an entity, only turning to self-examination once the work's meaning has been grasped. In short, the intellectual apprehension of the reader must be more finely honed than that of the hero. The hero experiences, thinks, and occasionally figures out his life-path. He determines where he is at that time and in that place and when he has a moment to reflect, because adventures usually come thick and fast, why he happens to be there. The reader, however, is not only invited to participate vicariously in the hero's adventures but also, more tellingly, with the poet in the process by which the work of literature comes to be. The reader examines the text/story line to recognize correspondences, divergences, and parallels, and to fit the pieces of the work into their places in the puzzle. Hartmann continually engages his reader in that process of reflection/understanding, for he often interrupts the narrative to question both characters' and narrators' motivations, as if to get the reader back on track or to lay to rest a nagging readerly doubt. The effect is, finally, that each of Hartmann's works exhibits, in the process of reading, the progress of a mind in the throes of self-examination, and, for the reader engaged in contemplating the work's design and execution, there emerges the picture of the author as a skilled creator, as a bringer of order, protestations of authorial inadequacy to the contrary.

Medieval romance literature shares with the literature of all periods and nations an active concern with mind, since it relates what goes on in characters' inner lives, and since it urges the reader to reflect while reading or listening. First, medieval literature gives a window into minds removed in time from its audience, and the sense is that the reader has access not only to what goes on *in* other minds, but also what goes on *outside* of one's own mind as a reader. Second, works of literature exercise readers' mental faculties, so that what obtains is a sense of mind looking at mind. What sets Hartmann's achievement apart, even cast against the general "given" background against which readers respond to literature, is his preoccupation not only with plots that tell the reader what occupies the characters' minds but also with the more abstract mechanics of how the mind works in and of itself as well as in tandem with the body. In this light Hartmann's use of what I shall call "mind-terms" is particularly telling. By mind-terms I mean those words ranging from explicit mental activity (such as, in Middle High German, the *denken, bedenken, gedenken* group and its derivations ("think, consider, reflect upon"), to knowledge (the *wizzen* group), to mental imaging (as, for example, *bilde*; "image, picture"), to casts of mind (*muot, sin*; "mind," "sense"), to perception-linked appearance (*schîn*; "appearance, look"), to evaluative reflection and assessment (*dünken*; "seems to be"), to advice (*rât*; "counsel," "advice," because those who know generally like to tell others what they know[9]), and finally to statements concerning others' assessment of one's mental abilities (*wîs, tump, tôr, kint*; "wise, experienced," "foolish, inexperienced," "fool," "child").[10] And when one notes Hartmann's further explicit concerns with those transformations that are tied to mind, the prevalence of terms such as *kêren, verkêren*, and *wandelbaere* ("to turn," "to make a change," and "changeable") makes good sense; the same can be said with respect to "obduracy" (*unwandelbaere*) or "constancy" (*staete*) and their derivatives. Just as each writer, be he/she medieval or modern, makes use of a particular set of vocabulary that overlaps that of contemporaries but retains its individuality, so Hartmann uses a high incidence of mind-terms precisely because they are, purely and simply, very much *on his mind*. I will spend little time on sources that may have contributed to Hartmann's understanding of mind, since they are poorly established and our knowledge about them is speculative. To focus on them detracts from the focus on Hartmann's *own* parameters of mind as well as those faculties he sees as related to mind. My intent is to suggest readings that are true to the individual poems as well as to the coherent concern of the body of Hartmann's work.[11]

A few words about my methodology and procedure seem in order. First, I do not adhere to the "critics on parade" school of academic writing, which means that references to other scholars will by and large be limited to the notes and to the bibliographical references. My focus is on the flow of the argument as it progresses over the text. Critical dragon-slaying is relegated to where it best belongs: in footnote wars. In addition, while we must consider how a "medieval" frame of mind received medieval texts, I feel that many critics who speak with certainty about what that frame of mind was are merely consciously or subconsciously echoing the constant medieval reliance on *auctoritas*. Often a modern reader's response to the text is overwhelmed by references to the *Patrologia latina* or Augustine or Bernard of Clairvaux and standard reference works. I find delight in these sources, but a middle ground approach seems better, not only because we cannot say with certainty what those "mislîchen buochen" ("diverse books") were upon which Hartmann based his works or who wrote them, but also because my approach to Hartmann does not demand the "antecedent model" favored by many medievalists today. Their papers and studies, though they are fascinating and deserve great respect, tend to ignore why we—twentieth-century readers—keep reading and enjoying medieval texts. The existence of a text over time of necessity engenders varying, and often equally valid, readings. We read medieval texts in the twentieth-century because they speak to us, albeit differently than to the audience of the twelfth or thirteenth centuries, with voices that are nevertheless penetrating and true to us now. We approach texts with a mixed perspective, so that our knowledge of the Church Fathers is tempered with a belief that many fundamental aspects of human nature remain constant over time. For example, my response to Hartmann's narrators' comments on woman's changeable nature draws from an historical knowledge of attitudes toward women, as well as insights derived from the growing field of women's studies, where women's roles, texts, and language come under scrutiny.

Furthermore, my stance is not to establish alternative sequences for the order of composition of the poems; I adhere to the accepted sequence,[12] except that I discuss *Iwein* as a whole in my last chapter, because its conclusion speaks convincingly to a progression apparent over the five poems. And I interpret Hartmann with a chronological perspective but nevertheless feel comfortable with accepting that a scene "looks forward" or "harks back" to other scenes within the work under discussion or to other of Hartmann's works. Finally, just as the writer knows which words are instinctively "right," I try as a critic to listen carefully to my intuitions, not just to trust the excitement felt when one has made sense of a difficult textual passage or an overall argument, but also to have the confidence to write, if necessary, "in a different voice."[13] If I exhibit "Stilbrüche" ("breaks in style"), I do so because Hartmann does so, and if I speak in the first person—for a long time a definite "no-no" in scholarly writing—I do so because Hartmann seems to have as little difficulty with that style as I do: it becomes my conscious interaction as critic with the text. Moreover, as an individual and as a woman scholar in America, my sense of language is unique. Over and above my foreign language competency, I have become multilingual in my own native language, in that I hear and use the standardized language of the male critical establishment, the student, the journalist, the regionalist, and a woman—this one. Recorded in a "Mischsprache" ("a mixed language"), my interpretation speaks to my own position as a woman writer who happens to know modern and medieval languages, Hartmann's own multiplicity of voices, and the very processes of experience, imagination, and conjecture. Like Hartmann, I, too, am fascinated with mind—how an artist's mind functions, how one learns and teaches, how other critics' judgments come to be made, and how my own assessments take their place in that chain of understanding, appreciation, and interpretation.

1

DIE KLAGE

A Mind in Conflict

In *Die Klage*, Hartmann's first poem in rhymed couplets, the poet presents the anatomy of a mind and analyzes the dissent that occurs in this mind. The literary format chosen is the debate poem, of which there are many in medieval literature, ranging from *Pearl* to the lay and clerical lovers' dispute in the *Carmina burana*, to the late medieval German *Ackermann aus Böhmen* (*The Ploughman from Bohemia* or *Death and the Ploughman*). Even the multiple interior monologue arguments in Chrétien de Troyes' works display that convention in microcosm.

Here the debate format is expressed through the time-honored, but in this case ultimately contrived, opposition of heart (*herze*) and body (*lîp*). The mind in *Die Klage* is one obsessively caught up in the process of decision-making, so that alternatives are tossed out for consideration, arguments by analogy are advanced, and consequences are weighed. The outer form of the debate genre, however, posits a diametrical opposition between the sparring partners and a necessary distance that Hartmann, unlike writers of other debate poems, in fact does not observe. For example, in *Pearl* the gap between the jeweler and the maiden narrows but never closes; in the *Ackermann* Death and the ploughman never see eye to eye. With *Die Klage*, however, the debaters do not restrict themselves to one side of the argument but actually incorporate both sides in their confrontation. Thus, Hartmann's heart, which often upholds rationality, nevertheless exhibits capriciousness, willfulness, and inconsistency, while the body, albeit highly emotional, reveals flashes of reason, sensibility, and cunning. It is not that one side, by dint of argument, wins the other over to its exclusive position, but rather that Hartmann shows the cooperation of all the faculties of mind in working its way out of a troubling problem, in finding an agreed-upon course of action, and in readying resolve so that action is possible. And because of the poem's direct dialogue format, there is immediate access to the functions of the mind,[1] in contrast to the third-person reporting of

Hartmann's narrative poems. To be sure, the opponents in *Die Klage* dissemble and put forth unsupported statements, but the absence of narrative action and the reliance on dialogue, on recorded thoughts, provide a unique window into Hartmann's concept of mind that the other works will not offer. The dialogue, unmediated by narrative action, is freed from the consequences that ensue when thoughts motivate actions, as well as bound by the limitations that obtain from the absence of consequences. The work is by its very nature solipsistic, while the narrative poems feature minds in conflict with each other. As such, *Die Klage* serves as the logical first work in the series due to its strictly defined scope; it establishes the various functions of mind that Hartmann later examines in detail.

The poem falls into four divisions, the first of which (ll. 1-484), after a thirty-two line introduction, features a lengthy speech by the body, the second of which (ll. 485-972) counters with an only marginally longer rejoinder by the heart, the third of which (ll. 973-1644) provides an alternating interchange between the two, and the fourth of which (ll. 1645-1914) constitutes a direct appeal, in a different rhyme pattern entirely, to the lady. In the process, the long monologues give way to a true dialogue—and one that is peppery in a way that the interchanges in *Erec* and *Iwein* are—and ultimately to a turning outward, in the fourth section, of the positions hammered out in the first three sections.[2] The thirty-two line introduction furnishes the circumstances against which the ensuing dialogue is to be seen: love has so overpowered a youth that he has offered his service to a lady who does not wish this burden. He suffers greatly in silence,[3] his plaint given voice by the poet, "der ouch dirre klage began / durch sus verswigen ungemach" (ll. 30-1; "who also took up this lament on account of unspoken pain"). Notable throughout these introductory lines is the emphasis on power and submission ("kraft"—l. 1; "force"; "sigehaft"—l. 2; "victorious"; "gewalteclichen"—l. 6; "powerfully"; "betwanc"—l. 7; "compelled"; "in ir gewalt ergeben"—l. 9; "to give over to her dominion"; "ir gebote"—l. 10; "her command"; "daz er ir waere undertan"—l. 15; "that he would be subject to her"; "sinen willen taete"—l. 22; "that [she] would do his will"), to be expected in medieval love terminology. This emphasis on power and on doing another's will runs throughout the poem, with body and heart continually jockeying for the upper hand in the argument.[4] Moreover, power is first an issue in the relationship between a man and a woman—so that he offers service while requiring "that she would do his will" (l. 22) and so that she reserves judgement (l. 16)—and subsequently a factor in the internal argument, so that the difference of opinion ("strit"—l. 18; "dispute, quarrel") between the man and the woman carried over into the heart-body debate:

> "Wer sol den strit nu scheiden
> under uns beiden"
> (ll. 411-2; "Who shall now resolve the dispute between the two of us?").

Thus, in prefacing the debate proper with an introduction that sets forth the two important concepts of power and conflict, Hartmann first shows *minds*, and then a *single* mind in conflict. There is a subtlety here that expands into a philosophy in Hartmann's longer works: the interior world of the protagonist's mind is not only influenced by external circumstances but also often reflects those circumstances. An external conflict engenders internal strife. And the presence of that internal strife guarantees the presence of the external conflict (the mind in concord finds harmonious relationships with other minds.) Finally, the protagonist's reticence ("disen kumberlichen strit / torst er nieman gesagen"—ll. 18-9; "he dared tell no one about this distressing quarrel") resonates in the difficulty with which the heart and body communicate: in short, the reluctance to trust in and confide in others accounts for the related initial uneasy interchange between the heart and body.

This uneasiness reveals itself in the verbs with which the body peppers its first speech. Subjunctives abound, and they are subjunctives indicating hypotheticality, rather than subjunctive forms required in certain grammatical constructions in Middle High German. Given this stress on hypotheticality, the frequent reference to the power possessed by the heart takes on significance, for both body and heart will later readily acknowledge the body's ability to bring death to the heart—as well as to itself in the process. It would seem that the body's opening speech becomes a veiled threat that is perfectly intelligible to the heart. Moreover, despite the body's protestations of powerlessness ("'daz ich [dinem gewalte] niht entwenken mac'"—l. 51; "'that I can't escape your control'"), the reader is quick to sense the power that derives from the name-calling and blame-laying in which the body promptly engages. True submission ought to produce silence. Ironically, there exists considerable strength in the outrage of the injured party, and the body exploits this in alternating evidence of its pain with proof of the heart's having caused it.

> ". . . wan dich wil nicht genüegen
> swaz du mir maht gefüegen
> nahe gender riuwe.
> daz ist ein untriuwe,

> sit du in mir gehuset hast
> und diu dinc an mir begast
> diu under friunden missezement,
> wan si mir freude gar benement"
>
> (ll. 53-60; "You are never satisfied with the amount of intense sorrow you have caused me. This is a betrayal, since you have resided in me, and do things that are inappropriate among friends, since these things take away all my happiness").

The "poor little me" stance masks the power that accrues from righteous indignation. And it also places the other party in a defensive mode.

In the next manuscript division the body reiterates its death threat, this time in the indicative mood. An additional indication that the body is striving to gain the upper hand through intimidation comes in its matter-of-fact and ominous comment to the heart that it is "'locked fast under my breast'" (ll. 64-5;). Previously the heart is said to have "'in mir gehuset'" (l. 57; "'have lived [housed] in me'"), which implies activity on its part, as well as submission to the enclosure of the body. With "beslozzen" ("locked"), the power scales tip in the direction of the body, and in the process the evaluative and transforming capabilities of the mind come into play; depending upon perspective, the unwelcome lodger (the heart) can become a hostage.

The attack on the heart is intensified in the next six-line stanza:

> "Du bist weizgot vil betrogen!
> dicke hast du mir gelogen
> unz daz du din übeler rat
> vil ungenislichen hat
> verleitet mich armen lip
> mit dinem gewalte an ein wip"
>
> (ll. 75-80; "God knows you are greatly deceived! You often lied to me until your wicked advice most treacherously and by force led me astray through a woman").

The common word-pair *betrogen/gelogen* ("deceived"/"lied"), taken with "'din übeler rat'" ("'your wicked advice'"),[5] the adverbial "'vil ungenislichen'" ("'quite hopelessly'"), which echoes "'din ungenist'" of l. 61; "your harm'"), and the loaded verb "verleitet" ("misled") at once attests to the heart's power to lead astray. If there is power, it is couched in terms of a capacity to do evil, to divide heart and body. Yet what the body conveniently ignores is any personal complicity in the matter, any willing participation on its own part in accepting the "advice" (l. 77) of the heart, while at the same time seeing itself as the center of the universe, wounded and suffering, misled by the heart and spurned by the lady. The body explains this attitude of mingled threats and despair in the subsequent manuscript grouping (ll. 81-9), where the heart is blamed for having raised pleasurable thoughts and expectations in the body, for having encouraged it in fantasies ("'und wie wol ez mir ergienge'"; "'and how well it would go for me'"). Yet in the next three lines sounds the theme that informs both the body's relationship with the heart and the man's relationship with the woman: disappointment. Just as the body expresses dissatisfaction with what it has received from the heart, so does the man receive what he does not want. Initially the reader knows the situation in as "bare facts" a tone the body can muster:

> "ja ist si leider ze guot:
> daz ist daz mir den schaden tuot,
> wan ich sin niht geniezen mac"
>   (ll. 87-9; "Unfortunately, she is indeed too
> good: that is what causes pain to me since I cannot
> benefit from that").

Subsequent exasperation, tinged with bafflement, causes the body to rephrase the situation:

> "sit si rehte wart gewar
> daz min freude also gar
> an ir einer gnade stet,
> sit enruocht si wiez mir get:
> daz ist ein starker wibes muot.
> ichne weiz wes si mir niht ist guot"
>   (ll. 93-8; "Since she became fully aware that
> my happiness is totally dependent on her favor, she
> has been unconcerned about how I am. This is a
> strong womanly spirit. I don't know why she doesn't
> favor me").

Hartmann will elaborate on what he calls "'wîbes muot'" ("'womanly spirit'"/"'the female mind'"), particularly in *Iwein*, where he sees justifications for an inherent changeability of woman's mind. In the subsequent stanza grouping, the body enlarges the state of affairs that led to the lady's estrangement, again concluding: "'ir muot ze fremder wise stat'" (l. 112; "'her spirit follows a different direction'"). What proves particularly noteworthy here is the body's continual shifting onto others anything besides praise for its own efforts (ll. 106ff.): the heart has provided bad advice (even if the body accepted it), and the woman has not responded correctly if she reacts in a manner contrary to what the body wished. The body occupies the center of its body-centered universe, where its sufferings and preferences are of utmost importance. Its very actions confer value. Has it not, after all, chosen this particular lady and placed no others ahead of her (ll.107-9)?

Moreover, it is the poor treatment of the body that occupies center stage in this section of the dialogue. The body has been grievously repaid for its service and has worsened its lot by expressing its thoughts, noting that its fortunes were better before it spoke its intent to the lady. Here the body could be associating silence with absence of pain. Further, because words have led to the lady's change of attitude, the body comes to devalue them, causing it to note pettishly at the outset of the next line cluster:

> "Friunt, wan deich die niht schelten sol
> der al diu werlt sprichet wol,
> so sagete ich ze maere
> daz si diu wirsest waere
> der ich ie künde gewan"
> (ll. 121-5; "Friend, were it not for the fact that I should not reproach her, the one who is praised by all, I would reveal that she is the worst one I've ever heard of").

Subjunctives notwithstanding, the body practices the verbal inconstancy with which the heart will later charge it, in that it reasons that if speaking brings ill, then speaking ill is called for. Yet so "divided of mind" is the body that it immediately pulls back from the pejorative statement (which is actually more self-descriptive than directed at the lady) and retreats from evaluation into hopeful musing:

> "nu ist der gedanc also fri
> daz si mir den niht wern mac,
> ichne si ir heimlich allen tac
> als mit gedanken ein man
> einem wibe beste kan.
> wan swaz mit werken mac ergan,
> daz han ich mit gedanke getan,
> daz doch ir eren wol gezimet:
> min muot im sin nicht fürbaz nimet.

> Daz ist doch min freude gar
> daz ich gedenken getar--
> ir ist ouch niht mere"
>
> (ll. 132-43; "Now thought is free, so that she
> cannot hinder me from doing it, from every day
> secretly possessing her in thought as best a man can
> in his thoughts. For what can be attained in deed, I
> have attained in thought, as is compatible with her
> reputation. My spirits do not go any farther in this
> matter. This is my joy after all: that I dare think:
> there is nothing more to them [the thoughts] than
> that").

Quite clearly the only thoughts that the body would choose to entertain are pleasurable, anticipatory, hopeful ones, and this helps explain the sudden shift which the lines take immediately thereafter, for the body is forced to recall the two obstacles to his pleasant reveries, that is, the lady's behavior and the heart's counsel:

> "nu wil sis haben ere
> daz ich von ir verderbe
> und gar an freude sterbe.
> heart, daz machet din rat
> der mich ir niht entwenken lat"
>
> (ll. 144-8; "Now she wants to obtain honor
> from the fact that I am perishing on account of her,
> and quite dying for joy. Heart, the advice you gave
> me won't let me escape her").

A parallel can be drawn to *Erec*, with which *Die Klage* is often linked, for both the body and Erec tend to displace their anger on others. Erec runs to silence and to a distrust of language, while the body resorts to a torrent of words to demonstrate how it has been wronged. Yet the effect is the same: Enîte, the messenger, has risked her life for the message she delivers, and the heart, whose counsel was earlier welcomed, is railed against and threatened.

So eager, in fact, is the body to discredit the heart's "advice" that it mentally sets up a situation that to show the heart's folly in having championed the lady. There, however, where the "'rede von guoten wiben ist'" (l. 152; "'where there is talk of fine ladies'"), where one might hear distasteful if not scandalous reports, the lady emerges unscathed—moreover, she is honored by the unanimous positive evaluation. This stanza ends with a direct appeal to the heart for advice:

> "herze, ob din gewalt erwunde
> daz ich ouch erkennen kunde
> ein guot wip als ein ander man,
> got weiz wol daz ich niht kan
> an ir erkennen wan guot,
> lieze si den einen muot
> den si wider mich nu lange hat.
> herze, nu sprich waz ist din rat"
>
> (ll. 173-80; "Heart, if only your power might extend far enough so that I too could identify a worthy woman as readily as any other man. God knows that I cannot see anything but good in her, as long as she desists from that disposition which she has had against me for so long. Heart, speak now your counsel").

The body's argument has virtually collapsed. Not only has the body turned to the heart for counsel (when it earlier decried the heart's advice), but it has also made a statement diametrically opposed to earlier ones. The body now uses "gewalt" in a more positive sense than before: power to discriminate, to perceive well, and to recognize is now intended, rather than power to oppress and to torture. Moreover, the subjunctive ("'erwunde'"—l. 173) is neither purely hypothetical nor threatening, but rather submissive: "'if your power might extend so far, that I . . . .'" Finally, the body, who has previously interpreted the sad state of affairs as stemming from bad advice, now moves tentatively to admit that it not only needs the tutelage of the heart, but it still follows the earlier advice of the heart to serve the lady, advice that is supported by the common assessment of the lady's excellence, reiterated by the body: "'got weiz wol daz ich niht kan / an ir erkennen wan guot'" (ll. 176-7; "'God knows that I cannot see anything but good in her'").

The sudden progress of the body does not imply that there will be no backsliding. Old habits die hard: in the ensuing stanza grouping the body reverts to gaining its success through the response of others, rather than on its own behavior. Were the lady so good as to speak to him, then the body's suffering would be mitigated. The body still reproaches the heart (ll. 198-9), for accustomed practices are comforting. Yet a request for direction is appended, along with appropriate obeisance to the deity:

> "gedenke an den richen got
> und bewise mich da bi,
> ob du iht weist . . ."

(ll. 200-2; "think of almighty God, and thereby show me if you know anything at all").

Shortly thereafter appears a ten-line cluster in which the body indulges in wishful thinking regarding its relationship to the lady and to God, whom the body has airily commended to the heart (l. 200), as well as referred to twice before in the context of divine knowledge (ll. 75; 176):

> "Noch ist si weiz got also guot,
> erkante si rehte minen muot,
> und ob ich waere ein heiden
> von der kristenheit gescheiden,
> daz si durch niemens raete
> so sere missetaete,
> swenne si bekante daz
> daz ich ir noch nie vergaz
> eines halben tages lanc,
> si sagte mirs etlichen danc"
>
> (ll. 207-16; "Even so she is, God knows, so fine, that if she truly knew my intention, she would not treat me so meanly on anyone's advice, not even if I were a heathen utterly separated from Christianity. If she realized that I have never forgotten her for even half a day, she would give me some praise for it").

The heart will later make clear to the body that God's role in the matter is more than perfunctory. Moreover, the reference to "heiden" ("heathen") suggests that the body is once more beginning to vacillate, to displace its anger, and to become carried away by its own rhetoric even as it pins hopes on the lady's response. One also notes the body's tendency to justify by quantification, which rings self-righteously in the context of the argument, and which, were the lady to hear it, might have an effect opposite of that intended. What, was she not remembered every hour, every minute, every second?

The body is suddenly assailed in the next cluster by the question of a man's sincerity toward a woman, and, not coincidentally, for the reader's response also runs along those lines, after having considered the assertion that scarcely half a day can go by without the body remembering the lady. Later the heart will chide the body for an exterior demeanor that does not reflect interior sorrow, and it is that very incongruence of the inner and outer man that the body now addresses:

Die Klage 17

"Nu ist ez leider ein slac
daz ein wip niht wizzen mac
wer si mit triwen meinet.
ouch ist in bescheinet
von mannen dicke solher list
der uns von rehte schade ist,
swaz man in mit eiden ie gehiez,
daz man des lützel war liez.
da von unsánfte ein wip getar
ir ere wagen also gar
uf solhe ungewisheit"

(ll. 217-27; "Now it is an unfortunate thing that a woman cannot know who loves her with loyalty. Also they are open to the deception practiced by man. Whatever was promised to them in oaths was seldom made a reality. That quite properly does us injury. A woman cannot lightly dare to risk all her honor on such uncertainty").

Interestingly enough, the man who practices such deception on a lady is motivated by "'swaches herzen lere'" (l. 245; "'a faulty guidance by the heart'"), which results in "'ein boeser muot'" (l. 243; "'a wicked disposition/spirit"). Considering that it is the heart that motivates in both the cases of the man who strives "'uf ein betrogen ere'" (l. 246; "'for a deceptive honor'") and the body itself, it would seem justified not only that the lady exhibit some uncertainty (l. 227) concerning a man's intent, but also that men themselves might well question the source of their inclinations. The body goes on to ascribe devilish motivation (l. 250) but does not go so far as to explain either how a man can be aware of the nature of the "muot" ("cast of mind") that compels him or how a lady can, another "muot" removed, so to speak, discern between those who are counseled by the devil and those whose hearts teach them truly. That answer is not forthcoming in the subsequent manuscript cluster either, which reiterates many of the previous charges against deceptive men. Like the previous stanza cluster, this one ends on a note of reward; earlier the body wanted to give false men a deserving reward (ll. 262ff.), and here he notes that deceivers hurt not only women but also honest men who deserve womanly rewards. What emerges from both stanzas, however, is a profound and pervasive sense of distrust on almost all levels: deceived women do not trust even trustworthy men, while men themselves do not trust the "'lere'" (l. 245; "'instruction'") given to them by their hearts.

This sense of distrust carries over into the next manuscript cluster, where it extends from man to man in a splendid delayed-impact sentence:

> "daz ich niht rehte wizzen mac
> waz oder wie mir ist geschehen
> od wes ich wider den sol jehen
> der mir denne als na ist bi,
> daz er mich fraget waz mir si;
> demne sag ich ouch niht me
> wan: 'geselle, mirst im herzen we"
>
> (ll. 300-6; "so that I cannot rightly know what has happened to me or how it has happened, or what I should say to the one who is so close to me, that he asks what is the matter with me. To him also I say no more than: '"Friend, I have pain in my heart"').

As the subsequent cluster reinforces, the sorrow of the body is to be internalized. It is not to be shared with other men, or even kinsmen (l. 316), and is not to be lightened by advice from other men (l. 313) or even from the heart itself (l. 319), of which the body has deep distrust, imagining that as it suffers in silence, the heart is merry as a bird:

> "wan so verest du dar inne
> (daz heize ich unminne)
> vor freuden als ein vogellin"
>
> (ll. 323-5; "for inside there you go along-- I call that hatefulness—in sheer joy, like a bird").

The body must feel some unease about depicting the heart's state as joyful, for in the next manuscript cluster it refers to itself as "'ein freudeloser man'" (l. 334; "'a joyless man'") and explains that any joy exhibited on account of other people was hollow, "'because it did not come from my heart'" (l. 343). The body seems oblivious to the contradiction raised between the heart as cheerful bird and the heart as sad source of distress under dissembling. Clearly, the body will give passing credit to the heart only if it suits the former's purposes. The gay exterior—although the body asserts the appropriateness of its appearance—is similarly rationalized:

> "min schimph mir also ane stat
> daz alle die beginnent jehen,
> die mich e habent gesehen,

so ich als ungefüege bin,
ich habe verwandelt den sin
und si worden unfruot"

(ll.433-9; "My happy appearance adorns me in such a manner that all of those who saw me before say, when I am so ill mannered, that I have gone through a change of disposition and have become despondent").

The body wants to have it both ways, to have *schimph* that lacks that special spark but is overly convincing even to those who observe it. At this point the body draws an analogy to nature (l. 367; "'That is like my own life'"). The effect is not unlike that in *Erec*, where Enîte announces "'des sol man bilde kiesen / an mir'" (ll. 6031-2; "'One should use me as an example of this'"—p. 100) after having created an analogy between herself and the transplanted linden tree (ll. 6008-30; pp. 99-100). Enîte's message is that she is not what she is perceived to be—this is also the import of the body's comparison, in which he likens himself to one who experiences emotional wave movements not unlike those that stir the sea even on calm days. The analogy and the gloss are unambiguous—there are depths of sorrow, wellsprings of powerful emotion that belie a calm surface or a smiling exterior—but the implications prove to be startling. If a smiling mouth can conceal hidden sorrows, then can it not also mask deceptive intent? How is a lady to know what to believe, particularly if the travails of the inner man are kept secret even from his friends? Moreover, the body has gradually come to the position that it actually speaks obliquely to include the heart in its statements—and possibly without recognizing that it does. It has come to posit the source of joy (ll. 340-2) as well as the seat of suffering (ll. 369-70) with the heart, and these emotions are seen to lodge in the inner man, just as the heart is said to be held fast in the body. The body here sees its bounds as encompassing an exterior and an interior, and that interior as housing those emotions that come from the heart. The reader sees the transition in Hartmann's mind from body and mind as a whole, rather than as fragmented entities.

Two subsequent analogies reinforce this integration of body and heart. The body stresses the analogies' importance in Hartmann's characteristic fashion by explicitly labelling them as instructive examples: "'bi disen zwein dingen / so nim ich dicke bilde'" (ll. 478-9; "'I often think about these two things'"). The first treats "'Diu nuz diu an dem boume stat'" (l. 451; "'the nut hanging on the tree'"), whereas the second concerns the "'kezzel'" and "'wazzer'" (ll. 465-6; "'kettle and water'"). In the first analogy, the body delineates the relationship of the nut shell to the kernel, stressing the protective role of the shell as well as the effects on the shell that are passed on to the kernel, as from the body to the heart:

> "witert iz der schalen als ez sol,
> da von gediht der kerne wol:
> swelch weter der schalen ouch we tuot,
> daz ist dem kernen kein guot"
> (ll. 459-62; "If the weather around the shell is as it should be, the kernal flourishes. However, weather that affects the shell is no good for the kernel either").

> "daz ich gedenke dar an
> daz du von schulden safte lebest
> als der kerne under der schalen"
> (ll. 446-9; "That I consider that you live comfortably under my breasts, just as a kernal under a shell").

The tone is no longer angry nor resigned, but conciliatory, as if the body had realized that there is little advantage to be gained by fighting in such close quarters with a too familiar adversary.

The second analogy reinforces the relationship by expanding on the "bad weather" metaphor in the first analogy, for the body is eager to know how the heart fares, while the body burns, for the water in a kettle cannot fail to heat if the kettle is placed "'an die gluot'" (l. 465; "'on the fire'"). If the analogies, in addition to noting the interrelationship between the heart and body, tend to stress the body's superior position, the body more than counters this by blandishments and protestations of regret. The body assumes the subordinate position ("'so diene ich dir als ich sol, / und kumt uns beiden also wol'"—ll. 425-6) and, instead of casting aspersions on the heart, it proves eager to settle the quarrel that it itself initiated:

> "wer sol den strit nu scheiden
> under uns beiden,
> wan du tuoz durch gotes ere"
> (ll. 411-3; "who is to judge the dispute between us, except that you should do it to the glory of God").

The body goes so far to inquire about the state of the heart in a compassioned rather than angry or sarcastic fashion: "'Waz wirretz dir, ob du mirz seist'" (l. 484; "'What's upsetting you, if you would tell me'"). The body's previous attempts to dissociate itself from the heart have gradually given way to a grudging acceptance of the fact it and the heart are yoked together, to a suspicion that all may not fare well with the heart, and, finally, to a request for communication.

The heart's response to the body's appeal is compressed and acid, evoking references in each speech to the words and behavior of the body. The first couplet demonstrates the shift in tone: "'Lip, ich wil ez gerne sagen, / wan ich möht ouch ze lange dagen'" (ll. 485-6; "'I will gladly tell it, lest I also keep silent too long'"). The "gladly" serves as an understatement, coming as it does after hundreds of lines of disregard and ill regard directed toward the heart. The formulaic *sagen/dagen* ("speak, tell"/"be silent") rhyme-pair, which Hartmann uses to advantage in *Erec*, here harks back in a dry way to the body's earlier reference to its silence (ll. 99, 157, 322); and "'wan ich möht ouch ze lange dagen'" ("'since I too like to keep silent for too long'") mockingly points out what the body has in fact *not done*: it has not remained silent, but has spoken, and at great length. The heart speaks, and its first request is that the body gain some control over its mouth. The heart goes on to label the body's orientation as "'lürzen'" (l. 494), as a deception, a misapprehension. Then, as the heart is given to proverbs in its speech, it cites one about adding insult to injury (ll. 496-8). In the process the heart has not only discredited the perceptions of the body but has also established itself as an authority that can lend veracity to others' utterances: "'ez ist et war daz man mir seit'" (l. 496; "'what one has told me is true'"). The heart thus establishes one of its prominent speech and thought patterns, that of making its points to the body by way of reference to a third entity that is somehow "like" the current subject of discussion. This pattern manifests itself not only in the number of uses of *glichen* ("to be like, to resemble"—the body uses it once, l. 367, but the heart employs it four times over a comparable number of lines in its first monologue—ll. 516, 652, 909, and 945) but also in the frequent use of *als* ("as") to provide those comparisons by way of a third entity:

> "du tuost als der schuldec man
> der sich wol uz nemen kan;
> also er den schaden getuot,
> so leret in sin karger muot
> (daz im ouch dicke frumet)
> daz er e ze hove kumet.
> sin schulde kan er wol verdagen
> und beginnet über jenen klage
> dem er den schaden hat getan:
> der muoz im dan ze buoze stan"

(ll. 501-10; "You act like a guilty man who well knows how to extricate himself. As soon as he has committed the misdeed, his clever spirit instructs him—to his frequent benefit—that he be the first to go to court. He can well conceal his guilt, and initiate a complaint about the one to whom he did injury, who will then have to compensate him").

In passing, I should note that the same tone is used in this passage as found in the opening parabolic segment later to be discussed in *Iwein*. There is clearly something of the atmosphere of a parable here, reinforced by the subsequent statement, "'dem glichet sich daz min leit'" (l. 516; "'his sorrow is like mine'"). This might be labeled the "Parable of the Innocent Perpetrator," and it tells the same story as the body's earlier outpourings concerning its alleged victimization by the heart yet the tone is more elevated, and the reasoning more sophisticated. One senses that the body's more rustic references to the nut and the kernel and to the kettle and water are, if not wasted on the more verbally adept heart, hardly intimidating or convincing to it.

The heart's linguistic cunning extends to picking up the language earlier employed by the body and using it to greater effect by compressing it, as in the cluster following the "parable":

"ichne weiz war umbe du ez last,
sit du ez gesprochen hast,
du wellest dich an mir rechen
unde ein mezzer in mich stechen?
daz haet ich vil wol versolt:
wan du mir daz gelouben solt,
waer ich gewaltec über dich
so du bist über mich,
daz ich hende haete,
din leben waere unstaete"

(ll. 521-30; "In as much as you did talk about it, I don't understand why you are dropping the matter of wanting to avenge yourself on me, of sticking a knife into me. I certainly would have earned it. But you should believe me when I say that if I had power over you, as you do over me, and if I had hands, your life would be of short duration").

And, in the process of ten lines, the heart has echoed the key vocabulary from the body's earlier speeches of ll. 33-74, has stripped away the body's verbiage, and has taken issue with the body's contention that the heart is powerful. The incongruous statement, "'daz ich hende haete'" (l. 529; "'if I had hands'"), that comes near the end of the cluster proves indicative of the course the heart will take: it will define itself by what it does *not* have.

> "Du gihst din kumber si min rat:
> du weist wol wiez dar umbe stat,
> daz ich so vil niht wizzen mac
> wenne ez si naht oder tac.
> ich erkenne übel noch guot,
> ich bin fro noch ungemuot,
> wan als mich von dir wirt ane braht.
> du hast dich der rede niht wol bedaht,
> daz du mich dar umbe sprichest an
> des ich schulde nie gewan"
> (ll. 535-44; "You say that my counsel is the source of your distress. But you know well how things really stand, and that I can't even tell if it is night or day. I perceive neither evil nor good. I am neither happy nor sorrowful, except insofar as what you bring to me. You have not thought out your words well. You are accusing me of things for which I have no responsibility").

The purpose of the heart is to disavow both knowledge and responsibility and to posit itself as morally neutral due to its dependency on the body, and it nearly succeeds, were it not for the phrase "'daz ich so vil niht wizzen mac / wenne es si naht oder tac'" (ll. 537-8; "'I don't even know if it is night or day'"), which sounds very like the heart's earlier wish for hands. Both jar slightly. There is something a little incongruous between the two. In the first statement the heart wishes for something extra, while in the second it backs off from any extra abilities it might have. The second statement is also pure bluff: the heart can and does discriminate between night and day. It asserts, "'den abent und den morgen ringe ich ie mit sorgen'" (ll. 691-2; "'evening and morn I always struggle with cares'"), and later waxes reflective:

> "swes ich von guoten sinnen
> ze freuden gedenken mac
> beide naht unde tac,
> daz muoz ich under wegen lan"

(ll. 852-5; "Night and day, I must abandon everything that I thought about for my joy, however well-intentioned").

One could argue that Hartmann here merely inserts the formula *naht unde tac* ("night and day") because it provides a good rhyme for "mac" ("can"), which is true, but his effect is far subtler than that, I believe, for the heart's disclaimer in ll. 535-44 that it cannot distinguish between night and day is joined with its profession of moral neutrality and innocence in the matter of advice-giving. Both of these assumptions will be speedily undercut. What the heart has done is exercise its skill as an arguer; it is a wordsmith that knows it can intimidate and silence some opponents with a confident bluff and can buy time for developing different strategies against others. This in part accounts for its vacillation—protesting that it knows nothing of the world except what the body tells it (ll. 555-7) and then assuming the role of advisor (l. 561). The heart then abandons its attempt to dodge sole responsibility and presses the issue:

"so weist du wol daz ich dich nie
boesiu dinc geminnen lie.
ze guoten dingen ich dir riet,
von allem valsche ich dich schiet;
dar umbe dulde ich dinen haz.
doch wil ich gerne liden daz
swaz mir da von geschehen sol:
ichne rat dir nimmer niht wan wol"
(ll. 563-70; "You know well that I never let
you love base things. I advised you to good things.
I kept you away from all falsehood. For this reason
I now endure your hatred. But I will gladly suffer
this, no matter what happens to me because of it. I
never recommend anything to you but the good").

Suddenly the position that the heart only perceives what the body shows it (ll. 555-7) is discarded, and references to what is known by whom (ll. 563, 573, 583, 584, 586) become nearly as numerous as those allusions to what is advised (ll. 561, 565, 570, 573, 580, 582, 588, 598) and are frequently found in promixity to each other. This clearly demonstrates the linkage between wisdom and advice-giving on which Hartmann frequently plays, especially in *Erec* and *Grêgôrius*: those who feel they know something generally cannot help sharing what they know with others, in the admonitory as well as in the informational sense. The mind reaches out, first to perceive, then to consider, and finally to advise, as the heart demonstrates in its justification to the body: "'ich rat dir niht wan rehten muot'" (l. 580; "'I am counselling you to assume nothing but an upright spirit'"). Moreover, the matter of complicity is dealt with squarely by the heart: "'ich riet dirz durch den willen din'" (l. 588; "'I advised you this for your own sake'"); the body is advised in the direction in which it would willingly go. Gone are the protestations of innocence, of neutrality: the heart has, undone by its own cunning, worked to salvage a stance so unworkable in the long run that even its maker realizes the advantages of its abandonment. In fact, the heart has neatly turned the tables on the body, transforming the earlier disadvantage of viewing the world through the eyes of the body (ll. 547-57) into a decided advantage: "'do ich si durch diniu ougen sach, / daz niht bezzers möhte sin'" (ll. 586-7; "'When I saw the world through your eyes, nothing could be any better'"). There is no mention made of the former inability to tell evil from good). Moreover, I would suggest that a note of positive chumminess replaces the sense of enforced togetherness previously communicated by the heart: suddenly the heart is eager to assert a close relationship with the body ("'du und ich, daz herze din'"—l. 602; "'you and I, your heart of hearts'").

And it is none too soon when the heart attempts to ingratiate itself to the body, for the heart is minded to give advice about what "minne" entails, initially broaching the subject not with the attitude of "you must" but rather "one who does such and such":

>"swer ahte hat uf minne
>der darf wol schoener sinne
>und swer ir lere rehte wil phlegen
>der muoz lazen under wegen
>swaz anders heizet denne guot
>und minnen rehtes mannes muot.
>da gehoeret arbeit zuo
>beide spate unde fruo
>und daz man vil gedenke an si"
>
>. . . . .
>"Swer ir ingesinde wesen wil,
>der darf solhes muotes vil,
>daz er gedenke dar zuo
>wie er mere guotes getuo
>dann er da von gespreche"
>   (ll. 607-15; 621-5; "He who casts an eye on
>love surely needs a fine sensibility. Whoever wants
>to rightly uphold the rule of love must leave behind
>that which is called other than good. He must love
>the upright manly spirit. This requires effort at all

times of the day, and also that one give much
thought to love . . . . Whoever wants to belong to the
entourage of love needs much of that sort of spirit
that makes him consider how he can do more good,
rather than merely speak of it").

The heart's function here is to instruct, and little would be gained in antagonizing the body by telling it immediately what it has done wrong or what it must do. Rather, the heart encapsulates the discipline of "minne" over two clusters (ll. 603-34) and only then resorts to catch-phrases: "'Du muost mit herten dingen / nach ir hulden ringen'" (ll. 635-6; "'you must struggle with difficult things for her loyalty'"). Integral parts of that discipline are attitude and concentration; "'gedenke'" ("'consider'") appears twice (ll. 615, 623), and it is not to be confused with the body's idea of "'gedenken'" (l. 142; "'thinking'"), which is to daydream and build fantasies about the beloved. Rather, the body is urged to consider, to think, to curb certain attitudes. Previously the body has, in effect, ranted and raved. Now it is told that there is rather more to the service of a lady than that. Verbal perspicacity is certainly in order, for service entails action, wise use of language, and considerable thought.

To give the body an idea of what such devotion entails, the heart details its vigilance with respect to "'unser beide ere'" (l. 667; "'the honor of us both'"), an apt parallel, since the relationship of heart to body throughout the poem runs along the lines of the relationship of *man* to *wîp*. The heart is quick to point out the direction in which its thoughts are ever inclined:

"wan min muot also stat
daz mich niht genüegen mac,
ichne flize mich naht und tac,
wie ich dir daz gefüege
des dich von rehte genüege
durch unser beider ere"
(ll. 662-7; "my spirit is so inclined that I
cannot be content unless I strive night and day to
furnish you what would rightly satisfy you, and the
honor of us both").

This effort is all the more commendable, the heart goes on to imply, because the body is otherwise occupied with "'singen unde sagen'" ("'singing and talking/recounting'"), "'beizen unde jagen'" ("'falconing and hunting'"), "'spilen und schiezen'" ("'playing and shooting'"—ll. 681-3), as well as with "'tanzen unde springen'" (l. 685; "'dancing and jumping'"). "'Ringen'" (l. 686) is also mentioned, but it is *ringen* as the weak verb, "to have an easy time of it," rather than as the strong verb ("to be maximally active, to be striving for") with which the heart has earlier associated love. Moreover, the heart is even active at night (which the heart scornfully refers to as "'daz halbe jar'"—l. 678; "'half of the year'"), bringing dreams of the lady because his thoughts are always with her (l. 703) and professes himself to be ever mindful of the mission to aid the body:

> "daz ich allen minen muot
> uf anders niht gewendet han
> wan waz ich der dinge müge began
> da von du liebe gewinnest"
> (ll. 714-7; "That I have directed my whole
> spirit to nothing other than what I can do so that
> you obtain love/joy").

This resolve is reiterated with slight variation in the subsequent cluster, where the phrase "'durch unser beider ere'" (l. 725; "'for the honor of us both'") is repeated. Reference is again made to the sufferings of the heart (l. 719), and the atmosphere of a "pep talk" prevails:

> "min ahte ist niht mere
> wan wiech dir müge gefüegen
> des dich sol genüegen
> freudebaerer wünne.
> Der allez mankünne
> schuof und in siner gwalt hat,
> der gebe uns heil unde rat
> daz ich noch daz erringe
> daz uns an ir gelinge"
> (ll. 726-34; "My sole intention is arranging for
> you that you should be satisfied with joyous delight.
> He who created mankind, and who has mankind
> under His dominion, give us now salvation and
> counsel, that I may now succeed through my efforts in
> gaining it [joy] for us").

It is the first time either heart or body refers to God's power or counsel, and these references, coming at the point when the heart calls for greater unity and effort, serve to underscore that the undertaking cannot be successful if power or counsel lodges with only one member: the message is that heart and body must be subordinate to a greater authority and must not squabble concerning relative power, as it will take the efforts of both, God willing, to guarantee success. In fact, pain and distress must be shared in the arduous task, and the heart, which previously vied with the body for the honor of having suffered the most, now asks for a double portion of suffering, as such suffering leads to blessedness: "'mit kumber saelde koufen'" (l. 754; "'buying blessedness with pain'"). What proves extremely interesting here, as the argument advances, is the manner in which one aspect of mind urges the other aspect to look upon what was a liability as an advantage. One aspect only bewails its pain, dwelling upon it, whereas another aspect, more practical as well as more visionary, looks beyond the pain to a reward. This division is in keeping with those faculties of mind Hartmann highlights, for the body has spoken a good deal of *muot*, that sense of inclination, mood, and mind that is primarily passive; the heart raises the issue of the mind as active, as having the sense necessary for right action:

> "so kan ich dir bescheiden wol
> wes ein man geniezen sol:
> tugende unde sinne,
> so sint ez reine minne"
> (ll. 777-80; "I can well explain to you what a
> man should enjoy: virtues and sensibility, as these
> are the true signs of love").

The body must practice virtue and sensibility, trust in God (ll. 807-8), and must be prepared for suffering, for "'ja enwaene ie dehein man / ane kumber liep gewan'" (ll. 791-2; "'I don't believe that any man ever won love without pain'").

At this point in the heart's counsel, Hartmann injects a less serious cluster, fully in keeping with his characteristic mixture of weightiness and whimsy, and also quite sound psychologically:

> "Behüete dich vor bosheit,
> daz dir got niht gebe leit!
> wische den mies von den ougen;
> der rede sin wir tougen:
> du weist wol daz du ie waere
> ein rehter slichaere:
> vil lere ich an dir verlos
> die din übeler muot verkos.
> ziph welche ein hovelicher lip!
> durch welchen tiuvel haete ein wip
> solches an dir ersehen,
> daz si dir liebe lieze geschehen?"
> (ll. 809-20; "Beware of evil, on pain of God's
> punishment! Wipe the moss from your eyes. Let's

Die Klage 29

>keep this to ourselves: you know well that you once
>were a real sneak: I wasted much teaching on you,
>which was rejected by your evil spirit. What a
>courtly being! By what devilish influence would
>a woman see anything in you that would let her give
>love to you?").

The teasing, almost backslapping, tone is perfect. The offhand "'let's keep this to ourselves'" is reminiscent of a fatherly punch on the shoulder: "'we don't need to let anyone know we've had this little talk, sonny.'" And "'you know well that you once were a real sneak'" might well be accompanied by a poke in the ribs (if the heart had hands!) and a wink. The tone marks tit for tat, with "'din übeler muot'" to counter and jokingly echo "'din übeler rat.'" Finally, the last three lines make light of what the body's entire speech and most of the heart's have made earnest: the love of the lady and the worthiness of the man. The entire cluster exudes cameraderie and works to several ends. First, it defuses the tension of an advice-giving session, which was getting heavy-handed. Second, it anticipates those humorous exchanges to come when the heart and body start trading one-liners. And, third, it bridges the way to the heart's next comparison, so elementary—not unlike the body's nut and kernel example—that one can almost hear the heart thinking, "'now here's one that you'll be able to understand, knuckle-head, the one about the flower under the snow!'"

The heart warms so to its comparison ("'Sich, lip, mir is als we /sam der bluomen underm sne'"—ll. 821-2; "'See, body, I am in pain, like the flower under the snow'") that it returns to its aggressive instruction, much of which focuses on instilling in the body a desire to do its part. In effect, the heart wishes to make the point that it cannot go it alone. Yet there is ultimately no question that the body is to remain in the subordinate role. The body is to provide the brawn and the heart the brains of the undertaking, and the argument would seem to be winding down. Yet at this point the heart stumbles in a manner not unlike the body's misstep. Until late the body maintained that the heart was foreign to it, estranged from it, and then realized that together they formed one entity. Ironically, the heart began by emphasizing its dependence on the body, by stressing that its meagre knowledge of the world was filtered through the body, and late in the argument, which asserted the necessary association of heart and body, it despairs and speaks for separation:

>"wir sin niht rehte zesamen geweten,
>wan wir ziehen niht geliche:
>man solte uns waerliche

> von ein ander scheiden:
> daz kaeme uns rehte beiden"
>
> (ll. 908-12; "we are not properly yoked together, since we do not pull equally: indeed, we ought to be separated. That would do us both justice [we probably would both find that acceptable]").

The heart's contention that the two are ill-yoked reflects its disgust with certain attitudes of the body but at the same time acknowledges its own weaknesses: its power is of a different nature than that of the body, and the heart laments this in words that hark back in language and theme to earlier contentions:

> "Stüende der gewalt an mir
> diu dinc ze verenden als an dir,
> des ez leider niht tuot
> (ichne han gewaltes wan den muot
> und den frien gedanc)
> du müesest under dinen danc
> nach gelobtem worte leben.
> Nune ist mir leider niht gegeben
> des gewaltes mere
> (daz schadet uns beiden sere)
> wan daz ich der ratgebe din
> ze allen dingen solte sin.
> nune bist du mir niht gehorsam.
> ich weiz wol daz ich nie vernam
> deheines mannes missetat
> so gar über sines herzen rat"
>
> (ll. 913-28; "If it were in my power, which it is unfortunately not, to change things the way you can—I have no power other than my mind/spirit and free thought—you would have to, against your will, live according to an oath sworn to me. Now, sadly, I have no more power—to our great mutual detriment—except to be an advisor to you in all things. But you do not obey me. I can certainly tell you that I have never heard of any other man's greater utter misdeed against the counsel of his heart").

This passage raises several interesting points. First, the lines "'ichne han gewaltes wan den muot / und den frien gedanc'" ("'I have no power other than my mind/spirit and free thought'") seem oddly placed; they sound almost as if the body had voiced them, for the body has earlier opined, "'nu ist der gedanc also fri'" (l. 132;

"'thoughts are free'") and has made frequent reference to the state of its "'muot'" ("'cast of mind'"—ll. 99, 208, 297, 351). This is not to say that the heart has not spoken of "muot," but rather to note that when it has, with few exceptions, it has been referring to the "muot" of others, often in the earlier noted third-person proverbs or parables (ll. 504, 612, 622, 760, 816, 860, 888). The heart has "'muot'" (ll. 714, 916, 953), but, more importantly, it is characterized by "'sinne'" (l. 894), that special discriminating sense that sees and reasons acutely. In casting the heart here in more of the role of the body, if speech patterns are any evidence—and are, as this poem consists almost entirely of dialogue—Hartmann deliberately blurs the distinction between the two halves of the one entity, wishing to show that rationality is not the sole property of the heart, nor that rash emotionalism is not limited to the body. Both heart and body fall prey to anger, rashness, sentimentality, and doubt; both cherish hopes (the flower under the snow is no more foolish than the contention that thoughts are free); both are petty and self-righteous; both chafe under the restraint the other provides; both are capable of reflection, evaluation, memory, fantasy, and imagination, all qualities of mind; and both contend not so much out of disagreement as out of a sense of inadequacy. Moreover—and this speaks to the second noteworthy point implied in the above passage—both crave control. In stressing its usefulness as an advisor, the heart possesses resolve and will to wield an alliance, and the body's obedience and ability to act pave the way for attaining the shared goal of the woman.

This joint resolve—neither can accomplish the task alone—is not agreed upon without some breast-beating ("'sit ich der werlt allez bin / der wolf an dem spelle'"—ll. 950-1; "'since everyone thinks I'm a lying wolf'"), accusation ("'lip, der schulde zihe ich dich'"—l. 940; "'body, I put the blame on you'"), and self-righteousness ("'uns dienet niht gelicher muot'"—l. 945; "'we don't share the same attitude'"). Yet the heart ends its speech, having made concessions and expressing a grudging willingness to try again:

> "wil ab du dich rehtes muotes
> noch zuo mir gesellen,
> wir enden swaz wir wellen.
> ich sage dir niht mere,
> wan merke mine lere:
> des gewinnest du noch ruom.
> sage mir, lip, ob duz wellest tuon"
> (ll. 966-72; "if from now on you want to be my companion in a good-willed way, we can accomplish what we wish to. I will tell you no more than that

you should mark my words: you will yet win recognition thereby. Tell me, body, if you want to do it").

The reader may well wonder why the heart gives the body another chance, if the body is indeed as insensitive, as perfidious as the heart makes it out to be. The motivation, pure and simple, is power. And the heart's power derives almost exclusively from its knowledge, which enables it to offer sound advice. This knowledge, as well as the accompanying confidence that comes from *knowing that one knows* gives it a distinct advantage over the body, that is borne out in the heart's employment of *wizzen* and related forms. To be sure, the body uses these forms more often in its first monologue than does the heart in its equally lengthy rejoinder, but the body generally uses them negatively, so that it calls attention to what it does not know (ll. 98, 182, 300, 403), what others do not know (ll. 218, 227, 308, 350), or, in rare instances, what knowledge the heart shares with it (ll. 198, 202, 483). The heart, virtually without exception, knows things unreservedly (ll. 556, 573, 584, 813, 898, 926, 930, 937, 941); and in those instances where *wizzen* is employed negatively, it is often with sarcastic or ironic intent (ll. 521, 536, 537). Accordingly, when the body reacts to the heart's monologue, it is not to question the body's "teaching" (l. 982) but rather to call attention to the rough way in which it is administered: "'nu strafst du mich als dinen kneht'" (l. 985; "'you reprimand me as if I were your servant'"). The body takes issue as well with the heart's choice of language, noting that friends should avoid "'reproachful words'" (l. 987) and "'threats'" (l. 1001) and should "'go to each other and take one another by the hand'" (ll. 989-90). This attitude, of course, does not cancel out the fact that the body has hardly behaved as a model of politeness and decorum. In effect, the body tries to save face by taking the successful style of the heart: by stating a strong position (no matter that it subsequently holds to it) in order to gain the upper hand. That position, voiced as it is in the context of an argument, is now to quarrel: "'wilst du dar umbe bagen, / der site ist dir niht guot'" (ll. 1004-5; "'if you want to argue about it, doing so will not be of help to you'").

Immediately the body takes another leaf, as it were, from the heart's book, by preaching what the heart has been asserting all along, but by presenting the statement as if it were being voiced for the first time:

"diu rede ist dir wol kunt
daz ez dem libe also stat
daz er helfe unde rat

> von dem heart nemen sol.
> da von so zaeme uns beiden wol
> daz wir lebten ane strit
> mit ein ander alle zit"
>
> (ll. 1008-14; "You surely know the saying that it is appropriate for the body to accept help and advice from the heart. It would profit both of us to live forever together without conflict").

On the one hand, this is a strong offensive tactical maneuver to tell an opponent what his/her job is, particularly when he/she has just finished elaborating at length of the nature of that job. On the other hand, such a statement reveals the body's naïveté in thinking that the heart must be reminded of its function? Or has the body simply not heard what the heart has been saying? This last possibility demonstrates Hartmann's dissection of stages of communication and non-communication, whereby both sides favor reiteration of complaints and restatement of issues, so that, by dint of repetition, point by laborious point is made as one party finally hears the other. The reader may determine which issues have been laid to rest to both parties' satisfaction simply by the fact that they are no longer discussed, but those issues that are repeatedly raised—such as the issue of power—necessarily remain open to ambiguous interpretations. To return to the question at hand, other possibilities come to mind: Has the body simply not understood the heart's frequent counsel? Has it heard it and presents it as new information in order to gain a strategic advantage? Or has it heard it and, in repeating it as its own, signals acceptance of this power relationship? The third interpretation seems the most profitable avenue to pursue now.

The body's taking the heart's argument as its own is immediately reinforced by phrases that emphasize the commonality between the two entities. The body suggests that both should consider that they are "'ein man'" (l. 1022; "'one man'"), that each needs the other (ll. 1023-4), and that it is willing to let bygones be bygones, upon the condition that

> "bist du mir guot sam bin ich dir,
> wan ane ein ander mugen wir
> deheine wile genesen:
> wir müezen immer sament wesen
> und mugen uns niht gescheiden.
> Got der hat uns beiden
> eine sele gegeben
> (anders möhte wir niht geleben)"

(ll. 1029-36; "If you are good to me, I will be the same to you, for separately we cannot survive for any time at all; we must always be together. We are in no position to be divided. God has given both of us one soul—without which we would not be alive").

Finally, the body implores the heart for advice, capping this request with yet another reference to their shared affairs. The particular significance of this altered attitude can be seen not only in the body's relationship to the heart, but also in its subsequent changed attitude with respect to serving the woman. It is virtually a trademark with Hartmann that a fundamental change of heart or mind toward one matter results in a marked shift in attitude toward others. This principle is readily seen in *Iwein*, where madness triggers a behavioral swing in the hero so that his very attitude toward knighthood and toward his wife is radically transformed for the better. In *Die Klage* Hartmann first allows the body to redefine its relationship to the heart, and, because the body has done this correctly, acknowledging God's role in the matter, the total man's relationship to the lady is redefined. Suddenly the body sees broader implications in love-service: that one's best efforts are to be directed to the good (ll. 1086-7), that words alone are not enough (l. 1095), and that the ultimate doing of good rather than the lady's reward is what counts:

> "enphahe ichs nimmer lon von ir,
> dannoch frümet ez mir
> daz mirz diu werlt ze guote verstat
> und mich deste gerner hat"
> (ll. 1099-1102; "Even if I never receive any reward from her, it still is advantageous to me that the world understands my effort in a positive way, and is therefore better disposed toward me").

The body's attitude wins immediate approbation from the heart (ll. 1126ff.), which responds with the example of two men, one of whom comes to an understanding of himself and is of a mind to change himself for the better (l. 1130-2), with the result that he seeks and cherishes good counsel, and the other of whom does not value advice and who in his deception is mocked by the world. The heart then places praise for the body's transformation where praise is due: with God: "'lip, da von lobe ich got / des ich von dir vernomen han'" (ll. 1148-9; "'body, I praise God for what I have perceived in you'"). On the body's part, the transformation results from reflection on past imperfect behavior, which points to yet another of Hartmann's ascriptions of mental faculties to heart and body. The heart possesses the capacity to advise, to evaluate the present and past with an eye to the future, while the body comes gradually to an understanding of the past, so that it may benefit from the advice of the heart. The body remains so hopelessly at sea in the first monologue precisely because it has not considered its past actions in sufficient light to enable it to determine a present course of action; it can only lament, going over the same ground repeatedly. Now, while both entities have the quality of reflection, only the body has the ability to act on the knowledge that reflection brings and the advice that wisdom dictates; the heart can motivate, but it remains for the body to act.

So closely enmeshed are motivation and action that Hartmann graphically reflects their proximity and interrelation in a tightly-packed interchange of primarily single-line remarks (ll. 1168-1268), with the body voicing one line of the rhymed couplet, only to have the heart chime in with the other half, or with a single line split ("'bistu siech?' 'nein ich'" (l. 1184; "'Are you sick?'" "'not I'") intervening to shift the order of the two, to allow the heart to begin the couplet. The effect is stunning, not only because of the sudden exchanges after the lengthy monologues, but also because of the range of emotion expressed in the interchange of one-liners. One finds brusqueness bordering on insult ("'din üppic frage tuot mich alt'"—l. 1176; "'your superfluous question makes me angry'"), the reassuring patter of lovers exchanging words of approval (ll. 1170-2), incisive comment ("'ich waen du fürhtest den tot'"—l. 1189; "'I believe that you fear death'"), sharp requests for direction (ll. 1216, 1222) or knowledge (ll. 1207, 1210), and warm, comfortable exchanges:

> "da volge den die wiser sint."
> "nu lere mich, ich bin din kint."
> "und ich din gwisser ratgebe."
> "so volge ich dir als gerne ich lebe"
> (ll. 1251-4; "Now follow those who are wiser." "Now teach me; I am your pupil." "And I your advisor." "Then I will follow you with the same enthusiasm I have for living itself").

In the process willingness and patience are decisively tested.

With this testing comes responsibility, as the subsequent four clusters emphasize: the heart is to guard and carry three precious herbs, "'milte, zuht, diemuot'" (l. 1303; "'generosity, good breeding/manners, humility'") and serve as the vessel for them, while the body is to impose the task upon itself taught to it by the heart:

> "wol in der ir hat künde!
> daz ist zer werlte ein saelekeit
> und ist gote niene leit,
> ez ist bedenthalp ein gwin,
> got und diu werlt minnet in;
> swer den selben zouberlist kan,
> der ist zer werlt ein saelec man"
> (ll. 1342-8; "Praise to him who has knowledge of these herbs. It is a blessing on earth and no sorrow to God; it is of profit on both sides, both God and the world love them. He who can practice this same magical cunning is a famed man in the world").

The example of the three herbs is puzzling, however, in its formulation. One would think that it would not be necessary to cloak such wisdom in allegorical form, since the heart and body have come to an understanding. Why does not the heart proceed, as have other advice-givers in Middle High German literature, and simply state, "'wis milte, wis züchtec, wis diemüetec'" ("'be generous, be decorous, be humble'")? Part of the answer lies in the heart's predilection for relying on examples (a predisposition shared with the body): some points are better made if they are presented obliquely and then glossed. And part of the motivation becomes clear in the heart's subsequent reference to those who misuse *zouber* ("magic"):

> "wan daz waer misselungen,
> wurde ein wip betwungen
> mit zouberlichen dingen"
> (ll. 1351-3; "For that would be a failed undertaking if a woman were won over by a magical device").

As has been the case, the heart offers options: here is how one behaves correctly, and here is how one behaves incorrectly. The body is to distinguish between use and abuse, and, if it does so, it understands the correct option. The heart notes: "'ist dir diu lere swaere, / so wizze daz du unsaelec bist'" (ll. 1374-5; "'if this teaching is painful to you, then be aware that you are unhappy'"). Like parables, where those who understand them are among the elect, the teaching of the heart is intelligible only to those who benefit from it.

The body's resolve is inclined in the direction the heart gives it, for it recognizes that the heart's teaching "'greatly improve[s]'" it (l. 1377). At this point the body takes a step backwards, having taken two forward, and begins to go over much the same ground covered earlier in its initial monologue, as it longs for the lady's greeting (ll. 1388ff.), notes how women are often deceived and lied to (ll. 1402ff.), and laments that the lady cannot know the inclination of the man's mind   (ll. 1397ff.).   Significantly, however, these comments are now interspersed with frequent reference to God's guidance (ll. 1423, 1448, 1475, 1487), a resolve to expend effort (ll. 1381ff., 1428ff., 1474), and, most telling of all, a reference to the lady's "'virtuous spirit'" (l. 1499) as a carbuncle:

> "Mir sagent manege daz [der karfunkel]
> des vinstern nahtes lieht ber
> und daz er alters eine
> lesche ander steine
> swa er bi in lit"
> (ll. 1503-7; "Many tell me that the carbuncle burns with light in the dark night and that it all by itself obscures the other stones that lie next to it").

The carbuncle, often associated with wisdom, suits the body's new perception of the lady, who becomes a beacon, an illuminator, and a source of insight rather than a burdensome thought clouding the mind. Contemplation of her no longer requires a litany of what she does not do, but rather comprises what a man must do to be worthy of her; awareness of her nature signals awareness of the steps that must be taken.

The effort, as the heart subsequently notes, is largely intellectual, since that resolve of mind must underlie the struggle to attain the lady's grace. The heart first states dryly that it shares a seriousness of purpose with the body (ll. 1537-9). What is important here is the tacit understanding that a commonality of purpose is of greater importance than equality of efforts; the powers of the heart and body are of necessity exercised in different spheres. Heart and body can be yoked equally—the heart's earlier reservations to the contrary—if the singleness of purpose drives them. The heart advocates constancy (ll. 1542ff.) and sets up one "'who is constant and fine of spirit'" (l. 1558) as an example. Then, by association, the heart skips from the proper state of the man's mind to "'woman's spirit'" (l. 1572), the motivational force behind which is admittedly "'completely hidden from me'" (l. 1588). The heart devotes a good number of lines (ll. 1572-92) to vain speculation on the matter before the body jerks it back to the main subject in a manner not unlike that used earlier by the heart to jog its sensibilities:

> "Du wirst von fremden leiden alt;
> daz du mir hast vor bezalt
> von wibes unbescheidenheit"
> (ll. 1595-7; "You are a worry wart: such as when you told me about women's lack of responsiblity").

The body bids the heart, and not too gently either, to return to the matter at hand (ll. 1609-12), to which the heart responds with a final analogy from nature, an analogy that expresses constancy: water wearing away stone (ll. 1615-21). To constancy must be added consistency, for the heart is quick to apprehend the advice that the body guard its tongue, so that the lady would never hear anything hateful (l. 636). That point is well taken, for in the body's earliest monologue the lady could have heard an ample number of statements that would give offense. Verbal caution is appropriate for the body, which is to serve as "'fürspreche'" (l. 1643; "'advocate'") to the heart's "'ratgebe'" (l. 1253; "'counsel'").

The remaining two hundred and seventy lines of *Die Klage* are given over to the man's direct appeal to the lady. The man's two opposing internal factions, body and heart, have finally come to rest, and the next opposition is external. Interestingly, the language of this appeal to the lady, while echoing many of the key terms found throughout the greater part of the work, is curiously bound and constrained. But this seems due in large part to the rhyme-scheme chosen. Each strophe alternates two rhyme-sounds, which creates a jouncing effect that is intensified the longer the strophe is—and some of the strophes are quite lengthy, particularly at the outset. The length of the strophes tapers off quite radically and rapidly after l. 1826, with the remaining eight strophes diminishing in size on a regular basis, so that they comprise, in order, of eighteen, sixteen, fourteen, twelve, ten, eight, six, and, finally, four lines. As the strophes become shorter, the appeal becomes less convoluted, as if the argument were stated in ever fewer words and therefore had to be increasingly refined. The rhyme-scheme also works to mirror the restraint exercised by the speaker; the control the rhyme provides is in keeping with the dictates of reason applied to passion.

The argument of this poem-within-the-poem covers many of the issues raised in the heart/body altercation: the pain of love, the devotion to the lady, the desire for the lady's grace are among them. What it does *not* do, however, is coherently develop these concerns in sequence, in the sense that heart and body earlier moved from one topic to another. With the heart and body one can see which thought triggered the next, but with the lover appealing to the lady the rhyme-scheme triumphs over orderly development. The first strophe begins with lip-service to temporal sequentiality (ll. 1645-51), but moves awkwardly from love's binding the lover and kindling his heart to a jarring image:

> "unheil mir über den wec schreit
>   gelich einem hunde.
> ze vaste ich mich dar uf verreit,
>   daz schadet mir an gesunde,
> sin zant mich sere versneit,
>   mir bluotet noch diu wunde"
>   (ll. 1671-6; "ill fortune crossed my path, like a dog. I rode too fast up to him, which hurt my health. His teeth cut into me deeply, and the wound is still bleeding").

The lady, who has been assured that she is in the lover's thoughts, may well wonder if things have not gotten out of hand rather rapidly, for the lover has a vivid ability to make comparisons. In fact, if anything unifies the lover's statements, it is the mind's capacity to hold a variety of thoughts, motives, and rationalizations. The mind of the lover thus ranges widely, from remembered pain (ll. 1645-8) to hoped-for reward (ll. 1662, 1668), from recollection of the period when he did not know love to earnestness of purpose (ll. 1659-60). If his intent is to convince the lady of his devotion, he employs rather a shotgun approach, alternating statements of reliance on her to heal him (ll. 1695ff.) with vivid descriptions of the pain he endures for her sake (ll. 1707ff.) and protestations of his loyalty with appeals to her better nature (ll. 1861ff.).

The appeal to the lady has a strained quality, which stems in part from the strictures imposed by the rhyme scheme. The appeal is also intended to be self-conscious in a way that the greater part of the poem is not. In the dialogue between the heart and the body there is, even in the most acrimonious moments, a basic ease between the two, despite the fact that they are, after all, warring body parts; each can act aggrieved, can confide, and can rail at the other, and each can do so on the basis of the freedom that comes from having cast its lot with the other for better or for worse. The dialogue, moreover, is between parts of one mind *represented by body parts*, parts that may not know each other perfectly but that know each other sufficiently to communicate successfully in the end. In the appeal to the lady, however, one hears only one half of a dialogue.

One learns exclusively of "'mannes muot'" (l. 1612; "'man's inclination'"), so that the lady is seen through man's eyes, becoming an image of his making, shaped by his words. Interchange is lacking, for in the bulk of *Die Klage* Hartmann wishes to focus on the contents and functions of *one* mind, which is also what he does in his love lyrics.[6] He is not interested here in showing interchange between the knight and the lady but employs the narrative perspective of the man to hint at the possibilities of increasing difficulties once a second person enters the picture. In *Die Klage* the sense is that of one mind mulling contradictory possibilities, recalling the past and hoping for the future, speculating and evaluating, turned almost totally inward. The lady provides more food for thought, more opportunity for the mind to suffer or rejoice. *Her* actions filter through *his* consciousness, and she is ever on his mind, which circles restlessly, examining not only events but also thoughts about events.

One of Hartmann's lyric poems from *Des Minnesangs Frühling*, the only one I will enter into this book's argument, demonstrates this sense of mind-centeredness particularly well, and the state of affairs is very like that in *Die Klage*, even to echoing language used in the longer poem. It proves useful at this point to consider several of the possibilities the poem raises:

205, 1   Sît ich den sumer truoc riuw unde klagen
          sô ist ze fröiden mîn trôst niht sô guot,
          mîn sanc ensül des winters wâpen tragen:
          daz selbe tuot ouch mîn vil sender muot.
5   wie lützel mir mîn staete liebe tuot!
          wan ich vil gar an ir versûmet hân
          die zît, den dienest, dar zuo langen wân.
          ich wil ir anders ungefluochet lân
          wan so, sî hât niht wol ze mir getân.
10   Wolt ich den hazzen der mir leide tuot,
          sô möhte ich wol mîn selbes vîent sîn..
          vil wandels hât mîn lîp und ouch der muot:
          daz ist an mînem ungelücke schîn.
          mîn vrowe gert mîn niht: diu schulde ist mîn.
15   sît sinne machent saeldehaften man
          und unsin staete saelde nie gewan,
          ob ich mit sinnen niht gedienen kan,
          dâ bin ich alterseine schuldic an.
       Dô ir mîn dienest niht ze herzen gie,
20   dô dûhte mich an ir bescheidenlich
          daz sî ir werden lîbes mich erlie:
          dar an bedâhte sî vil rehte sich.

zürn ich, daz ist ir spot und altet mich.
grôz was mîn wandel: dô sî den entsaz,
25   dô meit sî mich, vil wol geloube ich daz,
mê dur ir êre danne ûf mînen haz:
sî waenet des, ir lop stê deste baz.
206,10 Ich hân des reht, daz mîn lîp trûric sî,
wan mich twinget ein vil sendiu nôt.
swaz vröiden mir von kinde wonte bî,
die sint verzinset, als ez got gebôt.
mich hât beswaeret mînes herren tôt.
dar zuo so trüebet mich ein varende leit:
mich hât ein wîp genade widerseit,
der ich gedienet hân mit staetekeit,
206, 1   sît der stunde, daz ich ûf mîme stabe [reit].
Sî hâte mich nâch wâne unrehte erkant,
dô sî mich ir von êrste dienen liez:
dur daz sî mich sô wandelbaere vant,
mîn wandel und ir wîsheit mich verstiez.
sî hât geleistet swaz sî mir gehiez;
5   swaz sî mir solde, des bin ich gewert:
er ist ein tump man, der iht anders gert:
si lônde mich als ich sî dûhte wert:
mi[ch]ne sleht niht anders wan mîn selbes swert.[7]

(Ever since I carried grief and lament all summer long, my assurance of happiness is not so good, that my song will not also bear a wintery coat of arms. My yearning, love-sick spirit is doing the same. How little joy I have from my constancy! I have squandered it: the season, the service, also long cherished hope. I won't speak ill of her except to say she has not treated me well.

If I wanted to hate the one who does me pain, I would have to be my own enemy. My body, and also my spirit, have many faults: this is apparent by my misfortune. My lady does not desire me: the fault is mine. For intelligence makes a man happily virtuous, and lasting bliss was never obtained from stupidity. If I cannot serve with intelligence, it is solely my own fault.

When my service to her did not strike her heart, it seemed fitting to me that she did not give herself to me. She was quite right in coming to that conclusion.

If I become angry, that would heap scorn on her and
wear me out. My failing was great: she feared it
and therefore avoided me. I believe this without
doubt: she did it more to save her honor in others'
eyes, than because she hated me. She thinks that
she will thereby be more praised.

Great pain causes my sorrow. I've paid the taxes for
whatever joys I knew in my youth, as God required.
My lord's death has made me very sorrowful, and I
also carry a burden with me: a lady whom I have
served with constancy, since the very hour that I
made my choice, has denied me favor.

She apparently misjudged me from the very start of
allowing me to serve her: she found me very
mutable. My changeable aspect and her wisdom took
a wrong turn. She has done for me what she
promised, and I have paid for what she owed me.
It is an ignorant man who desires anything else. She
rewarded me as she thought I deserved: I have
simply fought against myself with none other than
my own sword).

The poem abounds in oppositions and juxtapositions—and not just in the conventional pairs of *sumer/winter* ("summer/winter") and "sinne/unsin" ("intelligence/stupidity") but also in the continued sounding of the relationships "'sî mich'" (ll. 205,21, 25; 206,1,2,3; "'she to me'") and "'sî mir'" (ll. 205,9; 206,5,6,8; "'she to me'"). It is not merely that the poet wishes to show a man and a woman not of the same mind, but also that that state of affairs is to be seen from the confused and self-contradictory perspective of the man, as is the case in *Die Klage*. It is his "'yearning spirit'" (l. 205,4) that mulls over behavior, that retraces the progress of his suit, and that comes to the conclusions that keep circling back to himself: "'michne sleht niht anders wan mîn selbes swert'" (l. 206,9; "'I fought against myself with none other than my own sword'").

Like the dual speakers of *Die Klage*, the speaker of the poem goes over the ground of self-reproach, impatience, anger, and veiled aggression directed at the lady, as well as despair and insight. Throughout, the tone is reminiscent of individual sections of *Die Klage*, and several lines employ identical terminology.[8] Moreover, like *Die Klage*, this poem conveys the strong sense of the mind talking to itself, of weighing possibilities and evaluating events, moving in the first strophe from an assertion of its misery to a bitter summation. The last two lines in particular hark back to the sniping by the body when it states that it did not want to say anything bad about the lady and then proceeds to do so (ll. 121ff.). The sense of the mind talking to itself is further underscored by the opening lines of the second strophe, where the expression "'mîn selbes vîent'" (l. 205,11) echoes l. 1453 of *Die Klage*: ("'I am not my own enemy'"). The obvious meaning is that one can do harm to oneself, but the additional implication would seem to be that one can be so divided of mind that one impulse can war against another, a situation graphically set out in the body-heart debate and mirrored in the poem's reference to the mind's changeability (l. 205,12). The antidote to the changeable mind is, in both the poem and *Die Klage*, *staete* ("loyalty/constancy"), and it is a constancy born of the mind at peace with itself, at ease with its resolve to serve. Yet, where the mind divided in *Die Klage* comes to a more complete recognition of what loyalty/constancy entail, the speaker of *MF* 205,1 apprehends his plight intellectually but not completely in an emotional sense, for the poem captures a mind arrested at what would be an early stage in *Die Klage*: caught up in self-reproach, despair, and bitterness. It is a mind at the point in which it sees others as only a type of reflection of its own inclinations, so that Hartmann writes: "'sî lônde mir als ich sî dûhte wert'" (l. 206,8; "'she rewarded me as she thought I deserved'"). Moreover, the mind in *Die Klage* has realized what the speaker of the poem has not—that is, that a lover must go beyond the stage of being preoccupied with reward to the point where he serves the lady because it is good to do so, and where it is assumed that reward (read: reciprocation) will come naturally.

In subsequent works Hartmann details the mind as it turns outward, both in light of its auxiliary functions and as it actively encounters other minds. Yet the principles of mind established in *Die Klage* are evident throughout the later works, although perhaps most accessible in *Erec*, where the interior monologues have much the same character as the musings of the heart and the body. The relationship between *Die Klage* and *Erec* is close, because of chronology, recognition of reliance on reason, manuscript order, shared language, and a widespread assumption that *Die Klage* provides the bones and *Erec* the flesh of a shared view on love.

Peter Wapnewski expresses the transition between the two works:

> Auf das Lehrstück folgt das Zeugnis der ersten Meisterschaft, auf die Didaxe das Beispiel, auf die Allegorie die Darstellung: die Geschichte Hartmanns des Dichters setzt ein mit dem ersten deutschen Artusroman, dem *Erek*.[9]

On Wapnewski's account, *Die Klage* serves as an "Etüde" that testifies to Hartmann's reliance on the power of reason, and, as such, forms a worthy prelude to *Erec*:

> Jetzt nimmt der Dichter die Fackel der lebensbewältigenden Verstandesklarheit und Erleuchtung und trägt sie in die eigentliche Dichtungswelt, in der sich dieser fromme Optimismus nun handelnd entfaltet: in das Reich des Königs Artus, in dem es immer licht ist.[10]

But *Die Klage*, as I establish in this chapter, concerns itself as much with irrationality and capriciousness as it does with rationality and order. As a mental debate, as a rendition through a conventionalized conflict between heart and body that portrays what the interior of a mind resembles, *Die Klage* cannot treat the physical world and the Arthurian world as *Erec* will, for *Die Klage* is concerned with mirroring mental progress exclusively. It sets out an anatomy of the functions of a mind as the seat of both reason and emotion, and as an entity capable of reflection, imagination, and problem-solving. Going a step further in the next chapter, I will show in the movement from *Die Klage* to *Erec* other significant developments in Hartmann's exposition of what mind entails.

In his first work Hartmann asks, among other questions, the following ones: how do two separate—but linked—halves of one entity communicate with each other? This focus widens in *Erec*, for, with the presence of plot and representations of the physical world, the consequences of communication—or noncommunication—of necessity become more complex, so that the ramifications of the issue extend beyond thought to the realm of action. Yet the first work provides the underpinnings for the second, and not only in the sense of functioning as evidence of apprenticeship, as Wapnewski has argued, but also in its deliberately limited scope: it shows a struggle of mind, with irrationality sometimes appearing on the side of the body and sometimes on that of the heart, with the resolution coming only when each side actually listens to the other and reflects on the other's viewpoint. *Erec*'s struggle will be similarly constituted and resolved, but, since the arena of that struggle is expanded to include the spiritually resonant Arthurian landscape, the hero's progress is marked not only in battles joined but also in words heard; the man who has ears but who cannot hear and who prefers silence to speech is transformed through the intervention of his wife into someone worthy of honor and kingship—but not without considerable conflict. What one sees, then, in both works is an entity in strife (heart-body in *Die Klage* and man-wife in *Erec*), and the torrent of words and total lack of external action in *Die Klage* actually speak to the same problem raised in the cyclical romance conventions of *Erec*: how does communication change the lover's mind, refine it, and strengthen it?[11]

2

EREC

Language, Perception, and Mind

Hartmann's von Aue's *Erec* draws on the fundamental meaning of *âventiure*—"that which comes to one"—for the physical world provides precisely the right incentives and obstacles that the protagonist requires for his development, and at exactly the times he needs them. As a result, Erec's encounters with giants, dwarves, and malign nobles in the mainly untouched forest that then covered Europe do not constitute a haphazard series of unrelated events, but rather form a carefully considered, structured,[1] and timed sequence of challenges that chart Erec's spiritual progress on his road to kingship. Yet there remains the deliberate illusion of randomness in Erec's adventures, and this is in part explained by the constitution of the audience (which I define here as readers/listeners) as well as by poetic design. Hartmann is very aware that part of the audience will analyze and discuss the story, and perhaps retell it, and part can simply lean back and uncritically watch the show—and what a show it is, with a succession of lecherous counts, a magically-bounded garden replete with impaled heads, and even a moveable court with a portable Round Table. The sense of spectacle characterizing *Erec*, as well as other Arthurian romances, serves a distinct purpose that cannot be over-emphasized: it is a feast for the ears if one cannot read and one for the eyes as well if one can read.

What Ulrich Gaier has shown to be true about the several centuries later Early New High German work, *Das Narrenschiff*, applies to *Erec*.[2] The Renaissance and Reformation German Humanists, a highly educated community with an appreciation for narrative technique, loved *Das Narrenschiff* and respected it for its advanced and complicated rhetorical presentation, but that sophistication of style did not diminish the work's appeal to the less literate, who could read the episodes and be amused or admonished, or to the barely literate, who could con out the meaning of the pithy couplets under the woodcuts, or, finally, to the illiterate, who could get some gist of the matter by examining the woodcuts. It was an inspired "high culture"/"popular culture" mix with eclectic appeal, and its success was astonishing, judging from the number of editions printed and translations into Latin and other European vernacular languages.

That literary breadth—"something for everyone"—underscores *Erec*, for Hartmann advances his rendition of a commonly known episodic plot with an eye to the various attention spans of different segments of his audience, as well as with an openness toward any synthetic, analytical ability that can be brought to bear on the work by listener, reader, or even modern day critic as he/she attempts to make sense of the order and sequence of the narrative segments in the work. On the one hand, the adventures move along at a good clip, so that Hartmann works to maintain entertainment, and the audience is kept as off-balance as Erec himself is as he moves from encounter to encounter. On the other hand, while seemingly random, Erec's adventures are not so many nor so dizzying that the audience senses incoherence and backs off from experiencing the story.

The illusion of randomness in *Erec* operates on one level only. I think that it is deliberately fostered and sustained by the poet. This not only allows the medieval audience and modern critic the pleasure of culling the fruit from the chaff, but it also allows the work's landscape, events, and characters to be seen through the protagonist's own eyes. Danger after unforeseen danger comes into sudden focus against unfamiliar scenery. Danger is heard approaching through Erec's ears, with ominous sounds magnified at times and/or slowly sorting themselves out of the background noise of court and forest, so that the narrative perspective frequently hones in on Erec's immediate surroundings in a horrifying way. What proves to be paradoxical is that the nature of Arthurian landscape is so infinitely accommodating to the needs of individual protagonists and yet they so often do not know where they are or where they are going. If in fact they are questing with some goal in mind, they generally do not know where to look for it, as is the case with Parzival, who is intended for the Grail but has no idea where to seek it. Things *befall* these heroes, things and people come *to* them in the senses of *âventiure*, and their courses through the Arthurian landscape often make sense once the protagonists attain the goal for which they are destined. They may take wrong turns, which implies faulty choices at forks in the path, but even these seeming missteps appear to be foreordained, for they, too, teach.

Hartmann, accordingly, charges the hero—and the audience—with making sense out of Erec's journey. However, the seeming randomness and disorientation Erec experiences are to be understood in a different way by the audience. The audience's task is to sort out the significance of Erec's seemingly disorganized adventures, much as it is to analyze the skipping nature of the body's and heart's mental activity in *Die Klage*. In *Erec* the audience is given a leg-up, because there is action on a physical level, as opposed to only dialogue;

"action" gives the illusion in literature of concreteness, a plot comes into being, and in *Erec* one discerns patterns and sees progress. Finally, to aid the audience, an obliging narrator provides commentary and assessments concerning the hero's progress, both straightforwardly and ironically, noting what he as narrator knows and does not know. In the former instance a situation obtains whereby Erec's perceptual limitations are pitted against the narrator's—and audience's—superior knowledge of the circumstance, as is the case when Erec and Enîte flee preciptiously and leave the audience to enjoy the comic scene in which the enraged count and outraged innkeeper trade insults. The audience knows then what Erec can only dread: pursuit and perhaps death. In the latter instance, where the narrator states that he does *not* know a detail or an outcome, the audience can construe this either as a sign of Hartmann's deviation from or disregard of his source or as an impetus for the individual to come to his/her own conclusions. For example, if one takes with a grain of salt the narrator's disclaimer concerning Mâbonagrîn, the audience can speculate profitably about that rash knight's chances, despite "'ich enweiz wie ez im ergie'" (l. 8886; "'I don't know what happened to him'"—p. 132). The audience suspects: trouble is on the horizon.

Erec is a work that, while building on the concept of mind that Hartmann established in *Die Klage,* does so with certain additional factors, the first two of which have been introduced here: 1) the presence of exterior landscape, which varies the backdrop for action, in addition to that interior mental space that generates thoughts, and 2) the addition of an omniscient narrator to comment upon what characters know, do not know, or think they know, and to provide the convention of a direct bridge to the audience. A third factor is an outgrowth of the previous two: *Erec* is concerned with the mechanics of how thought is transformed into action, and the audience is challenged to see that connection, which Hartmann poses in a subtle fashion even in the conventional rhyme-pair of *m u o t* ("mind/inclination") and *tuot* ("action/doing"),[3] between thought and action. What, then, is the relation of the interior world of mind to the outer world of action? For this question I will focus on Hartmann's understanding of two related functions of mind: perception and judgment.

For much of *Erec,* Hartmann characterizes his protagonist as a man plagued by disorientation. A close examination of the narrator's[4] justifications for Erec's perceptual failures gives access not only to Hartmann's concern with the interrelated functions of mind, but also to the work's thematic structure. Throughout the poem, the narrator calls attention to Erec's frequent difficulties with the landscape in which he maneuvers and with the people he encounters. The narrator repeatedly notes Erec's lack of familiarity with his surroundings: Erec is said to ride "wîselôs" (l. 250; Thomas, p. 34, translates as "forsaken," but I would opt for "without direction") and according to caprice ("nâch wâne"—l. 7808; "at random"—p. 120).

The narrator even notes that he rides "als in bewîste der wec, / er enweste selbe war" (ll. 5288-90; "Erec now just followed the road, not knowing where it led"—p. 92). His path takes him in "ein unkundez lant" (l. 4278; "a strange land"—p. 79), and it is not only the land that is "unkunt "(l. 4623; "unknown"—p. 83), but, at times, the path itself: "nû was der wec im unerkant" (l. 6737; "he did not know the way"—p. 108). His lack of familiarity with his surroundings extends to a nonrecognition of opponents—understandable in the case of his initial encounter with Idêr (l. 459; p. 36) or Guivreiz (ll. 4468ff.; p. 82) but more problematic when it comes to his second encounter with Guivreiz (ll. 6893ff.; p. 109), which occurs on a cloudless, moonlit night when visibility ought not to be impaired (ll. 6894-5; p. 109). Hartmann in *Iwein* rationalizes Iwein's nonrecognition of Gâwein partially on the grounds of nightfall (l. 7517; p. 140),[5] but Iwein is a better perceiver than Erec (his problems lie elsewhere, tied to another function of mind). Erec is as unaware of impending dangers in the forest (ll. 3123, 4150ff; pp. 66, 78) as he is of the dangers in the bedroom. He is the last to hear what others have been saying about him, so absorbed is he in his wife and in sensuality.

What proves interesting here is the narrator's compulson to provide disclaimers that minimize Erec's failings on the grounds of physical unaccountability. Thus, it is Enîte who sees the three robbers before her husband, and she does so, on Hartmann's account, merely because "si verre vor reit" (l. 3124; "Enite was some distance ahead"—p. 66). Yet this statement seems less a commentary on Erec's eyesight than on his lack of perception, particularly when it is considered along with the narrator's other excuses. The reader is told that it is Enîte who is able to ascertain the lecherous count's intent and parry his verbal thrusts, simply because she is sitting at some distance from her husband:

> . . . si sô besunder
> an dem tische sâzen
> und ensament niht enâzen
> (ll. 3731-3; . . . that the two of them should
> sit far apart instead of together—p. 73).

But here, too, the audience's immediate response is to question the given explanation, to wonder how Erec could *not* notice the count's advances to and flattery of Enîte, as well as Enîte's lengthy rejoinders. The audience is urged to take the bait the narrator offers and to speculate. Perhaps the most curious disclaimer comes in a narrative intrusion that approaches a rationalization. Enîte hears the approach of "a large company" (l. 4148; p. 78) and warns Erec, at which point the narrator hastens to note:

> nû endarf niemen sprechen daz:
> "von wiu kam daz diu vrouwe baz
> beide gehôrte unde gesach?"

> ich sage iu von wiu daz geschach.
> diu vrouwe reit gewaefens bar:
> dâ was er gewâfent gar,
> als ein guot ritter sol.
> daz gehôrte er noch gesach sô wol
> ûz der îsenwaete
> als er blôzer taete
>
> (ll. 4150-9; No one needs ask, "How did it happen that the lady could both hear and see better than the knight?" Because I shall tell you how it was. She was unarmed, while he, as is proper for a brave knight, was in full armor, which kept him from hearing and seeing as well as he could have without it—p. 78).

The audience's immediate response is that this is sound reasoning, medieval armor being what it was.[6] Yet, upon closer examination, difficulties arise, paramount of which is that all of Erec's opponents are armed and armed as he is, if Kâlogrenant's definition of a knight in *Iwein* is correct and yet they are cast as being more perceptive than he is, in that either they spot him before he sees or hears them or they are engaged in active pursuit of him.[7] Moreover, none of Erec's opponents sends out a woman as an advance guard as Erec does. One could be facetious and I will be and propose that, if knights were so hampered perceptually by their martial gear, each would have a woman in tow, not to provide decoration or motivation—and inspiration—for battle, but rather to act as a scout, much as a shark has a pilot fish as part of its defense system. Thus, the narrator's involved explanation of Erec's perceptual limitations, rather than settling the matter as it ostensibly sets out to do,[8] raises the issue of perception—what one knows through one's senses—in an impelling way. Suddenly the audience finds instances in which Erec's perceptual abilities are limited or even lacking: is this due to insensitivity or to what the narrator tosses off as a lack of physical accountability? Erec's problem seems to be not as much *martial* as *marital*. He simply does not pick up on the dangers that an unbalanced life presents, and Enîte does. She senses dangers where he does not, and her perceptiveness has nothing to do with where she is in relation to him.

Accordingly, in the cases where Hartmann shows Enîte operating perceptively while at a distance from her husband, the author cannot be implying that physical proximity to the dangers threatening his wife would make Erec a more perceptive individual, for it is when Erec and Enîte are in greatest moral danger and in proximity, as he succumbs to uxoriousness[9] early in the romance, that he is most unaware—and she particularly aware—of the dangers such "gemach" (l. 2967; "ease"—p. 64) presents.[10] Similarly, in the companion *Scheintod* scene at Lîmors, Erec is near his threatened wife but is, for most of the scene, oblivious to his surroundings and to the attendant danger due to his unconsciousness. The decisive factor here cannot be proximity, but rather the consciousness of a danger, whether it be on the battleground or in the bedroom, a consciousness that entails not only perception but also the correct interpretation of perceptions, as well as one that results in actions that can rectify a situation. The Erec at the outset of the romance possesses this consciousness, and he wisely perceives danger and acts prudently ("wîslîchen"—l. 100; p. 32) to avoid physical confrontation when he is unarmed and is, significantly, described by Hartmann as being "blôz sam ein wîp" (l. 103; "he wore no more armor than a woman"—p. 32). But Erec, in acquiring a wife and lover,[11] lapses.[12] Over the bulk of the romance, which occurs after Erec has won Enîte and has lost his perceptual acuity and has only eyes and mind for her, Hartmann charts the process whereby the hero is transformed from a man who cannot perceive correctly and, as example, to consider the implications of rash decision (his resolution to use his wife as bait for robbers and thieves), unconsidered word-giving (Mâbonagrîn's pledge to his wife), and precipitous action (Oringles' physical and verbal abuse of Enîte). He is given positive *exempla* of prudent behavior in the heightened perception and wise counsel of Gâwein, Guivreiz, Enîte's father, and especially his own wife, who speaks words of wisdom that Erec hears but initially cannot comprehend. Each adventure that befalls Erec teaches him and, at the same time, tests him in the translation of accurate perceptions into knowledge and, in turn, into sensible speech and wise action. Erec, who repeatedly and even brutally enjoins his wife to silence when she gives him information vital to his survival, becomes a man who learns that it is wise to employ a variety of responses, now speech and now action, and sometimes silence, and who protects his wife from, rather than exposes her to, danger. In order to examine the transformation of the hero, it is useful to consider Erec's changing attitude toward language, which serves as a mediator, on the one hand, between knowledge, so directly dependent upon perception, and, on the other hand, speech, that vocalization that so often precedes action and may follow considered thought.

Hartmann's most obvious concern with language in *Erec* is couched in terms of a speech/silence dichotomy. This concern is apparent in his frequent employment of variations on *sagen/verdagen* as couplet rhymes, since repeated rhyme-pair placement often serves as a way to focus on important oppositions. Moreover, the concern is placed before the audience in interior monologues, in the scrupulously presented debates in Enîte's mind, debates whose subjects treat the question of whether or not to speak, and whose resolutions break the silence. In fact, the very plot hinges on the presence and absence of speech, as well as on the perception and interpretation of language. Rarely do medieval romances eschew dialogue, but *Erec* is unusual in its use of dialogue as a thematic concern as well as a plot facilitator. In *Erec* are raised questions not only about the suitability of speech at certain times but also about speech as a vehicle for thought and as an expression of intent. Hartmann here takes a leaf from Chrétien's book, but he amplifies those concerns and, through narrative asides, gives the audience access to a mind aware of the uses of language and silence to tell the story of Erec and Enîte.

Accordingly, each of Erec's adventures contains at least one interchange concerning the use, value, or suitability of speech. Erec is, in the early part of the romance, a talker. He is often cast in the role of one who demands information or who admonishes others to remain silent when their words are foolish ("'sult ir stille gedagen'"—l. 577; "'say no more about it'"—p. 37), and it is Erec who responds prudently in the maiden's encounter with the alternately verbally abusive and taciturn dwarf (ll. 44-5; p. 31). Hartmann's intent in presenting Erec's encounter with the ill-mannered dwarf, over and above his decision to follow Chrétien's model, is to create an encapsulated portrait of Erec against which the audience can later judge the hero, a portrait that stresses Erec's initial wisdom with respect to speech and action.

First, it must be noted that the fundamentals of the opening sequence are startlingly like those of Erec's later adventures. The paradigm amounts to this: a woman rides forth alone into an unknown situation, while Erec initially remains at a safe distance and this is not at all unlike Enîte's repeatedly testing dangerous waters for her husband. The maiden, like Enîte, suffers the consequences. In the opening sequence, however, Erec quickly perceives the danger, the ugly nature of the strange knight and his diminutive minion, and the necessity of intervention, and caps this knowledge with a speech that stresses his eagerness to know more:

> Erec dô ahten began,
> der ritter enwaere dehein vrum man,
> daz er ez vor im vertruoc
> daz sîn getwerc die maget sluoc.
> er sprach: "ich wil rîten dar,
> daz ich iu diu maere ervar"
> (ll. 66-71; Erec thought that it was
> dishonorable of the knight to look on and do nothing
> while his dwarf struck the maiden. He said, "I'll
> ride over and find out for you"—p. 32).

In fact, Erec earlier asked the Queen if he should determine the identity of the knight (ll. 18-20; p. 31), showing not only a desire for knowledge but also deference to a woman's wishes. Erec's attitude here stands in contrast to his subsequent disinterest in the dangers facing his wife, as she alerts him to problems at court and in the forest; his standard reaction later on is to rebuke her for her admonitions. Furthermore, it is significant that Erec's request to the dwarf is one for speech ("'muget ir wêniger mir gesagen'"—l. 76; "'Tell me, little fellow'"—p. 32), reiterating the maiden's request for knowledge, which was summarily met with a demand for silence (ll.

44-5; p. 31) and a blow. Erec's request meets a rude enjoinder to silence ("'lâ dîn klaffen sîn'"—l. 83; "'Hold your tongue'"—p. 32; I would render it more strongly, as in "'Shut your trap!'" or "'Shut up!'") and an incorrect assessment on the dwarf's part: "'ir ensît niht wîse liute'" (l. 88; "'You people are fools'"—p. 32).

Often Erec's opponents characterize him with language that better applies to themselves, so that their assessment of his folly actually reflects upon their own. An additional example presents itself in the later episode where Erec confronts the two giants who are torturing a knight. One giant responds to Erec's request to free the captive with a rude "'dîn klaffen ist mir ungemach'" (l. 5477; "'Your chatter bothers me'"—p. 94; again, I would render "klaffen" in ruder terms), and this opponent, although vastly different in terms of physical dimensions, also possesses an attribute that Hartmann uses when he wishes to portray characters acting at their worst: *zorn* ("anger"). Both the giant and the dwarf express anger and mistreat others, and Erec's later anger (ll. 3049; 3416; 3956; 3969; 4263; 4704; 5068; 5070; 5074; pp. 65, 69, 75, 76, 79, 85, 89) underscores his psychic abuse of his wife; in displaying anger, he behaves like those undersize or outsize bullies that populate medieval romance and epic. In the opening sequence, however, there is only anger on the part of the dwarf, who will later, on Erec's account, suffer for his ill-mannered wrath. Erec, for his part, speaks politely and mildly to the dwarf and, moreover, is said by the narrator to have acted prudently ("wîslîchen"—l. 100; "wisely"—p. 32) in postponing conflict until he is armed. That is an understatement, to say the least.

Erec returns to the Queen and in a lengthy monologue (ll. 113-43; pp. 32-3) recounts the events that have occurred (which she has witnessed from a distance), interjects his perception and interpretation of them, and details his anticipated reactions to them. The composite portrait of the protagonist at this stage in the romance reveals Erec to be a man who perceives, thinks, and acts wisely and who relies on language's capacity to communicate, for he both requests speech of the dwarf and tells the Queen his thoughts of revenge (ll. 135-7; p. 32). And he has no trouble recounting what has happened. Unlike the man he will become, the Erec at the romance's outset lets others know what is on his mind and what has occurred and what course of action ought to be followed. Moreover, he is positively talkative in comparison to either the maiden or the Queen.

Erec also exhibits the ability to think before he acts, which he will later lose, for he considers whether he has time to return to court to fetch his armor before setting out after the strange knight:

> ouch dâhte der juncherre,
> im waere daz ze verre,
> ob er zen selben zîten
> hin wider wolde rîten
> dâ er sînen harnasch hâte,

> und daz er alsô drâte
> in nimmer genaeme
> (swie schiere er wider kaeme,
> sô waeren si im entriten gar),
> und îlte in nâch alsô bar
>
> (ll. 150-9; The youthful lord thought it would be too far for him to ride back to where his armor was, that he would never return with it in time: no matter how he hurried, they would surely get away from him. He therefore hastened after them as he was—p. 33).[18]

It is, significantly, when Erec is "blôz als ein wîp" (l. 103; "he wore no more armor than a woman"—p. 32) that he is most perceptive, and he sensibly stays "at a distance" (p. 33; l. 165) from the dwarf, knight, and lady as they proceed to Imâin's festival, so that "he could see them without being noticed" (p. 33; l. 166). The idea of distance seems to be important here: Erec is able to separate subject (Erec as hunter) from object (Idêr as quarry) and can thus also sort out his plan of action.

The narrator next describes Erec's actions in language that is nearly proverbial:

> er tete als dem dâ leit geschiht:
> der vlîzet dicke sich dar zuo
> wie erz mit vuoge widertuo
>
> (ll. 167-9; He acted as one does who has suffered injury and takes great care to even things up in a suitable manner—p. 33).

This phrasing resembles Iwein's: "'ouch enhebet er niht den strît / der den êrsten slac gît'" (ll. 871-2; "'Moreover, the man who strikes out does not start a dispute if the other lets it go'"—p. 65). Both heroes set out on their adventures because of a slight to themselves—coupled with a desire for honor in one of its guises ("heil"—l. 139, "honor"—p. 32 in *Erec*; and "riterschaft"—l. 913, "knightly combat"—p. 65 in *Iwein*)—and a precipitousness attends each departure. Of the two, Iwein will be seen to be the more rash at the outset.[19] He employs stealth (l. 945; p. 66) and dissembling (l. 955; p. 66), much as Erec will later, when he conceals his purpose as well as his armor (ll. 3064ff.; p. 65) and gives out only that he and Enîte are riding out for pleasure rather than leaving the court. At the beginning of the romance, Erec has not learned to dissemble, nor has he any reason to do so. He simply fares forth, significantly lacking those standard possessions of knights, that is, armor and a woman—and the audience is led to believe that he will soon be provided with them.

This "clean slate" state is further emphasized by the fact that Erec is ignorant of the reason for and ritual of the "hôchzît" (l. 184;

"festival"—p. 33) that Imâin celebrates: "nû enweste Erec niht / umbe dise geschiht" (ll. 218-9; "Erec knew nothing of these things"—p. 33). Young and untried, he is not recognized by the boisterous populace attending the fête (ll. 245-7; p. 34). Riding without direction, he manages to find lodging, and the manner in which he does so is noteworthy. The audience is given a rare glimpse into his thoughts, when the hero takes refuge in "ein altez gemiure" (l. 252; "an old ruin"—p. 34) that he assumes to be deserted:

> er gedâhte: "mîn dinc daz vert nû wol,
> wan ich in einem winkel sol
> belîben hinne unz an den tac,
> sît ich niht wesen baz enmac.
> des gan man mir doch âne strît:
> ich sihe wol daz ez oede lît"
> (ll. 264-9; He thought, "Things are going all right now, for I can stay inside in some nook until daylight, since I haven't anything better. Surely no one will object; I can easily see that it is vacant"—p. 34).

It is not only an unusual glimpse into Erec's consciousness of his situation—he will not have another interior monologue until nearly 8,000 lines have passed (ll. 8147-53; p. 124), when his thoughts are rendered in a prayer to God—but it is also important that Erec here makes what will be for him a characteristic misperception. Just as he will later not recognize the full value of his wife, "ein diu schoeniste maget / von der uns ie wart gesaget" (ll. 310-1; "the most beautiful of whom we have ever heard"—p. 34), so he here is unaware of the presence of inhabitants in what he takes to be an abandoned house; in each instance he takes control of, or occupies, a space/enclosure/woman before he has information on the nature of the person he comes to love or the house he enters. And, like Iwein, Erec stumbles in the ruin upon more than bargained for, just as Iwein finds in the enchanted spring area more than a frivolous adventure.

In this scene, once Erec has recognized his mistake in assuming a tumble-down castle is vacant, one finds the hero portrayed primarily in a positive mode, for he addresses Koralus and then later requests information (ll. 447-50; p. 36) and advice (ll. 479, 495; pp. 36-7) from the old man. It is Erec who comments upon Enîte's caring for his horse and offers to do it himself (ll. 344-6; p. 35), an attitude opposed to that which he adopts later when he demands that Enîte care for not one, but many horses. Moreover, it is Erec who convinces Koralus that his words are to be taken seriously (l. 565; p. 37) about wanting to marry Enîte, and who admonishes her father to silence about the matter of Enîte's poverty:

> "ir armuot hoere ich iuch klagen:
> der sult ir stille gedagen.

> ez enschadet iu niht gegenmir,
> wan ich ir guotes wol enbir"
>> (ll. 576-9; "You lament her poverty: say no more about it. I shall not hold it against you, because I can easily do without her dowry"—p. 37).

Throughout the whole greeting sequence and bride-bartering interchange Enîte has been surprisingly taciturn, having been limited by Hartmann to one obedient phrase ("'herre, daz tuon ich'"—l. 322; "'I shall do it, sir'"—p. 35), which stands in direct contrast to her later speeches.[20] Rather, attention has been primarily paid to her looks, which are apparently spectacular. The reader learns that "der megede lîp was lobelich" (l. 323; "the maiden's figure was lovely"—p. 35) and that "man saget daz ni kint gewan / einen lîp sô gar dem wunsche gelîch" (ll. 331-2; "They say that no other maiden was so perfectly formed"—p. 35). Her obedience, too, is stressed, so that her actions congrue to the wishes of others (ll. 352-3; p. 35). She seems to have, other than her remarkable physical personage, no existence outside of how others perceive her and command her. None of her thoughts are recorded, and she takes no part in the conversation in which Erec assesses the contest at Imâîn's festival and then, coupling his desire for Enîte with the necessity of having a beautiful woman in order to take part in the sparrow hawk festivities, proposes to marry her.

The narrative focus is on Erec, and the audience is occupied with his curiosity and verbal ability. He is more than eager for information:

> den wirt er vrâgen began
> waz der schal von den liuten
> möhte bediuten
> den er in dem markete hete gesehen
>> (ll. 447-50; Erec asked the meaning of the large crowd he had seen in the market town—p. 36).

So eager, in fact, is Erec that Hartmann indicates his protagonist's intensity with repetitive language, so that, "dô vrâgete er aber vürbaz" (l. 457; "Erec questioned [him further]"—p. 36) is echoed in "mit vrâge er vürbaz kam" (l. 471; "Erec made further inquiries"—p. 36). He takes the initiative not only through his questions but also through his domination of Koralus, who initially feels mocked by Erec's proposal, both in the sense of using Enîte as a beauty contest entrant and in the sense of marrying her. Erec urges Koralus to to banish any thoughts that include mockery ("'durch schimph'"—l. 563; p. 37) on Erec's part, and to leave off speaking of his poverty. Mollified, Koralus grants Erec his daughter and throws in a suit of armor that he has kept around "'nâch wâne'" (l. 597; "'with the thought [that a friend might need it]'"—p. 38). Suddenly Erec is provisioned with the necessary equipment—armor[21] and a woman—

for knightly adventure. In the tradition of *âventiure*, things come to Erec.

But my concern is with the bride-to-be. Enîte must have been present during the interchange between Erec and his host, but the audience does not know her thoughts. Attention is focused on those of the man and on his willingness to communicate them: "'ich sage iu wie mîn muot stât'" (l. 501; "'I'll tell you what I have in mind'"—p. 37). Enîte is given no recorded speech until her outburst in the bedroom during the honeymoon period:

> si sprach: "wê dir, dû vil armer man,
> und mir ellendem wîbe,
> daz ich mînem lîbe
> sô manegen vluoch vernemen sol"
> (ll. 3029-32; "Alas for you, poor man," she
> said, "and for me, wretched woman, that I should
> hear so many condemn me"—p. 65).

This is not that she has had nothing to say; rather, she has had no direct speech. The audience learns that she laments as Erec fights Idêr (ll. 802, 852; pp. 40-1), but the overall impression of a nonverbal Enîte is reinforced in the vignette that occurs after the sparrow hawk incident:

> in ir schôz leite in
> daz kint vrouwe Enîte
> ze ruowe nâch dem strîte.
> ir gebaerde was vil bliuclîch,
> einer magede gelîch.
> si *enredete* im *niht vil* mite:
> wan daz ist ir aller site
> daz si zem êrsten schamic sint
> und blûc sam diu kint
> (ll. 1317-25, my italics; The young Enite laid
> his head in her lap so that he could rest from battle.
> She acted very shy, as maidens do, and said little to
> him. That is the way they are: at first they are as
> bashful and timid as children—pp. 46).

The scene comes across as a tableau, part chivalric, part pièta, but, for the purposes of this argument, one more than indicative of Enîte's passive, nonverbal role at this stage in the romance.

Furthermore, that Enîte's one thought before the outburst is also Erec's thought raises interesting implications. Hartmann notes:

> ir beider gedanc stuont alsô:
> "jâ enwirde ich nimmer vrô,
> ich engelige dir noch bî
> zwô naht oder drî"

> (ll. 1872-5; Each thought, "I shall never be happy until I have lain two or three nights with you"—pp. 51-2).

The shared thought is unblushingly sensual, and it suggests that Enîte is perceiving herself as the sexual being Erec sees her to be. In fact, Erec's initial interest in her is aroused solely by her beauty, and he frankly counters Imâîn's cordial offer of better clothing for Enîte with a cool statement of what he feels is worth noting in a woman:

> "er haete harte missesehen,
> swer ein wîp erkande
> niuwan bî dem gewande.
> man sol einem wîbe
> kiesen bî dem lîbe
> ob si ze lobe stât
> unde niht bî der wat"
> (ll. 643-9; "Whoever judges a woman only by her clothing is greatly deceived. One should decide on the basis of her person, not her dress, whether or not a woman is beautiful" —p. 38).

In Middle High German, *lîp* ("body, person, being") is, to be sure, a loaded word,[23] but, given Erec's subsequent tendency to uxoriousness and Enîte's repeated association with horses, frequent icons for lust and the flesh during the Middle Ages,[24] it is reasonable to assume that Erec's interest is with *lîp* on the literal, rather than the abstract, level. In fact, this seems to be the standard response to Enîte, with the result that even her uncle perceives her as contents that one can enhance by the vessel that surrounds it: "'ouch volget mîner lêre / und lât mich si vazzen baz'" (ll. 639-40; "'take my advice and let me dress her better'"—p. 38). Imâîn's assessment of and Erec's interest in Enîte's *lîp* is shared by the Arthurian court, which, after one collectively dazzled glance at her person, selects her as "die schoenste" (l. 1742; "the fairest woman"—p. 50). Her physical beauty even makes a self-professed lover of the narrator, who describes Enîte's new clothes, which include "a gleaming ruby" (l. 1562; p. 48) as ornament,[25] and then affects an inability to do justice to them on account of her beauty:

> "doch bescheide ichz sô ich beste kan
> und als ichz vernomen han,
> sô was ûzer strîte:
> ez was vrouwe Enîte
> diu aller schoeniste maget
> diu ie, sô man saget,
> in des küneges hof kam"
> (ll. 1604-10; "Lacking experience, I cannot do her justice, but shall nevertheless proclaim her

beauty as best I can and as I have heard it: Lady Enite was without question the loveliest maiden ever to enter the king's court"—p. 49).

That such a beautiful woman should have any thoughts other than sensual ones (ll. 1873-5; p. 52) or concern for her spouse's physical safety (ll. 802, 852; pp. 40, 41) comes as a shock both to Erec[27] and, for that matter, the audience, which has heard what Erec has to say and is aware that he does in fact think (ll. 264, 582, 931, 1806, 1872, 2249, 2254, 2545, 2788; pp. 34, 38, 41, 51, 56, 61-2) but who has found Enîte to be decorative but essentially vacuous. If the audience is unprepared for Enîte's subsequent portrayal as an extremely verbal wisdom figure, one can readily imagine Erec's astonishment at getting more than he expected in the person of Enîte.[28] And just as Enîte begins to think and talk, so Erec reverts to minimal use of language[29] and, with one exception over thousands of lines (ll. 3004-6711; pp. 65-107), to thoughtlessness, both in the sense that he is not reported to have thoughts and in the sense that he exhibits reckless disregard for the physical person he previously so cherished. The exceptional thought ("gedanc"—l. 4239; Thomas, p. 79, translates this freely as "anxiety") that Erec does entertain is a prayer to God that he—there is no reference to Enîte—might be delivered without harm "'von disem lande'" (l. 4235; "'out of the land'"—p. 79). Erec, who is led by "der wec" into "ein unkundez lant" (ll. 4277, 4278; "the road . . . into a strange land"—p. 79), needs Enîte to escape, but he cannot perceive the full extent of this need, nor is he capable of expressing it now. And he will only orient himself in the physical landscape once he knows Enîte on more than the carnal level.[30]

Hartmann emphasizes the sudden glimpse into Enîte's inner thoughts, expressed vocally much more than does his predecessor Chrétien.[31] Chrétien, like Hartmann, makes much of his heroine's beauty, but Enide's beauty is said to be surpassed by her wisdom; she is *sage* ("wise"), and the reader is thus prepared for her prudent assessment of her husband's lapse, her reasonable commentary, and her wise actions as they journey through the forest. Moreover, Chrétien sets the stage for such wisdom, in that every character in his romance is judged according to his or her wisdom or folly. Hartmann, however, prefers the sharp disjunction between silence and language in his portrayal of Enîte, probably because of its effect on an audience; Enîte's verbal transformation is so unexpected that the audience has the opportunity to see her through Erec's shocked and angry eyes.[32]

There has been some intimation that Enîte has entertained thoughts concerning Erec's transformation, cued by the ominous *exempla* of Solomon, Absolom, Samson, and Alexander (ll. 2815-21; p. 62),[33] and those thoughts come in the mental conflict she has as to whether she wants a coward or a warrior for a husband (ll. 2845-8; p. 62). But these thoughts have not been voiced, and, as a result,

Erec has not been a party to them. But, more than that, Erec's mind has been elsewhere. As Hartmann notes:

> Erec was biderbe unde guot,
> ritterlîche stuont sîn muot
> ê er wîp genaeme
> und hin heim kaeme:
> nû sô er heim komen ist,
> dô kêrte allen sînen list
> an vrouwen Enîten minne
> (ll. 2924-30; Erec was upright and capable, and, before marrying and returning home, had had a knightly spirit. Now, however, he thought only of Enite's love—p. 64).

He spurns society, preferring to be "'von den liuten'" (l. 2950; "'[away from] the others'"—p. 64) and becomes not only so absorbed in his wife but also so caught up in himself that he ceases to hear or see what others might be—and are—thinking of him. Yet, as his perceptual acuity declines, Enîte's increases, and with it her mental activity, so that references to perception (ll. 3001, 3007; p. 65) occur along with those to thought ("und gedâhte manegen enden"—l. 3004; "she tried to think of some way"—p. 65 and "dâ begunde si denken an"—l. 3024; "chanced to think"—p. 65) and finally culminate in Enîte's vocalization of her thoughts.

Erec, oblivious to the court's talk that had progressed to the point that even his wife heard it (ll. 2999ff.; p. 65), suddenly apprehends the situation: "dô vernam Erec die rede wol" (l. 3033; "Erec heard her plainly"—p. 65). His immediate response is a speech studded with language terms: 1) "'saget'" (l. 3035; "'spoke up'"—p. 65), 2) "'klaget'" (l. 3037; "'replied'"—p. 65); 3) "'gelougent'" (l. 3038; "'deny'"—p. 65); 4) "'lât die rede stân'" (l. 3039; "'Stop that!'"—p. 65); 5) "'die rede'" (l. 3041; "'what you were talking about'"—p. 65); 6) "'sagen'" (l. 3042; "'tell me'"—p. 65); 7) "'klagen'" (l. 3043; "'[what it is that I heard you] bewailing'"—p. 65); 8) "'verswigen'" (l. 3044; "'and keeping from me'"—p. 65), and capped with a terse "'der ist genuoc getân'" (l. 3052; "'I've heard enough'"—l. 65). His reported speech thus is a talk about talking—and not talking—about language and silence, and it sets the stage for the many debates on the wisdom or folly of speaking out that occur in the romance. Erec's immediate response, too, involves a verbal deception, and this is the first time that his manner is less than straightforward. As Erec becomes taciturn and bids Enîte to do likewise, his actions become covert. He keeps his thoughts to himself (ll. 3077-9; p. 65). He dons armor in secret, leaves instruction with the cooks that dinner is to be ready upon his return, and gives out that he "wolde rîten /ûz kurzwîlen" (ll. 3061-2; "to a tournament [or for pleasure]"—p. 65). The change in Erec is not only signalled by Hartmann's overt comments that it has occurred (ll. 2931-4; 2966-7; 2984; p. 64), but also by his sudden command to his wife that she should don "daz beste gewaete" (l. 3056; "her best clothing"—p. 65). Erec, who earlier self-righteously spurned fine garb for his wife,[35] now attempts to tell her through his command to dress well just how little he values her person.[36]

Erec does not value Enîte,[37] not only because he feels that she does not value him because she criticizes him, but also because she speaks, albeit reluctantly, words of reproachful wisdom that he does not want to hear. She possesses a heightened sense of perception, shown in the court's derogatory assessment of her husband filtered through her consciousness and, after thought (ll. 3004, 3024; p. 65), conveyed to Erec. Yet it initially seems as if she has made one drastic misperception, for "si wânde daz er sliefe" (l. 3026; "believing him asleep"—p. 65). Since it is Erec's and Enîte's custom to make love in the middle of the day, one would expect Enîte to know whether her husband is sleeping or not. Rather, in allowing Enîte such an outburst, Hartmann indulges in a sophisticated deception on Enîte's part. She behaves as if Erec cannot hear her and in fact depends upon it, so that in vocalizing her thought she anticipates no danger of it being heard and yet seeks that very feeling of possible danger and being found out. Her speech is not an involuntary slip but rather the logical culmination of her thoughts ("da begunde si denken an"— l. 3024; "Then Enite chanced to think"—p. 65), for Hartmann later examines the thought/speech linkage in Enîte's interior monologues and in her lament and suicide attempt.[38] Furthermore, events bear out the necessity of Enîte's misperception concerning her husband's "sleeping" state; there are times when misperception brings benefits, just as the pair will learn that there are times when it is wise to lie. True wisdom, as the concept is developed in *Erec*, entails the development of varied responses to individual situations and looks toward the greater good to be attained, rather than to the sometimes correct and sometimes flawed responses to various circumstances. Thus, here Enîte makes what first appears to be an error of judgment but what is in the final analysis a necessary, if chastizing, function of wisdom. The ultimate wisdom of Enîte's reproach lies in its results, for both Erec and Enîte learn that actions have consequences, that wisdom is an active virtue that must be cultivated, and that unpleasant but necessary experiences must be undergone in order to correct unconsidered behavior and rash action.

Enîte, in effect, communicates to Erec an unpleasant truth that he does not wish to hear, as evidenced by the fact that his immediate response is an attempt to silence the voice that has expressed this truth.[39] And he begins to engage in a series of contradictory actions that serve to reveal how complex is the truth that Enîte speaks. One must first question the degree to which Erec understands Enîte's words. Hartmann states, "dô vernam Erec die rede wol" (l. 3033; "Erec heard her plainly"—p. 65), but one does not find Erec mulling over in his mind the words his wife has spoken; as earlier noted, Erec suddenly stops having reported thoughts, and Hartmann makes an assessment of what will be characteristic of Erec for the bulk of the romance:

> dô enwas aber niemen
> der sich des mohte verstân
> wie sîn gemüete was getân
> 	(ll. 3077-9; No one could have guessed what he had in mind—p. 65).

Since we do not know the contents of Erec's mind, we cannot ascertain how much of Enîte's message Erec has understood. Hartmann's companion piece to *Erec*, *Iwein*,[40] affords an interesting insight, however, with respect to the reception of language, and it is one that can be directly applied to Erec's situation. One recalls that Kâlogrenant engages in a verbal sparring match with the troublesome Keiî—ironically over whether or not the former should speak—and delivers an admonitory salvo before he tells his tale:

> "man verliuset michel sagen,
> man enwellez merken unde dagen.
> maniger biutet diu ôren dar:
> ern nemes ouch mit dem herzen war,
> sone wirt im niht wan der dôz,
> und ist der schade alze grôz,
> wan si verliesent beide ir arbeit,
> der dâ hoeret und der dâ seit.
> ir muget mir deste gerne dagen,
> ichn wil iu deheine lüge sagen"
> 	(ll. 249-58; "Many words are to no purpose if one does not keep still and pay attention. Some lend their ears, but if they do not understand with their hearts, it is only sound. And that is too bad, for both he who speaks and those who hear are merely wasting time. You may listen all the more readily because what I tell is true"—p. 58).

The situation is eerily akin to that of Erec and Enîte, except that Kâlogrenant incorporates the roles of both one who tells something of significance and one who requests silence before telling. While it is Enîte who makes an important remark, it is Erec who demands silence from the one who makes the remark. In Kâlogrenant's case, it is silence that is first requested before the crucial statement is made. Yet Kâlogrenant's very enjoinder to silence is fraught with importance for the cases of Erec and Enîte, for it details levels of perception throw light on the problems in the marriage in *Erec*. Quite clearly, one may have ears and yet not perceive anything more than sound, and Erec's immediate response to Enîte's words of wisdom seems to be precisely that.[41]

Yet there is a further sense in which Kâlogrenant's words are applicable to Erec's and Enîte's situation. Kâlogrenant both requests silence and then speaks words of import, while these roles are shared—and presented in reverse order, as Enîte speaks and Erec demands silence—by the Arthurian couple in *Erec.* This breaking up of the roles is more than a device to further plot. It reinforces the fact that the audience is dealing with a collective being in the persons of Erec and Enîte. Together the couple forms one entity, so that the several and related functions of perception, thought, speech, and action are parcelled out variously to each member of the couple and shift over the course of the romance. This is not at odds with the idealized concept of marriage in the Middle Ages, where the husband and wife form one entity, although this oneness is couched in the divided and weighted terms of the hierarchical stance of the husband to the wife and, abstractly, the soul to the body, the spirit to the flesh, and the reason to the will.[42] In *Erec* this concept of the unity of man and wife is explicit in Enîte's long lament when she thinks her husband is dead and accordingly addresses God in despair:

> ". . . aller werlde ist erkant
> ein wort daz du gesprochen hâst,
> und bite dich daz dûz staete lâst,
> daz ein man und sîn wîp
> suln wesen ein lîp"
> (ll. 5823-7; "Lord, the well-known teaching you have proclaimed which I beg you to support, that a man and his wife should be one body"—pp. 97-8).[43]

Moreover, the idea that the two form one, established earlier in the body-heart dichotomy in *Die Klage,* informs *Erec* on several levels,[44] not the least of which is the narrative level, where the husband and wife split up functions between themselves, so that Enîte perceives, thinks, and speaks when Erec primarily acts. She counters Erec's demands for silence with its opposite—speech—and meets his rashness with her hesitant consideration. On a more abstract level, Enîte functions as a voice of reason in comparison to Erec's willfulness, so that she tempers his headlong actions with admonitions, and his lust with her moderation.

But most importantly that Hartmann sees Erec and Enîte as a composite entity[45] draws credence from the division of language functions. In fact, the movement of the hero toward *mâze* ("moderation"), so often seen as one of the keys to the romance,[46] finds its reflection in the interplay of language and silence on the part of Enîte and Erec. Erec, initially so prudent in his speech and actions, is succeeded by an Erec who not only cannot temper his rashness but who also imposes silence upon one whose words were for his benefit, and, ultimately, by an Erec who can learn from admonitions and who can frame words—and structure situations—to his benefit. Correspondingly, Enîte's garrulousness and verbal perspicacity are in their ascendancy when Erec's are at their nadir, so that her wisdom is seen to consist in her ability to translate her perceptions into knowledge and speech at those times when Erec remains his most unaware and taciturn. Similarly, Enîte is portrayed as being speechless when Erec is seen to be wise and, correspondingly, most vocal at the outset of the romance. As he lapses into lustfulness, she becomes increasingly more vocal, until Erec finally comprehends the wisdom and loyalty/love expressed by her repeated outbursts concerning his safety. At that point Erec begins to take over many of the perceptual functions previously fulfilled by his spouse, so that by the end of the romance he is often seen as recognizing danger before Enîte does, and so that her reported speech dwindles and finally disappears, just as his perception and vocalization increase. The key, then, to the balance between the two halves of the marriage entity—that is, between Erec and Enîte—is the balance between language and silence, sifted through the awareness of what constitutes prudent behavior. The turning point is the bedroom scene in which Enîte is so startlingly vocal and Erec so surprisingly speechless. Here Erec has ears but cannot hear in the fundamental sense, and Enîte must repeat her admonitory/revelatory speeches over the course of several adventures until the significance of her words penetrates Erec's consciousness and he stops misperceiving her.

In each of these adventures Enîte is forbidden to speak (l. 3099; p. 66) and to report on what she sees or hears (ll. 3101-2; p. 66). This sentiment is reiterated in ll. 3963ff. (p. 76). One finds here Hartmann's use of word-pairs to strengthen the perception-to-language association: "vil drâte si hin umbe sach, / zErecke si mit vorhten sprach" (ll. 3378-9; "She turned around quickly [looked behind] and spoke fearfully to Erec"—p. 69) and "als si sînen ernest sach / und daz erz von herzen sprach" (ll. 3838-9; "Seeing that he meant it [when she saw his seriousness, that he spoke from his heart]"—p. 74). One also sees the manner by which Enîte perceives, then inwardly debates concerning language or silence ("[ge]sagen/[ver]dagen" in ll. 3146-7, 3184-5, 3374-5; pp. 66, 67, 69), and then speaks. Her thought process is presented to the reader in some detail:

> dô si in solhem zwîvel reit,
> ob si imz torste gesagen
> oder solde gedagen,
> nû redete si in ir muote
>
> (ll. 3145-8; As she rode on in despair, unable
> to decide whether to risk telling Erec or to keep
> silent, she thought—p. 66).

She sees a choice whereby she will lose her husband or her life, and she chooses to sacrifice her life ("'bezzer ist verlorn mîn lîp'" (l. 3168; "'It would be better that I die'"—p. 66), because "'wir wegen ungelîche'" (l. 3173; "'we are not of like value'"—p. 66). This sense of "weighing unevenly" creates much the same effect as the statement of the heart in *Die Klage:* "'uns dienet niht gelîcher muot'" (l. 945; "'we don't have the same inclination'"). While Enîte's unease stems from a self-imposed lack of worth—although society does much to reinforce this by perceiving her one-sidedly—that unease can be tied to a temporary feeling of subordination, fostered by her lamentation and brow-beating in which it has engaged for the better part of a thousand lines. In both instances, disregard for one half of the team—man and wife or heart and body—creates an imbalance signalled by an inability of one part to hear or comprehend the other. In *Die Klage* the rectification of this imbalance takes the form of a gradual shortening of extended monologues, so that, as the body and heart come to hear what each other has to say, the monologues are replaced by a true dialogue. In *Erec* the process is subtler and not as exclusively dependent on length or frequency of speeches. Rather, Hartmann embeds Enîte's message reiteratively in her speeches, so that by dint of recurrence Erec finally hears it. Even in her first warning to him, Enîte mentions her motivation. Erec does not have access to the workings of her mind, although the audience does, but he is repeatedly told that Enîte exhibits *triuwe* ("loyalty"). In her very first infraction of Erec's gag rule, Enîte tells Erec her motivations ("'wil ich dir durch triuwe sagen / dînen schaden enmac ich niht verdagen'"—ll. 3184-5; "'Permit me to tell you in loyalty—for I can't be silent when danger threatens you'"—p. 67), and yet it appears that he does not hear her, for in his reproach he does not mention her motivations but instead concentrates on what he perceives to be her characteristically female disobedience:

> "wie nû, wunderlîchez wîp?
> jâ verbôt ich iu an den lîp
> daz ir iht soldet sprechen:
> wer hiez iuch daz brechen?
> daz ich von wîben hân vernomen,
> daz ist wâr, des bin ich komen
> vol an ein ende hie:
> swaz man in unz her noch ie
> alsô tiure verbôt,
> dar nâch wart in alsô nôt
> daz sis muosten bekorn.
> ez ist doch vil gar verlorn
> swaz man iuch mîden heizet,
> wan daz ez iuch reizet
> daz irz enmuget vermîden:
> des sult ir laster lîden.
> swaz ein wîp nimmer getaete,
> der irz nie verboten haete,
> niht langer si daz verbirt
> wan unz ez ir verboten wirt:

sô enmac sis langer niht verlân"
(ll. 3238-58; "How is this, marvelous woman? I forbade you to speak on pain of death. Who told you to ignore my order? I have found out here that what I had heard about women is true, that whatever was strictly forbidden them is just that which they had an urgent longing to try. It is a waste of time to tell you not to do something, because this only entices you until you can't abstain. You therefore deserve scorn. What a woman would never think of doing if it were permitted, she will do at once as soon as it is forbidden: she simply can't resist then"—p. 67).

In responding, Erec not only fails through selective hearing to perceive the truth given him—Enîte's loyalty—but also engages in an antifeminist tirade like those in *Iwein* that treat the changeability of woman's mind. Women's fault, purely and simply, lies in their continued flouting of men's wishes, yet Enîte's continual disobedience, coming after a lifetime of obedience to men's wishes, is serious and significant: it guarantees Erec's safety and his life. On the surface Enîte goes against his wishes, but in a deeper sense she demonstrates a far-reaching loyalty.

Enîte's second outburst does not mention *triuwe*, but she urges Erec "'durch got'" (l. 3380; "'for God's sake'"—p. 69) to listen to her, and the audience knows that she speaks out because she fears that on account of "'untriuwen'" (l. 3367; my translation: "'disloyalty'") something might happen to Erec. The audience's attention is also drawn to the conclusion of her interior monologue: "'ich waene ez solde verdagen / entriuwen niht, ich sol imz sagen'" (ll. 3374-5; "'Should I keep still? No, certainly not, I must tell him'"—p. 69). Clearly, *triuwe* is at the heart of Enîte's actions, and it dictates whether she speaks or, in fending off the lecherous count's advances, dissembles. Yet even when Enîte reiterates to Erec that she has again acted "'durch triuwe'" (l. 3415; "'because I was loyal'"—p. 69), Erec once more does not listen to what he hears and promptly saddles her with the care of the horses, an apt indication of his perception of her at this time, as earlier noted.[47]

At this point in the narrative Hartmann injects a sequence in which a youth is presented as an accurate perceiver—his phrases are studded with "'mich dunket'" (ll. 3520, 3523, 3532; "'seem'" is the common phrase here—pp. 70-1)—who assesses the couple's situation at a glance and who speaks to Erec concerning his mistreatment of Enîte, only to receive a curt reply: "'knabe, daz sult ir lân'" (l. 3590; "'You will have to forgo that, youth'"—p. 71). The youth is further cast in the role of a wisdom figure when he communicates his experience with Erec and Enîte to his lord, who, struck with Enîte's beauty, begins to ruminate ("gedâhte . . . manecvalt wart sîn gedanc"—ll. 3669, 3672; "began to regret . . . began to consider"—p. 72) until Hartmann announces:

> der enwas dar an niht staete,
> wan in vrou Minne betwanc
> ûf einen valschen gedanc
> (ll. 3717-9; He was not steadfast in this, so Dame Love could urge on him an evil thought—p. 73).

Enîte has obviously measured up to the youth's assessment:

> "jâ muget ir an der vrouwen
> daz schoeniste wîp schouwen
> die wir ie gesâhen"
> (ll. 3620-2; "You will find the lady to be the most beautiful woman either of us has ever seen"—p. 72).

The count is so smitten with her that his mind takes a disloyal turn (ll. 3668-71; p. 72). Hartmann tells us that this count is normally a man of good character (l. 3689; p. 72) and that his sudden fancy for Enîte is effected by love, which caused him to abandon reason (ll. 3684ff.; p. 72). Yet the fact that this "love" is actually lust is underscored by Hartmann's subsequent comment that the count was steered "ûf einen valschen gedanc" (l. 3719; "[toward] an evil thought"—p. 73).

Throughout Erec is oblivious to what is going on. He is not wary of the count ("dô enhete Erec deheinen wân / daz er im schaden solde" (ll. 3727-8; "Erec had no idea that he wanted to harm him"—p. 73). He is virtually taciturn, snapping at the count concerning the fact that he and his wife are dining apart: "'herre, mîn gemüete stât alsô'" (l. 3745; "'Sir,' answered Erec, 'that is simply my desire'"—p. 73). Erec here is not only a man of few words but also one whose utterances communicate nothing that might be illuminating to a situation. The count's ensuing discussion with Enîte reflects the perception/language nexus examined throughout this work. The count essentially misperceives Enîte in a way in which Erec also misperceived her. He, like the Erec who visited the impoverished household of Enîte's parents, sees "armuot" (l. 3765; "poverty"—p. 73)[48] and "body" (l. 3759; Thomas renders this here as "fair lady" in context—p. 73) to the exclusion of Enîte's deeper nature, which encompasses *triuwe*. The count's speeches, blunt and forceful, reflect his desire for her, and he repeatedly expresses his self-centeredness in terms of mental activity: "'ich sage iu, vrouwe, mînen muot'" (l. 3781; "'Lady, I'll let you know my will'"—p. 73) and "'ich sage iu wie mîn dinc stât'" (l. 3785; "'I'll tell you how things are with me'"—p. 74), and, finally, in an ominous repetition that links mental activity and physical action: "'ich sage iu mînen muot: / dar nâch beweget iuch was ir tuot'" (ll. 3828-9; "'Listen to my intentions and judge by them what action you should take'"—p. 74). He closes his speech with a command for silence ("'diu rede sol ein ende hân'" (l. 3837; "'And that is that"—p. 74). Despite his harshness and basic oblivion to Enîte's nature and situation, the count does accurately assess the sad condition of Enîte's "'êre'" (ll. 3756, 3779; "'honor'"—p. 73) and her suitability to rule a land (ll. 3793-4; p. 74). The count is, moreover, a flatterer who inadvertently speaks the truth concerning Enîte: "'und ist daz ir sô wîse sît'" (l. 3782; "'which you would be wise not to oppose'"—p. 73). Enîte is indeed wise enough to realize that what the count cannot gain by speech, he will take by force. She has made an attempt to correct his misperceptions concerning her relationship to Erec, and it has been unsuccessful. The language she uses to try to dissuade him—before she realizes that language is of no avail— proves revealing and worthy of examination. She responds to the count's contention that she has been given to an unworthy man with an assertion of mingled pride, hope, and desperation that encapsulates the underlying movement of the romance:

>"unser ahte stât gelîche:
>wir ensîn beide niht rîche,
>wir komen wol ze mâze.
>got mir in leben lâze!"
> (ll. 3822-5; "My husband and I are suited to
>each other. We are of like station, and neither of us
>is wealthy. May God preserve him for me!"—p. 74).

At a time when she is physically removed and emotionally estranged from her husband, she nevertheless expresses devotion to Erec when he has almost total disregard for it. She wisely shifts her tactics and contrives a "list" (l. 3842; "guile"—p. 74) whereby she can extricate herself and her spouse from the dangerous situation that has developed. Her following speech to the count, complete with reference to eye contact and smiles (ll. 3840-2; p. 74), thus becomes a marvelous combination of lies and truth that bears close examination.[49]

Enîte begins with a disclaimer reminiscent of her father's words to Erec when the knight asked him for his daughter's hand. Koralus perceived Erec's request as mockery ("'spot'"—l. 532; p. 37), a "'schimph'" (ll. 546, 559; "'jest,'" "'joke'"—p. 37), and a "'wân'" (l. 558; "'unless I am quite mistaken'"—p. 37). Enîte echoes her father:

>si sprach: "ich waene iu ernest ist.
>herre, enzürnet ir niht:
>wan iu der rede unnôt geschiht.
>ez was zewâre mîn wân,
>ir hetet die rede durch schimph getân.
>wan ez ist iuwer manner site

> daz ir uns armiu wîp dâ mite
> vil gerne trieget
> (ich entar gesprachen: lieget),
> daz ir uns vil ze guote
> geheizet wider iuwerm muote"
>
> (ll. 3843-53; "I believe you are in earnest."
> she said. "Sir, don't be angry at me, since it is not
> necessary. I truly thought you were only joking,
> because you men are accustomed to mislead—not to
> say, deceive—us poor women by making great
> promises which you do not expect to keep"—p. 74).

And she assures him : "'ich wânte diu rede waere iuwer spot'" (l. 3891; "'I fancied you were speaking in jest'"—p. 75), thus further echoing her father. The link between Koralus' reactions and his daughter's dissemblings is strengthened by the fact that Koralus discussed Erec's winning of Enîte, the very subject Enîte next raises with the count:

> "vil rehte wil ich iu bejehen
> wie mich von êrste mîn man
> im ze wîbe gewan.
> ichn bin im niht genôzsam:
> mînem vater er mich nam,
> wan der ist waerlîche
> edel unde rîche.
> in des hof er dicke reit.
> nâch kinde gewonheit
> lief ich dâ hin und her.
> eines tages spilte er
> mit uns. dô schein wol daz kint
> lîhte ze triegenne sint
> mit liste er mich vürs tor gewan"
>
> (ll. 3865-78; "I'll tell you just how my
> husband got me for his wife, because we are not of
> like station. He stole me away from my father, who
> in truth is noble and wealthy. He often rode into our
> court, where I ran about with others as children do.
> One day he played with us, and it then became clear
> how easily children are deceived. He tricked me
> into going out of the gate with him"—pp. 74-5).

Her lie is all the more successful because it contains several truths: children *are* easily duped, Erec *did* ride into Enîte's parents' house, and Enîte's father *is* noble and *is* now, through the efforts of Erec, rich. Yet Enîte, described earlier as a child (ll. 309, 331; pp. 34, 35), is not so easily tricked and is rather, in the later and ironic assessment of Oringles of Lîmors, a "'wunderlîchez wîp'" (l. 6160; "'marvelous woman'"—p. 101) who, through acute perception and wise thought, can transform bad situations into good ones. She accomplishes this end here through the giving of a double-edged counsel to the count, so that he concludes, "'iuwer rât der ist guot'" (l. 3937; "'It is good advice'"—p. 75), but the audience knows that it is this "advice" that will save her husband and herself.

Swift flight saves Erec and Enîte, leaving an enraged count to argue over language, silence, and information with the host, reported in a characteristically peppery exchange of one-liners. Here, too, Hartmann draws in the count's subsequent lament an ironic parallel to Erec, who has already been noted to have similarities to the count in his essential misperception of Enîte. The count cries out:

> ". . . mir enwas êre
> niht ze teile getân,
> daz ich sus verlorn hân
> daz schoeniste wîp durch gemach
> die mîn ouge ie gesach,
> vremde oder kunde.
> vervluochet sî diu stunde
> daz ich hînaht entslief"
>   (ll. 4087-94; "Fate would not grant me honor,'
> he said. 'How could I have lost the most beautiful
> woman I ever saw anywhere only because of comfort!
> Cursed be the hour I went to sleep tonight!"—p. 77).

He appends to this assessment—which applies equally well to Erec (who "wente sînen lîp / grôzes gemaches durch sîn wîp"—ll. 2966-7; "Erec turned to a life of ease because of his wife"—p. 64)—a statement of a principle of which he and Erec are both instantiations:

> ". . . swer sîne sache
> wendet gar ze gemache,
> als ich hînaht hân getân,
> dem sol êre abe gân
> unde schande sîn bereit.
> wer gewan ie vrumen âne arbeit?
> mir ist geschehen vil rehte"
>   (ll. 4096-4102; "Who arranges his affairs
> according to convenience, as I did tonight, ought to
> lose honor and win shame. Who ever gained
> something of value without effort? I got what I
> deserved"—p. 77).

The count's attitude of regret nevertheless conceals a truth important for an understanding of the romance—*gemach* ("ease, convenience") can lead to danger—but there is no evidence that he profits from the wisdom of his words, for shortly thereafter he is depicted by Hartmann as misassessing Erec's relationship to Enîte, because he believed Enîte's trumped-up tale. True to Hartmann's pattern, the one who mentions folly is the one seen to be acting foolishly:

> "ez möhte an dirre vrouwen
> ein tôre wol schouwen
> daz si iu niht enist ze mâze"
> (ll. 4188-90; "A fool could see that this lady is not suitable for you"—p. 78).

Erec's reaction is terse, stuffy, and accurate:

> "ir enthöveschet iuch," sprach Erec,
> "an mir harte sêre.
> von wem habet ir die lêre
> daz ir scheltet einen man
> der ie ritters namen gewan?
> ir sît an swachem hove erzogen.
> nû schamet iuch: ir habet gelogen.
> ich bin edeler dan ir sît"
> (ll. 4197-4204; "You are forgetting all courtly manners," replied Erec. "Where did you learn to revile a knight this way? You were brought up in a boorish court. Shame on you for your lie: I am of more noble birth than you"—p. 79).

Erec's statement of his noble status is the first step toward acting nobly. Moreover, Erec's speech correctly evaluates the count's words and is not the first instance of his changing attitude toward perception, assessment, and language.[50] One would think that it belabors the obvious to have Erec understand, "er weste wol, man rite im nâch" (l. 4119; "He knew that they would be pursued"—p. 78), but it is a clear indication that Erec is coming to see consequences of actions and to prepare for contingencies.

Erec's progress is not without lapses, for Erec is aware that he will be pursued and yet unobservant of the actual approach of his pursuers (ll. 4139ff.; p. 78), with the result that Enîte once more gives voice to her perceptions immediately after Erec has forbidden her to do so. There is no reported dialogue as she breaks her word in this scene, and even Erec's delayed reproach is not given in recorded speech (ll. 4258-67; p. 79). But Erec is clearly on the road to wisdom, for after Enîte warns him of his next assailant's approach, Hartmann states: "dô wart im aber ir triuwe erkant" (l. 4319; "Enite once more showed her faithfulness to her husband"—p. 80). Finally Erec starts to regain his former perceptual acuity; he hears Guivreiz's approach and realizes that, much as he would like to avoid it, there is going to be a fight. Guivreiz has precipitated the fight by noting Erec's possession of armor ("'dar zuo sît ir gewâfent wol'"—l. 4336; "'Moreover, you are well armed'"—p. 80) and of "'daz aller schoeniste wîp / der ich ie künde gewan'" (ll. 4333-4; "'the most beautiful woman, on my soul, I ever met'"—p. 80), capping this observation with: "'wer gaebe die einem boesen man?'" (l. 4335; "'who would have given her to a worthless fellow?'"—p. 80).[51] Erec remonstrates, but sees ("gesach"—l. 4378; p. 81) that battle is imminent. It is during this fight that Enîte's cry is succeeded by Erec's correction ("'vrouwe, iuch triuget iuwer wân'" (l. 4429; "'You are mistaken, lady'"—p. 81) and his rapid defeat of Guivreiz, labelled "der wênige man" (l. 4436; "the little man"—p. 81). Overcoming this man who is small in stature harks back to Erec's own poor treatment at the hands of Idêr's dwarf, but also looks forward to a renewed, more open Erec. Erec and Guivreiz subsequently exchange names and discuss antecedents, and Erec becomes positively talkative in reponse to Guivreiz's requests for information, although he does not react favorably toward Guivreiz's suggestions concerning his need for medical attention, a response that has grave consequences. Guivreiz also raises the issue that Erec is unfamiliar with the land in which he finds himself: "'dar zuo ist iu daz lant unkunt, / und mac iu vil wol missegân'" (ll. 4623-4; "'you . . . do not know the country. Things could easily go badly with you'"—p. 83).

Erec's wounds and his unfamiliarity with the territory afford yet another opportunity for Hartmann to present situations in which perception and language are seen as the cornerstones of right action. One recalls that Keiî, "der quâtspreche" (l. 4664; "the Slanderer"—p. 85), comes upon Erec, assesses his situation, and announces sensibly that he is severely injured: "'ich sihe wol, ir sît sêre wunt'" (l. 4629[47]; p. 84). Keiî is a good perceiver in this instance, and it is no coincidence that he later recognizes Erec by his voice (ll. 4854-7; p. 87) and that he, unlike Erec, is familiar with the physical terrain through which he rides ("'der künec Artûs mîn herre / enliget hie niht verre'"—ll. 4629[48-9]; "'My lord, King Arthur, is camped not far from here'"—p. 84). Keiî may be perceptive, but he attempts to build on these perceptions a plan that depends on others' misperceptions:

> alsus was im gedâht:
> hete er in ze hove brâht,
> daz er danne wolde sagen,
> er hete im die wunden geslagen
> und er solde gevangen sîn
>   (ll. 4629[56]-4632; Here was his plan. Once he had brought the knight to the court, he would say that he, Keii, had wounded and captured him—p. 84).

Keiî, riding a borrowed horse and thinking sly thoughts, is refreshingly brash. His downfall, however, comes in the transfer from his perceptions to his thoughts on his perceptions; accordingly, his words and deeds will be flawed:

> alsô daz er vor *valsche* was
> lûter sam ein spiegelglas
> und daz er sich huote
> mit *werken* und mit *muote*,
> daz er immer *missetaete*.
> des was er unstaete,
> wan dar nâch kam im der tac
> daz er deheiner triuwen enphlac.
> sô enwolde in niht genüegen,
> swaz er *valsches* gevüegen
> mit allem vlîze kunde
> mit *werken* und mit *munde*:
> daz *riet* im elliu sîn ger
>
> (ll. 4642-54, my italics; He . . . was as free
> of falseness as a shining mirror, and avoided every
> evil word or deed. But his mood would change so
> that he soon forgot all decency. Then his only desire
> was to carry out zealously some deceit of word or
> deed—p. 85).

Keiî's mistake comes, then, when he uses language unwisely and tries to act, by trying physically to bring Erec to court. Erec soon reduces Keiî to "ein sac / under dem rosse" (ll. 4730-1; "he fell from the horse like a sack"—p. 85) and later elicits from him information concerning Keiî's point of origin and the circumstances surrounding the borrowing of Gâwein's horse. Erec refuses to give Keiî his name, however, but Keiî deduces Erec's identity from his voice. There remains yet another point to be considered in this Keiî episode, for Keiî still exhibits the admirable quality of telling what he knows, of detailing his encounter with Erec, even though he must be aware that it will only reflect detrimentally on him at Arthur's court:

> Keiîn hin ze hove reit
> und twanc in des sîn wârheit
> daz ers doch niht verdagete
> wan daz er rehte sagete
> sîn schemelîchez maere,
> wiez im ergangen waere
>
> (ll. 4836-41; Keii rode to the court, where
> his promise forced him not to keep silent but to relate
> truthfully the shameful story of what had
> happened—p. 87).

Finally, Keiî's brush with Erec results in the greater good that Gâwein is able to effect, through his recognition ("erkande"—l. 4908; "knew who he was" —p. 87), consideration ("gedâhte"—l. 4935; p. 88), and true perception of Erec's situation (ll. 4984-5; p. 88). Like Enîte, Gâwein must resort to a "list" (l. 4998; "ruse"—p. 88), arrived at after thought (l. 4998; p. 88), in order to guarantee Erec's physical safety and ease. Erec himself expects nothing until he sees the peripatetic court, which maneuvers with ease in a landscape in which he seems to be continually disoriented: "ouch erkande er si wol, / wan er si dicke hete gesehen" (ll. 5041-2; "He recognized them at once, for he had seen them often"—p. 89). His immediate reaction to Gâwein echoes his reproaches to Enîte's counsel:

> "ir enhabet niht wol an mir getân.
> her Gâwein, diz ist iuwer rât.
> nû hân ich iuwer missetât
> selten alsô vil vernomen.
> daz ich dâ her bin komen,
> des was mir vil ungedâht.
> ir habet mich übele her brâht"
> (ll. 5045-51; "This was your idea, Sir
> Gawein, and you haven't treated me well. I never
> heard of your playing such a mean trick before. I
> didn't intend to come here at all, and it was wrong of
> you to bring me"—p. 89).

Yet Gâwein *has* acted in Erec's best interests, as had Enîte, so the issue becomes one of whether Erec can know what is good or bad for himself. In this sense Gâwein, and, to a far greater extent, Enîte function as a type of early warning system for Erec, who is primarily depicted as a man of action. As wisdom figures, Gâwein and Enîte provide the admonition, moderation, and correction that the often rash Erec requires, and it is these two characters who must endure Erec's "zorn" ("anger"; l. 3049 for Enîte—p. 65; and l. 5068 for Gâwein—p. 89)[52] and who must nevertheless speak words and voice sentiments that he may not wish to hear:

> "waz mac ich nû gesprechen mê?
> wan sol ich iuch beswaeret hân,
> daz hân ich doch durch got getân"
> (ll. 5077-9; "What more can I say? Although
> I may have offended you, my intentions were good"—
> p. 89).

Old habits die slowly for Erec so that he takes two steps down the road to wisdom, only to retreat one step. Having been tricked by Gâwein, even though it is for his own good, Erec lapses into taciturnity in his overnight visit at Arthur's court. While Enîte speaks with Ginovêr,

> dâ wart vil wîplîche
> von in beiden geklaget,
> vil gevrâget und gesaget

> (ll. 5107-9; They exchanged many questions
> and answers and lamented Enite's unusual troubles at
> length, as women do—p. 90),

Erec exchanges no dialogue with those who removed his armor and is portrayed as being perceived rather than as being a perceiver ("vil schiere kam diu künegîn / in klagen unde schouwen"—ll. 5129-30; "The queen soon came with all her ladies to visit him and express her sympathy"—p. 90).

Erec is, however, shown to be thinking ("dô hügete er wider ûf die vart"—l. 5249; "[he] began to think of resuming his journey"—p. 91),[53] and his insistence that they depart, thought by the court to be a mistake (l. 5273; p. 91), proves to be fortunate, since, despite the fact that he does not know where he is going, his path leads him to where he is most needed. The very nature of his adventures begins to change, as has been noted in Hartmann scholarship, and the earlier adventures—which in very basic terms can be reduced to an encounter with an unruly dwarf, a fight over a bird, two unsuccessful robbery attempts, a pre-dawn escape from an inn, and an unprovoked challenge from a macho-minded dwarf—give way to adventures in which the issue is not something Erec has or wants but is rather a matter of life and death, not only for Erec, but also for those he aids. Moreover, these subsequent adventures are ones in which he can exercise his atrophied perceptual skills. Thus, Hartmann allows Erec to perceive before Enîte: it is Erec who "hôrte . . . eine stimme" (l. 5297; "heard . . . [a] scream[s]"—p. 92) and who queries the frightened, grief-stricken maiden, and who sets about to free a man who is as silent, although for different reasons, as he was at a certain point in the past:

> er was geslagen unz ûf daz zil
> daz er des bluotes was ersigen
> unde nû sô gar geswigen
> daz in schrîens verdrôz
> (ll. 5417-20; He had been whipped until he
> was faint from loss of blood and too weak to cry
> out—p. 93).

Hartmann's intent is to show how Erec's verbal skills are being honed throughout this *âventiure* to save the tortured knight, so that he is demonstrated to be wise in the manner in which he manipulates language. He speaks before he acts, first requesting information (ll. 5436ff.; p. 93) and then resorting to verbal deception ("dannoch redete er mit listen"—l. 5458; p. 94) with the giants who assess him, quite wrongly, to be "'tump'" (l. 5448; "'[a] fool'"—p. 94). Moreover, in order to demonstrate the giants' lack of wisdom, Hartmann gives them a disregard for language that harks directly back to Idêr's dwarf's retort to Erec, when he barked: "'lâ dîn klaffen sîn'" (l. 83; "'Hold your tongue'"—p. 32). Here one giant tellingly attempts to silence Erec with the statement: "'dîn klaffen ist mir ungemach'" (l. 5477; "'Your chatter bothers me'"—p. 94). Furthermore, the fact that this entire interchange reflects Erec's path to wisdom is stressed in an oblique glimpse into Erec's motivations; he must act to save the knight, even though such action involves raising the giants' ire (l. 5493; p. 94). Like Enîte and like Gâwein, he must risk *zorn* if he is to accomplish anything that is for the greater good.

Having defeated the giants—and it should be recalled that the Erec in the earlier part of the romance had a bad enough time of it with dwarves—Erec further demonstrates his perceptual abilities by locating the wounded knight, whose horse had stayed with him during the previous fracas, despite the fact that Hartmann intones: "niemen kunde gesagen / wâ er im ze vindenne wart" (ll. 5573-4; "no one could have known where to find him"—p. 95). A positive transformation is wrought as Erec restores the wounded man to his lover, and Erec speaks at length with the pair concerning their identities, gives advice ("'diz ist mîn rât'"—l. 5676; "'I would advise you'"—p. 96), and caps his performance by moving confidently through the once confusing landscape in order to rejoin Enîte:

> ouch schiet harte balde
> wider ûz dem walde
> der tugentrîche Erec
> und suochte den wec
> dâ er vrouwen Enîten
> sîn gehiez bîten
> (ll. 5710-5; The noble Erec quickly left the forest and looked for the place where he had told Enite to wait for him —p. 96).

Erec's wounds open (ll. 5716ff.; p. 96)[54] and he tumbles head-first from his horse. It is not merely the unusual physical effort that exhausts Erec, for his verbal exertions have also been exceptional. Now "der halptôte man" ("half-dead man"—p. 97) lapses into silence, and it is no coincidence that Enîte becomes again most vocal:

> von jamer huop diu guote
> ein klage vil barmeclîche,
> herzeriuweclîche.
> ir wuof gap alsolhen schal
> dan ir der walt wierhal
> (ll. 5743-7; "In her misery she raised a pitiful, despairing cry which was loud enough to resound from the forest—p. 97).

Such is the shifting balance between the characters of Enîte and Erec that Enîte now reproaches God for His "'zorn'" (l. 5779; p. 97) and calls Him to task for giving her such a bad example of His consideration of her ("'wie swachez bilde'"—l. 5783; p. 97). In the final analysis, Erec's *Scheintod* scene will have instructive benefits, but Enîte now is in the position Erec was when he was made party to his wife's assessment of his situation: something is happening, but the person to whom it is happening cannot, through lack of perception or foresight, see its ultimate good consequences, so clouded are the perceptions by the present pain.

Enîte is so prostrated by grief that she proposes the solution of being devoured by animals. Here Hartmann's skill is such that he couches even this possibility in terms of wisdom and perception. Enîte calls upon "'ir tier vil ungewizzen'" (l. 5844; "'foolish beasts'"—p. 98) and then suggests that they would be "'wîse'" (l. 5850; "'clever'"—p. 98) to feed upon her and her spouse. Yet the romance's landscape, earlier portrayed as teeming with dangerous creatures, both human and otherwise, cannot produce an animal that sniffs the bait Enîte so readily and eagerly offers ("daz dehein tier ez vernaeme"—l. 5858; "no wild beasts heard them"—p. 98).[55] Clearly, there are times when even lack of perception, like verbal deception, is wise, if greater good is to be attained, even if it is only animals here who fail to perceive. Moreover, Enîte may lapse, too, as she does here, and the greater wisdom of God will hold life-threatening dangers in abeyance while she calls upon God and, later, Death, whom she accuses of providing bad examples (l. 5917; p. 99), as she earlier did God, and of giving bad advice (l. 5924; p. 99). Her verbal recklessness increases to the point that she even assesses herself incorrectly regarding the speech act toward Erec that resulted in the current situation: "'ich tete als die tôren tuont, / unwîses muotes'" (ll. 5965-6; "'I acted like the fools who stupidly . . .'"—p. 99). Hartmann's point is not that Enîte was a fool, but rather that here she is not able to perceive herself correctly and falls victim to the problem that afflicts Erec: lack of foresight and trust. She cannot see any benefits down the weary road she travels, and, neither, in fact, can Erec until that path leads him to Mâbonagrîn's castle, at which point Erec is given an example of his own former situation in terms that he cannot help but understand, so that he can then state confidently:

> "ich weste wol, der Saelden wec
> gienge in der werlde eteswâ,
> rehte enweste ich aber wâ,
> wan daz ich in suochende reit
> in grôzer ungewisheit,
> unz daz ich in nû vunden hân.
> got hât wol ze mir getân
> daz er mich hât gewîset her"
> (ll. 8521-8; "I knew that there was a road of Fortune somewhere in the world," said King Erec, "but I didn't know just where. So I rode forth at random to look and now have found it. God has shown me his kindness in leading me here"—p. 128).

Erec's path leads him to strife in the "boumgarte" (l. 8700; "park"—p. 130; I would also gloss "orchard" and "garden"), and it is strikingly appropriate that the next topic upon which Enîte focuses in her protracted lament is her "'bilde'" (l. 6031; "'example'"—p. 100) of the fruit tree in the "'boumgarten'" (l. 6017; "orchard"—p. 100). Enîte interweaves her *exemplum* with thoughts of her own childhood, so that she first thinks of her parents,

> "ouwê liebiu muoter
> unde vater guoter!
> nû ist iu ze dirre stunt
> mîn grôzer kumber vil unkunt"
>   (ll. 5974-7; "Oh, dear mother and father! You don't yet know my great sorrow"—p. 99).

Then she develops the transplanted tree idea, and finally she announces: "'des sol man bilde kiesen / an mir vil gotes armen'" (ll. 6031-2; "'One should use me as an example of this, Godforsaken as I am'"—p. 100). The audience must ask what it is about this orchard that one must perceive, so that Erec must go to it in the form of accepting Mâbonagrîn's challenge and Enîte must refer to it in her *exemplum*. In a very fundamental sense Erec's ultimate *âventiure* will involve Mâbonagrîn because Mâbonagrîn, like Erec, took to wife "ein kint" (l. 9467; "child"—p. 139)[56] with a remarkable physical personage (ll. 9469; p. 139), a woman who used language to work changes upon her husband, although in a fashion diametrically opposed to the manner in which Enîte uses language to effect positive changes.[57] Thus, in Enîte's lament over her supposedly dead husband one finds a reversion to her betrothal to Erec. She states that her parents do not now know the situation in which she finds herself, and what she implies is that she did not know *then* in what circumstances she was to fall. Thus, in marrying, it is not only Erec who does not know the full nature of his bride (Enîte as a wise person) but also Enîte who does not know the full nature of her husband (Erec as a man who will lapse and then, through trial and error, become wise).

But in order to bring Erec to the point that he can undergo the crucial Joy of the Court adventure, Hartmann must first detail the essential waking of Erec's consciousness, and he does so in a sequence that gathers its shape from the use and abuse of language. One recalls that Enîte's voice resounds through the land (l. 6084; p. 100), so that the Count of Lîmors hears it (ll. 6140, 6142; p. 101) and prevents Enîte from acting upon her "wort" (l. 6110; "she meant this"—p. 101; literally: "word"), that is, her *thought* to commit suicide ("'entriuwen, ich hân nû wol gedâht'"—l. 6061; "'Truly, I have made the right decision'" —p. 100). Enîte asks for death, and it obligingly arrives in name, in *Lîmors*, and in actuality, as the count of Lîmors will be dispatched by the end of this episode. That the count is in some way to mirror Erec's previous predilections becomes apparent in his first words, where he addresses her, as did the imperceptive, mocking Erec, as "'wunderlîchez wîp'" (l. 6160; "'marvelous woman'"—p. 101). He goes on to characterize her as an image, as "'daz schoeniste bilde'" (l. 6164; "'the loveliest creature'"—p. 101) that exists, and the audience suddenly apprehends that this is the crux of the matter: the first impression Enîte makes is that of an exterior without an interior, so that any thoughts and speech she might exhibit come as a total surprise. She is a *bilde* ("image")[58] in the sense that she *becomes* an image for those who see in her what they themselves are; if lustful and occupied with the flesh, her perceivers apprehend her primarily in terms of lust and the flesh. And finally, looking back to Enîte's own *bilde* of the tree, one may state that men do not see her in the sense of an instructive example; she is just another tree to be transplanted into men's pleasure gardens. The sad thing is that she is a *bilde* that can enable other characters to learn from her wisdom, yet not everyone perceives this. She is beauty, to be sure, but beauty, as St. Augustine noted, must be used and not abused. Thus, Enîte's cry, "'des sol man bilde kiesen / an mir vil gotes armen'" (ll. 6031-2; "'One should use me as an example of this, Godforsaken as I am'"—p. 100), proves to be a thematically loaded statement: Enîte simply *is*, and the essential issue is *how she is perceived*.[59]

That the count of Lîmors misperceives Enîte is emphasized throughout. He is a man who hears only what he wants to hear from his advisors, in other words, that he marry Enîte. He is also one who promises unnecessary transformations from poverty to richness (l. 6262; p. 102), which Enîte, being already rich, does not need. The count also tends to think in clichés, tossing off Enîte's distress and refusal to submit to him with a world-weary assessment:

> "diu wîp suln reden alsô.
> dâ von man irz niht wîzen sol:
> si bekêret sich wol
> von ir unmuote"
> (ll. 6303-6; "That is how women talk . . . so one shouldn't reprove her. She will get over her despondence"—p. 103).

He does not view Enîte as an individual, but rather as a manifestation of womanhood, albeit a singularly beautiful specimen. Women are expected to lament when their husbands die, but they are also expected to be accommodating and change their minds and adjust to situations. This attitude, in fact, informs the entire plot of *Iwein*, and it is therefore no coincidence that the count's speech on the expediency of marriage foreshadows Lûnete's rationalization of Laudîne's marriage to her husband's murderer. Actually, the count overtly seems to be making a sexist statement here, but what Hartmann actually shows is the dehumanizing aspect that arises when either sex treats members of the other sex as expendable and interchangeable.

The count of Lîmors states with cool precision: "'ich enhân wîbes niht: ze wîbe wil ich iuch genemen'" (ll. 6271-2; "'I am not married and want to have you as my wife'"—p. 102). He entertains fond hopes of the pleasure that Enîte can give him: "er gedâhte, des lîhte niht geschach, / mit ir vil guote naht hân" (ll. 6355-6; "he was looking forward to the night, which he expected to spend most pleasantly with the lady"—p. 103). However, the count's attitude toward Enîte and toward language has additional ramifications. Here, perception is once again bound up with language, so that most of the count's energies are occupied in silencing Enîte and much of her time is spent in lamentation. The one who will ultimately triumph is seen as being verbal, while the one who is held by even his retainers to be "'toerlîch'" (l. 6532; "'stupid'"—p. 105) is seen to be urging silence (ll. 6420, 6458; p. 104), accusing her of folly (ll. 6491, 6505; p. 105), and delivering a blow, out of foolish anger ("sîn zorn in verleite / ze grôzer tôrheite"—ll. 6518-9; "his anger led him to great folly and crude behavior"—p. 105) to Enîte on the appropriate—and *only*—part of her body that offends him: "an den munt" (l. 6579; "on the mouth"—p. 106). Lîmors, like Erec, not only wishes to silence the reproachful voice that he hears, but also essentially misperceives the owner of that voice, for he rationalizes Enîte's lament as coming from a child (l. 6451; p. 106). Children, on Hartmann's account in *Erec*, cannot be expected to be verbally accountable for themselves; they are easy to trick, they lie ("'lüge ich, herre, ich waere ein kint'"—l. 4063; literally: "'if I were to lie, lord, I would be a child'"), and, implicitly, they are to be seen rather than heard. If Enîte is to be perceived as a child, then these are the kinds of misperceptions that will be continually made about her. And the physical punishment that the enraged Lîmors metes out to her is virtually the chastisement given abusively to a child, and it is received with horror even by his retainers. One must here note yet another ironic parallel between the count and the lapsed Erec, in the count's angry speech to those retainers who verbally question his treatment of Enîte:

> "ir herren, ir sît wunderlich,
> daz ir dar umbe strâfet mich
> swaz ich mînem wîbe tuo.
> dâ bestât doch niemen zuo
> ze redenne übel noch guot,
> swaz ein man sînem wîbe tuot.
> si ist mîn und bin ich ir:
> wie welt ir daz erwern mir,
> ich entuo ir swaz mir gevalle"
>
> (ll. 6540-8; "It is strange that you lords should find fault with the way I treat my wife," he said fiercely, "for no one has a right to say anything,

good or bad, about a man's actions toward his wife. She belongs to me and I to her. How will you keep me from dealing with her as I please?"—p. 105).

In essence, Oringles feels that no one has the right to question what goes on between a man and his wife. This mirrors Erec's earlier stance as he angrily reacts to his own court's assessment of his preoccupation with Enîte. Judging by Erec's learning process over the course of the romance, such an attitude toward one's wife signals that the count is about to be re-educated.

The education process for the count of Lîmors begins with Erec's hearing Enîte's cry and ends with Oringles' swift death at the hands of the hero, who now knows fully how to transform his perceptions into right action. Curiously, Enîte's final outburst, which is her penultimate recorded speech (the ultimate is ll. 6946ff., p. 110, where she again aids Erec's physical well-being), makes reference again to the ambiguous term *lîp*, but she employs the word differently from the lapsed Erec or the count of Lîmors. She shrieks:

> ". . . wê mir vil armen wîbe!
> waere mîn geselle bî lîbe,
> diz bliuwen waere vil unvertragen"
> (ll. 6584-6; "Oh, my dear lord! You are dead, and I cry for help in vain"—p. 106).

For Enîte, *lîp* is more than a beautiful or handsome form: it is *life itself*. And in Erec's hearing these precise words, Hartmann draws the audience's memory back to the scene in which Erec was physically "bî lîbe" in that he was lying in his wife's arms (l. 3015; p. 65), but could not appreciate her words of wisdom. Enîte's words both catapult him into the series of adventures and help extricate him, just as Enîte's guidance will accompany him on the path he does not recognize: "nû was der wec im unerkant" (l. 6737; "he did not know the way"—p. 108). Hartmann's treatment of a physical event thus stands as an apt assessment of a spiritual process: "wan si in den wec lêrte" (l. 6746; "Enite . . . guided him"—p. 108).

When Enîte cries out at Lîmors, thinking to provoke the count into killing her and ending her misery, it is not so much the volume of her lament as it is the intensity and frequency of her distress signals that finally penetrate Erec's consciousness as he lies "senseless and as if dead, although he was not" (p. 106; ll. 6590-1). Hartmann describes Erec's waking in terms of a mixture of perception and disorientation, with concern for Enîte helping Erec make sense out of a situation in which he "enweste wie er dar kam" (l. 6602; "wondering what had happened to him"—p. 106) and yet know that his wife "was in some sort of danger, but did not know what or where it was (p. 106; ll. 6610-2). What proves important here is that Erec does not need to know precisely where he is in order to employ right action. He merely needs correct perception, and he is well supplied with that at this stage of the romance, so that Hartmann tells the audience not only that Erec "begunde mit den ougen sehen" (l. 6600; "looked about"—p. 106) and recognizes his wife's voice: "er erkande ir stimme" (ll. 6614; "he knew who she was as soon as Enite called to him"—p. 106). Enraged ("er hâte zornes genuoc"—l. 6620; literally: "he was angry enough")—and it is justified anger this time—he rises up, a sword comes promptly to his hand (note the construction: "der kam im einez in die hant"—l. 6619; literally: "one of them came to his hand," which implies almost an inanimate volition, p. 106), and mayhem ensues, until Lîmors "liutlôs beleip" (l. 6663; "Limors was left deserted"—p. 107; literally: "left without people").

At this point the narrator pauses to consider how he would have acted in a similar situation, which is at the same time an appeal to the audience to do the same. Then, after Erec hurries his wife outside the castle, the reader is given a glimpse into yet another mind, embodied in the form of the page, singing to himself, who ambles up with Erec's horse just when it is needed. Erec, who spies the horse from afar, manages to grab the horse's bridle, capture it, and mount, all without any additional reference to the fate of the lad who sat on it. One has a sense that the mind of the placid boy registers his changed circumstances somewhere in the middle of a flight into a hedgerow, but Hartmann gives no indication. The child vanishes from the narrative as suddenly as he has appeared, his function in the work having been carried out. The focus returns to Erec and Enîte, as they ride out into a landscape that is "unerkant" (l. 6737; "he did not know the way"—p. 108) to him, but familiar to her, so that she guides him.

When Erec once again knows where he is, he asks Enîte how he came to Lîmors (ll. 6763-7; p. 108), a sure sign that he is on the road to recovery, for he is regaining that openness to language's ability to communicate that he had at the romance's outset. The watershed in Erec's transformation is also signalled by his apology to Enîte (ll. 6781ff.; p. 108) and is mirrored in his subsequent perceptual responses. He is the first to hear the approach of an opponent, who turns out to be Guivreiz, significantly from a distance (l. 6872; p. 109). To be sure, he is not aware that it is Guivreiz, but he does communicate this perception of impending danger to his wife:

>dô si noch wâren verre,
>der ellende herre
>wart vil wol gewar
>der gewâfenten schar,
>wan der schal und der dôz
>was von den schilten grôz.
>er sprach ze vrouwen Enîten:
>"vrouwe, ich hoere rîten
>engegen uns ein michel her"
>
>(ll. 6872-80; He became aware of the armed band while it was still far off because of the loud

clatter of the shields. "Lady, I hear a large troop riding toward us," he said to Enite—p. 109).

Even in his desperate physical condition, he is prepared to wrestle an opponent if need be, but Enîte's wise intervention and her appeal to Guivreiz obviate the need for conflict. Moreover, Erec begins to be a more considerate man in general, as is evident in his speech with the newly recognized Guivreiz. Guivreiz regrets having wounded Erec, and Erec replies with words that show the extent of the lesson he has learned:

> Erec sprach: "des sult ir gedagen
> und ûz iuwer ahte lân.
> ir enhabet an mir niht missetân.
> swelh man toerlîche tuot,
> wirts im gelônet, daz ist guot.
> sît daz ich tumber man
> ie von tumpheit muot gewan
> sô grôzer unmâze
> daz ich vremder strâze
> eine wolde walten
> unde vor behalten
> sô manegem guoten knehte,
> dô tâtet ir mir rehte"
>   (ll. 7007-19; "Say no more and don't be concerned about it. You didn't treat me wrongly. If a man behaves foolishly, it is fitting that he receive a fool's reward. Since I was so imprudent and arrogant as to want to take control of someone else's road and hold it alone against many brave knights, you gave me what I deserved"—pp. 110-1).

In effect, Erec has learned to look at himself through others' eyes and, having admitted in his apology to Enîte that he has been found wanting, is restored to health and society, so that the passage in which Erec, "als . . . ein schefbrüchiger man"(ll. 7063-4; "like a shipwrecked man"—p. 111) finds shore, is immediately followed by his physical reconciliation with Enîte, as they sleep together but apart from others of Guivreiz' retinue (l. 7093; p. 111) under "drî buochen" (l. 7085; "three beeches"—p. 111):[60]

> dem unbescheiden hazze
> wart ein ende gegeben
> und kurn in ein bezzer leben
>   (ll. 7099-7101; The foolish discord came to an end, and they began a better life—p. 111).

The fourteen-day idyll that follows at Guivreiz' castle provides a time for healing and for Enîte to be equipped with a new horse and saddle, fashioned by "der wercwîseste man / der satelwerkes ie began" (ll. 7468-9; "the most skillful saddler who ever lived"—p. 115). The saddle is remarkable for its workmanship. Depicted is the story of Piramus and Thisbe, a singularly appropriate choice considering Enîte's near-suicide and Erec's *Scheintod* in the forest near Lîmors. In addition, other ornamentation seems particularly apt, especially "der liehte carbunculus" (l. 7744), the only jewel of a group of twelve mentioned by name, as the carbuncle has traditionally been seen as a stone that illumines darkness, much as wisdom shines through misconception and ignorance.[61] And it is only fitting that the carbuncle be given to Enîte, who has guided her husband through so many dark times. Enîte is not only the most beautiful woman but also a prudent lady who has taught Erec something about the nature of wisdom.

Having learned, Erec must now teach. Mâbonagrîn, who represents an unprogressed Erec, is the pupil on which Erec can test his wisdom.[62] That Mâbonagrîn is a formidable opponent is proven by Guivreiz' obvious reluctance to talk about the nature of the Joy of the Court challenge as well as by his subsequent advice not to accept the challenge the affair offers. Guivreiz' counsel must be assessed in light of two other wisdom figures who employ speech either to prevent or to correct mistakes. Imâîn, Gâwein, and Guivreiz all counsel Erec, who does not avail himself of their advice for various reasons. Imâîn and Gâwein see situations that can be rectified (Enîte's shabby dress and Erec's weakened physical condition, respectively), in order to prevent further unpleasant situations from developing. In rejecting their wisdom, Erec errs. However, in the case of Guivreiz the audience finds a different situation. Guivreiz counsels Erec to avoid confrontation with Mâbonagrîn (ll. 8479, 8510, 8582; p. 128), but here Erec is wise to ignore Guivreiz' advice, since fighting Mâbonagrîn will rectify a bad situation. The difference between the interpretations of Erec's refusal to abide by Imâîn's, Gâwein's, and Guivreiz' counsel lies in the fact that Erec is wrong in ignoring Imâîn's and Gâwein's prudent advice and is right to spurn Guivreiz' suggestion. Imâîn and Gâwein rightly perceive and assess situations, and Erec's refusal to take their advice is rectified by an action of the Arthurian court: if Erec will not take advice to clothe his wife properly, then the Queen will have to do it, and if Erec will not come to the court to rest, then the court will simply have to pack up its Round Table and come to him.

Guivreiz, however, is not a good perceiver; Hartmann notes concerning Guivreiz' assessment of his opponent Erec: "der herre gedâhte: 'er ist verzaget, / sît er sîne arbeit klaget'" (ll. 4366-7; "'He is lamenting his troubles because he is afraid,' thought the lord"—pp. 80-1). Since Erec laments, Guivreiz concludes falsely that his opponent is a coward, and it may be that some lingering vestige of this assessment explains Guivreiz' reluctance to speak of the matter of the Joy of the Court. Hartmann seems to imply this in his description of Erec as "'ein unverzageter man'" (l. 8425; "'a bold man'"—p. 127) who listens to Guivreiz' advice and sensibly disregards it. Guivreiz, who earlier held his guest to be a coward and was summarily defeated, once again misperceives Erec's abilities and comes to the wrong conclusions.

The example of Guivreiz is nevertheless instructive for Erec—and for the audience—because it economically shows the process on which Hartmann focuses at length in Erec's and Enîte's relationship: the linkage of perception to thought, thought to knowledge, knowledge to speech, and speech to action. At each stage in the movement from perception to action there is the possibility of a breakdown in either a cessation or an incorrect move. Guivreiz errs on the level of perception. Because his perception is inaccurate, he rashly challenges Erec. Guivreiz is trounced, but Hartmann shows his audience that Guivreiz may argue differently the second time around but will make the same mistake in his assessment of Erec's chances against Mâbonagrîn. Since Guivreiz' judgment is inaccurate, his counsel is faulty. Moreover, he must be urged to speak and tell what he knows to Erec, who urges:

> "nû war umbe tuot ir daz
> daz ir sô lange mich verdaget
> daz ir mirs niht ein ende saget?"
> (ll. 7991-3; "Why have you so long avoided giving me a full account of the matter?"—p. 122).

Here one finds an Erec eager for knowledge and desirous of speech, an Erec who digests and thinks about what information he finally wrings from Guivreiz, and an Erec who is not, as Mâbonagrîn states, a "'tumber gouch'" (l. 9044; "'a stupid fool'"—p. 134) who acts "'toerlich'" (l. 9030; "'foolish'"—p. 133). Thus, Erec at the end of the romance stands in direct contrast to his mentor, Guivreiz; Erec is seen to act "als die wîsen tuont" (l. 8633; "as wise men do"—p. 129).[63] Hartmann shows this to consist of not only his accurate perceptions and physical actions but also his receptivity to language and thought, while Guivreiz is seen at the romance's end to be physically inactive, verbally reluctant, and perceptually inaccurate.

In disregarding Guivreiz' counsel, Erec enters into battle with an opponent possessing faults he once had and into a situation in which he can demonstrate his new-found wisdom. Accordingly, before the battle one finds Erec actively questioning (ll. 8368, 8777; pp. 126, 131), thinking (ll. 8294ff., 8350ff., 8400; pp. 126, 127), and exhibiting prudent temerity (ll. 8619ff., 8633ff.; p. 129) in contrast to his former rashness. He is described as "der muotveste" (l. 8119; literally: "firm of mind") and as "ein unverzageter man" (l. 8425; "[an] undaunted [man]"—p. 124), but there is an important difference in the man to whom these epithets are now applied, for Erec's makeup now includes an antidote for his rashness: "er tete als die wîsen tuont, / wan hie gehôrte vorhte zuo" (ll. 8633-4; "he did as wise men do— because there was reason for concern"—p. 129). Furthermore, in contrast to his wife at this point, Erec is portrayed as perceptive; while Enîte falls into unconsciousness at the sight of the eighty head-bedecked stakes, Erec remains quite alert and receptive. Moreover, he waxes positively loquacious in his comforting speech to Enîte (ll. 8839-73; pp. 131-2), in which he voices his dependence on her and assures her that thoughts of her will aid him:

> "swenne mich der muot iuwer mant,
> sôst sigesaelic mîn hant
> wan iuwer guote minne
> die sterkent mîne sinne"
>   (ll. 8868-71; "The thought of you makes my hand victorious, for your love gives me such strength"—p. 132).

During the battle his perceptions are further heightened, and his thoughts return again and again to Enîte:

> Erec, ze swelhen zîten
> er gedâhte an vrouwen Enîten.
> sô starcten im ir minne
> sîn herze und ouch die sinne
>   (ll. 9182-5; Whenever he thought of Enite, her love strengthened his heart and sharpened his wits—p. 135).

And the audience is told: "der gedanc an sîn schoene wîp / der kreftigete im den lîp" (ll. 9230-1; "[Erec] gain[ed] strength from the thought of his beautiful wife"—p. 136). Here the audience sees that the man who could previously not think of adventure because he was so occupied with his wife has been transformed into a man who is now able to have adventures while at the same time being mindful of his wife. Erec survives his encounter with Mâbonagrîn as much from the courage he gets from thinking of his wife as from an old skill he learned "as a boy—in England" (p. 137; ll. 9282-3), that is, wrestling ("ringen"—l. 9284; p. 137). Having granted Mâbonagrîn his life, he sits down with the man and extracts from him information that bears on a series of situations in the work. Initially Mâbonagrîn turns a deaf ear to Erec's entreaties to tell him who he is and only acquiesces when Erec's own ancestry proves to be impeccable enough to prevent Mâbonagrîn's defeat from being shameful.

At this point it is useful to examine Hartmann's description of Erec's and Mâbonagrîn's discussion. In a particularly medieval way, hostilities vanish between the two mortal enemies once a pact has been reached:

> hie wurden si beroubet
> hazlîchez muotes:
> êren und guotes

> gunden si ein ander wol,
> als ein geselleschaft sol
> (ll. 9393-7; Their enmity vanished and they wished one another honor and well-being, as friends should—p. 138).

It is as if the mind has been purged and, like a vessel, newly filled with different intent. Erec is curious to know more of Mâbonagrîn's situation, and it is with some surprise that the audience hears Erec, the man who formerly preferred to be "von den liuten" (l. 2950; "[away from] the others"—p. 24) and who fled from the court and was enraged when it found him again, now asking Mâbonagrîn how he passes the time with no other people around (p. 138; ll. 9415-6), and telling him how nice it is to be in society: "'wan bî den liuten ist sô guot'" (l. 9438; "'it is very nice to be with other people'"—p. 138).[64]

Mâbonagrîn's answer makes clear that his lifestyle is not dictated by choice ("'ich enhân mir diz leben / von deheinem vrîen muote erkorn'"—ll. 9445-6; "'I didn't choose this life of my own free will'"— p. 138)[65] but rather by a rash promise he made to an eleven-year old child/woman (l. 9467; p. 139) whom Erec himself has already deemed to be the most beautiful he has ever seen, except that she is clearly surpassed by Enîte (ll. 8926-30; p. 132). Erec, in defeating Mâbonagrîn where eighty other knights failed, frees that knight from his constricting promise, but there remain yet matters to be settled.

One may well ask how much Mâbonagrîn has learned from Erec, who has obviously learned considerably over the course of the romance. A reckless, albeit triumphant note creeps into Mâbonagrîn's speech when he cries: "'nû var ich ûz und swar ich wil'" (l. 9589; "'I'll go out and travel wherever I wish'"—p. 140). This is as precise a reflection of Erec's own earlier actions as one can imagine, for did not Erec leave his court with a similar compulsion and lack of specific direction? The key to understanding Mâbonagrîn's intent may lie in his wife's assessment of their physical situation as "'daz ander paradîse'" (l. 9542; "'a second Garden of Eden'"—p. 139). The Fall of Man, which addresses the theme of knowledge, precedes the exodus from Paradise, and Paradise can only be attained again through the redemptive acts of the second Adam, Christ. Having sinned, man must work to repent and must be aided in this task.[66] One finds in Hartmann's *Erec* resonances of this process. The implication is that Mâbonagrîn, who rashly gave his word and then was shocked at what his wife said, may have to travel the same difficult road by which Erec has come to "'daz ander paradîse.'"

Optimism prevails, however, for the audience has seen Erec make that journey, with setbacks and disappointments, until Hartmann can finally say of him: "er tete sam die wîsen tuont" (l. 10085; "as the wise do"—p. 145). The inner transformation is further reflected in the fact that Erec, who is repeatedly noted by the narrator to be in unfamiliar territory or even disoriented, suddenly has no difficulty in getting home to Karnant. Once Erec knows *who* he is, that is, part of an entity with Enîte ("'daz ein man und sîn wîp / suln wesen ein lîp'"—ll. 5826-7; "'a man and his wife should be one body'"—pp. 97-8), he knows *where* he is.

Hartmann, having shown Erec's relationship to Mâbonagrîn, appends a scene in which it is revealed that Enîte and Mâbonagrîn's wife are related. It is not merely that each has been described repeatedly as "a child," but also that they are cousins who were born at the same place (l. 9724; p. 141). At the outset of the scene, the narrator notes:

> ir gemüete was gescheiden,
> diu under der pavelûne saz
> und dirre der dâ baz
> an dem strîte gelanc:
> in sweic der munt, ir herze sanc.
> diu eine vreuden krône truoc,
> diu ander hâte leides genuoc
> geladen mit herzensêre
> dâ von daz si niht mêre
> in dem boumgarten solde sîn
> und ir âmîs Mâbonagrîn
>
> (ll. 9685-95; I will swear that the moods of the two ladies — the one who gained most from the conflict and the one sitting under the tent — were not the same: neither spoke, but the heart of one was singing. She was as happy as she could be, while the other wrung her hands at her husband's defeat and was filled with grief because she and Mabonagrin were no longer to remain in the park—p. 141).

However, by dint of "ein wîplich gemüete" (l. 9702; "a womanly heart"—p. 141)[67] and "talk[ing] back and forth" (l. 9707; p. 141), Enîte brings her cousin around so that she cries and laughs for joy. Whatever the future brings, Mâbonagrîn's wife is reconciled to make the best of the present, spurred by the sign that God miraculously brought her together with her cousin in "ein alsô vremdez lant" (l. 9743; "in a foreign land"—p. 141).

These transformations from sorrow to joy, both of Mâbonagrîn and Erec and of Enîte and Mâbonagrîn's wife, occur with almost dizzying speed, and the romance rapidly comes to its end with Erec conducting the eighty bereaved widows to Arthur's court, which he has no difficulty whatsoever in finding, whether it be, in Guivreiz' words, "'ze Karidôl / oder benamen ze Tintajôl'" (ll. 7806-7; "'at Karidol or perhaps at Tintajol'"—p. 120), and then moving on with his own wife to Karnant. The series of adventures comes to a conclusion,[68] with each adventure having served as a signpost on Erec's spiritual journey, so that, as they impress themselves on his consciousness, he comes to orient himself with respect to proper perception, thought, speech, and action.

Whereas we have seen in *Die Klage* the anatomy of a mind divided, we note in *Erec* the position that Hartmann sees mind to occupy in the chain that stretches from perception to action. Word frequency alone stresses Hartmann's preoccupation with mind and its auxiliary functions in *Erec*, for there are hundreds of references to mind terms in the work, ranging from knowledge (*wizzen*)[69] to thought (*denken*)[70] to cast of mind (*muot* and *sin*)[71] to recognition (*erkennen*)[72] to wisdom or folly (*wîs*, "*tump, tôr,* among others)[73] and to advice (*rât*).[74] Finally, I would include verbs indicating speech or silence (*sagen/dagen, sprechen/swîgen*) in this group for the purposes of examination of this romance.[75] In *Grêgôrius*, treated in the next chapter, Hartmann maintains this intensity of mind terms but focuses more explicitly on the nature of knowledge, on what the mind knows and how it knows what it knows, with the result that the very plot and the work's thematic structure revolve around these facets of Hartmann's concern with mind.

3

" ir wizzet wol "

Knowledge in *Grêgôrius*

Grêgôrius is the most overtly intellectual of Hartmann's longer narratives, not only in the sense that each character is uniformly delineated and evaluated in terms of what he/she does or does not know, but also in the sense that the reader is continually challenged to contrast the workings of divine wisdom with the flawed and incomplete processes of human reasoning. Each scene reflects the tension between knowing and not knowing, and the theme of knowledge becomes the overarching principle that unifies the poem's involved cycle of losing and finding, hiding and revealing, forgetting and remembering, and, ultimately, sin and redemption. Moreover, just as the theme of knowledge informs the plot, so does the concept of knowledge prove central in the reader's response to plot events: the audience, which knows certain circumstances before characters are fully aware of them, develops expectations accordingly. Since the audience benefits from the prologue in which Grêgôrius' salvation is assured, it knows at the outset what the protagonist only comes to learn over the course of the work. The poem becomes a window opening onto a person's growing self-knowledge, as well as an instructive mirror for the audience. Examination of Hartmann's use of the concept of knowledge—and the term "knowledge" here expresses a range of functions from nonreflective apprehension to self-conscious wisdom—gives access to the deep structure of *Grêgôrius*, and the strategy works best chronologically, because the very plot hinges, almost in mystery story fashion, on *who knows what and when*.

The narrative proper[1] begins with the deathbed scene of Grêgôrius' grandfather. In addition to placing Grêgôrius in a rich and powerful lineage—for much of the poem will treat his search for knowledge of his roots—the scene is essential for setting out basic attributes of the knowable, as well as by-products of knowledge. The dying king, judged by Hartmann to have acted wisely ("dô tet er sam die wîsen tuont"—l. 194; "[he] did then as all wise men will do"—p. 33), calls his retainers and children to his bedside, where he acts as do all other Hartmann characters who feel they know something: he proceeds to give advice.[2] The advice, besides being formulaic and conventional, is sound; yet, on Hartmann's account, knowledge possessed by one person may not always be transmittable to another. The father tells his son, in part:

> "wis den wîsen gerne bî,
> vliuch den tumben swâ er sî.
> vor allen dingen minne got,
> rihte wol durch sîn gebot.
> ich bevilhe dir die sêle mîn
> und diz kint, die swester dîn,
> daz dû dich wol an ir bewarst
> und ir bruoderlîchen mite varst:
> sô geschiht iu beiden wol"
> (ll. 255-63;
> "Frequent the wise man willingly,
> And flee the fool wherever he be.
> First love God, and with just hand
> Rule men because of God's command.
> My soul I now to you commend
> And bid you this fair child befriend—
> Your sister cherish as you should,
> Protecting her in brotherhood.
> Then with the two of you it will
> Fare well"—p. 37).

The father's advice, well intended, is imperfectly received, in the sense that it is both selectively heard and selectively followed. Later actions reveal that the son has not taken this advice to heart, for, far from avoiding "foolish" people, he is drawn to his sister, and does not behave "in a brotherly fashion" with her. Yet if the brother acts unwisely—he is, in fact, called "der unwîse" (l. 357; "the foolish lad"—p. 43)—it is only upon the counsel of the Devil, according to the poem's narrator (l. 339; p. 41). Here Hartmann again sets up a disparity between those who know and those who do not know, for the sister clearly sees in her brother's actions and intent devilish motivation: "'lâ dich von dînen sinnen / den triuvel niht bringen'" (ll. 382-3; "'Don't let the Devil and his crew / Deprive you of your wits'"—p. 45). The brother, however, does not see anything wrong with his incestuous love for his sister,[3] and Hartmann significantly does not state that the brother is aware of "des tiuvels rât" (l. 339; "the Devil's counsel" would be a better rendering) as an inspiration for his actions. The brother is depicted as thinking ("daz er benamen gedâhte / mit sîner swester slâfen"—ll. 330-1; "the thought / Of sleeping with his sister"—p. 41), and although the audience can see that this thought mirrors an earlier satanic thought ("sus gedâhte er . . ."—l. 314; "so he planned . . ."—p. 41), the brother himself does not indicate that he himself could feel that his intended course of action might be wrong or sinful. The four "explanations" for his sin ("diu minne," "sîner swester schoene," "des tiuvels hoene," and "sîn kintheit"—ll. 323-7; "concupiscence," "her beauty," "the Devil's insolence," and "his childishness"—p. 41) are given for the benefit of the audience, and there is no indication or evidence that the brother sins in any way other than unwittingly. The sister's case is a different matter entirely, for she recognizes and states that the Devil has had a hand in this enterprise. Yet she errs in that she does not protest loudly. Instead,

>si gedâhte: "swige ich stille,
>so ergât des tiuvels wille
>und wirde mînes bruoder brût,
>und wirde ich aber lût,
>so haben wir iemer mêre
>verloren unser êre"
>   (ll. 385-90;
>"If I keep silent," thought the lass,
>"The Devil's wish will come to pass,
>And I'll become my brother's bride.
>But if I shout aloud and chide
>We shall have lost forever more
>All fame and honor that we bore"—p. 45).

The audience immediately thinks back to another of Hartmann's bedroom sequences in which a woman *does* speak up—and in the cause of her husband's honor—with quite different consequences. Enîte, it must be recalled, has been, like Grêgôrius' royal pair, called a child and she has spent considerable time in the bedchamber with a man who wrestled ("ringen"—l. 9284; p. 137) in his youth. Significantly, one of the sister's first utterances during the seduction scene in *Grêgôrius* is: "'waz diutet diz ringen?'" (l. 384; "'What aim / Or meaning has this wrestling game?'"—p. 45), and it is a type of wrestling match that occurs in privacy ("nû begunde er si triuten / mê danne vor den liuten"—ll. 375-6; "More than his wont in the eyes of men / The brother showed his love, and then / Grew intimate in fond caress"—p. 43), echoing Erec's lapsing into uxoriousness when he is "von den liuten" (l. 2950; "[when he] left the others"—p. 64). Finally, the sister sees the strength of the brother's intent ("hie verstuont sî sich mite / daz ez ein ernest solde sîn" (ll. 378-9; "Now she perceived to her distress / That his behavior was no sport"—p. 43), but she lacks the experience, intellectual capacity, and saving verbal deviousness that Enîte possesses when she acts to protect herself and her husband from the count. Enîte, purely and simply, knows how to keep from going to bed with someone, and she knows how, when in bed, to sound a verbal alarm. The sister in *Grêgôrius* is untried in these matters, and she foolishly opts for a course of silence that she feels will safeguard the good reputation that she and her brother must maintain.

The desire that others not know what is going on will sound again and again in the poem, and this scene in which the two siblings gain carnal knowledge effectively begins the rich and complex interlaced cycle of concealment/revealment and sin/redemption from which the poem gathers its meaning. Moreover, through use of shared language, Hartmann allows this scene to foreshadow and parallel in an inverted fashion a scene that occurs later in the poem. One recalls that Hartmann voices an authorial intrusion just prior to the incest sequence, when he notes the children's separate beds and the boy's movement from his bed to that of the girl, and then states: "jâ laege er baz besunder" (l. 366; "far better that he lay apart"—p. 43). The situation of *besunder ligen* ("lying apart") anticipates with variations the subsequent scene in which the two wise Roman men do in fact sleep apart ("Dâ sî besunder lagen"—l. 3171; "As each was in his home"—p. 201) and are given not Devil-inspired carnal knowledge, but rather divinely-inspired revelation. Yet it can be asserted that the fruit of the physical union and that of the shared message voiced by "the voice of God" (p. 201; l. 3173) are one and the same: Grêgôrius himself. The parents get a child, the cardinals find a pope, and the sinful conception of Grêgôrius is reflected but significantly altered in the more fortuitous meeting of the minds that leads to the discovery of the pope. In the process, both the sinful and the redeemed Grêgôrius are seen to result from the thought of a suprahuman being: the boy, counseled by the Devil, engenders a child lost both in the physical and spiritual senses of the word, while the wise Romans, advised by God, share a revelation that finds the lost Grêgôrius, locates him as well as aids in his salvation.

Loss figures heavily in the subsequent experiences of the brother and sister, coupled with a strong desire that other people not know the true nature of their relationship. The sister laments to her brother:

> "wande ich hân durch dich verlorn
> got und ouch die liute.
> daz mein daz wir unz verstoln
> daz enwil niht mêre sîn verholn.
> ich bewar vil wol daz ich ez sage:
> aber daz kint daz ich hie trage
> daz tuot ez wol den liuten kunt"
>   (ll. 440-7;

"Because of you I am forlorn:
I've lost men's favor and God's grace.
How we have sinned in our embrace,
That till this day we've not revealed,
Can no longer be concealed.
My tongue I will guard cautiously,
Yet will the child I bear in me

Make manifest to all our sin"—p. 47).

It is not merely that they are lost in the eyes of society if they are found out that troubles the sister but also that a spiritual diminishment has occurred: she has lost God (l. 441; p. 47). Moreover, she shortly thereafter expresses her fear that their child, too, may be damned. Yet the sister consoles herself with the folk wisdom that events in the poem later belie.

> "ouch ist uns ofte vor geseit
> daz ein kint niene treit
> sînes vater schulde"
> (ll. 475-7;
> "Often, too, we've heard declare
> That children do not ever bear
> Their father's guilt"—p. 49).

But the immediate actions of the guilty pair and their mentor, described as wise (p. 49; l. 491), are to encumber that child with written evidence of his father's guilt that he will quite literally carry with him for much of the narrative.[4] Ironically, those concerned with keeping society ignorant of Grêgôrius' existence and the circumstances of his conception unwittingly do the most to ensure that his shameful birth will later be found out, although care is taken not to reveal his exact land of origin or lineage, an omission that subsequently proves that what Grêgôrius does not know can indeed hurt him. The alternative, that of keeping Grêgôrius totally innocent of the circumstances of his birth, is not feasible, for Hartmann's didactic intent is to show that spiritual growth entails knowing enough to recognize that one does not know all that one should or that God knows. Grêgôrius must be given a certain amount of information, so that he can be made aware of his sinful heritage, yet he must not be given enough to prevent him from sinning himself, for, on Hartmann's account, only through sin is redemption seen to be possible in the poem. Grêgôrius must be hurt in order to be helped, just as he must sin in order to be saved.[5] Accordingly, all the counsel of Grêgôrius' parents' mentor—and "rât" and its derivatives appear eighteen times in ll. 465-625 (pp. 49-57)—cannot avert Grêgôrius' own disaster, nor can it do more than patch up as quietly and quickly as possible the current bad situation. Moreover, the advice given to the parents cannot make up for that which is lost, for, as Hartmann describes it, wisdom is not easily transferred from one person to another but rather must be laboriously acquired on an individual basis. Had the brother and sister been wise, they would not have strayed into sin, yet neither can their father's well-intentioned advice forestall their sin nor can the action of their mentor allow the pair to escape the consequences of their behavior.

It is the paradoxically individual as well as universal nature of sin[6] that links the fortunes of Grêgôrius' parents with his own. The infant is supplied with a comprehensive but necessarily incomplete account of his origins, so that he may, upon reaching the age of reason, contemplate and "überhüebe . . . sich niht" (l. 752; "[remain] free from arrogance"—p. 65). By implication, he is to learn not to sin by being given an example of what sin produces. Yet the fundamental incompleteness of the account of Grêgôrius' birth proves to be ultimately responsible for his falling into sin. Thus, man is born to sin, not necessarily because the sins of the father are visited upon the son, but rather because the father's acquired knowledge of the consequences of sinful behavior seem to be passed on incompletely to future generations. The individual person of necessity sins and by doing so joins the general mass of sinful humanity. As a result, the relationship of the individual sinner to previous generations of sinners seems to be predicated upon a lack of knowledge. Grêgôrius sins, purely and simply, because he does not know certain facts about his past, such as his exact lineage. Yet, because the by-product of this sin is knowledge, Grêgôrius is ultimately richer spiritually for his experience.

At the point at which the infant Grêgôrius is consigned to the mercy of the waves[7] and is driven into an uncertain future by an auspicious breeze, the narrator injects a curious disclaimer that again raises the issue of the transfer of knowledge. Having just established the circumstances for the transmission of knowledge over time by ensuring that Grêgôrius will unwittingly take knowledge of his past with him into his future, the narrator now turns to what is essentially the same problem, but expressed this time in general artistic terms. Instead of questioning, in effect, how one man's sin affects another person, the narrator now questions how one man's experience can be shared with others. The passage in question is considerably more sophisticated in intent and in implication that has previously been assumed.

> Ir wizzet wol daz ein man
> der ir iewederz nie gewan,
> reht liep noch grôz herzeleit,dem ist
> der munt niht sô gereit
> rehte ze sprechenne dâ von
> sô dem der ir ist gewon.
> nû bin ich gescheiden
> dâ zwischen von in beiden,
> wan mir iewederz nie geschach:
> ichn gewan nie liep noch ungemach,
> ich enlebe übele noch wol.
> dâ von enmac ich als ich sol
> der vrouwen leit entdecken
> noch mit worten errecken
> wan ez waere von ir schaden
> tûsent herze überladen
>   (ll. 789-804;

> This you know full well: he who
> Has never felt a joy that's true,
> Or a deep sorrow, will be less
> Apt to find words to express
> These feelings justly than will he
> Who has felt both in full degree.
> Now equally remote from me
> Are both, for I was always free
> Of them, since I have never felt
> Great joy or deep distress. Life dealt
> Me neither evil nor great good.
> I cannot, therefore, as I should,
> Convey or find words to depict
> Her grief, so great it would afflict
> A thousand hearts that all would be
> Weighed down by such calamity—p. 67).

The immediate effect of the passage is oddly reminiscent of that of the earlier passage in which the young mother hopes, bolstered by past advice, that the sins of the father are not visited upon the son.[8] This very wish signals the audience that that dreaded course of events will in fact come to pass. Similarly, the above passage, in which the narrator affects the inability to do justice to the mother's grief, only prepares the way for the following description of grief. In both instances the assumption is undercut, if not immediately, then within a short period of time. But in the passage just presented the reader is appealed to directly. The audience "well knows" that ability to write of painful experiences or their joyous counterparts rests upon experiential grounds. Yet the reader finds himself/herself rather in the earlier position of Grêgôrius' mother, for what he/she "knows" is in fact contradicted by subsequent actions: the narrator disclaims any such experiences, yet the mother's grief is beautifully detailed. And the mother, who hopes that what she has been told is true, finds out, to her dismay, that it is not. In effect, both the mother and the reader in this passage are played false by what they are told they know and, therefore, think they know. The passage of time proves the mother's assumption wrong, and the author's control over his own medium marks his deference to the reader's knowledge as merely perfunctory. The reader "well knows," and yet must rely on the narrator for additional information, which is promptly given in an enumerative sequence that resembles the earlier authorial intrusion in which the underlying motivation of the parents' sin is arithmetically detailed.

Here the narrator lists the three sorrows (p. 67; l. 805) that cloud the mother's immediate and distant future, and knowledge—or, rather, lack of it—figures prominently among them: sin with her brother, frailness, and anxiety. The mother must contend with the immediate pain her actions have caused, and, if that is not enough, she faces uncertainty as to her son's fate. And it is the narrator's pointing out of this missing piece of knowledge that both foreshadows the mother's later nonrecognition of her son and speaks to her ignorance of the consequences of her sin. It is as if, by consigning her son to the waves, she has rid herself of the visible fruits of her sinful actions—and is not her husband/brother similarly dispatched from her sight?[9] But the consequence is that her not knowing *how* life treats her son will result in her not knowing *him* when they again meet. The implication is that if the fruits of sin are cast away, they will not be recognized when again encountered, which accounts for the curious puzzle posed by *Grêgôrius*: why characters can sin again while believing that they are atoning for past sin. Grêgôrius' mother sins again because she has given in to a counsel that, in the interests of present expediency, ransoms the future and hobbles her, by removing from her thoughts the tangible result of her sin, in her subsequent confrontation with her son.

The narrator details the surface means by which the mother does penance after describing the "helt" ("hero") whom the mother now loves:

> Si hete zuo ir minne erwelt
> weizgot einen starken helt,
> den aller tiuristen man
> der ie mannes namen gewan.
> vor dem zierte sî ir lîp,
> als ein minnendez wîp
> ûf einen biderben man sol
> dem si gerne behagete wol.
> swie vaste ez sî wider dem site
> daz dehein wîp mannes bite,
> sô lac si im doch allez an,
> so si des state gewan:
> mit dem herzen zaller stunde,
> und ouch mit dem munde:
> ich meine den gnaedigen got
>   (ll. 871-85;
>
> As her love a Man she chose,
> A mighty Hero, Heaven knows,
> A Man dearer than any man
> Who has been loved since time began.
> For Him her body she made sweet,
> As for a loving wife is meet
> Who wants to please and honor, too,
> A husband who is good and true.
> Though custom strongly has eschewed
> That man by womankind be wooed,
> She failed no opportunity,
> However often that might be,
> To court Him with each word and phrase.
> Her heart sang always in His praise,

By Him I mean the Gracious Lord—p. 71).

The effect is subtly like that of the "'mîn gert ein vrîer bûman'" speech in *Der arme Heinrich* (ll. 775ff.; "'I am courted by a free farmer'"—p. 29), in which the grace of Jesus is the motivating factor for the young girl who wants to sacrifice herself for Heinrich. In both instances, this fervent spiritual devotion to God or Christ is supplanted by an earthly marriage which each female professes not to want. The sister's dedication to her celestial hero is succeeded by an incestuous marriage with the son she tried to save by sending him away, and the maiden's intense desire for death and the heavenly ploughman is met with a marriage to the man she so earnestly wanted to save by sacrificing herself. Clearly, the prognosis is not good for the long-range celibacy of either the maiden or the sister, whose kingdom is gradually chipped away.

By comparison, Grêgôrius appears, at least on the surface, to be better provided for. His physical needs are met, although his seagoing accommodations cannot have been spacious, and he is sustained in his journey, which is overtly analogous to that of Jonah (ll. 931ff.; p. 75), by God. Yet the pattern set up in his parents' and their wise counselor's actions proves to be repeated. First of all, the weighted "lost/found" juxtaposition surfaces again. One recalls that Grêgôrius' mother's lament that she has lost God and society (ll. 440-1; p. 47) is succeeded by the father's finding of advice (l. 487; p. 49). Here in the later paired passage, Hartmann details the diminishment of the mother's kingdom so that only one city remains, and that only through the grace of God. This loss is followed immediately by the finding of Grêgôrius, contained and sustained in the small vessel, which is seen as "ir vundene sache" (l. 974; "their find"—p. 77) by the fishermen.[10]

The fishermen also share a mental orientation common to Grêgôrius' parents, when they attempt to conceal the little chest from others' eyes. This clumsy concealment is not a rash but rather a considered action ("wan si hâten des gedâht"—l. 971; "For they had planned and had in mind"—p. 77), as is the more elaborately designed decision to conceal arrived at by Grêgôrius' parents and the wise counselor. And, because the fishermen are less adept at deception, the small mound under the "gewant" (l. 975; Buehne, p. 77, translates this as "gear," but an equally good rendering is "clothing") in the boat is more immediately obvious to scrutiny than is the child swelling under the mother's clothes as it grows in her womb, since the mother has been spirited off to wait out her term at the home of the counselor, who is, not coincidentally, "der rîchiste" (l. 590; "the mightiest"—p. 55; alternatively, "richest") among his respected countrymen. Grêgôrius will, significantly, be passed off as the grandchild of one of the fishermen: the fisherman who is rich. In such a manner, Hartmann links the two actions centered around the same child, and the scene with the fishermen thus serves not only as a foreshadowing of the paired scene at the end of the narrative, where fishing skills net a long lost key, but also as a reinforcement of the earlier behavior of Grêgôrius' parents and their advisor. The common thread of concealment runs through both of these early scenes and lays the groundwork for the subsequent undoing of both plans to conceal. All of the emphasis on concealment (ll. 685, 738, 766, 1100; pp. 61, 63, 65, 85) and on lying and deception (ll. 1076, 1084; p. 83) prepares the reader for the opposite, for revelation and for the truth. Since the concealment is so obvious, the reader's expectations focus upon the inevitable reversal that the narrative promises. Whether inept or involved, the procedure of concealment in *Grêgôrius* triggers revelation.

Although the infant Grêgôrius carries with him the tangible seeds of his own undoing in the tablet inscribed with his partial background, it is not until years after his discovery, adrift in the small vessel,[11] that even some degree of what others know is revealed to him. In the meantime Grêgôrius has become "der witze ein man" although "der jâre ein kint" (l. 1180; "He was in age / A child; in mental life, a sage"—p. 89); he is described in terms of quality of mind: "er was getriuwe unde guot / und hete geduldigen muot" (ll. 1239-40; "Loyal, patient, good, and true"—p. 91); and he has studied subjects "diu guot ze wizzenne sint" (l. 1171; "About whatever would permit / A blessed child to benefit"—p. 89) and is furthermore said to possess "wisdom" (p. 93; l. 1257) and to walk "on wisdom's road" (p. 93; l. 1254). Yet, just as the knowledge Grêgôrius has mastered is that of things external to himself ("grammaticus, dîvînitas"—ll. 1183, 1187; p. 89), so is the picture presented to society by Grêgôrius one that emphasizes his external circumstances—that of being the fisher's relative—rather than his internal makeup, although it is apparent to all that he is not blood-related to the fisherman.

Hartmann here calls attention to the external, rather than internal, perspective on Grêgôrius for two essential and related reasons. First of all, the poet wishes to undercut the reader's expectations, what the reader thinks he/she knows. Having given the reader a picture of a favored child who gains and never loses friends (ll. 1245-6; p. 93) and who acts "ze rehter mâze" (l. 1248; "Not . . . excessively"—p. 93), the poet next turns to the view of Grêgôrius as a youth who, moved by a foreign and uncharacteristic impulse ("ez enkam von sînem willen niht"—l. 1290; "It happened quite without intent"—p. 95), strikes his unwitting "relative" in hardly a friendly fashion. Secondly, the picture of Grêgôrius as seen from an external viewpoint, in addition to being a surprising and experientially inaccurate portrait—what buried impulse could cause this perfect child to strike another?—is also shown to be an incomplete portrait, and for the same reason as noted before: it lacks that essential element of his true heritage. The foster mother's assertion, given in the E manuscript, "'jâ enweiz niemen wer er ist'" (ll. 1320, 1332; "'For where he comes from, none here know'"—p. 97), reveals the standard by which Grêgôrius is to be judged. The past, like the workings of Grêgôrius' own mind, is absent from the portrait. And Hartmann's intent to interlock knowledge of the past with the development of introspection is borne out by the fact that, for Grêgôrius, knowledge—even partial knowledge—of his heritage gives divine wisdom in the matter ("wizze Krist"—l. 1348; "God [more accurately, Christ] knows"—p. 97); she has no idea what caused the tiff. The blow Grêgôrius gives his "brother" is tantamount to a sudden, uncomprehended thought or apprehension, here expressed first in the foster family's startled reaction and then in Grêgôrius' attempts to make sense of what occurred during play that bears upon what happened years earlier. And the underlying assumption, that Grêgôrius' total background is unintelligible except to God, is underscored by the situation in which the "ungewizzen wîp" (l. 1217; "unreasonable [unknowing] wife"—p. 91) and the fisher find themselves: they have *found* someone (the "vuntkint," "er vundene dürftige"—ll. 1323, 1337; the "foundling child," "That foundling, he!"—p. 97), yet they have no idea who he is nor what manner of man he fundamentally is.[12]

Grêgôrius' partial past is, of course, accessible to the abbot, who deliberately keeps the fisher and his kin ignorant of it. It is likely that even if the fisher family were to examine the tablet, they would not be able to make sense of the markings on it, as, given their class, they are probably not literate. Grêgôrius has been schooled, however, and has access not only to the past of those historical figures who wrote but also to his own text, and it is no wonder that he decides to go to the abbot, who named him after himself and wrote on his mind a text of past masters of grammar and divinity. But before he goes to the abbot, Grêgôrius considers the new-found situation—that he is not who he thought he was—at length on his own. The information proves too much for him:

> er gedâhte im grôzer swaere,
> ob disiu rede waere
> ein lüge oder ein wârheit
>   (ll. 1377-9;
> He pondered over every word
> His foster mother had just said—
> Was it false, or true instead?—p. 99).

He rushes to the abbey and pulls the abbot aside—and "von den liuten sunder dan" (l. 1384; "aside, apart from men"—p. 99), indicates the seriousness of his mission as well as the privacy necessary for the information to be communicated, and bluntly asks of his origins. He is, interestingly enough, not uncertain as to the validity of his "mother's" charges, almost as if he had suspected all along the certainty of what he will later assert: "'ich enbin niht der ich wânde sîn'" (l. 1403; "'I'm someone other than I believed'"—p. 101). His fear is not of the possible unworthiness of his origins, but, rather of what people will say, and significantly, this fear is directed toward women's alleged volubility:

> "diu wîp sint sô unverdaget:
> sît si ez iemen hât gesaget,
> sô wizzen ez vil schiere
> drîe unde viere
> und dar nâch alle die hie sint"
> (ll. 1427-1431;
> "All women tattle so and prate.
> Since once my tale she did relate,
> No time will pass before first three,
> Then four hear it, and presently
> Everyone will know it here" (pp. 101-3).

Yet, it must be noted, that had a woman been more voluble in the past, Grêgôrius' own conception would not have occurred. In addition, Grêgôrius here blames others for telling him the truth, which is a stance that many of Hartmann's heroes will take, having equal difficulty with bare facts and more far-reaching wisdom. In coming to the abbot, Grêgôrius seems to be asking not only for painful corroboration of what his "mother" has said are his origins, but also for advice on how to live with his new-found knowledge that he is not the fisherman's child.

To a degree the abbot enlightens Grêgôrius as to his past. Yet this scene, too, is informed by the sense that Grêgôrius' mind has hitherto been unfathomable to his teacher and mentor, just as his origins have been concealed from the island's inhabitants, for Grêgôrius' announcement that he "'würde gerne ritter'" (l. 1503; "'I've always wished to be a knight'"—p. 1500), while a logical culmination of *his* immediate reasoning, comes as a surprise to both the abbot and the reader. Yet, quite clearly, Grêgôrius has gleaned from his study a healthy respect for knightly life as well as for grammatical and divinical studies, and he has daydreamed considerably on the matter of knighthood.[13] His monologue on the subject, given the paucity of his earlier reported thoughts and speech, is positively astounding, both in length and richness of imagination. Hartmann's reasons for revealing this side of his protagonist in such a fashion are sound, however. First of all, oblique hints as to Grêgôrius' future have been given, for, in addition to the more ominous signals that what has been concealed will be revealed, the reader expects fine things from a youth so well formed by nature (ll. 1263ff.; p. 93). But, more than that, Hartmann reveals Grêgôrius' heretofore secret wishes to become a knight at the time when the abbot tells Grêgôrius what he knows of his heritage, not merely because the plot dictates that revelation of Grêgôrius' "geburt" and "guot" (l. 1502; "rank" and "means to live"—p. 107) will facilitate his entering the knightly ranks, but also because, once again, communication of information about a character's internal state is tied to knowledge of that character's past. Access to the mind here is tantamount to recognition, recognition, of the past.

Yet, however bright Grêgôrius' hopes are for becoming a knight—and he details them at length (ll. 1539ff.; p. 109)—the indications for a prognosis of unqualified success in this venture are mixed. Grêgôrius will indeed perform prodigious feats as a knight; yet the total outlook proves to be marred, for Hartmann resorts to three methods he has employed earlier in the work for foreshadowing complications. First of all, he has the abbot stress Grêgôrius' foolish anger (l. 1454; p. 103), recalling Grêgôrius' grandfather's admonition. Moreover, Hartmann places the abbot in the role the reader has come to expect of wise people: the abbot feels constrained to give advice and to give it at length. He urges Grêgôrius, "'volge mîner lêre'" (l. 1451; "'follow all my teaching'"—p. 103), and paints himself in the role of the wise greybeard. The abbot has assured Grêgôrius that he has been given "'vrîe wal'" (l. 1439; "'freedom of the will'"—p. 103), although there is considerable indication that he does not want the youth to exercise choice, and that people in his country respect him, and that "'einer toerinne klaffen'" (l. 1475; "'a foolish woman's chat'"—p. 105) should not make any difference to him. Yet the reader is fully prepared for the hero to decide to disregard his elder's advice, not only because Grêgôrius' grandfather's advice fell on deaf ears, but also because Grêgôrius' parents' counselor's advice could not help but have disastrous, if delayed, consequences. Finally, Grêgôrius himself chooses to enumerate his reasons for disregarding the abbot's advice, and enumeration has in the past been demonstrated to be a narrative device whereby Hartmann warns the reader that surface meaning is not sufficient for predicting short or long-range implications of an action. In other words, Hartmann here prepares the reader for a reversal in fortunes. Thus, Grêgôrius states the three things that necessitate his departure: shame, uncertainty as to parentage, and the possibility of knightly heritage (ll. 1487-1503; pp. 105-7). And the reader, while anticipating that Grêgôrius will have success as a knight, since this child excels at all things, senses that this success will be undercut, for the pattern has been established that unsolicited advice betokens the opposite behavior of that desired, and that enumeration implies subsequent confirmation of the reader's—as well as of the character's—expectations. Moreover, as an enumerator, Grêgôrius is seen as a true child of his parents' lineage, for the father's motivation to sin was of a four-fold nature, and the mother's burdens were three-fold. The implication is, then, that the parents' blighted future is quantified in the son: he is the sum of their union in more than one way.

Yet, in a sense, the nature-versus-nurture question is very much alive in the person of Grêgôrius, despite Hartmann's numerical foreshadowings, for the youth is obviously both his parents' child and the product of the abbot's rearing. As such, he demonstrates an admixture of traits, so that his lack of knowledge of his past mirrors his parents' fundamental ignorance, and so that his erudition in matters grammatical and divinical reflects the abbot's tutelage. Yet nurture is not totally to have its way with Grêgôrius, for all that he knows ("book-learning") is nothing compared to that which he does *not* know (his heritage). And Hartmann's intent in the scene in which the abbot and Grêgôrius differ concerning the youth's future is to cast the nature-versus-nurture conflict in the light that Grêgôrius' mental training may prepare him for—and may even cushion him from—the challenges that life has in store for him, but that it is no defense against situations demanding experiential wisdom rather than theoretical knowledge. Thus, while Grêgôrius is expansive and overambitious, the abbot is more cautious, advising the youth to change his mental outlook: "'Sun, dîn rede enist niht guot: / durch got bekêre dînen muot'" (ll. 1515-6; "'My son, you speak not wisdom's part. / For God's sake, change your mind and heart'"—p. 107), a sentiment reiterated in l. 1673: "'noch bekêre dînen muot'" ("'Change your mind'"—p. 115). But the abbot's reliance on religion is scorned as the ranting of "a false monk's life" (l. 1535; p. 107) who does not believe that one can acquire from books the necessary knowledge of knighthood. Grêgôrius, however, tosses aside that possibility and, in fact, exudes overconfidence:

> "herre, ich bin ein junger man
> und lerne des ich niht enkan.
> swar ich die sinne wenden wil,
> des gelerne ich schiere vil"
>   (ll. 1543-6;
> "Sir, I am young and shall still grow;
> There's time to learn what I don't know.
> No matter to what my mind I turn,
> In short time I shall that learn"—p. 109).

There is a fine irony to this, for Grêgôrius does prove to be a quick learner as far as worldly skills go, while an extremely slow learner—and one taught in the school of hard knocks—in grasping the meaning of sin and repentence. Grêgôrius further subscribes to the belief that what he has learned under the abbot will stand him in good stead in the outside world:

> "herre, iu ist vil wâr geseit:
> ez bedarf vil wol gewonheit,
> swer guot ritter wesen sol.
> ouch hân ich ez gelernet wol
> von kinde in mînem muote hie:
> ez enkam ûz mînem sinne nie"
>   (ll. 1563-7;
> "Much you have heard, sir, is quite right.
> Whoever would be a good knight,
> Great knowledge must that man possess.
> But I have learned it nonetheless,

> And myself in spirit taught
> From earliest childhood; for the thought
> Has never left me"—p. 109).

Interestingly, Grêgôrius employs the "'ist . . .geseit'" ("'have . . . heard'") formulation that his mother relied upon. But "knowledge" is more than just "what one has been told." The knowledge Grêgôrius has gained, because it crucially lacks the one piece of information that might have saved him from sin, will be inadequate. It is a cerebral knowledge—note the repeated references to *gedanc* and related words in his monologue (ll. 1569-73, 1578, 1584, 1587, 1593; pp. 109-11)—rather than a deep-seated understanding, and it is this factor upon which the abbot plays when he urges the youth to devote himself to the life for which he has the most practical training: the religious life.[14]

Yet even the abbot must give in[15] when it becomes obvious that the child he has nurtured virtually since birth is a stranger to him. Certainly a good deal of the estrangement has to do with Grêgôrius' adolescence and awakening adulthood; fathers, like mothers, selectively forget and remember this period as they see it in their offspring, and the effects run the range in perceivers from the self-indulgent to the jarring. After listening to Grêgôrius' revelation of what in fact has been going on in his head, it is no wonder that the abbot is at a loss:

> "Sun, dû hâst mir vil geseit,
> manic diutsch wort vür geleit,
> daz mich sêre umbe dich
> wundern muoz, crêde mich,
> und weiz niht war zuo daz sol:
> ich vernaeme kriechisch als wol"
>   (ll. 1625-30;
> "You've told me much, son. I'm confused
> By many German words you've used.
> These words I am amazed to hear,
> *Crede me*, from you; not clear
> Is what they mean, and as you speak
> I might as well be hearing Greek"—p. 113).

It is not merely that Grêgôrius' terms are "Greek" to the abbot, who ironically salts *his* phrases with Latin, but also that the youth and the abbot do not speak the same language in the sense that words should lead to understanding. The abbot's lack of comprehension reflects the absence of a deeper understanding of the contents of Grêgôrius' mind. And this admission on the abbot's part, followed by a brief attempt at concealment of the tablet foreshadows the bafflement of Grêgôrius' mother/wife, who similarly does not know the secret inner recesses of sorrow in Grêgôrius' mind. In each case, the surprise at Grêgôrius' behavior is followed by the revelation of the contents of the tablet. The information given on the tablet is revealed to Grêgôrius only after the abbot has displayed the diversionary tactic of promising his namesake "'ein alsô rîche hîrât'" and a good life (ll. 1663-4; "'You'll wed / As wealthily as you desire; / I'll see to that. What you require / I'll give you, so that you, indeed, / A very pleasant life will lead'"—p. 115). That passage is fascinating, as it contains some of Hartmann's most obvious and yet delicate word-plays about *hirat* ("marriage) and *rât* ("advice").[16] Moreover, a change of Grêgôrius' mind ("muot"—l. 1673; p. 115) should make him mindful of his poverty ("armuot"—l. 1666; p. 115), just as the abbot's "rât" (l. 1656; "counsel"—p. 115) is to produce "ein alsô rîche hîrât" (l. 1661; "[a marriage] as wealthily as you desire"—p. 115); the mind is to ruminate on advice and conclude with marriage and recalling one's poverty will effect a change in mind. This scene is not only self-referential but also looks ahead to the scene in which Grêgôrius learns of his identity.

The parallel between the abbot's revelatory scene and the scene in which Grêgôrius' mother/wife apprehends his identity becomes complete, because that revelation comes hard on the heels of the youth's actual marriage. Thus, the scene between Grêgôrius and his spiritual father cannot help but look forward to the events at the court of his biological mother, with the reader having the advantage in the later scene of having anticipated the outcome: that which has been hidden shall be revealed. Furthermore, the interchange between the abbot and the youth is related to that between mother/wife and son in the same manner that Grêgôrius' thoughts are related to his actions. For, at the abbey, Grêgôrius can only have knowledge as intellectual apprehension: he reads of knighthood much as he reads on the tablet of his partial heritage, which is not to discount the pain the revelation of his incestuous heritage brings him. But his actual experience of knighthood and incest brings him more than intellectual apprehension: it translates book-learning—for is not the tablet a type of history book, albeit it a personal account?—into actuality, instantiating the process with which the poet has been concerned throughout, which is how one person's knowledge/wisdom can be passed on. Hartmann is not optimistic as to the transmission of knowledge over generations, from one person to another, but in his protagonist he affirms the manner whereby for one person knowledge becomes wisdom through the laborious, clarifying processes of sin and redemption. Grêgôrius reads and re-reads, then sins through that piece of information left out of the account and, having sinned, lives what he has before only read. The reader, too, reads and re-reads the poem, the *tavel* that Hartmann writes, and searches for the missing information in the narrative, for the thread that connects the generations, and for the experience that translates knowledge into wisdom. Yet, having read, the reader is forwarned—and is not the purpose of the poem's lengthy prologue with allusions to the biblical Good Samaritan story a type of parable?—but must yet choose the correct path himself/herself.

Thus, Hartmann sets up this problem of transmission on several levels, so that the reader looks for continuity and diversity not just between the generations but also between the scenes. The question becomes not only how Grêgôrius resembles his parents and unknowingly repeats their sin, but also how the poem's individual scenes look forward to and backward from each other, mirror each other with variations, and present the same problem over narrative time that Grêgôrius poses over his own life. Moreover, just as Grêgôrius longs to know of his origins, so the reader seeks to gain his/her orientation to the work: how, then, knowing what is now known, can the reader use this knowledge to better his/her life and to avoid sin? And in the process, through constant subtle and not-so-subtle reminders, the reader is urged to see in Grêgôrius' situation a paradigm of sinful humanity transformed, a template of individual man's sin and redemption. Thus, *Grêgôrius* displays in microcosm over three generations the ongoing process over the centuries since Creation: the hero is Jonah, the saved sinner, as well as the man rescued by the Good Samaritan; he is Adam; he is Christ re-born; he is Everyman; he is proof of God's forgiveness. Therefore, it is not merely the fact that Grêgôrius is born in sin that proves to be significant, but also that he sins himself, thus falling into the pattern that characterizes the human condition.[17] It is not for nought that Grêgôrius is repeatedly referred to as "der ellende" (ll. 1825, 1855, 1906; "exiled"—pp. 125-9), an exile from the Garden as well as a stranger in a new land.[18]

Since Grêgôrius, born in sin, must sin himself, Hartmann charts the journey that takes the youth back to the land he left as an infant. The "wunschwint" (l. 787; "fairest wind"—p. 67) that sped the child to an existence in which he would be kept ignorant of his origins is balanced by the gale and winds (ll. 1832, 1835, 1837, 1840; p. 125) that blow him back to confront—physically, intellectually, and emotionally—these origins. Grêgôrius must go back, and, although he does not know this, the reader does. The reader knows that, like a mind that returns again and again to a thought not fully worked out or to an insight that has been quickly forgotten, the narrative will circle back to a meeting of Grêgôrius and his mother/wife. When he and she first part, the stage is set for his return. After their marriage and the revelation of the double incest, it is only a matter of time until their final meeting. Moreover, these meetings between mother/wife and husband/son demonstrate the different qualities of mind that each possesses. Grêgôrius acts out of ignorance, hindered by what he does not know; as he comes to know, he keeps this knowledge constantly before him by exercising contemplative repentence. He is viewed as actively exercising his mind, learning by degrees and retaining what he learns. The wife/mother, however, exhibits behavior that shows that she is not mindful of her earlier vows, as she is swayed by her courtiers' specious advice that "ein sô rîchez lant" (l. 2212; "so great a realm"—p. 145) must have an heir and, accordingly, agrees to marry the man who has just saved it from ruin. Moreover, the fact that she is so easily convinced of the wisdom of her retainers' advice is underscored by the course in which her thoughts are already running:

> dô gedâhte diu guote
> vil dicke in ir muote
> wen sî nemen möhte
> der baz ir muote töhte
> dan den selben man
> (und geviel vil gar dar an)
> den ir got hete gesant
> ze loesen sî unde ir lant
>   (ll. 2235-42;
> The thought would enter in her mind,
> What better husband could she find
> Who'd be more fitting than that knight
> Whom God had sent her in her plight,
> Who had not only freed her land,
> But rescued her from the duke's hand—p. 147).

Furthermore, the fact that she does not dwell on the ominous coincidence that the fabric of her defender's garb is identical to that which she placed in her son's vessel indicates that hers is a mind that does not make connections, that does not go beyond surface facts or that perhaps chooses to ignore the obvious. The narrator notes, concerning her realization that the fabric is "like" ("gelîch"—l. 1949; p. 131) that cloth that she had placed about her son, so that "daz ermante sî ir leide" (l. 1954; "The sight / Recalled to her her grievous plight"—p. 131), but that is as far as it goes. She seems incapable of making that one step of reasoning that would avert disaster, and once again she does not speak, does not ask the origin of the cloth, and, even more importantly, does not inquire as to her husband's origins.[19]

In general it must be said that the mother/wife is not very perceptive or communicative; she neither notices that Grêgôrius regularly withdraws to a private chamber and becomes deeply upset upon returning—in other words, that he harbors a secret—nor does she share her own past with him. As he is her child and shares her heritage, he possesses these traits as well, although not to the extent that she does; he does not enlighten her as to his uncertain parentage before they marry,[20] nor is he perceptive enough to detect any indications on her part that her past was anything but unblemished, but he does not display her inability to pick up on simple clues such as the telltale fabric. The difference between mother and son is that he is only imperceptive about that which he does not know, whereas, for the mother, a little knowledge makes her blind to the greater implications of that knowledge. She knows that she has seen the fabric before, and she knows that the recollection of having seen it before gives her pain, but that is the extent of her knowledge. The fabric reminds ("ermanen"—l. 1954; p. 131) but does not warn ("manen") her, for she is simply not cast as a reflective person in this part of the poem. As earlier noted, the tangible fruits of her incest were quickly removed from her, and she is not, after that first enumeration of her grief, portrayed as pining away in contemplation of her past sin while her kingdom is being whittled down around her. Rather, she is described as "schoene" (l. 1897; "fair"—p. 129) as well as "junc" (l. 1897; "young"—p. 129), and her excellent physical condition as well as the single reference to her past sorrow (l. 1954; p. 131) suggests that contemplation on her sin/son has not weighed heavily upon her mind. Nor has it resulted in the debilitating physical transformation that the reflective Grêgôrius will later undergo. Here she so typifies the "out of sight, out of mind" mentality that she is not described as having thoughts about her son during the period of his growth and maturity while at the monastery but is only reminded of his existence when he in fact stands before her, although she does not recognize him.

It must be noted, though, that Grêgôrius, too, suffers from an inability to recognize fully his situation. He, who earlier decried that others should know that he was a foundling, takes pains to conceal his heritage from those in his new land. Having earlier wished,

> "jâ vinde ich eteswâ daz lant
> daz da niemen ist erkant
> wie ich her komen bin"
> (ll. 1417-9;
> "Somewhere, perhaps, I may suppose,
> There is a land where no one knows
> How I first came here to you"—p. 101),

he maintains the secrecy of his origins in the land of his origin to the point that he takes elaborate precautions to make sure that no one knows nor finds out the tangible record of his heritage. He feels safe, in that he has taken refuge in a land where he is unknown and where he initially does not know how events stand ("daz er des niene weste"—l. 1863; "That he could be so unaware / And ignorant of this affair"—p. 127), yet it is the very land that, had he known the full story of his origins, he would have avoided. And here Hartmann makes use of the underlying assumption that relates physical journey to spiritual progress, with an added temporal dimension, for Grêgôrius journeys in a sense to the past in going to the land of his origin and there committing the same sin as his parents. Grêgôrius goes to his mother's land, where he regresses spiritually, where he sins as did his forefathers, while reading of

> ... die süntlîche bürde

> sîner muoter und sînes vater.
> unsern herren got bat er
> in beiden umbe hulde
> und erkande niht der schulde
> diu ûf sîn selbes rücke lac,
> die er naht unde tac
> mit sîner muoter uopte,
> dâ mite er got betruopte
> (ll. 2286-94;
> Of how in sinful circumstance
> He had been born, and weeping read
> Of what parents he was bred,
> Who both were burdened with such sin.
> Then in prayer he would begin
> To beg the Lord that He bestow
> His grace on them. He did not know
> Or recognize in any way
> The guilt that rested night and day
> On him, as with his mother he,
> To God's offense, lived sinfully—pp. 149-51).

His knowledge is incomplete, as is that of his mother, and, so for that matter, is that of the maid who later engineers the revelation that drives Grêgôrius from the court.

The theme of partial knowledge sounds repeatedly throughout the poem. An examination of the revelation scene gives insight into later scenes, where the established pattern repeats itself with variations. The basic premise, that of the incompleteness of knowledge, takes two forms, the first of which is illustrated by the maid's knowledge. Note the terms used to describe her actions: "gemarhte" (l. 2304; "marked"—p. 151); "ersaehe" (l. 2311; "ascertain, see"—p. 151); "gesach" (l. 2317; "watched"—p. 151); "ervarn" (l. 2326; "learned"—p. 151); "ersach" (l. 2328; "saw in a 'completed' sense"— my translation); "ersach" (l. 2386; "witnessed"—p. 155); "gesach" (l. 2395; "seen"—p. 155); "erkande" (l. 2397; "became plain"—p. 155 or "recognized"); "sach" (l. 2403; "saw"—p. 155). Cast as a perceptive and curious individual, the maid knows well that Grêgôrius is sorrowful, but she does not know the cause. As such, she exemplifies the following pattern: here is a fact, but since the underpinnings of that fact are obscured, the fact cannot be fully comprehended. The mind seeks to know more. This paradigm manifests itself most readily in the circumstances of Grêgôrius' birth: Grêgôrius had parents, but their identity is not named. Another way of stating this paradigm would be to say, colloquially, that we know something is out there, but we don't know what it is. We can also express that variation of the theme in this way: we know what is out there, but we don't know where it is. This variation manifests itself not only in the cardinals' partial revelation of Grêgôrius' existence, but also in the certain knowledge that the key to Grêgôrius' shackles exists, even though its exact location is unknown. In both variations one starts out with the known and ends up with the unknown, and this state of affairs is invariably resolved in this poem by revelation, both human and divine.

The revelation that the maid brings about is resisted on several levels by her mistress, who is loathe to contemplate the implications of what might be revealed. Her speech is sprinkled with knowledge terms such as "'weizgot'" (l. 2416; "'God knows'"—p. 157), "'weiz'" (l. 2431; "'I know'"—p. 157), "'ze wizzen'" (l. 2436; "'to learn'"—p. 157) "'ze wizzene'" (l. 2438; "'to know'"—p. 157), "'gewis'" (l. 2446; "'certain'"—p. 159). But there is still a reluctance on her part to find out the cause of Grêgôrius' sorrow, lest she lose him in the process (l. 2430; p. 157). And her own past sorrow, which she has repressed, surfaces in a four-line comment:

> "jâ engeschach mînem lîbe
> nie deheiner slahte guot
> unde ouch niemer getuot
> niuwan von sîn eines tugent"
> (ll. 2418-21;
> "Good luck has never
> In all my life, nor will it ever,
> Come my way, and I have known
> No luck except through him alone"—p. 157).

Even after the maid's advice to her mistress to do a little detective work on her own, which of course results in the discovery of the damning evidence, the mother/wife holds out faint hope that Grêgôrius might have come by the tablet and fabric in all innocence. And here Hartmann does not take refuge in his earlier disclaimers, where he pleaded inadequacy to describe the extent of her grief, for he details, through first-person lament and third-person descriptive commentary, the emotional and intellectual effect of this revelation upon the mother/wife. Hers is a mind forced not only to comprehend but also to remember, albeit reluctantly, and to exercise its forward-looking abilities toward consequences ("si gedâhte daz sî vür wâr / zuo der helle waere geborn"—ll. 2488-9; "Not could she from the thought forbear / That for Hell she had been born"—p. 161) as well as its reflective capacities upon past causes ("und erkande sî zehant . . ."—l. 2476; "knew at once . . ."—pp. 159-61).Her grasping of this revelation necessarily proceeds in stages, and not without some nice touches on the part of Hartmann in the way of echoing with variations language that harks back to previous scenes. The narrator notes in somewhat hackneyed terms:

> Ir vreuden sunne wart bedaht
> mit tôtvinsterre naht.
> ich waene ir herze waere
> gebrochen von der swaere,

> wan daz ein kurz gedinge
> ir muot tete ringe
> und stuont ir trôst doch gar dar an
> (ll. 2499-505;
> Now was the sun of her delight
> Gone down in deadly black of night.
> Grief surely would have caused her heart
> To break at once beneath the smart,
> I do believe, had she not eased
> Her mind with one faint hope and seized
> Her only comfort . . .—p. 161).

The first rhyme-pair gives the clue that the revelation's roots lie in the past, for the brother's seduction of his sister begins:

> nû vriste erz unz eine naht
> dô mit slâfe was bedaht
> diu juncvrouwe dâ si lac
> (ll. 353-5;
> Then he delayed his action till
> One night when the maiden lay quite still
> And slumbered fast in deep repose—p. 43).

The parallel becomes even more striking when one notices that "ringe" (here: "easy") echoes the sister's earlier cry: "'waz diutet diz ringen'" (l. 384; "'What aim / Or meaning has this wrestling game?'"—p. 45). There the overt meaning of the strong verb "ringen" was "to wrestle," while in the latter passage the adjective "ringe" corresponds to the weak verb "ringen" ("to relieve, ameliorate") but the linguistic nexus set up here is too strong to ignore. Once again Hartmann calls attention to two types of knowledge: carnal and intellectual. And in both instances the mother/wife hedges after thinking the matter over. She initially thinks to hold her peace:

> si gedâhte, "swîge ich stille,
> sô ergât des tiuvels wille
> und wirde mînes bruoder brût,
> und wirde ich aber lût,
> sô haben wir iemer mêre
> verloren unser êre"
> (ll. 385-90;
> "If I keep silent," thought the lass,
> "The Devil's wish will come to pass,
> And I'll become my brother's bride.
> But if I shout aloud and chide
> We shall have lost forever more
> All fame and honor that we bore"—p. 45).

The bewildered girl-child has been supplanted by the woman, and, while her manner of perceiving danger has not changed fundamentally, her response to it and reaction to it have. As a result, she wavers but then acts. Her thoughts, while holding out a faint hope that is more bad faith than actual hope, turn eventually to speaking out, as the enormity of the situation comes home to her:

>si gedâhte: "waz ob mînem man
>disiu tavel ist zuo brâht
>anders danne ich hân gedâht?"
>(ll. 2506-8;
>[She thought] "What is this tablet once was brought
>To my dear husband otherwise
>Than I was first drawn to surmise?"—p. 161).

His history has become her story. She speaks this time because she realizes that her initial failure to raise an objection to her brother's "wrestling," on account of possible loss of reputation has resulted in a far greater loss: "'ist mir diu sêle nû verlorn'" (l. 2677; "'If my soul, too, is lost to me'"—p. 171), a loss she earlier feared, yet of which she grew unmindful after the tangible result of her sin, Grêgôrius, was given over to the waves and presumably banished forever from her life. This time Grêgôrius will again leave, but the mother/wife, in truly repenting, will remember him and what he represents.

Grêgôrius' reaction to his mother/wife's revelation adds yet another dimension to Hartmann's concept of mind:

>er was in leides gebote.
>sînen zorn huop er hin ze gote,
>er sprach: "diz ist des ich ie bat,
>daz got mich braehte ûf die stat
>daz mir sô wol geschaehe
>daz ich mit vreuden saehe
>mîne liebe muoter.
>rîcher got vil guoter,
>des hâst du anders mich gewert
>danne ich an dich hân gegert.
>ich gertes in mînem muote
>nâch liebe und nâch guote:
>nû hân ich sî gesehen sô
>daz ich des niemer wirde vrô,
>wande ich sî baz verbaere
>danne ich ir sus heimlich waere"
>(ll. 2605-22;
>Beside himself, through sorrow dazed,
>His angry voice to God he raised.
>"Always have I prayed," he said,
>"That God my wandering bestead

And lead me to that very place
Where through good fortune I'd embrace
My mother happily at last.
O Gracious Lord, in power vast,
My wish now Thou hast granted me
So otherwise than wished of Thee.
For in my heart's deepest recess
I longed for love and happiness.
Now I have seeen her in such way
That I shall ever rue the day.
Would that on her I'd never set eyes
Than that I know her in this wise!"—p. 167).

Grêgôrius' response harks back in a sense to Enîte's lament in *Erec*, where her request for death is answered in short order in name ("Lîmors") and then in actuality, in Oringles' death. Here Grêgôrius has repeatedly prayed—and is not prayer a hopeful communication between the human and divine minds?—and has been given exactly what he asked for. He has seen his mother. His anger, then, is directed at the literalness with which God has answered his prayer. Hartmann once again underscores the linkage of thought and action: thought of the mother means a return to the mother.

The mother, on her part, reacts with a curious mixture of hope and fatalism. In a sense, she sees her predicament as an example of "'der heize gotes zorn'" (l. 2678; "'God's flaming wrath'"—p. 171; literally "anger") falling on her, as something her body did to her (l. 2682; p. 171), and as a set of circumstances that can be ameliorated if one just knew how. She appeals to her learned son for aid, and there is an implicit edge of suicidal feeling in her speech. She does not pick up a handy sword, as does Enîte, but she longs for and fears the end of her life. Grêgôrius' response speaks to the life they have unwittingly led and, in effect, urges her to build a new life of penance that will soften God's angry mind (l. 2734; p. 173) and that will not consist of "'gemach unde vreude'" (l. 2710; "'comfort'" and "'pleasure'"—p. 173) but will rather concentrate on less worldly things:

"dem lande und dem guote
und wertlîchem muote
dem sî hiute widerseit"
    (ll. 2745-7;
"Now let my realm and my possessions,
Let the world and its professions
Be renounced this very day!"—p. 175).

And immediately prior to Grêgôrius' departure, the hero notes, "'wir waeren baz gescheiden ê'" (l. 2744; "'Better that we had parted earlier'"—my translation), with the "baz" ("better") echoing the "baz" in "jâ laege er baz besunder" (l. 366; "Far better that he lay apart"—p. 43) that was the commentary on his father's actions. It would have been "better," but "better" in earthly terms is not always "better" in the long run of heavenly terms, for Grêgôrius' wish,

> "wir suln ez bringen dar zuo
> daz uns noch got gelîche
> gesamene in sînem rîche"
> (ll. 2740-2;
> "We may yet bring it to pass
> That our Lord, no longer loath,
> In his realm will unite us both"—p. 175),

will come true, but not before the pair has been reunited on earth.

The next thousand and eighty lines, a little over a quarter of the narrative, are given over to Grêgôrius' activities after leaving his wife/mother and before his reunion with her at the close of the poem, when the altered physical appearance of both will attest to a positive spiritual transformation. His initial three-day wandering (l. 2770; p. 177) points toward the Harrowing of Hell motif, earlier alluded to in the infant's journey that is compared to that of Jonah, a traditional type of Christ, and additional indications are given to show that Grêgôrius' suffering is to bear good fruits: he treads the narrow path, the difficult road to salvation. Seemingly without direction ("der wîselose man"—l. 2822; Buehne translates "helpless," p. 181, but I opt for "directionless, without knowledge," as it is more in keeping with Hartmann's wordplays), he is nevertheless led precisely where he needs to go to do penance. Described as wise (l. 2890; p. 185) and able to give advice to his mother (l. 2688; p. 171), he turns increasingly inward in his repentence, and this is reflected in the fact that he speaks sparingly and, when he does, acknowledges his limitations and inadequacy:

> "herre, ich bin ein man
> daz ich niht ahte wizzen kan
> mîner süntlîchen schulde"
> (ll. 2955-7;
> He said, "I am a man, good sir,
> Who is not able to aver
> How far his sinful guilt extends"—p. 187).

In comparison to the inner-directed and relatively taciturn Grêgôrius, the fisher whom the protagonist meets is vituperatively garrulous and verbally abusive. Hartmann purposefully draws him broadly, not only to fashion him as a foil to his good and considerate wife, but also to show him in his unregenerate state so that his subsequent repentance will be all the more striking. Yet, however unpleasant the fisher is, he is just what Grêgôrius needs, in medieval literature's tradition of providing precisely the necessary obstacles and incentives to a hero's progress. The fisher is callous enough to test Grêgôrius' resolve to turn the other cheek, impatient enough to pay little heed to Grêgôrius' physical needs, and cruel enough to place Grêgôrius in a situation from which he can be extricated only through miraculous means. Moreover, as an advice-giver/provider (l. 2988; p. 189), he says just what the penitent Grêgôrius wants to hear:

> swie erz mit hônschaft taete,
> sô wâren im die raete
> rehte als er wünschen wolde.
> ob er wünschen solde
> (ll. 3015-8;
> Though jeeringly the fisher taunted,
> Just this Gregorius had wanted.
> If he'd been wishing for advice,
> This he'd have wished for in a trice—p. 191).

He does not provide Grêgôrius with comfortable accommodations. The hero "vant dar inne swachen rât" (l. 3039; "found little provision there"—my translation—with the pun on "rât" clearly accessible to the reader). Furthermore, the fisher nearly leaves without Grêgôrius on the morning when he is to convey him to the rock, which causes Grêgôrius to leave his tablet behind (ll. 3080-2; p. 195). The fisher's final action in this episode caps a sequence of slights, insults, and misperceptions, for, after he heaves the key into the waves, he taunts:

> "daz weiz ich âne wân,
> swenne ich den slüzzel vunden hân
> ûz der tiefen ünde,
> sô bistû âne sünde
> unde wol ein heilic man"
> (ll. 3095-9[21];
> "If ever I find this key again
> From out the deep, assuredly
> I'll know," he said, "that you are free
> Of sin, a holy man instead"—p. 195).

Grêgôrius will, the fisher to the contrary, be shown to be a holy man, but only through the grace of God, who not only miraculously sustains him through seventeen years on the rock, but also forgives Grêgôrius' sins. What proves incredible is that these seventeen years are dispatched in a matter of one hundred and fifty lines in which Hartmann primarily occupies himself with describing how Grêgôrius received what little water he had to drink. There is no mention made of any mental activity on Grêgôrius' part, neither ruminations on his past behavior nor voiced prayers for forgiveness. This absence is akin to that period in Iwein's life when he is described as having no thoughts, but the reader of *Grêgôrius* knows that a man who spends seventeen years chained to a rock, with only his own thoughts for companionship, is likely to be having insights concerning himself, God, and the world. Yet Hartmann is stubbornly and characteristically silent here, and to good purpose, letting Grêgôrius' inner pain and penance be evident on his body. What is important is not a word-for-word access to Grêgôrius' mind at this point but rather the fact that God does indeed forgive Grêgôrius' past behavior. Here again Hartmann's language proves highly significant, for the narrator notes, "unde got vergaz / sîner houbetschulde" (ll. 3140-1; "the Lord / Forgot his deadly sin"—p. 199), a circumstance later voiced in similar language by the protagonist when he speaks with his mother at the end of the poem:

> "swie grôz und swie swaere
> mîner sünden last waere,
> des hât nû got *vergezzen*"
> (ll. 3927-9, my italics;
> "Oppressive as my great sins were,
> God has now forgiven me"—p. 243; literally:
> 'forgotten').

The close proximity of the first mention of God's "forgetting" to Grêgôrius' neglecting to remember his tablet (sixty lines) cannot help but call attention to the point Hartmann wishes to make concerning sin and redemption[22] in light of divine and human remembering and forgetting. In *Grêgôrius* the human mind is seen to resemble the divine mind in that it is capable of selective forgetting, but where the human mind forgets in the *in malo* sense in failing to recall and reflect, the divine mind forgets in the *in bono* sense in that it, through grace, overlooks sin if proper penance has been done and repentence exercised.

Grêgôrius' failure to remember his tablet—the written, book-learning record of his heritage—in addition to highlighting the difference between the human and divine minds, also indicates that it is *his* sin on which he will concentrate in his seventeen years of penance. The tablet remains safe in his absence, despite the destruction of the hut in which it lay forgotten, and this state of affairs indicates not only Hartmann's contention that things hidden or forgotten do not stay hidden or forgotten, but also that, in accepting the call to the papacy, Grêgôrius brings to that office not only the sins he has committed but also those of his forebears. For that reason it is essential that he find again the record of his birth. Grêgôrius' adamant assertion to do so reflects the gravity of the situation:

> got er im sô helfen bat,
> er enkaeme niemer von der stat,
> ob er ir niht vunde
> (ll. 3723-5;
> [he] then maintained,

Unless the tablet he regained,
So help him God, there he would stay—p. 231).

Finding his tablet serves as the capstone of a series of findings that clear the way for—and, indeed, impel—Grêgôrius' ascent of the papal throne. First of all, as those in Rome are stymied concerning the selection of a new pope, it is decided that the choice be left to God:

> nû rieten si über al
> daz si liezen die wal
> an unseren herren got
> (ll. 3155-7;
> Then one and all reached this accord:
> To let the choice rest with our lord—p. 199).

And the human proposal ("rieten"—l. 3155; "accord" here—p. 199) is promptly countered by divine counsel: "got . . . der ie der guoten vrâge riet" (ll. 3164-5; "God . . . / Who always heeds the righteous' plea"—p. 201). In seeking advice the Romans appeal to divine authority. Because human knowledge is necessarily incomplete, they receive a partial response and learn that the next pope is a man named Grêgôrius who sits on a cliff in Aquitaine. No one knows him, but the cardinals are undeterred and set off to seek him in a landscape in which they are continually disoriented and in which they frequently despair of finding him (ll. 3220, 3227-8; p. 203).

Although well provided for ("wol berâten"—ll. 3263, 3268; p. 205), they are "wegelôs" (l. 3231; "without direction"—p. 203) and only stumble upon the fisher's house by following their inclinations (l. 3232; p. 203), which, being divinely guided and counseled, are unerring, even though the two men may not be aware of this fact. It is their presence that prompts the greedy fisher, who well "knows" (l. 3264; p. 205) a chance for profit,[23] to offer them a splendid fish that he has only caught that day. Of course, the fish, true to fairy-tale fashion,[24] contains the lost key to Grêgôrius' shackles (ll. 3294-5; p. 207), which triggers the fisher's recognition, repentance, and willingness to transport the Romans to the man. Moreover, the fisher's new-found humility causes him to seek counsel in atoning for his misdeed ("daz si im etelîchen rât / taeten vür die missetât"—ll. 3335-6; "Imploring help that he be shown / How for his sin he might atone"—p. 209). The atonement proves to be directions and conveyance to Grêgôrius. The sequence in which the Romans, Grêgôrius, and the fisher exchange information about each other functions in such a manner as if piece after piece were added to a puzzle, so that separate bits of knowledge, from recognition to wisdom, are joined together: the Romans have their dream, the fisher has the key, and Grêgôrius the divine sanction; while these factors separately mean little, they collectively account for a great deal, specifically for the crowning of a pope.

The pope is experientially schooled in "des heiligen geistes lêre" (l. 3795; "the Holy Ghost['s teaching]"—p. 235) and can well give "geistlichen rât" (l. 3875; "counsel of religious worth"—p. 241) to all who seek it. At this point the narrative returns in cyclical fashion to the final meeting of mother and son, [25] where neither initially recognizes the other (ll. 3853, 3877; pp. 239-41). Grêgôrius is the first to grasp that the penitent woman before him in the confessional is in fact his mother, and it is curious that he does not do so until she mentions the one fact that previously stood between him and awareness of his origins: the land of his birth, "Equitânja" (l. 3855; "Aquitaine"—p. 239). Yet one would think that she had presumably told him more than enough to make him aware that the participants in "ir houbetmissetât" (l. 3838; "mortal sin"—p. 239) include himself. The probable answer to this dilemma would seem to lie in the woman's extreme physical and spiritual transformation. Grêgôrius does not recognize her, simply because she is no longer what she was. Even more curious is the interchange between Grêgôrius, who speaks guardedly, and his mother, who in a sense plays Laudîne to Grêgôrius' Lûnete. But her ignorance here proves to be essential if Hartmann is to make his point concerning knowledge. Only by showing characters acting out of ignorance, out of partial knowledge, or out of inaccurate information can Hartmann contrast the workings of the human mind with the paths of divine wisdom, and he appends a gloss to his tale of Grêgôrius that speaks to the same limitations of human reasoning. One might, the narrator notes, be tempted to read the wrong moral from *Grêgôrius*, to assume that if the work's "sündaere" (l. 3960; "sinners"—p. 247) can be redeeemed, then one might as well live wildly and repent at leisure. Yet that is to read the tale incorrectly and take "boesez bilde" (l. 3965; "an evil precedent"—p. 247; literally: "a bad, base image") rather than "ein saelic bilde" (l. 3984; a "moral"—p. 247; literally: "a blessed, good image") from it. To read the tale aright is to view it as an admonition, as an instructive mirror, and as a deterrent.

Finally, in the multifaceted theme of knowledge Hartmann binds up his interconnected concerns with losing and finding, concealing and revealing, and forgetting and remembering, in order to couch sin and redemption in terms of perspective. Overall, the human perspective entails an incompleteness of knowledge (in the case of Grêgôrius) or an incapacity to remember all that is necessary in order not to continue sinning (the wife/mother). The divine perspective, however, is all-encompassing and involves selective forgetting in order to redeem mankind. The human perspective interprets events, people, and places as mysteries, as baffling and often seemingly unrelated bits of information, whereas the divine perspective is ever-mindful of interrelationships and wider-reaching significances. For the reader, who is shown those who are "wegelôs" ("without direction") and those who tread "der saelden strâze" (l. 87; "the road to heavenly bliss"—p. 25), the poem, then, becomes a type of road map for a fascinating journey through a landscape fraught with develish detours, [26] a window into one man's grave recognition of God's all-encompassing forgiveness, and an instructive mirror for the reader, who, if he/she ponders upon what he/she has read and contemplates his/her sin through repentance, may yet come to take the good counsel offered by the story of Grêgôrius, "der guote sündaere" (l. 176; the "good sinner"—p. 31).[27] In reading, the reader may apprehend intellectually what is required of him/her: in practicing penance, he/she may come wisely to know of God.

Grêgôrius is a poem that contrasts the inscrutable workings of the divine mind with the necessarily flawed processes of human reason. The reader—and, one suspects, Grêgôrius himself—could be tempted to question the logic of the fantastic and rapid coincidences at the poem's *dénouement*, where prophetic dreams, a miraculously restored key, and some lucky wandering conspire to place on the papal throne a man who, himself the child of an incestuous union, has committed further incest with his mother. Furthermore, how can it be reasonably explained that, out of all the possible besieged kingdoms that crowd the romance world, Grêgôrius lands on the shores of his mother's territory? Yet one of the primary messages of this poem is that what may to man appear to be chance or even arbitrary choice actually results from an incomplete understanding of divine intentions. Grêgôrius *must* undergo the adventures and sorrows he does precisely because, for him, sin and repentance form the necessary prerequisities for comprehending divine wisdom.

If one takes knowledge as the work's overarching principle, the poem is seen to be even more tightly unified than previously supposed, for Hartmann, never one to include superfluous scenes in his narratives, crafts each exchange in *Grêgôrius* so that one character's knowledge is juxtaposed to that of another character or to that of God. Often Hartmann flags a character's knowledge through the use of the formulaic contrast-pair *wîs/tump* ("wise, learned"/ "inexperienced, ignorant"), but often he leads the reader, through undercutting, to an ironic appeal to a seeming wisdom figure. And, because people who "know" generally feel qualified and obligated— even constrained—to give advice, Hartmann allows the reader to assess the work of the advice solicited and rendered throughout the work. In fact, the continual emphasis on intellectual apprehension may account for that leanness, that spareness that characterizes this work, in contrast to Hartmann's other poems. For *Grêgôrius'* plot possesses a certain simplicity, on the one hand indicative of Hartmann's debt to the structure and conventions of romance, and on the other hand stripped of the conventions of romance and attired in the trappings of fairy tale. The cyclical movement of romance—its phases of departure, struggle, and return—is present, as is the sense of the outer world of landscape's harmony with the hero's inner world, yet lacking are the standard details that crowd contemporary romances: the elaborate court rituals, battles, and feasts, the involved interior monologues, the extended nature descriptions, and the stylized physical renderings of lovers. *Grêgôrius* displays a bare-bones narrative, with the skeleton of romance,[28] as it were, so exposed—not unlike the hero's emaciated frame must have appeared to the cardinals and fisher—so that the reader intellectually considers the pull that draws the hero back to his origin, his mother, the subsequent distancing, and then the reasserted pull that unites them, albeit chastely this time, in their final reconciliation. These meetings, moreover, seem to illustrate in yet another way Hartmann's concern with the fragmentation of entities, so that the final reconciliation of mother and son reflects a variation in the union experienced by heart and body in *Die Klage* and by Erec and Enîte in *Erec*: there is a proper way for each entity to exist as one, and it will only come, in *Die Klage*, after a good deal of arguing, in *Erec*, after considerable misunderstanding, and in *Grêgôrius*, after unwitting union and separation.

4

DER ARME HEINRICH
Admonition and Expectation

Der arme Heinrich bears Hartmann's characteristic stamp not only because of its first misleading impression of simplicity but also because of its fundamental concern with mind. Like the two romances and the didactic *Grêgôrius*, *Der arme Heinrich* charts the process whereby physical transformation speaks to spiritual growth.[1] However, more than the other poems, this work uses the characters' mental and physical journeys to play with the reader's expectations—with what the reader knows or thinks he/she knows. The reader is challenged to make a rapid succession of mental assessments, establishments of inevitability, and then double-takes when expectations are momentarily undercut, only to be re-established at a later time. More so than *Grêgôrius*, where a fated atmosphere obtains, *Der arme Heinrich* calls attention to the reader's expectations—the reader *knows* that the protagonist both will suffer and will be saved—but, as is not so noticeable in reading *Grêgôrius*, the reader of *Der arme Heinrich* is continually brought up short, repeatedly led to wonder *why* he/she knows, or thinks he/she knows, the outcome of any number of instances where the plot hangs in the balance. In other words, the interest lies in both the characters' adjustment to ever-changing situations in a story and the reader's adjustments to that story: each asks, "What is likely to come of this?" but each asks for different reasons.

As in reading *Grêgôrius*, the two romances, and *Die Klage*, reading *Der arme Heinrich* is best served by a sequential approach, since Hartmann's technique relies upon comparisons made over time, as new knowledge is added to what is already known. The work's prologue provides the foundation for subsequent additions.

> Ein ritter sô gelêret was,
> daz er an den buochen las,
> swaz er dar an geschriben vant:

> der was Hartman genant.
> dienstman was er zOuwe.
> er nam im manige schouwe
> an mislîchen buochen;
> dar an begunde er suochen,
> ob er iht des funde,
> dâ mite er swaere stunde
> möhte senfter machen,
> und von sô gewanten sachen,
> daz gotes êren töhte
> und dâ mite er sich möhte
> gelieben den liuten.
> nu beginnet er iu diuten
> ein rede die er geschriben vant
>
> (ll. 1-17; A knight called Hartmann, who was a vassal of the Lords of Aue, was so learned that he could read whatever was written in books. He often looked into different ones, searching for something that would make troublesome hours more pleasant and was of such a nature as to endear him to men and honor God. He will now begin to tell you a story he found written—p. 23).

Hartmann's skill is here demonstrated in that what initially appears to be a fairly straightforward exposition of his motive is, upon reflection, hardly ingenuous. In a twist away from the conventional humility formula with which prologues to medieval works often abound, the reader faces a narrator who, after some seventeen lines, is seen trumpeting his own erudition, rather than that of some third person, an "er" ("he") who happens to be called "Hartman" and who resides "zOuwe" (ll. 4-5; "at Aue"). The matter of book learning, over and above what clues it may give us about Hartmann, works first to create in the mind of the reader the impression that one is dealing with an informed source and, moreover, with one who will not tell from where he derives his information but readily admits to having a source, thus substantiating, in that particularly medieval way, the validity of what he is to write as well as his own credentials as a writer. Hartmann reinforces the concept of the authoritative narrator, too, through the use of the third person, for "er" distances more effectively than *Grêgôrius'* "ich" and creates the superficial impression of objectivity. The import of first-person narration, colored as it is with potential misperception and conjecture, gives way to the weight of "objective" third-person reporting. Hartmann, in writing of himself in the third person, effectively has it both ways: "objectivity" cloaks subjectivity if one is an "ich" disguised as an "er."

Moreover, in associating himself with books, both as a reader and a writer of them, Hartmann establishes not only the idea of access to valuable information (which is valuable enough to be written down, and *because* it is written down is perceived to be valuable), but also the power to give others access to that information, to pass on what one perceives as important and to disregard what one does not hold to be germane to the story. Of course, that selectivity of vision is common to all authors: one writes about what one considers important. But what Hartmann is doing here is nothing less than establishing his authority, only subsequently to cast this authority in doubt, ultimately, before the final authority that he sees lodged in God. Significantly, all the book-learning in the world is of no help to Heinrich, nor is it, for that matter, to Grêgôrius, whose wide reading does not prepare him for maneuvering in the noncloistered world. God alone delivers both Heinrich and Grêgôrius, and if He is a reader, it is not of "mislîchen buochen" (l. 7; "different [books]"—p. 23) but rather of the book that is His world, His creation. Thus, the reader's expectation, which the narrator has fostered in the prologue—that is, that book-learning has its advantages (after all, it allows one to compose works to God's honor and man's delectation (ll. 10-15; p. 23)—is belied by events within the work itself as well as in other contexts in which education does not stand a character in good stead.

This analysis does not belittle Hartmann's self-professed educational accomplishments, but rather lays the groundwork for us to examine the sophisticated technique of contrastive undercutting which Hartmann not only uses but also enjoins his reader to use— implicitly here, called forth through close analysis and reflection, but explicitly elsewhere, as, for example, when *Iwein*'s narrator and "'vrouwe Minne'" ("'Lady Love'") challenge each other's perceptions and motives. Hartmann urges his reader, best expressed with a sports term, to "follow through," that is, to take an idea to its logical conclusion—in short, to think and reflect. In part this is accomplished in admonitory speeches—the close of *Grêgôrius* comes immediately to mind—and in part it is effected by what might be called a temporal "follow through." And in fact, Hartmann next turns to this concept in *Der arme Heinrich*:

> dar umbe hât er sich genant,
> daz er sîner arbeit
> die er dar an hât geleit
> iht âne lôn belîbe,
> und swer nâch sînem lîbe
> si hoere sagen oder lese,
> daz er im bittende wese
> der sêle heiles hin ze gote.
> man giht, er sî sîn selbes bote
> und erloese sich dâ mite,
> swer vür des andern schulde bite
> (ll. 18-28[3]; He gave his name in order to be rewarded for the pains he has taken with it and so

that whoever reads it or hears it told after his death might pray to God for the welfare of his soul. They say that he who intercedes for others is his own messenger too and thereby redeems himself—p. 23).

In effect, if one hears Hartmann's tale told—or, better yet, if one rubs shoulders with erudite authority and *reads* it—one is asked to pray for the poet's soul, to think of him after his death, to keep him in mind, to extend the original life over time, in thought. Also, the hearing or reading of the tale of Heinrich, coupled with compliance with the poet's request for prayers, confers upon the listener or reader some of the blessing of authority, for authority naturally seeks to perpetuate itself. "I have read," states Hartmann, to which the reader answers, stating, "I, too, have read."

What Hartmann has written, and what the reader will read, is a tale in which knowledge is seen variously as expectation and admonition, a story that gathers its shape from the interplay of writer and audience, and a recounting of surprising reversals of fortune that cannot help but give a courtly audience—and a modern audience—pause. The unexpected fall and equally astonishing restoration of leprous Heinrich thus serves as a warning to a courtly audience aspiring to knightly virtues such as Heinrich is said to possess: noble birth (ll. 39, 42, 45; p. 23), wealth (l. 39; p. 23), honor (l. 46; p. 23) and spirit (l. 46; p. 23). Hartmann's very litany of Heinrich's praiseworthy qualities should trigger in the perceptive reader the sense that Heinrich is in some way being "set up" for a fall, in the time-honored manner whereby the methodical piling up of positive qualities at one end of the value spectrum makes the reader increasingly aware of the possibilities awaiting the hero at the opposite end of the spectrum. Good thus becomes intelligible not in terms of an absence of evil but rather in spite of evil; evil must coexist in order for good to be defined as its opposite. In Heinrich's case the virtually formulaic listing of the protagonist's elevated status draws the mind to the possibility of degradation,[4] and the two lines in which the fall is effected seem, as a result, long anticipated and, in their brevity, sufficient not only in terms of dramatic quality but in terms of the reader's preparedness for such an occurrence: ("sîn hôchmuot wart verkêret in ein leben gar geneiget"— ll. 82-3; "His high self-esteem vanished as his station became very humble"—p. 23). Yet the critic familiar with Hartmann's other works will notice a foreshadowing that initially appears harmless on a superficial level of meaning. Twice Hartmann stresses the seemingly positive qualities of his protagonist by means of a familiar rhyme-pair. First he notes:

> an dem enwas vergezzen
> nie deheiner der *tugent*
> die ein ritter in sîner *jugent*
> ze vollem lobe haben sol

>(ll. 32-5, my italics; [he] lacked no virtue a
>young knight should have in order to gain the
>highest renown—p. 23).

Some twenty lines later the "tugent"/"jugent" nexus appears as the first element in a series of conventional but powerful metaphors:

>im was der rehte wunsch gegeben
>von werltlîchen êren:
>die kunde er wol gemêren
>mit aller hande reiner *tugent.*
>er was ein bluome der *jugent*
>   (ll. 56-60, my italics; He had all the
>worldly fame one could wish for, and with his many
>splendid qualities, could easily add to it. He was a
>flower of youth—p. 23).

The two qualities of youth and virtue, as well as those of noble birth and good reputation will be precisely those that characterize not only Iwein but also Laudîne in *Iwein*; the two are seen to be suited for each other not only because the qualities each possesses indicate worthiness, but also because they share the *same* qualities. And it will be shown by analysis of *Iwein* that this sharing extends as well to qualities of mind, which makes the mention of the term "vergezzen" (l. 32; "forgotten, omitted") in the earlier passage from *Der arme Heinrich*—a fine and probably unconscious—allusion to a tale in which the protagonist must lose his mind and wife in order to find them again. It is no coincidence that the plot of *Der arme Heinrich*, as well as those of *Erec*, *Grêgôrius*, and *Iwein*, could be reduced to the similar terms of possession, loss, and restoration. Therefore, while the most accessible meaning of ll. 32-5 is that nothing praiseworthy was omitted, the critic, mindful of Hartmann's continuing concern with the mind, catches intimations that all is not well under the surface. In stating, "an dem enwas vergezzen / nie deheiner der tugent" (ll. 32-3; "[he] lacked no virtue"—p. 23), a sense obtains that is not unlike that communicated by the effect of Hartmann's listing of Heinrich's praiseworthy qualities: the reader is readied for subsequent undercutting. Despite the negatives ("enwas"—l. 32; "deheiner"—l. 33)—or radically, *because* of them— the net effect remains with "vergezzen" ("lacking, forgotten"). After having been told that *nothing* was left out, or forgotten, the reader wonders, both before and after, just *what* was, in fact, missing.

On the surface of the matter, the omission cannot be glaring or even noticeable. Heinrich, in fact, seems almost too good to be true. Yet once again Hartmann's pattern of undercutting becomes apparent in the use of a negative quality being negated ("im wart über noch gebrast"—l. 67; "neither too much nor too little"—p. 23): the hint of something not entirely positive remains, even after the disclaimer of the negative quality and the series of positive—and positively expressed—statements that follows. This analysis would be hairsplitting if it did not demonstrate the central principle that will be illustrated by the didactic Latin passage and gloss that follow Hartmann's brief passage describing Heinrich's fall (ll. 82-9; p. 23). This passage affords insights into Hartmann's concern with knowledge as expectation and admonition:

> als uns diu schrift hât geseit.
> ez sprichet an einer stat dâ:
> "mêdiâ vitâ
> in morte sûmus."
> daz bediutet sich alsus,
> daz wir in dem tôde sweben
> so wir aller beste waenen leben
> (ll. 90-6; So the Scripture has told us. In one place it says there: "media vita in morte sumus," which means that, when we fancy we are living better than ever before, we are on the brink of death—p. 23).

The narrator's erudition is showing, of course, in the Latin and its somewhat elaborated-upon Middle High German translation. The knowledge shared with the reader is more than a facility or familiarity with languages, so that the real issue becomes the correct perception of the relationship that interlocks life and death. Death lurks in life, just as gall swims in honey and precisely as negation floats in a sea of positive statements. In other words, Hartmann expresses stylistically what he focuses upon thematically: one's perceptions often play one false, and the undercutting of expectations occurs precisely because of what one believes one knows. And, in order to underscore the precarious stance toward death, Hartmann recreates that sense of disregard of (read: drawing attention to) the fly in the ointment. Nothing was omitted (*what* is left out, asks the reader?), youth and virtue carry the day (but how do they help Heinrich in the final analysis?), and life seems to be dealing Heinrich such a splendid hand (but does not the narrator—and now the reader—know that death holds the trump card?). Heinrich's fall, in short, is a consequence of the way the world is ordered and of the way a mind works to grasp that ordering: warning and expectation come from knowledge of that ordering. If one knows what is to be, one expects it.

Heinrich's fall, accomplished in the space of a very few lines, is thus glossed with liturgical authority, as well as restated by the narrator in Middle High German. Yet Hartmann is not through. He appends to these lines another example chosen to reinforce the correct nature of his perception of the world:

> Dirre werlte veste,
> ir staete und ir beste

>   und ir groeste magenkraft,
>   diu stât âne meisterschaft.
>   des muge wir an der kerzen sehen
>   ein wârez bilde geschehen,
>   daz si zeiner aschen wirt
>   iemitten daz si lieht birt
>
>   (ll. 97-104; The firmness of this world, its constancy and its greatest might are powerless. We can see a true picture of that with the candle, which turns to ashes as it gives off light—pp. 23-4).

Hartmann's reference to "ein . . . bilde" (l. 102; p. 24) is noteworthy not only in its context in this poem but also in its appearance elsewhere in Middle High German. For Hartmann, as well as for other writers of Middle High German romance and lyric poetry, *bilde* ("picture, image, representation") communicates both an admonitory significance and an establishment of a relationship between representation and reality. In *Erec* we have seen that much of Enîte's predicament—which she did not bring upon herself—is that she is perceived primarily as a *bilde*, as a beautiful form incapable of formulating thoughts and judgments; and she herself draws the analogy of the transplanted tree ("'des sol man bilde kiesen / an mir vil gotes armen'"—*Erec*, ll. 6031-2; "'One could use me as an example of this'"—p. 100). As a *bilde*, her experience is to educate the reader to look to her plight and see in her rendition of the example of the transplanted tree a reflection of reality. As it turns out, Enîte has not drawn a true picture of her position in her choice of imagery, for she is eminently suited to the status she holds. The image may initially seem to reflect reality, but it becomes suspect on some grounds at second glance.

And this is precisely what Hartmann again seems to be suggesting in the previously cited passage from *Der arme Heinrich*. At the outset one is tempted to take the passage purely as a conventional voicing of the inconstancy theme, itself an offshoot of the concept of fickle fortune. Yet the *bilde* itself does not reflect the message stated in the first four lines of the passage. The reader is told, in effect, that the constancy and splendor of the world are "âne meisterschaft" (l. 100; "are powerless"—p. 24; I would append a variant: "out of control"), yet the image of the candle that follows does not speak directly to this quality. Instead, Hartmann's "wârez bilde" (l. 102; "true picture"—p. 24) is that of a candle giving light as it in fact consumes itself. The issue of splendor may be reflected in the light itself, but the matter of control or power seems not to enter in. One could argue that it is perhaps too much to hold Hartmann accountable for every transitional or supportive nuance of argument—can't he be a little off in the formation of a supportive *bilde* (here: "literary image")? I would counter that close analysis of past precedents in which Hartmann brings irony into play would rather argue for a subtle message in this minor disjunction. Once again, reader expectations come to the fore: Hartmann has made a statement about the nature of the world, and now he backs it up with an image, not just a poetic image, but also a representation of the message communicated in his previous assessment of the way the world is. When the message of his "wârez bilde" does not exactly congrue with his previous assessment, the reader may well wonder if the subsequent portrait of Heinrich's fortunes is entirely true to the *bilde* (here: story, parable) Hartmann advances. To be sure, once Heinrich's fall has been established, the protagonist's fortune run a good deal "zeiner aschen" (l. 103; "to ashes"—p. 24) when leprosy strikes, but the overall message of the narrative is less of the corruptibility and fragility of the world than it is of God's redemptive powers. God, as it were, intervenes to add a few more inches of tallow to Heinrich's candle.

But before redemption can be brought about, the reader, knowing full well that it *will* be effected, expects a good story, and Hartmann is prepared to provide it, complete with comfortable familiar comparisons to figures in Biblical history who suffered falls similar to that of Heinrich ("Absalôn"—l. 85; p. 24; "Jôb"—ll. 128, 139; p. 24) and unexpected small twists of plot that keep the reader alert. Throughout, Heinrich depends upon the tension that exists between what one knows will happen eventually and the uneven progress by which it comes to pass. The reader becomes involved, checking his/her knowledge against the movement of the narrative, cognizant of what must happen, and anticipating what will occur, while at the same time open to a series of checks that delays the anticipated actions. Hartmann establishes this tension by means of a variety of techniques, two of which—simple verbal repetition and reference to exemplary figures—are apparent in the passage that immediately follows his *kerzen-bilde* ("candle"-"image") analogy. The standard oppositional pairs ("weinen"/"lachen"—ll. 106-7; "to cry"-"to laugh"—p. 24; "süeze"/"gallen"—ll. 108-9; "sweetness"/"gall"—p. 24) give way to an expanded reiteration of Heinrich's tumble from universal esteem and, we learn, from grace as well (l. 115; p. 24). Yet this expanded version picks up on language that has appeared earlier, so that ll. 116-7 ("er viel von sînem gebote / ab sîner besten werdekeit"; "he fell from his position of great honor"—p. 24) echoes ll. 86-9:

> daz diu üppige krône
> werltlîcher süeze
> vellet under vüeze
> ab ir besten werdekeit
> (ll. 86-9; that the vain crown of worldly
> pleasure can fall from its highest splendor into the
> dust —p. 23).

Moreover, the sententious statement, "unser bluome der muoz vallen / so er aller grüenest waenet sîn" (ll. 110-1; "our blossom must fall just when it thinks itself most fresh"—p. 24) substantiates what the reader has expected will happen to Heinrich, who is not for nothing called "ein bluome der jugent" (l. 60; "a flower of youth"—p. 23). A temporal sequence is clearly established—flower, to flower that must be plucked, to flower that must die—and a linkage that is time based is a natural outgrowth: from the passage of the flower that is the man, now, in the narrative at hand, to the passages of the men, then, in the touchstone narrative, the Bible. First Absalom and then Job[5] surface as the *exempla*. Hartmann further soothes the reader's expectations by subtly referring back, in Job's fall, through language, to the liturgical gloss on Heinrich's fall, yet it is a subtlety accessible only to those knowledgeable in Latin as well as Middle High German—yet another opportunity for the learned and observant reader to note, "*I* know":

> als ouch Jôbe geschach,
> dem edeln und dem rîchen
> der vil jamerlîchen
> dem miste wart ze teile
> mitten in sînem heile
>   (ll. 128-32[6]; So too it was with the noble and rich Job, who, in the midst of his happiness, was consigned in misery to the dunghill—p. 24).

The association of "mitten in sînem heile" with "mêdiâ vitâ" is not forced.

This idea of "mid-ness" sets up other resonances as well, and Hartmann explores another consequence of Heinrich's fall in his noting that Heinrich is no longer the center of his social universe (ll. 122-7; p. 24). Suddenly this man, who enjoyed such high repute and who was so loyal and generous to kinsmen and those in need, is ostracized. People cannot bear the sight of him, and this visual shifting away from the once favored protagonist is accompanied by a physical distancing, when Heinrich leaves the surrounding area, first to seek medical aid and then to live his last days away from courtly society. One notes the corresponding spiritual estrangement as well, which comes after the reader has been led to the comparison of Heinrich with Job. The expectation is that Heinrich, afflicted to the degree of Job, will bear his burden as patiently as the exemplary figure does (l. 145; p. 24). Hartmann informs us tersely that this is not the case with Heinrich (ll. 146-7; p. 24) and goes on to deliver another litany that contains a spiritual variation on the "mid-ness" theme:

> sîn swebendez herze daz verswanc,
> sîn swimmendiu vreude ertranc,
> sîn hôchvart muose vallen,
> sîn honec wart ze gallen.
> ein swinde vinster donerslac
> zebrach im sînen *mitten* tac,

> ein trübez wolken unde dic
> bedahte im sîner sunnen blic
>
> (ll. 149-56, my italics; His soaring heart ceased to fly, his swimming joy drowned, his pride fell, his honey became gall. A mighty, fierce thunderclap destroyed his midday as a heavy dark cloud covered the gleam of his sun—p. 24).

The day/life, night/death analogy comes immediately to mind, but the essentials of Heinrich's plight are communicated more graphically if the sun as a conventional symbol of the divine is taken into account. Heinrich is distanced not only from his fellows but from God as well, and the use of landscape to reflect man's inner state reveals the flaw in Heinrich. Held in esteem and concerned with worldly matters, Heinrich has seen himself and not God as the center of things. He has fundamentally misperceived, and, if he has been dealt a blow and a fall from favor, he is not likely to understand why. Here, word choice is again significant, and Hartmann's concern with mind comes into play in the phrase "ein trübez wolken unde dic / bedahte im sîner sunnen blic" (ll. 155-6; "a heavy, dark cloud covered the gleam of his sun"—p. 24), which is reminiscent, both in language and situation of *Iwein*, where "ein . . . donreslac" (l. 651; "a thunderclap"—p. 62) heralds the blocking of the sun by clouds. The sense of covering ("bedahte"—l. 156; "covered"—p. 24) recalls the subsequent scene in Iwein, where the narrator notes how nightfall and armor conceal ("bedaht"—l. 7518; p. 142) Iwein's and Gâwein's identities. As it will later be demonstrated, Iwein cannot *know*—that is, recognize—Gâwein until he knows himself (knows the contents of his own mind as well as his relationship to society), and the light of Heinrich's mid-day shall be blocked until he understands the source of that light.

The parallels between Heinrich's and Iwein's plights are striking, not only in shared language but also plot. Iwein, described in terms reminiscent of the litany of Heinrich's virtues ("der ie ein rehter adamas / riterlîcher tugende was"—*Iwein*, ll. 3257-8; "he who had been a diamond of knightly virtue"—p. 94; "hövesch unde wîs"—l. 3521; "well-mannered and clever"—p. 97), suffers a physical and spiritual reversal that, while different in its bodily manifestation than that visited upon Heinrich, is equally devastating. It is a reversal that separates him from society, just as Heinrich's leprosy makes him repulsive to his fellows. Both share conventional praiseworthy epithets in their glory and both suffer from a type of sickness, Iwein's a brain-inspired malady and Heinrich's a bodily deterioration. Finally both are cured and restored to society, and even this expected oucome is marked by those little touches of language that characterize Hartmann's artistry. For Heinrich, the fall is a thunderclap that darkens his midday (l. 154; p. 24), while for Iwein physical restoration of sanity comes at noon. For Heinrich the fall is a type of negative covering up of the sun, while for Iwein restoration involves covering in the positive sense as he dons clothes indicative of his restored status: "als er bedahte die swarzen lîch, / dô wart er einem riter glîch" (ll. 3595-6; "as soon as his black body was covered, he looked just like a knight"—p. 98). This striking use of shared language points to Hartmann's contention that Iwein's and Heinrich's sicknesses have much in common and reinforces the reader's expectations that Heinrich will be cured.

Heinrich shares this expectation, for he holds out hope for a cure, to his credit,[7] but the reader knows from the moment Heinrich opens his mouth that the protagonist's hope derives more from obduracy rather than from firm faith. When the second doctor consulted explains that a cure exists but that, paradoxically, it is impossible to gain access to this cure, Heinrich blurts out a response that reveals his mind to be one that dwells on only the surface meaning of the doctor's words:

> "wie mac daz wesen?
> diu rede ist harte unmügelich.
> bin ich genislich, sô genise ich:
> und swaz mir vür wirt geleit
> von guote oder von arbeit,
> daz trûwe ich volbringen"
> (ll. 188-93; "How can this be?" exclaimed Heinrich. "What you say is impossible. If I can be healed, I shall be healed, for I expect to do whatever is prescribed for me, regardless of the hardship or the cost"—p. 24).

There is nothing to indicate any recognition of dependency on God's will, nor is there a spiritual dimension to the forces that Heinrich is prepared to bring to bear to facilitate his recovery. Rather, Heinrich announces himself ready to expend toil and goods to regain his health, and there is a matter-of-factness to his statement that speaks neither to the reality of the situation nor to his perception of that reality. Heinrich's belief that material goods and effort can purchase a cure is no doubt an outgrowth of the system of obligation, protection, loyalty, and reward that stands him in good stead in those feudal relations that made him "a shield for his clan" (l. 65; p. 23) and "an even scale of generosity" (l. 66; p. 23). Heinrich, like Erec, demonstrates the selectivity of hearing that indicates a spiritual deficiency, for it clearly does not register upon him when the doctor indicates that only God can provide a cure. Heinrich, in return to this fairly pointed statement, makes no rejoinder that takes into account God's pivotal role in the whole matter, and instead he reiterates his offer of goods to ensure a cure, and sounds his earlier theme, with variations, "'jâ hân ich guotes wol die kraft'" (l. 207; "'I have great wealth'"—p. 24). It is as if Heinrich wants the world to play by *his* rules, rather than by its, and he takes out on the messenger the anger he has at the message. Comfort is what he wants, and one has the sense that Heinrich will settle for an answer—any answer—that offers him hope: he is ripe for being duped. The doctor, however, is above that and wisely gives Heinrich a spiritual lesson that the protagonist does not unfortunately internalize. The doctor first notes concerning Heinrich's materialism:

> "und waere der arzenîe alsô
> daz man si veile vunde
> oder daz man si kunde
> mit deheinen dingen erwerben,
> ich enlieze iuch niht verderben"
> (ll. 216-20; "and if the remedy were of a kind that one could buy or obtain in any way, I would not let you perish" —p. 24).

Then, after telling the hero that a maid's life will purchase his, he makes a wry understatement: "'nu enist ez niht der liute site / daz ez ieman gerne tuo'" (ll. 228-30; p. 24). Heinrich's mental reaction to the doctor's revelation gives his literalist understanding of the message as well as his limited spiritual comprehension. The obvious, expected thought—that of Christ, after whom martyrs pattern themselves—does not occur to Heinrich, but the reader would not have anticipated that it would spring to his mind, as the pattern of Heinrich's personality has been set in the way that certain insights given to others are denied to him. Whereas Heinrich's mental reaction seems to be predictable, his physical actions are not. Rather than jealously holding onto his considerable material possessions, which he could very easily do, he divides them among less prosperous kinsmen and poor people. For the first time, God is mentioned: "daz sich got erbarmen / geruochte über der sêle heil" (ll. 254-5; "so that God might be pleased to have mercy on his soul"—p. 25). To be sure, it is not only Heinrich's inclination but also the "wîser rât" (l. 249; "wise counsel"—p. 25) of others that motivates him to seek to find favor with God by divesting himself of his possessions. Nevertheless, if such behavior is calculated to trigger a compassionate, healing response from God, it does not succeed, and the reader would be caught off balance if it did. For Hartmann's heroes, there is more to conversion and transformation than an external show of changed behavior: change must be wrought in the inner chambers of the heart as well.

Heinrich's inner conversion takes place while the protagonist is removed from society, as is also the case in *Erec*, *Grêgôrius*, and *Iwein*, and parallels to the last work are telling in this respect. In *Iwein* the protagonist, after aimless wandering, comes to set up a home base of sorts ("an ein niuwe riute"—l. 3285; "a new clearing"—p. 95) that he stumbles upon, once again "umbe einen mitten tac" (l. 3284; "about noon"—p. 95). The cleared area boasts one inhabitant, a hermit, who establishes an uneasy reciprocal relationship with Iwein, who supplies him with game in exchange for bread and water. In *Der arme Heinrich* the protagonist repairs to "ein geriute" (l. 259; "a clearing"—p. 25[8]) where he shuns all people except for "ein vrîer bûman" (l. 269; "[a] free farmer"—p. 25) and his family, who meet his physical needs and teach him lessons he is much in need of learning. As in the case of Iwein and the hermit, reciprocity forms the basis for behavior, for it appears that the farmer is inclined to treat Heinrich well because Heinrich, as his lord, had always dealt with him protectively and fairly. Heinrich, in fact, rates as an exemplary lord:

> Der ê diz geriute
> und der ez dannoch biute,
> daz was ein vrîer bûman
> der vil selten ie gewan
> dehein grôz ungemach,
> daz andern gebûren doch geschach
> die wirs geherret wâren
> und si die niht verbâren
> beidiu mit stiure und mit bete
> (ll. 267-75; The free farmer who had always worked this tract and never suffered the hardships endured by other farmers who had harsher lords and were spared neither taxes nor fees—p. 25).

What proves especially interesting here is that the farmer is, in his own way, in an analogous position to pre-fall Heinrich, for he enjoys special status among his fellows: "des was deheiner sîn gelîch / in dem lande alsô rîch" (ll. 281-2; "no one in his country of his station was so prosperous"—p. 25). Moreover, the reader is told: "Got hete dem meier gegeben / nach sîner ahte ein reinez leben" (ll. 295-6; "God had given the farmer a happy life for one in his position"—p. 25). This man, favored by God and Heinrich, gives back as he has received, in marked contrast to the earlier Heinrich, who evinced much concern for his kinsmen and for his own worldly honor but none for God. The reader will later learn that Heinrich's host's motives are not completely pure, but what is important here is that the farmer provides a place of refuge in which the further recuperative actions of a female, in this case, his daughter, can take place. This is not unlike the situation in *Iwein*, when the hermit, hoping to stay alive in the presence of a madman, provides a home for Iwein, until a female (or three females—three Marys, as it were!) can heal the protagonist.

Restoration of health does not come overnight, but the reader knows that it is in the offing, when, with ever-narrowing focus, the center of expectation moves from the farmer to one of his daughters:

> er hete ein wol erbeiten lîp
> und ein wol werbendez wîp,

> dar zuo hete er schoeniu kint,
> diu gar des mannes vreud sint,
> unde hete, sô man saget,
> under den eine maget,
> ein kint von ahte jâren
>
> (ll. 297-303; He was able-bodied and had an upright wife and handsome children, which are indeed a true joy to a man. Among them, it is said, was a girl of eight years—p. 25).

The time-gaining, suspense-building interpolation, "sô man saget" (l. 301; "it is said"—p. 25), only heightens the supposition that here, then, is the particular "eine maget" ("a maid, a girl") foretold in the similarly positioned—at the end of the line and, therefore, highlighted—"eine maget" (l. 224) prescribed by the doctor at Salerno. One could argue that such expectation could be subsequently unmasked by the poet as unfounded, yet what Hartmann is doing here is giving in to expectation: that is, this condition is needed for a cure and, lo and behold, the means for a cure is readily—indeed, almost too readily—at hand. Then he is in the position to play with that expectation down the road a bit. A maiden has been found, but there are still surprises in store for the reader and for Heinrich as well: the nature of this maiden proves to be considerably more complex than could be anticipated. Even at the outset the relationship between Heinrich and his foster family's girl-child seems marked for special consideration, since the focus is unrelentingly upon her. She alone, of all the children of the farmer, does not avoid leprous Heinrich. Rather, she seeks out his company and assumes the supplicant position characteristic of incidents in the Bible, for she is repeatedly described as being at her master's feet. Hartmann first notes that "diu wolde nie entwîchen / von ir herren einen vuoz" (ll. 306-7; "She never wanted to move a foot's distance from her lord"—p. 25), and subsequently states, "daz man si zallen zîten vant / under sînem vuoze" (ll. 324-5; "she was always at his feet"—p. 25). It is not merely that she is *underfoot*, as it were, although this is no doubt instrumental in Heinrich's growing affection for her, but also that from the outset she conveys subordination, a willingness to please as well as to be accommodating, a trait that Hartmann sees as being characteristic of children in general: "ouch half in sere daz diu kint / sô lîhte ze wenenne sint" (ll. 333-4; "Since children adapt easily, it was not hard to please her"—p. 25). This statement may be true, but Hartmann interposes it to comment upon something more specific than general behavioral traits of children. One recalls that Enîte in *Erec* has had made a very similar statement—both in syntax and content—concerning children: "dô schien wol daz kint / lîhte ze triegenne sint"—ll. 3876-7; "how easily children are deceived"—p. 75).

Her observations, as noted earlier, address a specific danger, from which she can extricate herself and Erec only through a lie that is partially true, but they give the background against which Hartmann's broad hint in *Der arme Heinrich* can be understood. Heinrich's youthful companion can be seen as a type of Enîte, who is characterized as a child (ll. 309, 331; pp. 34-5) and who is linked thematically to Mâbonagrîn's bride—who is also nameless as is Heinrich's young friend—"ein kint" (l. 9467; "a child"—p. 139). What is particularly striking is the fact that Mâbonagrîn's bride is "wol einlif jâr alt" (l. 9467; "only eleven"—p. 139), the precise age attained by Heinrich's "gemahel" (l. 341; "bride"—p. 25) at the point she determines to sacrifice her life for him. Clearly, the age and the circumstances of Heinrich's future spouse's attachment to him indicate a serious relationship, and subsequent events will bear this out. Woman's speech—in the instances of Hartmann's child-women, Enîte, Mâbonagrîn's bride, and Heinrich's soon-to-be wife—will effect profound changes, whether they be for better or worse. In Mâbonagrîn's case, woman's words bind him to a self-destructive pact in which he cannot act to improve his mental attitude and relationship; he literally kills men as if they were intrusive thoughts on his consciousness. In Erec's case, Enîte's words motivate the hero to chart a rash course and behave in a manner that places the pair in constant danger. With Heinrich the matter proves to be somewhat more complicated, although tied, as in the previous instances to female admonition, for woman's ability to intervene sucessfully in the life of man is seen here to be very much a matter of life and death. With both Enîte and Mâbonagrîn's wife, female intervention or pre-conditions have functioned to provide the hero with setbacks necessary for his spiritual growth. However, with Heinrich's "bride," the female advances the cure for his disease as the result of her intervention. She stands, nevertheless, in subordinate position to the hero she helps on his physical/spiritual quest. What is of importance here is the fact that she, as woman, is seen as a help and not as a hindrance: she, by her very nature—virginal and young—is capable of providing Heinrich with the help he needs.

The cue that the maiden offers precisely what ailing Heinrich needs comes not in the general medicinal prescription of a virgin—anyone will do—but rather in this particular maiden's heightened perception—or is it misperception?—of Heinrich's nature. Attracted to him, so that she seldom leaves him alone, she assesses him: "er dûhte si vil reine" (l. 344; "he seemed without fault or blemish"—p. 25). Superficially she misperceives, in not noticing the ravages of his disease, and the reader asks why she seeks out what others shun. Can it be that Heinrich has once again bought a supporter with his generosity:

> er gewan ir swaz er veile vant,
> spiegel unde hârbant

und swaz kinden liep solde sîn,
gürtel unde vingerlîn
(ll. 335-8; He got her everything a child might like that was for sale — mirrors, hair ribbons, belts and rings—p. 25).

Is this Heinrich's way of conducting social relationships—an empty trading of goods for devotion, or, at least, a semblance of devotion—or are his giving and her reciprocating indications of a depth of *caritas* not achieved in Heinrich's past? Hartmann's calculated ambivalence demonstrates Heinrich's well-intentioned but essentially empty behavior toward his kinsmen and supports his concern for the one person who remains loyal to him despite his disability. What proves interesting is the fact that the reader is not made privy to any mental reflection in which Heinrich might be engaged during this time. Surely one as aware of his disease as he is must be drawing connections between the requirements for its cure and the proximity of the means for that cure. The means are within his reach both literally and figuratively, yet denied him. Certainly his thoughts must dwell on the disparity between the hope that is unreasonable expectation and the despair that is actuality for him. Yet his thoughts are not recorded by Hartmann, which is consistent with other instances where internal transformations are effected without the reader being given a glimpse into the mental processes that mark these changes. Hartmann is provokingly unforthcoming about his hero's ruminations during those times the reader expects and wants access to a protagonist's thought process, as, for example, during Grêgôrius' lengthy stay on the rock. One would expect at least an interior monologue, or a vocalization in the manner of Iwein's post-madness speech, or Enîte's outpouring after Erec's "death." What Hartmann gives in *Der arme Heinrich* is instead access to the thoughts of the family with which Heinrich spends what are expected to be his last days: "si gedâhten alsô verre" (l. 366; "they kept thinking about this"—p. 26).

The thoughts of the farmer and his family are almost refreshingly pragmatic. Heinrich's death would indeed leave them badly off, and their concern stems less from greed than from a rational appraisal of the facts. It is the same reasonableness, given the circumstances, that will characterize the daughter's subsequent appeal to her parents and the man for whom she would give her life. The father, having thought, turns to inquiry, expressing what is commonplace knowledge: cannot a cure for Heinrich's malady be found at Salerno, where there are many doctors (ll. 372-6; p. 26)? Heinrich's reply addresses several themes: his own unworthiness, his fall, the possibility/impossibility of a cure, and, interestingly, the effects one human's actions can have on another. The monologue treats the concept of knowledge as expectation and admonition and falls easily into three parts: Heinrich's recognition of the reasons for his fall, his thoughts on the good care he is receiving, and his bitter reflections on a cure that cannot come but could come. The tone of the monologue becomes increasingly pragmatic as the metaphoric language shifts to a more bare-bones account that echoes the surgeon's earlier statement concerning a cure, in keeping with the movement over the course of the monologue from the spiritual causes to physical deliverance.

The first part of the monologue reveals that Heinrich has in fact done a good deal of thinking of, if not discussing, his plight in the three years he has spent with the family:

> "Ich hân den schämelichen spot
> vil wol gedienet umbe got.
> wan dû saehe wol hie vor
> daz hôch offen stuont mîn tor
> nâch wertlîcher wünne
> und daz nieman in sînem künne
> sînen willen baz hete dan ich:
> und was daz joch unmügelich,
> wan ich enhete in niht wan gar,
> dô nam ich sîn vil kleine war
> der mir daz selbe wunschleben
> von sînen gnâden hete gegeben.
> daz herze mir dô alsô stuont,
> als alle werlttôren tuont
> den daz raetet ir muot
> daz si êre unde guot
> âne got mügen hân.
> sus trouc ouch mich mîn tumber wân,
> wan ich in lützel ane sach
> von des gnâden mir geschach
> vil êren unde guotes.
> dô des hôchmuotes
> den hôhen portenaere verdrôz,
> die saelden porte er mir beslôz.
> dâ kum ich leider niemer in:
> daz verworhte mir mîn tumber sin.
> got hât durch râche an mich geleit
> ein sus gewante siecheit
> die neiman mac erloesen.
> nu versmâhe ich den boesen,
> die biderben ruochent mîn niht.
> swie boese er ist der mich gesiht,
> des boeser muoz ich dannoch sîn.
> sîn unwert tuot mir schîn:
> er wirfet diu ougen abe mir"
>
> (ll. 383-417; "I have well deserved this shameful humiliation from God," he said, "for you yourself have seen that my gate formerly was wide open to worldly pleasure and that no one ever had

his own way among his kinsmen more than I. This could not be, because I did everything I wished. I paid little heed to Him whose grace had given me such a happy life, for my heart was then like that of all fools who think they can have esteem and riches without God's help. My foolish fancy deceived me because I had little regard for Him by whose grace much honor and wealth was mine. When the high gatekeeper lost patience with this pride, He closed the portals of bliss before me, and I shall never come in. My foolish wit has cost me that. God has punished me with a sickness from which no one can set me free. The exalted pay no attention to me, and the petty scorn me. However base he may be who catches sight of me, I must be even more worthless; he shows me his disdain by turning his eyes away"— p. 26).

Heinrich has correctly identified the source of his problems—he failed to perceive that his "'wunschleben'" (l. 393; "'such a happy life'"—p. 26) was given to him by God—but he perhaps goes too far in seeing God as vengeful. Heinrich labels himself a fool (l. 396, p. 26) in having held a false perception that honor and goods may be maintained without thought to God as their source and sustainer. This happy life was illusory and nonpermanent, in short, because it was not grounded in respect to God. Hartmann employs the loaded term "wunschleben" ("happy life" or "a life that was all that one could wish for") most notably elsewhere in *Iwein*, when he refers to Arthur's court: "ouch wart in dâ ze hove gegeben / in alle wîs ein wunschleben" (ll. 43-4; "And their life at the court was in every way all that one could wish"—p. 55). It may well be an ideal, wished for existence, but the subsequent portrayal of Arthurian ideals in *Iwein*—such as the court's fundamentally empty definition of adventure—reveals that this existence stands on shaky grounds. A pattern thus establishes itself in Hartmann's works whereby the mention of "wunschleben" carries in it the seeds of its own undercutting. There is, moreover, an additional resonance of "wunschleben" to be considered, and that is its inclusion in a passage that contains the following lines:

"dô des hôchmuotes
den hôhen portenaere verdrôz,
die saelden porte er mir beslôz"
(ll. 404-6; "When the high gatekeeper lost patience with this pride, He closed the portals of bliss before me"—p. 26).

The "wunschleben" comes to be identified with what Hartmann will elsewhere call "daz ander paradîse" (*Erec*, l. 9542; "a second Garden of Eden"—p. 139); and *Iwein*, l. 687; "as if in paradise"—p. 63), which is a pre-Fall state characterized by misperception, incomplete knowledge, and an obliviousness to the possibility of an existence predicated on spiritual growth rather than on stasis.

In *Iwein* this pre-Fall state characterizes the flawed existence of individuals like Kâlogrenant, whose adventures are purposeless, but whose sobering tumble/fall (ll. 743-5; pp. 63-4) is necessarily accompanied by the post-Fall revelation of his folly: "'ich hân einem tôren glîch getân'" (l. 795; "'[I] was foolish'"—p. 64). This episode in *Iwein* exhibits shared features with the Mâbonagrîn episode in *Erec*, as both are planned to show falls—literal and metaphoric—and expulsion from paradise, a situation that figures heavily in Heinrich's discomfort as well. In *Erec*, one recalls, Mâbonagrîn accuses Erec of folly ("'ez ist et vil toerlich'"—l. 9030; "'It is very foolish'"—p. 133), in the classic stance of the fool attributing to an opponent his own chief weakness,[9] and it is Mâbonagrîn who stays in the elaborate cage fashioned for him, significantly labelled a paradise, until he is conquered (read: educated, in the sense of being informed and being "led out") by Erec. Erec can effect Mâbonagrîn's release, too, because, unlike Heinrich, for whom "die saelden port" are closed off, he has trod "der Saelden wec" (l. 8521; "[the] road of Fortune"—p. 128). Mâbonagrîn hails Erec as God-sent (l. 9587; p. 140), precisely because this intruder in his self-made garden effects his release: "'sît mich von disem bande / hât erloeset iuwer hant'"— ll. 9585-6; "'since you have set me free'"—p. 140). Heinrich, on the contrary, has come to the conclusion that he is forever to be excluded from "saelde":

> "got hât durch râche an mich geleit
> ein sus gewante siecheit
> die neiman mac erloesen"
> (ll. 409-11; "God has punished me with a
> sickness from which no one can set me free"—p. 26).

The term "erloesen" ("to deliver from, to effect salvation") points to Mâbonagrîn's realization of and Heinrich's unawareness of the fact that one must leave paradise in order to return to it: deliverance only comes as a result of a fall, and salvation only occurs when the awareness of one's own particular prison surfaces in one's consciousness.

For Heinrich, the immediate consequences of his fall are grasped in terms not only of his exclusion from the life he found to be paradisical, but also of his diminished status in the eyes of other people, a sign that he has not entirely separated himself from the mode of thinking that caused him to thoroughly enjoy—and talk about—the high regard in which he had been held by those around him. This concern is addressed at the very end of the first part of his monologue, so that it forms an effective bridge to the monologue's second part, which treats both his altered status and his new found understanding of his need for relationships with others. Suddenly Heinrich explains to others that he is not just a "giver" but also a "taker." He first laments how others perceive him, how others cannot bear even to look at him, and the visual element of the shunning comes immediately into play.

Hartmann here comments upon a common occurrence. The visually unappealing or even repulsive is often avoided, and much of Heinrich's story hinges upon how one plane of reality—the physical—often reflects the spiritual. In addition, Hartmann here introduces the theme of sight, of seeing (that is, visual perception as well as mental acuity) that will become so important later in the work, when Heinrich looks at the naked girl, ready to be operated upon (read: slaughtered) and finally *sees*.[10] But the underlying thought structure in this passage seems to be that exclusion from "die saelden porte" triggers the thought of exclusion from human circles, and this, in turn, leads to Heinrich's pitiful praise of his host for having not excluded him. Yet throughout, despite the praise for those who include him and the implicit contempt, mingled with understanding, for those who exclude him, this part of Heinrich's lament demonstrates that the protagonist has not yet come to terms with his altered condition. He has, to be sure, passed from the stages of disbelief and aggression (represented in his curt assurances to the physician that any necessary goods or resources would be forthcoming) to the stages of mourning and rationalization, where he expresses his innermost thoughts in language that is more metaphorical and convoluted than that of his earlier conversation with the doctor in Salerno. But Heinrich, for all his understanding of the cause of his fall, still thinks in terms of a world in which he has control. Thus, while intellectually comprehending his change in social status, he emotionally rejects people's reactions to him; he still talks in terms of human measures of worth, not recognizing that, to God, these distinctions are meaningless. Heinrich equates a move in the human hierarchy (the host's elevation as a result of Heinrich's degradation) with a boost in one's spiritual status. He is correct in that charitable acts are commendable, but he retains the rich man's outlook that salvation, like any other commodity, can be purchased (l. 430; p. 26).

Something quite complicated involving hierarchies and exchanges appears in the work at this time, with the reiteration of the surgeon's diagnosis in the third part of Heinrich's lament. One recalls that Heinrich doubts that anyone would want to die for him, and he has couched this impossible cure, again, in terms of exchanges: "'in der werlte nieman / mit nihte gewinnen kan'" (ll. 443-4; "'that no one in the world could possibly get'"—p. 26). A picture emerges in which the linked concept of giving and gaining has various manifestations: God gives to Heinrich with no intent to gain; Heinrich gives materially to others but, because he does not give heed to God, ultimately loses; the peasant family gives to Heinrich out of a sense of gratitude for his past behavior, but with a practical eye as to how gain is tied to give; Heinrich seeks to give goods to gain a cure but learns that that kind of giving cannot produce a gain, although he states that a giving of earthly service can result in a gain in spiritual terms; and a maiden can give life for a life (that is, suffer death on another's account). What proves significant here in this toting up of balance sheets is that Heinrich does not complete the progression and sketch any gain a maiden might derive from such a sacrifice. Hartmann will leave it to the girl herself to bring forth arguments pointing to spiritual as well as material gains.

Hierarchies enter into this giving/gaining complex in two ways. First, the built-in feudal hierarchy establishes a legitimate conduit for the mutual exchange (read: giving and gaining) to take place on a material level, but, unless corresponding attention is paid to non-material matters, any gains made may not be permanent. Class status determines whether the giving is out of largesse that has worldly repute as its gain, or out of service to a lord who accordingly treats his servant well. In other words, the feudal hierarchy both sets up the framework according to which exchanges can occur and maintains the hierarchical stratification by dictating how those exchanges will be viewed: the gift of a peasant is still not worth the gift of a lord. The giving, therefore, is *milte* ("generosity") if performed by one high in the social hierarchy, and it is *dienst* ("service") if performed by one lower on the scale. Now, where a second view of hierarchy and exchanges proves valuable to an understanding of how *Der arme Heinrich* works lies in the very situation at the core of the work: the exchange of a life for a life—which Heinrich ultimately rejects for all of the right reasons—cuts across the social, feudal hierarchy. The true motives of love for one's fellow man know no social class. A well-born maiden does not make the offer to die for Heinrich, nor is a low-born maiden summarily sacrificed.[11]

Heinrich's lament, which touches upon many topics and bears wide implications, has direct reported effect not only on the maiden, although it was directed exclusively to the father, but also upon both parents. Hartmann first reports:

> sîner rede nam si war
> unde marhte si gar:
> si enkam von ir herzen nie
>   (ll. 467-9; She noted carefully what he said
>   and kept it in her heart—p. 26).

She hears it ostensibly because she is in close physical proximity to Heinrich: "ir lieben herren vüeze / stânde in ir schôzen" (ll. 462-3; "[she] was holding the feet of her beloved lord in her lap"—p. 26). Yet she hears it not only for that reason but also because her heightened ability as a perceiver marks her as the one intended to hear it, much as Enîte is meant to hear the criticism leveled by the court at her unwitting husband.

This statement about the maiden is supported by Hartmann's technique. First of all, the sense throughout Hartmann's works—and throughout medieval literature in general—is that help or hindrance is built into the stories of spiritually foundering protagonists, so that the mere note that the maiden takes his speech to heart is crucial: she understands it precisely because she is the means to the end of helping Heinrich. Moreover, this "kint" ("child") with her lord's feet in her lap calls to mind the similar tableau of "daz kint vrouwe Enîte" (l. 1318; "the young Enîte"—p. 46)[12] with Erec reclining in her "schôz" (l. 1317; "lap"—p. 46), and Enîte, several times described as a child (as is Mâbonagrîn's bride, the eleven-year-old child),[13] instructs Erec over the course of the romance in perceptiveness.

Furthermore, the glimpse of Heinrich's feet in the lap of the maid has immediate verbal resonances in the text of *Der arme Heinrich*, resonances that by their frequency call attention to a part of the human anatomy that has traditionally borne symbolic significance: the foot. One recalls that the child has been said frequently to be at Heinrich's feet (l. 325; p. 25) and she will wet her parents' feet with tears (l. 479; p. 27) as she prepares to go to sleep at "ir vater vüezen" (l. 471; "at the feet of her father"—pp. 26-7) that night after hearing Heinrich's story. She, moreover, will later pick up language that Hartmann has earlier employed when she fears "daz mich der werlte süeze / zuhte under vüeze" (ll. 701-2; "'I fear that the charms of the world would drag me down to its feet'"—p. 28), echoing with variation Hartmann's account of how "werltlicher süeze / vellet under vüeze" (ll. 87-8; "worldly pleasure can fall . . . into the dust [under foot]"—p. 23). The child's association with feet ties in with concerns that Hartmann has earlier exhibited. The hierarchical aspect comes first to mind, suggesting a suppliant posture on the part of the girl who is both a child to her parents and a "spouse" to Heinrich, and the plummeting sweetness of the world indicates a fall from status. The foot's symbolism of relative level accounts for this hierarchical aspect as well as for terms like "footfall"; feet go down, and they connect to the earth, to the dust.

But there are other aspects of the foot as a symbol that make the child's association with it significant: as support for the entire body, the foot not only "grounds" the body to the earth, but also, if Greek myths may be drawn upon here—and Heinrich, in his *Grêgôrius*, clearly shows his familiarity with them—represents the soul: "it serves as the support of the body in the sense of keeping man upright . . . . in Greek legends, lameness usually symbolizes some defect of the spirit, some essential blemish."[14] Hartmann's familiarity with and reworking of the Oedipus legend in *Grêgôrius* make this reading plausible. On this account, the maiden's closeness to feet indicates that she somehow is associated with the soul—the English and German puns "soul"/"sole" and "Seele"/"Sohle" come readily to mind, as language orders response to the world. Puns often can tell a reader or listener hidden stories that weave together associations not always accessible to the conscious mind. What the maiden, associated with feet and the soul, teaches, both through her very existence and through her will to sacrifice himself for Heinrich, is nothing less than a spiritual lesson.[15] She "grounds" Heinrich in giving him renewed hope, and she, with her feet literally and metaphorically on the ground, knows what her sacrifice means: that she should go below ground in order that he should stay above ground.

There is every reason to believe that her first response to Heinrich's plight is based on true compassion, rather than exclusively on any selfish motive.[16] She exhibits the standard exterior manifestations of distress ("manigen sûft tiefen / holte si von herzen"—ll. 474-5; "she breathed many deep sighs"—p. 27; and a rain of tears—ll. 478-9; p. 27) and only later is forced to explain to her parents in terms that they can understand why Heinrich's immanent deterioration and death cause her so much pain. If one relies on her previous actions, which have amounted to deep devotion to a man repulsive to virtually everyone else, as well as upon Heinrich's actions, one sees that there must be some very strong attraction present. The maiden quite literally sees something different in him than others see, and he is closer to her than he is to anyone else in the family, if physical proximity is a clue—no one else is described as been as "underfoot" as she is. Moreover, if the fact that his host has waited, out of deference, three years before broaching the subject of a cure is indicative of the level of verbal communication between Heinrich and the family, then Hartmann, in describing the physical closeness of Heinrich and his "gemahel," is attesting to an unusual degree of attraction and communication at some deeper level. Now, one can argue that children are charmed by attention, but the key interpretative factor is Hartmann's reluctance to add anything superfluous to the narrative. Each scene contains just those factors needed to advance the plot, while at the same time weaving its part of the overall thematic and symbolic web. In less abstract terms, if Hartmann offers detail, he does so consciously, and it is likely to be important. The maiden's association with feet thus indicates an intimacy with Heinrich, both on a conscious and on an unconscious level. And her sleeping at her father's feet and later raining tears on her parents' feet represent attempts to communicate her perception of Heinrich's situation and her compassion for him. As such, she functions as Lûnete will in *Iwein*, forming a communicative bridge between minds, for it is not until the maiden voices her fears that her parents give any indication that they have heard Heinrich's answer to the father's query.

The maiden's formulation of an explanation for her distress is pragmatic, not unlike Lûnete's practical counsel to her mistress at the time that Laudîne is faced with the dilemma of the defenseless spring area. The maiden, too, has surprising verbal ability, coupled with her perceptiveness and subsequently developed rationality. Beginning with her first reluctant speech, her presentations become longer and more developed, yet still contain the germ of the argument that she first advances as a lament about loss (ll. 490-8; p. 27). Incidentally, loss has been an important factor in Enîte's and Grêgôrius' wife/mother's motivations, and the maiden's speech could easily be put into their mouths, as well as into the mouth of Laudîne. On the next night in her second outburst, the maiden draws the logical loving conclusion ("'ich wil ê vür in sterben'"—l. 564; "'I would rather die for him'"—p. 27) that follows from her exposition of Heinrich's goodness. Each outburst is followed by a parental appeal, or command, for silence, yet the force of the maiden's argument will not be stilled. Accordingly, her third speech picks up on the first two, reiterating the esteem and property (p. 28; l. 617) that Heinrich confers, as well as her willingness to give up her life for Heinrich, and even echoing earlier language (ll. 563-4; p. 27; and ll. 623-4; p. 28). What she introduces here, however, is a line of reasoning to which her parents must listen: she can gain "'daz êwige leben'" (l. 610; "'eternal life'"—p. 28) and can do so at a young age, thus sparing herself a long and painful life and being of benefit to her parents at the same time. It is a seductive argument for people who live a hard life and believe in the hereafter. Eventually her argument overrides the parents' appeals for silence, much as Erec finally listens to what Enîte has to say. In *Der arme Heinrich*, the mother is the first to break away in a significant manner from the parental pattern of urging silence on the daughter—another echo of children being seen but not heard? She does so in a statement as psychologically apt today as it was in Hartmann's time (ll. 631-5; p. 28).

The sentiment of, in effect, "we don't want to hear it" ("'wan lâzestû uns slâfen?'"—l. 549; "'Why don't you let us sleep?'"—p. 27), has been replaced by something like, "I hear you, but I most certainly don't like what I hear . . . . with all the trouble I've gone to bear you, I certainly deserve better than that! But I am listening." As a result, the mother's appeal to her daughter is an emotional rather than a reasoned one, whereas her daughter has tempered her sentiments with self-conscious rationality: "'swie tump ich sî, / mir wonet iedoch diu witze bî'" (ll. 593-4; "'as simple as I am, I have still enough sense. . . .'"—p. 27). The mother actually shifts the grounds of the argument from the measures needed to save Heinrich to what she sees as the higher authority dictated by the Ten Commandments ("'daz man muoter unde vater / minne und êre biete'"—ll. 642-3; "'[He] bade us love and honor mother and father'"—p. 28), which, she feels, out of a sense of order and self-interest, to have applicability here. Her speech ultimately comes down to urging an end to her daughter's argument, but not before she has expressed her love and concern: "'daz dîn vater unde ich / gerne leben, daz ist durch dich'" (ll. 651-2; "'you are the reason your father and I enjoy life'"—p. 28). By charting the parents' reaction to the maiden's contention, it becomes apparent that the force of her argument is sufficiently strong and that it cannot effectively be countered by a perfunctory command for silence. The reader expects that the parents will continue to implore the daughter to drop the subject, but knows that she will not.

Judging from the parents' reactions, the maiden has surprised them with her intention as well as persistence. That she is about to turn their minds to her purpose comes as no surprise to the reader, however, for the mother's speech contains indications peculiar to *Der arme Heinrich* that a favored individual is about ready to become unreliable. In a manner reminiscent of the narrator's metaphorical litany of Heinrich's good qualities (ll. 60ff.; p. 23) and of Heinrich's own description of his elevated position *vis-à-vis* worldly "wünne" (l. 387; p. 26), Hartmann prepares for a change in the maiden's status, when he places in the mother's mouth this series of qualities:

> "unser beider vreude sîn,
> unser liebe âne leide,
> unser liehtiu ougenweide,
> unser lîbes wünne,
> ein bluome in dînem künne,
> unsers alters ein stap"
>   (ll. 653-7; "our happiness, our carefree
> pleasure, a bright feast for our eyes, the delight of
> our lives, a flower among your kinfolk, and a staff of
> our old age"—p. 28).

Heinrich, too, is called "ein bluome" (l. 60; "a flower"—p. 23), and the mother's identical description of the maiden is another of Hartmann's indications that the two are intended for each other, a technique he later employs in *Iwein* in the case of Iwein and Laudîne. Heinrich and the maiden share yet another quality, which is both descriptive and predictive: they both have an obduracy of mind, which accounts on her part for total devotion or total disappointment and on his part for either elevation or denigration, with literally nothing in the middle; crises may occur in times of "mid-ness," but the reactions to crises fashioned by Heinrich and the maiden always take place on edges. As such, both Heinrich and the maiden are admirable subjects for Hartmann in his ongoing concern with the changing of mind over time. Both are of such a mind that they hew hard and fast to what is believed to be the most direct route to a cure, and Heinrich's last-minute mind-changing signals a radical alteration that is accompanied, in delayed reaction fashion, by a corresponding change wrought on his body. In other words, these are characters with an extraordinary capacity to suffer, to serve, to sacrifice, and to act from the courage of their convictions. These tendencies are evident in the maiden's speech in which she wins her reluctant parents over to her way of thinking (ll. 683-854; pp. 29-30). The reader, expecting that the maiden will best her parents in this argument—and the plot would grind to a halt otherwise—and that she will offer her life for Heinrich's, is now in the position to watch just how the maiden argues her points.

The first fifteen or so lines are intended to allay the parents' fears of insubordination on the maiden's part (ll. 663-80; p. 28). Here she is not telling her parents anything that they do not already know, but the fact that *she* is telling *them* these things speaks to a stance of superiority on her part. While assuring them of her obedience to them, she nevertheless resorts to a not-so-subtle form of flattery along the lines of "apples don't fall far from the tree." She knows full well that she is the fairest child and explicity gives credit to them ("'nâch gote'"—l. 677; "'after God'"—p. 28), for this. The "'nâch gote'" is significant, though, for it introduces the awareness of hierarchy and of the ultimate source of the "'genâde'" (ll. 665, 670, 676; "'grace'"—p. 29) that motivates the maiden, yet at the same time it does not place undue emphasis on the divine at that point in time when it is the parents who must be appealed to and mollified: they must first be assured of their authority over the maiden before she can communicate to them that this authority must defer to a greater demand. To this end, the maiden reiterates her dependence on her parents for the grace that they have given her by bringing her into existence. She then contrasts God to the Devil (l. 686-7; p. 28) before sounding the major theme of her argument: the nature of the world and the nature of man are such that a rapid departure from the former can only be beneficial to the latter. Deftly the argument has been turned from the narrow subject of filial obedience to a broader perspective against which the parents can view her request.

The maiden's observations about the mundane, while convincing to her parents and thoroughly conventional to medieval literature, are nevertheless startling, for, like Enîte, the maiden has presented a placid, child-like façade and has not volunteered anything that would give those around her—or the reader, for that matter—any indication that she had come to some profound conclusions about life. The visual picture that she has presented, with Heinrich's feet in her lap, corresponds neatly to that image of Enîte cradling a battle-weary Erec in her lap, and her speeches astound the reader for a different reason than they baffle and irritate her parents. They seem to come from mid-air. And they reveal to others the many thoughts that the maiden has been having at the time when she has been presented as least verbal. She notes:

> "nû wil ich gote gnâde sagen
> daz er in mînem jungen tagen
> mir die sinne hât gegeben
> daz ich ûf diz broede leben
> ahte harte kleine"
>
> (ll. 693-7; "I want to deliver myself up to God's power thus unstained and thank God for giving me in my youth the wisdom to hold this feeble life of little account"—p. 28).

Yet all other indications she has given with respect to her understanding and appreciation of life are to the contrary, for she is earlier said to have gladly received many gifts of mirrors, hair-ribbons, belts, and rings from Heinrich, which points to a clear acceptance of material, ornamental things. Moreover, it does not appear that hers is a household in which otherworldly matters are routinely discussed, if the three-year hiatus between Heinrich's arrival and his host's solicitous inquiry is taken into account. Now, this sceptical analysis is not intended to cast doubt on the maiden's sincerity—she *is* deeply in earnest—but rather to call attention to Hartmann's technique of raising expectation (here, that the girl will offer her life for Heinrich's) and then undercutting it (here, the argument that she fields does not appear to derive from her own experience). The reader is prepared to watch the maiden's parents gradually be convinced, but it would be difficult to anticipate the strength or precise direction of the maiden's argument, which is notable in its reiterative emphasis on the unreliability of the world:

> "wir hân niht gewisses mê
> wan hiute wol und morgen wê
> und ie ze jungest der tôt"
> (ll. 713-5; "We can be sure of nothing more
> than that today's well-being will be tomorrow's pain
> and that death always comes at last"—p. 28).

Coming from a maiden whose previous impression was that of a petted, charming child, these sentiments, and others such as "'mir behaget diu werlt niht sô wol'" (l. 708; "'the world pleases me little'"—p. 28), can only be explained in terms of a suddenly altered perception of the world. Having heard Heinrich's account of his fall, disease, and lack of hope for a cure, the maiden can no longer view the world as amicable, but rather as invidious: her diatribe on the nature of the world may be a conclusion drawn after thought, but it is also a reaction to the possibility of losing Heinrich. And it can also be dogma filtered through a pubescent mentality. Curiously, it is an accurate mimicry of Heinrich's own description of the world, in content if not in phraseology. Accordingly, in both speeches, God is the source, the giver of all. Both speakers ask for a speedy death, and both are deeply appreciative of the care others have given them. Where the maiden surpasses Heinrich is in the degree of her condemnation of the world and in her reaction to the "disease" with which *she* is afflicted.

The maiden's "disease,"[17] although never explicitly stated, is quite obviously puberty,[18] for she discourses on one cure for it—that is, marriage—and couches the other possible cure, death, in terms of Christ as Bridegroom (ll. 775-812; p. 29). Much is made of the fact that she is without a man (l. 747; p. 29), and the option of giving her to one (ll. 753, 760; p. 29) causes distress, even if the marriage were a good one: "'wirt er mir liep, daz ist ein nôt: / wirt er mir leit, daz ist der tôt'" (ll. 765-6; "'If I get to like him, it will be because I must and, if I dislike him it will be the death of me'"—p. 29). The maiden argues that Heinrich might die before she could be married off, and that the family's resultant poverty would put a financial crimp in any wedding plans. These are very real considerations, but they need not be the only ones raised in an analysis of this part of the poem. In other words, the maiden's speech, in focusing upon her availability, be it to an earthly spouse or to the heavenly ploughman),[19] calls the reader's attention to her growing sense of sexuality, and this bears far-reaching implications for the understanding of the poem.

It can be no coincidence that the resolution of *Der arme Heinrich* exhibits that fairy tale motif of the socially superior bridegroom choosing a lesser-born woman as a wife,[20] and that fairy tales often highlight that emotion-charged, confusing period of one's life during which one undergoes puberty and experiences awakening sexuality. Students of fairy tales have noted that quite often there comes a freeze-framing effect, frequently expressed in a death-like sleep, whereby the pubescent heroine is suspended in a virginal state until awakened, saved, or otherwise freed by the prospective bridegroom, as is the case in the tales of Snow White, Sleeping Beauty, and others.[21] For the maiden in *Der arme Heinrich*, death is seen as the perfect answer to troublesome sexuality, which clearly occupies her mind, if her reference to the plough of Christ the Bridegroom ("'im gat sîn phluoc harte wol'"—l. 779; "'his plow tills well'"—p. 29) is any indication.[22] To her, metaphoric defloration is preferable to actual penetration, the maiden feels. Even more telling is the possibility that she does *not* raise: marriage to Heinrich, who already calls her his bride. In what she says and what she does not say, the reader gains a glimpse of a mind in conflict: the maiden is very aware of Heinrich as a sexual being, yet, whether put off by fears of consummation or by doubts as to social acceptability and Heinrich's mortality, she is not ready to offer herself in that way to him. Sex and death are so often linked in literature, particularly in works of this period,[23] that these speculations are not far-fetched, particularly when one takes into account the additional linkage, on Heinrich's part, of leprosy and sexuality. Another related aspect, that of temporality and change, enters into the picture at this point, for the maiden's ideal "marriage" deliberately excludes mutability: "'da enwirt von jâren nieman alt'" (p. 784; "'nobody gets older'"—p. 29). Change, death, and decay in fact comprise the inconstancy that the maiden decries throughout her speech: "'unser staete bibet als ein loup'" (l. 724; "'our firm support trembles as a leaf'"—p. 29).[24] The world suddenly appears dreadfully complicated, changeable, and her easy companionship with Heinrich vanishes the moment he speaks to her father and she hears. Her reaction is a way of holding those dangerous elements of sex and mutability at bay.[25]

It would be a mistake to contend that the maiden is aware of the implications of her remarks on marriage. She is not. She merely says what comes into her mind, as Heinrich will later note (ll. 949-54; p. 30), with a natural ease of transition from filial obedience to dependence on God, to the nature of the world from which God can deliver man, to one problematic aspect of that world (her marriageability), to the preference of a "marriage" in Heaven, to God's commands as having precedence, and, finally, to her responses to her mother's dread of standing over her grave. In this last point one sees clearly the maiden's style of argument: she prefers one-upmanship, and her summation, which posits that her death is beneficial to all, is, indeed, so thought-out,[26] so strong, and so commandingly delivered, that it leaves her parents speechless: "ir dewederz enkunde / ein einic wort gesprechen" (ll. 882-3; "neither could speak a single word"—p. 30). They are no match for her, not only because they are unable to voice effective counterarguments, but also because they cannot conceive of them either: "wan si doch niht enkunden / ir niemer werden âne baz" (ll. 894-5; "at least they could not lose her in a better cause"—p. 30). The maiden has, purely and simply, out-argued them in both the content and form of her discourse. She has anticipated objections that could be raised and laid them to rest in advance, she has brought her elders around to her opinion while lulling them with assurances of obedience and love, and she has caught them off-guard in a way reminiscent of Balaam's ass. So astonished are they by her utterances that they automatically assume that there is divine intervention in the matter:

> Dô si daz kint sâhen
> zem tôde sô gâhen
> und ez sô wîslîchen sprach
> unde menschlich reht zebrach,
> si begunden ahten under in
> daz die wîsheit und den sin
> niemer erzeigen kunde
> dehein zunge in kindes munde.
> si jâhen daz der heilic geist
> der rede waere ir volleist,
> der ouch sant Niklauses phlac,
> dô er in der wagen lac,
> und in die wîsheit lêrte
> daz er ze gote kêrte
> sîne kintlîche güete
>
> (ll. 855-69; When they saw that the child
> was eager to die, and when she spoke so wisely and
> contrary to nature, they began to think that no child's
> tongue could bring forth such views and such wisdom.
> They told each other that the source of her words
> was the Holy Spirit, who also cared for St. Nicholas
> as he lay in the cradle and taught him to turn his
> infant virtue to God—p. 30).

The comparison to Saint Nicholas is apt, not merely because it speaks to his age relative to the maiden's, but also because this saint is frequently associated with children.[27] One must remember, however, that this comparison is drawn by the parents and not by the maiden. The parents have simply not expected this kind of a disquisition from their daughter, who is presumably not formally educated. Such wisdom can only be explained by reference to a tried and true *exemplum*, as the girl cannot have dreamed all this up by herself: God's hand must be in it (l. 874; p. 30). It proves useful to recall that other talkative children in Hartmann's works come in for similarly extreme reactions on the part of others when they vent sentiments that reveal them as acute perceivers (Enîte) or independent thinkers (Grêgôrius). Enîte is summarily silenced (l. 3039; p. 65), and Grêgôrius is chided (ll. 1515ff.; p. 107). All three are children wise beyond their years—can one even imagine Parzival holding forth in this manner at this age?—and all three work ultimately to aid others (Heinrich is helped by the maiden, Erec by Enîte, and Grêgôrius' wife/mother by her husband/son), even though the value of their contributions is not immediately recognized. In the immediate case of the maiden's parents, their acquiescence is accomplished in short order (ll. 855-902; p. 30) in the stunned silence as their daughter's words sink in.

In comparison with the parents, Heinrich is not so easily convinced. Initially he is touched by the maiden's concern but does not really take her heartfelt assertion to die for him all that seriously, attributing it to childish whims:

> "gemahel, du tuost als diu kint
> diu da gaehes muotes sint:
> swaz den kumet in den muot,
> ez sî übel oder guot,
> dar zuo ist in allen gâch
> und geriuwet si dar nâch"
> (ll. 949-54; "Little bride, you are acting as
> children do: they are impatient and eager to attempt
> whatever comes into their heads, good or bad, only to
> regret it later" —p. 30).

What proves interesting is the fact that the maiden does not feel the need to turn on Heinrich the same battery of argument that won over her parents, despite the fact that Heinrich would no doubt be more familiar with and receptive to the theological niceties of her presentation than would her uneducated parents. Instead, she couches her desire and intent in very simply terms, perhaps unwittingly aware that, while her parents can be swayed by an adult argument coming from a child's mouth, this approach would be lost on Heinrich. She progresses from a recognition of his distress (ll. 910-11; p. 30) to a restatement of conditions for a cure (ll. 921-4; p.30), to a simple announcement: "'diu wil ich weizgot selbe sîn'" (l. 925;

"'God knows that I myself want to be the one'"—p. 30). She communicates her desires forthrightly, with the simplicity of a child, and the tone in which Heinrich replies is speech modulated for a child's ears:

> er sprach: "gemahel, jâ enist der tôt
> iedoch niht ein senftiu nôt,
> als dû dir lîhte hâst gedâht.
> dû hâst mich des wol innen brâht,
> möhtestû, dû hülfest mir.
> des genüeget mich von dir.
> ich erkenne dînen süezen muot:
> dîn wille ist reine unde guot,
> ich ensol ouch niht mê an dich gern.
> dû maht mich des niht wol gewern
> daz dû dâ gesprochen hâst.
> die triuwe die dû an mir begâst,
> die sol dir vergelten got"
> (ll. 931-43; "Little bride," he said, "death is not a light pain, as you perhaps think. You have convinced me that you would help if you could, and that is enough for me. I know your kind heart and that your purpose is honest and good, but I will not ask more of you. Although you cannot give me what you have promised, God will repay you for the loyalty you have shown me"—p. 30).

He very much needs at this point to perceive her as a child, perhaps because he subconsciously fears confronting her as a woman, and this need shines through his rejoinder to her suggestion to sacrifice herself for him. He sets about to cast her in the role of child-as-misperceiver and child-as-misconceptualizer. Next, he appeals to that sense in which children are particularly vulnerable, suggesting that mockery or scorn would be likely to follow another of his vain attempts at "remedies" (l. 946; p. 30). Finally, he suggests that her offer is an unconsidered one, made by a mind quick to sieze upon a concept to act upon it. Accordingly, he asks her to reconsider her rash offer.

Throughout, Heinrich's attitude is kindly, tempered with a smile (l. 968; p. 31), yet characterized by a grown-up type of authority that takes for granted superior knowledge of the situation. It is only when the girl's parents corroborate her desire to sacrifice her life that Heinrich begins to take the matter seriously and recognize that the maiden is in earnest (l. 989; p. 31). Their report of her deliberations, undertaken over three days ("'si enhât sich kurze niht bedâht: / ez ist hiute der dritte tac'"—ll. 980b-1; "It is not a passing fancy, for this is the third day'"—p. 31), spurs him to think ("gedenken"—l. 1000; "consider"—p. 31), and then to act with dispatch. The speed with which Heinrich reaches his decision to accept the maiden's sacrifice proves to be a typical feature of Hartmann's decision-making heroes. Heinrich does not agonize over alternatives, nor does he give vent to long interior monologues on the subject, just as Erec moves swiftly to avenge his honor, with Enîte as bait, just as Iwein blithely agrees to Gâwein's counsel to go on the tournament circuit, and just as Grêgôrius precipitously leaves his wife/mother's castle for the solitude of his cliff. The reader is left, in all four cases, rather breathless, almost as if Hartmann is hurrying one over a difficult spot in the narrative where one is most tempted to linger to hear the protagonist's inner thoughts. At the point in which so much is presumably going on in his characters' minds, Hartmann is purposefully, maddeningly, and tantalizingly silent, calling attention to mind but not allowing the reader access to it beyond the brief descriptives, "dô bedâhte sich . . . der arme Heinrich"—ll. 1011-2; "poor Heinrich considered the offer"—p. 31), and ("to the maiden's great joy"—p. 31; l. 1016). Emphasis is all on the visible signs of consternation at parting (ll. 1027-48; p. 31), which decidedly distances the reader from the internal distress undergone. Once the maiden, the parents, and Heinrich have agreed upon a reasonable course of action, the mechanics of fulfillment are of secondary interest, as the focus of the narrative shifts anticipatorily to the next stage of events.

So forward-directed is the thrust of the narrative that the long journey to Salerno is astonishingly effected in the space of six lines (ll. 1049-54; p. 31). There is no mention of any conversation or adventures along the way, but one gathers from a brief reference that Heinrich's thoughts have run a good deal on his possible cure: "und dô er si vol brâhte / hin als er gedâhte . . ." (ll. 1055-6; "and when the lord had finally taken her [to where the master was]"—p. 31). As if reiterating the concern with mind, the Salernese doctor, a thorough diagnostician, is quick to ask the maiden if she has thoroughly considered her intended course of action ("'kint, hâstû dich / dises willen selbe bedâht'" (ll. 1064-5; "'My child, did you come to this decision by yourself?'"—p. 32), before twice urging her to envision what her resolve will necessitate: ("'daz dû dich bedenkest baz'"—l. 1077; "'My child, you must consider the matter more carefully'"—p. 32; "'bedenken disen smerzen'"—l. 1091; "'then think of this anguish'"—p. 32). In so doing, the very "bedenken" ("consider, think upon") displays a range from the reflective to the imaginative, fully in keeping with Hartmann's accustomed usage. The maiden's reply is studded with mental terms that communicate her understanding of what to expect and why ("'ich weiz wol durch wen ichz tuo'"—l. 1158; "'I know well for whom I do this'"—p. 32; "'*ich weiz wol*'"—l. 1162; "'I know'"—p. 32), her firmness of resolve ("'wan daz ich mich weste / des muotes alsô veste'"—ll. 1135-6; "'if I had not known myself to be resolute enough'"—p. 32; and "'ein muot alsô vester'"—l. 1140; "'a spirit . . . which is so strong'"—p. 32), and the sense of needing to brow-beat the doctor into going through with the operation. On the last account, she feigns a mental uncertainty (here: "'zwîvel'"—l. 1115; "'misgiving'"—p. 32) that is rapidly seen to reflect unfavorably on him. She upbraids him for temerity, for cowardice, and does so with an insult that reflects on sex roles, a technique not uncommon for Hartmann: "'iuwer rede gezaeme einem wîbe'" (l. 1122; "'your words are those of a woman'"—p. 32). Yet within ten lines the stereotypical picture of "weak womanhood" gives way to a blunt assessment of woman's strengths:

> "ich bin ein wîp und hân die kraft:
> geturret ir mich snîden,
> ich tar ez wol erlîden"
>   (ll. 1128-30; "Although a woman, I am strong: if you have the courage to cut me, I trust myself to endure it"—p. 32).

The self-characterization is noteworthy in two ways. First of all, the assertion of woman's strength both looks back to Enîte's courage in riding as bait/sacrifice ("vil wîplîchen si dô leit / dise ungelernet arbeit"—ll. 3280-1; "In a most womanly manner she endured the unfamiliar work"—p. 68) and forward to Lûnete's hardnosed realization of the extent of woman's power: "'ez ist vil wîplich daz ir claget'" (l. 1800; "'You lament as a woman should'"—p. 76); "'ir sprechet eht als ein wîp'" (l. 1921; "'You talk just like a woman'"—p. 78); and "'ir sît ein wîp'" (l. 1955; "'even though you are a woman'"—p. 78). Events in *Erec* have already demonstrated and in *Iwein* will show woman's ability to change man's mind for the better, and this is no less the case in *Der arme Heinrich*. Yet, in the instance under discussion, the maiden succeeds in convincing the doctor to go on with the operation, first, by taunting his masculinity and, then, by holding her strength and daring up to his. In other words, the emphasis is on the quality of courage, with the sexual element serving as a means to bring the mind to bear on that quality. The sexual stereotyping, while attention-getting, is still secondary. However, this sexual self-characterization proves crucial in a second major interpretation of the passage in question. On the one hand, the maiden's reference to herself as a woman serves to galvanize the doctor's will and permits matters to move toward the maiden's sacrifice, while, on the other hand, this self-description indicates a progression in the maiden's own awareness of herself as a sexual being, and this progression can have taken place only during that hazy time-period between leave-taking and arrival at Salerno. The reader knows "daz der wec sô verre was" (l. 1053; "it was so far away"—p. 31). Somewhere along that long way, the girl ceases to describe herself as maiden, although others will continue to view her as such (ll. 1060, 1177; pp. 31, 32) and as a child (ll. 1033, 1076; p. 31), and calls herself instead, "wîp" (l. 1128; p. 32).

To be sure, there are none of the standard indications of mutual sexual interest, such as occur during Erec's and Enîte's ride to Arthur's court (l. 1500; p. 48). No such passage occurs in *Der arme Heinrich*, but something happens nevertheless: the maiden, who is fondly called a bride, now calls herself, unabashedly, "a woman." What I am suggesting here is not any actual consummation—indications are that Heinrich has been oblivious on the ride to Salerno of everything except his thoughts of the maiden as a means to an end, as he does not really *see* her until ll. 1234ff. (p. 33)—but rather a process whereby the maiden sublimates sexual interest. Earlier she praises the plough of Christ over mundane marriage, and in Salerno she begs for the knife. What the maiden wants is not a conventional lovers' exchange of hearts, but rather a death that negates the possibility of that exchange, while guaranteeing a sense of lover's sacrifice without the toll wrought in loss of virginity. For the maiden, sacrifice as death must be less traumatic in some sense than sacrifice in the marriage bed. Yet interest in Heinrich and in the marriage bed lies at the heart of the matter,[28] and that subconscious realization, reached somewhere on the road to Salerno—not as dramatic as Saul's revelation on the road to Damascus but just as irreversible and wide-reaching—accounts for her new view of herself as "woman," as "wîp." Heinrich is very much on her mind, as well as her intent to sacrifice herself for him, although she does not seem to realize that the process will sacrifice her youth. When he sacrifices himself for her, she reacts emotionally, unthinkingly, failing to realize that love and healing cannot be one-sided. Heinrich's love and cure are bound up in her love and cure, and in her aging and undergoing adult, rather than childish, experiences.

At the time, however, her mind is only on the cure she hopes to facilitate for Heinrich, and it is to this end that she convinces the doctor to proceed. The reader nevertheless anticipates a last-minute stay of execution,[29] and Hartmann accordingly engineers the scene with an eye of a showman: the girl is stripped, first in the mental walking through of the procedure (ll. 1085ff.; p. 32), and subsequently in actuality (ll. 1190-200; p. 32); touches such as the locked and barred door are added; and finally, the last minute considerations are not untinged with titillation:

> Dô si der meister ane sach,
> in sînem herzen er des jach
> daz schoener krêâtiure
> al der werlte waere tiure
>   (ll. 1197-1200; When the master looked at
> her, he thought to himself that there was no more
> beautiful creature in all the world than she—p. 33).

Heinrich is duly sequestered away from the place of the operation, yet not far enough from hearing the sound of the whetted knife, not unlike the Middle English *Pearl*-Poet's Gawain in *Sir Gawain and the Green Knight* hearing the axe being sharpened that is to sever his head. Gawain must rely only on his own sharpened sense of hearing, but Heinrich in the Middle High German poem is able to find visual access to the proceedings. A handy "loch" (l. 1230; "crack"—p. 33) gives the protagonist a glimpse of the maiden's beauty, much in the way that a window conveniently gives on Laudîne's despair (l. 1450; p. 75) and changes the direction of Iwein's thoughts. Heinrich sees ("nû sach er"—l. 1234; "he looked"—p. 33) and, in effect, *sees* for the first time, not coincidentally after he *hears* ("erhôrte"—l. 1221; "heard"—p. 33). After seeing and hearing, Heinrich begins to exhibit qualities of the truly perceptive when evidence and interpretation begin to fill his mind, and the reader recognizes that a change of mind is in the offing.[30]

Heinrich peering through the hole, and his new perception puts one in mind of two scenes in *Iwein*, although the immediate connection may not be obvious. Let us first look at the passage in *Der arme Heinrich*:

> nu begunde er suochen und spehen,
> unz daz er durch die want
> ein loch gânde vant,
> und ersach sie durch die schrunden
> nacket und gebunden.
> ir lîp der was vil minneclich,
> nû sach er si an under sich
> und gewan einen niuwen muote
>   (ll. 1228-35; He searched until he found a
> crack in the wall and through it caught sight of her
> lovely body, naked and bound. He looked at her and
> at himself, and had a change of heart—p. 33).

The hero *sees* in a way that he has not before, and that is not at all unlike what occurs when Iwein gets his initial glimpse of Laudîne, when Hartmann notes succinctly:

> swâ ir der lîp blôzer schein,
> da ersach sî der herre Iwein;
> dâ was ir hâr und ir lîch
> sô gar dem wunsche glîch
> daz er im ir minne
> verkêrte die sinne,
> daz er sîn selbes gar vergaz
>   (ll. 1331-7; Sir Iwein caught glimpses of her
> bare form, and her hair and body were so beautiful
> that love robbed him of reason, to the point that he
> quite forgot himself—p. 71).

That Iwein's mental transformation comes as a direct result of something that he has seen—and significantly what he has seen is partially naked female anatomy that very much attracts him—does not differ in its essentials from Heinrich's sudden pulling up short at the sight of the maiden earlier described as "nacket unde blôz" (l.

1195; "naked [and bare]" —p. 33). Just as the thought of Laudîne displaces Iwein's earlier fears of discovery and death (ll. 1169ff.; p. 71), so does the sight of the maiden trigger a new mental attitude on Heinrich's part:

> in dûhte dô daz niht guot
> des er gedâht hâte
> und verkêrte vil drâte
> sîn altez gemüete
> in eine niuwe güete
> (ll. 1236; What he had intended now seemed wrong, and his former spirit was quickly transformed into a new kindness—p. 33).

The "old" cast of mind, to sacrifice the maiden for his own survival, is replaced by the "new,"[31] that is, in effect, to sacrifice his chances of living so that she might live. Heinrich had intellectually convinced himself of the reasonableness of the maiden's sacrifice, but he now "sees," both in the perceptual and conceptual senses, that his attitude was misguided. A nobler impulse takes over, the doctor is hailed "durch die want" (l. 1267; "through the wall"—p. 33), and the operation is called off.

In fact, it is the very existence of a wall that is breached, to good ends, that harks to the second related scene in *Iwein*. Iwein, one recalls, has contracted to fight two giants, but the battle is not joined until he has agreed to sequester his lion in a shed where it could still see the fight in the courtyard through a crack in the wall. The shared language with *Der arme Heinrich* extends to the rhyme-pairs, linking scenes not only thematically but formally:

> dô dise slege herte
> der lewe sîn geverte
> beide erhôrte und ersach
> dô muote in sîn ungemach.
> nûne vander loch noch tür
> dâ er kaeme hin vür,
> und suochte al umbe unz er vant
> bî der erde an der want
> eine vûle swelle
> (ll. 6737-45; When his comrade, the lion, heard and saw the fierce blows, it was greatly disturbed by the danger he was in but could find no way to get out. It searched everywhere and at last found a decaying foundation beam—p. 134).

The lion, which has been understood to represent a noble quality acquired by Iwein, moved by what it has seen through the wall, escapes and comes to Iwein's aid, literally saving his life. While the lion must make its way by force through a weak place in the wall, Heinrich is able to negotiate verbally with the doctor for admission, having, like the lion, seen a situation that needs to be rectified. Because the lion is a physical manifestation of a mental trait, it is perhaps more fitting that it cracks open the wall dramatically, whereas Heinrich uses language to go to the girl's aid. It is the wall as threshold, though, that obtains final importance: right perception necessitates passing over a significant threshold, so that right action can occur. And the scene in *Der arme Heinrich*—incorporating as it does the sexual aspect of the first *Iwein* scene discussed above, the breaching of the wall in the second *Iwein* scene, and the perception/change of mind nexus that informs both scenes—serves as the turning point of the work.

The change in Heinrich is described almost entirely in terms of mind, with reference as well to the sense of hierarchy whereby God grants both burdens and blessings:

> Nû er si alsô schoene sach,
> wider sich selben er dô sprach:
> "dû hâst einen tumben gedanc
> daz dû sunder sînen danc
> gerst ze lebenne einen tac
> wider den nieman niht enmac.
> dû enweist ouch rehte waz dû tuost,
> sît dû benamen ersterben muost,
> daz dû diz lasterlîche leben
> daz dir got hât gegeben
> niht vil willeclîchen treist
> und ouch dar zuo niene weist
> ob dich des kindes tôt ernert.
> swaz die got hât beschert,
> daz lâ allez geschehen.
> ich enwil des kindes tôt niht sehen"
>
> (ll. 1241-54; When he saw that she was so beautiful, he said to himself, "You are foolish to want to live a single day against the will of Him whom no one can hinder. Since you must indeed die, you don't know what you are doing by not gladly enduring the odious life that God has ordained for you. Moreover, you also don't know whether the child's death will heal you. Let everything come that God has assigned you. I don't want to see the child die"—p. 33).

The reader, who has access to Iwein's axiomatic statement,

> "er ist ein vil wîser man
> der tumben gedanc verdenken kan
> mit wîslîcher tât"

(ll. 1499-1501; "It is a wise man who can put an end to foolish whims with sensible deeds"—pp. 72-3),

sees Heinrich at the point of changing his mind and, accordingly, his behavior for the better. The reader, who knows that Heinrich has given considerable thought to the maiden's sacrifice, has not been privy to those thoughts, and there is reason to believe that Heinrich's thoughts have run more on what the maiden has offered to do *for him* than on what he is about to do *to her*. Her loyalty (l. 1001; p. 31) has been noted, as well as her resolve (l. 989; p. 31), yet these qualities are by their very nature directed toward Heinrich, who, in his selfishness, has given only perfunctory thought to what the maiden's sacrifice entails. It takes the sight of the maiden, bound and naked at the moment of sacrifice, to jar Heinrich's sensibilities, so that he realizes, regardless of what she can do for him, what he can absolutely *not do* to her. His trip to Salerno is seen to rest on what is held to be a false mental premise: "ein tumber gedanc" (l. 1243; "[a] foolish [thought]"—p. 33), and he must now consider what he knows to be true: that the death of the maiden is a cheap way out of a burdensome existence intended for him, and for him alone, by God. Injury to her would only compound his predicament in the eyes of God.

Heinrich's reversal is not all that unexpected, for the suspense that Hartmann builds into the narrative gathers its shape from the undercutting of plot assumptions. From the moment the maiden offers herself as a sacrifice, the reader knows both that Heinrich will, albeit with reservations, accept her offer and that she, in turn, will be prevented from making good on her promise to die for him. To this end, Hartmann speeds up the narrative to convey the pair from Swabia to Salerno in a matter of a few lines, in order to rush on to a dreadful *dénouement*, and then deliciously retards the action, so that the doctor questions, the maiden responds, the doctor ritualistically locks and bolts the door, the maiden strips, and the doctor binds her and whets his knife in a sequence that is cinematic in its narrowing focus[32] and melodramatic in effect. Hartmann creates the medieval equivalent of the modern maiden bound to the tracks, with the locomotive bearing down, overpowering in sight and sound, and the rasp of the whetstone rings as loudly as another whetstone does in *Sir Gawain and the Green Knight's* Green Chapel episode.[33]

Both Gawain and the maiden are prepared to meet their maker, and the reader revels in the expectation that death is likely to occur and yet is certain not to. Death is so anticipated that it calls forth its opposite. This tension is effected by the juxtaposition of what the reader is told (that is, the surface movement of plot) and what he/she nevertheless knows (the questions that he/she asks at every plot juncture). In effect, death and life balance and unbalance each other on several levels. First, over-emphasis on one of them evokes the other: Heinrich's vibrant life invites a fall and death, and the maiden's repeated desire for death binds her to life, despite her protests. Second, the subtle introduction of one term in a mass of repetitions of the other term signals the shift in the surface plot that lags behind the reader's expectations. By way of support for this contention, the episode at Salerno contains frequent references to death, (ll. 1079, 1081, 1109, 1165, 1216, 1253, 1256; pp. 31ff.) and very few to life. The maiden twice uses the term "'daz êwige leben'" (ll. 1148, 1154; "'eternal life'"—p. 32), but she means by it "death." Life enters the text briefly in two references to Heinrich, first when he regrets "that he should never again see the maiden alive" (p. 33; ll. 1226-7), and then when he speaks of his own burdensome life (l. 1249; p. 33). These two references, coming as they do before the dual reference to "des kindes tôt" (ll. 1253, 1256; "the child's death"—p. 33), attest to the new direction of the text, which dovetails with the reader's expectations, met when Heinrich cries out: "'ir sult die maget lâzen leben'" (l. 1280; "'you must let the maiden live'"—p. 33). The scales tip toward life, and the maiden lives, to the relief of the doctor as well (ll. 1281ff.; p. 33).[34]

The maiden's reaction to this turn of events is vehement:

> Dô diu maget rehte ersach
> daz ir ze sterbenne niht geschach,
> dâ was ir muot beswaeret mite.
> si brach ir zuht und ir site.
> si hete leides genuoc:
> zuo den brüsten si sich sluoc,
> si zarte unde roufte sich
> (ll. 1281-4; When she realized that she was not to die, the maiden's heart was troubled. In great sorrow she went beyond the bounds of decorum and manners as she beat her breast and tore her hair—p. 33).

And, just as her actions are directed against herself, so too does her subsequent speech reveal a notable self-orientation:

> "wê *mir* vil armen unde ouwê!
> wie sol ez *mir* nû ergân,
> muoz *ich* alsus verlorn hân
> die rîchen himelkrône?
> diu waere *mir* ze lône
> gegeben umbe dise nôt.
> nû bin *ich* alrêst tôt.
> ouwê, gewaltiger Krist,
> waz êren uns benomen ist,
> mînem herren unde *mir*!
> nû enbirt er und *ich* enbir
> der êren der uns was gedâht.
> ob diz waere volbrâht,

> so waere im der lîp genesen,
> und müese *ich* iemer saelic wesen"
>
> (ll. 1290-1304, my italics; "Oh! Oh, poor me," she cried bitterly. "What will happen to me now? Must I thus lose the splendid heavenly crown that would have been my reward for this ordeal? Now I am dead indeed. Oh, mighty Christ, what glory has been taken from my lord and me? He and I are deprived of the honor that was intended for us. If this plan had been carried out, he would be cured and I would be forever happy"—pp. 33-4).

Her first concern is *her* loss, rather than Heinrich's gain, and this suggests that she has been dwelling more on the rewarding consequences of her actions than on motivation. Also, in the violation of her expectations, she has lost sight of the fact that the power to heal Heinrich lies not in her hands or in her heart's blood but rather in the hands and heart of Christ. In fact, she is not at all unlike the earlier Heinrich, who expresses shock at his fall, for her reaction is one of disappointment at the loss of seeming control over her existence. Just as prosperity implies to Heinrich continued prosperity, so the comforting thought of honor sustains itself in the maiden's mind. Both are at a loss when matters do not continue on their expected course, and this undercutting of expectations is a necessary part of their spiritual growth. Both need to see that, while they may not get just what they want when they want it, they may in fact get what they need, if I may paraphrase the Rolling Stones.

At this time, however, the maiden is hardly in any state to realize—as the reader is—that events will take a fortuitous turn. Instead, she vents her anger on Heinrich and in tones that are increasingly more adult, and with language that builds on the earlier impression, gained in her response to the doctor, that she has left childhood behind and perceives herself now as a woman. One recalls that her early speeches, when she was convincing her parents and Heinrich, while exhibiting a rationality that belied her chronological age, still were the words of a child, and part of their impact drew from the fact that a child was coming forth with such subtlety and logic. The *topos*, of course, is that of the *puer senex*, or what could be called the "Daniel Syndrome" in a religious context: one is all the more likely to take the child seriously when he/she does not speak like a child even though he/she obviously is a child. In the maiden's angry discourse after Heinrich has called a halt to the operation, she no longer sounds like a child—albeit an unusually wise one—but rather like a woman, not only because she takes a longer view of matters over time (note her use of "'ie'"—ll. 1314, 1318; "'always, again and again'"—p. 34, and her scornful reference to "'alle iuwer tage'"—l. 1319; "'all your life'"—p. 34), but also because she casts aspersions at Heinrich's "'mannes muot'" (l. 1316;

"'manly spirit'"—p. 34). This latter formulation, when viewed in light of her earlier contention, "'ich bin ein wîp'" (l. 1128; "'[I am] a woman'"—p. 32), suggests that she is beginning to view her relationship with Heinrich as something other than child and adult. Heinrich, needless to say, perceives her in a considerably less avuncular light, if his reaction to her loveliness can be interpreted as an action that will culminate in his taking her to wife some two hundred lines later. Finally, the maiden's angry diatribe is refreshingly illogical, for she flatly contradicts the people (l. 1314; p. 34) who all praise Heinrich, and she presents a startlingly revisionist view of Heinrich's character that is clearly not upheld by his behavior: "'ir wâret alle iuwer tage / und sît noch ein werltzage'" (ll. 1319-20; "'for all your life you have been an abject coward, and you still are'"—p. 34). She castigates him for his cowardice and, in so doing, makes a statement that can be read literally or ironically: "'ez was doch ein dickiu want / enzwischen iu unde mir'" (ll. 1326-7; "'After all, there was a thick wall between us'"—p. 34). Certainly the wall was there, but it is now gone, for he has seen (l. 1234; p. 33) and she has seen (l. 1281; p. 33), and things will never again be the same between them.

The return journey to Swabia is accomplished with the same swiftness that marked the trip to Salerno.[35] The protesting maiden is bundled into her clothes, the doctor is paid for his troubles, and Heinrich and the maiden set off for home. The reader is told that Heinrich has some second thoughts,[36] occasioned by his awareness of his countrymen's probable reaction to his failure to find a cure (ll. 1348; p. 34). But Heinrich, formerly so sensitive to his standing in the world, dismisses this thought summarily and for the right reason: "daz liez er allez an got" (l. 1352; "he left all that to God"— p. 34).[37] That one-line admission of dependence tells the audience more than pages and pages of repentent monologues could. And it is, significantly, exactly when the hope for a cure is most absent that the once longed-for cure comes. The absence of expectation on Heinrich's part counterbalances increased anticipation on the reader's part. Surely, now that Heinrich has demonstrated compassion and selflessness, the cure will come, *must* come, and a transformation in the doctor's presence would not be too dramatic. Yet this expected transformation of the ailing Heinrich into a rejuvenated nobleman does not occur at the moment the reader expects it to, that is, at Salerno, at the time Heinrich "sees" the maiden,[38] and Hartmann postpones the cure for two reasons. First, the pattern of undercut expectation must be maintained throughout the work, in order to make any encompassing statement about mind, which Hartmann fully intends to do in this study of the juxtaposition of the human and the divine minds, filtered through the mind of the reader. But even more than that, the reader recognizes that the maiden must be seen as having been, like Heinrich, tested by God. Accordingly, the maiden, like Heinrich, is brought near death (l. 1355; p. 34), only to be spared that death. The agency for redemption, as well as for fulfilling the reader's expectations *vis-à-vis* the pair, is Christ, to whom the maiden has earlier appealed in her outburst. Hartmann notes:

> dô erzeicte der heilic Krist
> wie liep im triuwe und bärmde ist
> und schiet si dô beide
> von allem ir leide
> und machete in dâ zestunt
> reine unde wol gesunt
> (ll. 1365-70; Our Holy Christ then showed how dear to Him faithfulness and compassion are by freeing both from all their sorrows and at once making the lord handsome and completely healthy—p. 34).

Christ the Transformer, who was Christ the Sustainer in *Grêgôrius*, is cast as perceiver as well: "dô erkande ir triuwe und ir nôt" (l. 1356; "[He] perceived her faithfulness and her distress"—p. 34). The reader sees once again an instance in which a being—here, more than human, but elsewhere in Hartmann's works quite human and fallible—brings about a change by seeing what has been internalized, by reflecting upon this, and then by acting.

The physical restoration of Heinrich, which is tantamount to a rescue of the maiden as well, is accomplished, again, with extraordinary swiftness: once the interior is found to be pure, the cleansing of the exterior proceeds apace. That the purity of the interior takes precedence is underscored by language, for Heinrich, who once lamented, "'[He] closed the portals of bliss before me'" (l. 406; p. 26), is cured by one "vor dem deheinez herzen tor / vürnames niht beslozzen ist" (ll. 1358-9; "to whom indeed no heart's gate is closed"—p. 34). Heinrich fears exclusion, and his self-imposed exile stresses this state of mind, and he needs to learn that faith in one's inclusion in God's grace is of more importance than virtually anything else. As soon as Heinrich ceases his self-centered laments, exhausts his earthly possibilities for a cure, and "left all that to God" (l. 1352; p. 34), and as soon as the maiden, too, reaches the watershed that represents her own inability to effect her salvation and Heinrich's restoration, then can Christ intervene and alter the physical, so that it aligns with the spiritual. Then, and only then, at the point when despair over the missed opportunity for sacrifice of the maiden is at its greatest and when tried and true remedies (one maiden's heart = one cure) are seen to be less preferable to abandonment to the disease, can the divine step in. There is no rational argument to explain divine behavior; neither the reasoned appeals of the maiden, nor the seemingly infallible and unattainable recommendations of the Salernese doctor bear fruit in the final analysis, for absence of suffering appears to result from a total passivity on Heinrich's part and from an obstinate persistence of grief on the maiden's part. Neither has done the "right thing"—Heinrich has not gone through with the distasteful operation, and the maiden has not acquiesced to the unchanging state of affairs—and each has, like Jonah, reached Nineveh, in effect, by sailing in the opposite direction. Christ tests them (l. 1360; p. 34), tries them (l. 1362; p. 34) even as Job was tried (l. 1364; p. 34), and restores them miraculously.

The reader is not told directly why God tests Heinrich and the maiden, but there is reason to believe that He does so in order to make them mindful of Him, both to keep Him in mind and to ground their lives in Him. Once this change of attitude has been brought about, the poem moves rapidly to its conclusion, complete with romance and fairy tale touches that satisfy the expectations of the reader. The maiden does marry Heinrich[39] even though there is last-minute consultation of wise kinsmen and vassals who offer advice that Heinrich does not take. He follows his own inclinations: "'nû raetet mir al mîn sin / daz ich si ze wîbe neme'" (ll. 1498-9; "'I intend to have her as my wife'"—p. 35). She is the logical choice, in his mind, as she is directly responsible for his restored good health (ll. 1494; p. 35) and is eligible (l. 1497; p. 35).[40] Yet the real reasons probably have little to do with such logic, if one reads between the lines the obvious and growing attraction between Heinrich and the maiden.[41] The fairy tale ending depends upon this attraction, for it legitimatizes the union between the two and accords with Heinrich's restored high status within his community. The "happy ending" of fairy tale becomes at the same time a Christian commentary:

> nâch süezem lanclîbe
> do besâzen si gelîche
> daz êwige rîche
> (ll. 1514-6; After a long and happy life, both went to dwell in the kingdom of Heaven—p. 35).

And the religious overtones of the pair's experience tie directly into traditional romance conventions, for they are said to return to Swabia within three days (l. 1391; p. 34), echoing the three-day period of crucifixion, Harrowing of Hell, and resurrection, the period upon which medieval romance is based.[42] Heinrich and the maiden have harrowed hells of their own making, and their journey away from and return to society is planned so that what they learn can be put to use as they resume their places in society. Because those who harrow Hell bring back something that society needs,[43] elevation in status often occurs,[44] as is the case with Erec's kingship, Grêgôrius' papacy, and Parzival's Grail Kingship. In *Der arme Heinrich*, the protagonist regains—no, surpasses—his former wealth and status: "er wart rîcher vil dan ê / des guotes und der êren" (ll. 1430-1; "He became much richer than before in both property and honor"—p. 35). Why goods and a revered position in society should result from

Heinrich's miraculous cure remains a point for the reader to ponder, and the implicit conclusion drawn by Hartmann is that Heinrich and the maiden have learned something about God from their experience: dependency on God frees the maiden from the prideful thought that she can orchestrate her destiny and provides a firm extra-mundane ground for Heinrich's earthly status. Both come to see that status, goods, and salvation come from God; the first two are meaningless without Him, and the last cannot be entered into as one would a pact. God takes away that which is essentially empty without Him, and He gives back—and more—that which He has taken.

Hartmann closes the work with a sentiment that, true to the direction of the poem, speaks to admonition and expectation:

> alsô müezez uns allen
> ze jungest gevallen!
> den lôn den si dâ nâmen,
> des helfe uns got. âmen
> (ll. 1517-20; May this at the end be our lot.
> God help us to gain the reward they received.
> Amen—p. 35).

With God's help, the reader may look forward to the same reward granted Heinrich and his wife, which is at the same time a powerful incentive toward a pattern of behavior that includes, rather than excludes, God. The consequences of failure to set God as a priority are evident in the warning given in Heinrich's illness and simultaneous fall from grace and social status, and the benefits of attention to this priority come in Heinrich's restoration. For the reader, the knowledge of Heinrich's past serves as an admonition, while knowledge of his future translates into an expectation of eternal life that can be shared by Hartmann, the reader, and all who while away their "troublesome hours" (l. 10; p. 23) with it. As text, the tale of Heinrich and the maiden becomes at once warning and hope,[45] and Hartmann's concern with mind here assumes several dimensions. First of all, Heinrich's experience is to serve as food for thought, so that the reader may learn from it, just as Hartmann has learned from reading books. Moreover, just as Hartmann's intent is to educate his readers or listeners while spinning a pleasing story, so is the text to couch a serious message that may be intellectually apprehended even while the reader is carried along by the narrative surface.

In fact, it is not farfetched to contend that Hartmann in *Der arme Heinrich* conceives of the reader *as mind*, as reflective, reactive, cogitative response to the narrative. The reader becomes, more than in Hartmann's other poems, a focus and functions as another mind that the poet wishes to reach: to teach through admonition, to divert, and, finally, to recruit prayers for the poet (ll. 22-8; p. 23). This does not mean that Hartmann, in including the reader, loses interest in charting the manner in which his characters' minds operate. On the contrary, Hartmann draws a wide circle that encompasses not only the maiden's theological reflections and Heinrich's change of mind, but also the reader's presence as an active mind that considers turns of plot, moral implications, and the overriding rule of the divine. The plot and structure of *Der arme Heinrich* may be considerably simpler than those of his other narratives,[46] but Hartmann's focus here is wider, as the reader is drawn mentally into the narrative in a way that does not happen in the other works. And what is striking, in addition, is that this reader involvement is effected without the standard devices whereby the reader is invoked in a consciously rhetorical fashion. The task for the reader of *Der arme Heinrich* is not the effort of taking the seemingly random succession of Erec's adventures and extrapolating from them the principles of thematic structure that inform the work, nor is it the identification of a common characterization device in *Grêgôrius*. Rather, in *Der arme Heinrich*, the reader-as-critic is urged to engage in an abstract dialogue with the work's maker, knowing where the narrative is heading—so that the writer's task in holding the reader's interest is to maintain the delicate balance between expectation and undercutting.

5

IWEIN

Strife in the Landscape of the Mind

Hartmann's last work,[1] *Iwein*, relies on the language, situations, and conventions established in the other four poems, but its tone is darker and its stylistic features are more sophisticated than those of *Die Klage, Erec, Grêgôrius,* and *Der arme Heinrich*. Even given the somewhat sensational subject matter of *Grêgôrius, Iwein*'s plot elements of murder, serial monogamy, exploitation in the workplace, and madness produce a different type of thematic texture than those of Hartmann's earlier works, and, while the conflicts in *Iwein* are resolved at the end of the poem—Laudîne and Iwein *are* reunited—*Iwein* lacks the characteristic tidiness of resolution between man and woman (or between heart and body) of the other poems. Laudîne reconciles with Iwein, but only because she feels she must keep her word, and the reader senses that Iwein and Laudîne still have considerable difficulties to work out in their relationship. Iwein may have come to some peace of mind regarding how he balances knighthood and love, but the romance ends before the reader sees how Iwein will communicate to his wife what he has learned over a sustained period of stress and introspection. And Hartmann, through the repetition of "waenlich" (ll. 8148, 8159; "I believe" and "one may suppose"—p. 149)[2] and the disclaimer concerning the lovers' continued life together ("'ichn weiz aber waz ode wie / in sît geschaehe beiden'"—ll. 8160-1; "'I don't know for certain what happened from this time on'"—p. 149) leaves the possibility of a happy ending up in the air. There is no culminating marriage (as in *Der arme Heinrich*) or explicitly happy royal rule (as in *Erec*) or chaste reunion of mother/wife with husband/son (as in *Grêgôrius*) or even unanimity of mind (as in *Die Klage*). What obtains instead is demonstrated by the work's last disturbance at the fountain area, which presages a stormy relationship to come.

In fact, this interrelationship of landscape and mind proves to be the predominant narrative technique of the poem. The poem's inner and outer worlds both inform and reflect upon each other so that the physical progress of the hero meshes with his spiritual itinerary. The outer world of landscape produces the hindrances and rewards that the inner world of mind requires, and the mind modifies and comments upon the challenges offered by the physical world.[3] No character or incident is superfluous or out of place;[4] each is cued precisely when the hero can gain from it. Hartmann thus calls the storm-making spring into being each time that its appearance can teach Iwein something, and he provides timely messengers, both admonitory and inciting, to move his hero on his path to *mâze* ("moderation"), much as Wolfram von Eschenbach allows the Grail Castle's materialization and Sigune's advice only at those points in Parzival's journey when they can be instructive. Hartmann, moreover, represents qualities of mind in terms of objects, so that the lion becomes a physical representation of a modification that is taking place in Iwein's interior.

As in Hartmann's other works, the inner and outer landscapes gather their shape from the poet's meticulous use of language, a finely honed sense of word connotation that offers to the audience both literal and figurative meanings. In effect, Hartmann sets up a dual vocabulary that includes "strîten" ("to fight, argue"), "kêren"/"bekêren"/"verkêren" ("to turn, convert"), "kennen"/"erkennen" ("to know, recognize"), "strît" ("wâfen") "strît" ("worten") ("to fight with weapons"/"to fight with words"). In the process, corporeal movement, recognition, and conflict set up resonances on the spiritual level as well. Moreover, Hartmann's physical landscapes are so constituted to express one of the central themes in *Iwein*: how, on Hartmann's account, does the mind (and the heart must be included here) function in its capacity to evaluate perceptions, to weigh alternatives, to change, and to control the content of its thought? This problem repeatedly surfaces in the work's interior monologues that give the reader access to characters' decision-making processes, Iwein's road to and from insanity, and even the manner in which the hero and his lady fall in love. It is a problem worked out not only in the chambers of the mind (and heart) but also in every pitched battle joined by the romance's characters. The landscapes of the mind and of the physical world are characterized through shared language and congruent structures in terms of choices to be made, courses of action to be pursued, and strife that must be resolved. For this reason Hartmann creates his two landscapes so that, while they do not possess identical features, they do share a common reliance on conflict and on the setting of conflict. He then carefully walks his reader over these two landscapes, over the terrain of the Arthurian world with its vague geography and ever-present battles, and over the inner topography of the mind, where love and honor, memory and forgetfulness, dream and reality, and recognition and incomprehension clash. These are related landscapes so informed by dispute, argumentation, and change, that conflict and the resolution of conflict are underlying and central themes in the romance.

Virtually every scene in *Iwein* contains some sort of strife,[5] whether it be Keiî's war of words, the inheritance dispute between the daughters "of Black Thorn" (l. 5629; p. 121), the battle between the lion and the dragon, or the skirmishes into which Iwein enters. On the physical level this constant conflict is resolved in the outcomes of battles. In the spiritual dimension, resolution is expressed in Iwein's mental and spiritual transformation over the course of the romance. Iwein is led from the romance's outset, where the only way he knows to conclude a battle is to destroy his adversary, to the work's conclusion, where his combat with Gâwein is resolved without death and defeat of his opponent, and with regret on both sides that the conflict had to occur. Iwein will come to the realization that he fights not *merely to fight* but rather to achieve good for others, whether it be to deliver one maiden from her enemies or three hundred ladies from their tormentors. Moreover, Hartmann's hero is brought to the point in his amorous conflicts that he remembers his obligations to his wife and also understands what these obligations entail; in short, leaving Laudîne's physical presence need not be tantamount to forgetting her. Over the romance, the hero's physical adventures will keep pace with the process whereby his mind is transformed from an arena of troubled contention into a serene receptacle of memory and obligation.

Throughout, Hartmann, as did Chrétien before him,[6] employs the concept of enclosure, so that the mind (or the heart) becomes a vessel and an arena unto itself, not unlike the fields of battle that appear in the work. In *Iwein*, the concept of enclosure provides a series of settings into which foreign elements can enter and either be defeated and subsequently expelled or integrated.[7] To put it simply, Hartmann takes a basic situation, the breaching of an enclosure, and repeats it with variations throughout the poem. The enclosure may be physical (such as a castle),[8] or it may be the vessel of the heart, or even the body that contains the heart.[9] The breaching of the enclosure occurs through the senses if the enclosure is a vessel of the mind/heart and by way of gates, doors, and windows if a physical edifice.[10] Thresholds thus obtain importance, because they provide openings in the wall of defense. Hartmann therefore details the gates as Iwein enters into and is trapped within Ascalôn's fortress (ll. 1075-134; p. 68) and then within the gates guarded by the recalcitrant porter at the castle holding the three hundred ladies (ll. 6171ff.; p. 128). Iwein's eyes also function like windows, conducting Laudîne's beauty into his heart (ll. 2340-55; pp. 70-1), and it is no coincidence that windows give on sights that affect Iwein's mind and subsequent actions (ll. 6190ff.; p. 128). Orifices in buildings thus correspond to the perceptual organs in the body, and the penetration of the mind comes to have implications as important as the breaching of physical edifices. Often the person, thing, or sight entering the enclosure takes possession and changes the old order, signalled by a transformation of emotions over the course of a narrative segment. For example, the entrance of Iwein into his rival's stronghold, hard on the heels of the dead knight, brings woe to Laudîne that can be supplanted by joy only after she weighs alternatives and allows Ascalôn to slip from her mind and Iwein to enter it. By way of contrast, woe can be transformed into joy by Iwein entering a castle or battle arena and fighting to defeat those who control the fortunes of those within.

This chapter examines Hartmann's transformation of the contents of his interrelated enclosures, so that Iwein's mental metamorphosis is charted through the breaching of physical enclosures and the alterations that are brought about by the ensuing altercations. The strife in the landscape of the mind, as the new displaces the old, is mirrored in the constant physical conflict joined within enclosures, castle walls, battle arenas, and the charmed bounds of the storm-making spring. It even involves the *persona* of Hartmann in his ongoing dispute with "vrouw Minne." The manner and outcome of these battles provide apt commentary on the state of Iwein's mind, and, to a lesser degree, Laudîne's mind. The reader, too, is indirectly enjoined to exercise his/her mind to fathom the meaning of Iwein's actions and, ultimately, of the work itself.

Iwein begins with an idyllic picture of the Pentecostal festival held at Arthur's court. The narrator assures the reader of the presence of many noble knights and describes them at their courtly occupations, which include dancing, singing, chatting, and bragging. It is truly "ein wunschleben" (l. 44; "all that one could wish"—p. 55), and yet the picture is marred both by the waspishness of the narrator, as he contrasts the festivities to those in his own day, and by the slothful ease with which Keiî dozes in the midst of the activity (ll. 74-5; p. 56). Shortly thereafter Arthur and the Queen are seen retreating to a private chamber in a manner reminiscent of lapsed Erec and his bride, holding hands on their way to a bit of mid-day lovemaking ("ze handen si sich viengen"—*Erec*, l. 2942; "ze handen gevangen"—*Iwein*, l. 79; "hand in hand"—p. 56). The "wunschleben" suddenly begins to take on the color of "daz selbe wunschleben" (l. 393; "happy life"—p. 26) of *Der arme Heinrich*, whereby the pinnacle is detailed in order to make the subsequent fall more dramatic. The Arthurian court has chinks in its armor; not merely is the smooth surface of that idealized society about to be disturbed in the verbal fracas that erupts, but also the "wunschleben" for the protagonist is going to come to an end, just as Heinrich's did. To be sure, Hartmann is milder than many medieval writers in their ironic treatment of the "perfect" Arthurian society—the Middle English *Pearl*-Poet's linkage of Arthur's court to Belshazzar's through the use of shared language is much more pointed—but he does insert details that stress Arthur's foolishness and the court's lack of accountability. The mention of "wunschleben" works in this sense to raise the reader's expectations that the fly in the ointment is about to be discovered.

Kâlogrenant proposes to tell his audience a tale "that had caused him a great deal of trouble without increasing his fame" (ll. 94-5; p. 56), and almost immediately conflict begins. Angered at Kâlogrenant's rapid recognition of the Queen's arrival, Keiî unleashes a tirade that starts with sarcastic praise for Kâlogrenant's courtliness and ends with a disparaging remark that suggests Kâlogrenant would have done well not to let his behavior reflect unkindly on the other knights present. The Queen chides him in a statement that makes explicit the principle to which Hartmann has adhered in many of his earlier exchanges where characters insult each other and cut each other with their own words. Keiî's behavior only reflects upon himself in the final analysis: what he says to another speaks to his own emotional makeup. Keiî, not to be outdone, responds with a speech that is as insulting to the Queen as his castigation of Kâlogrenant was to that knight, and Kâlogrenant notes:

> "ez ensprichet niemans munt
> wan als in sîn herze lêret:
> swen iuwer zunge unêret,
> dâ ist daz herze schuldec an.
> in der werlte ist manec man
> valsch und wandelbaere,
> der gerne biderbe waere,
> wan daz in sîn herze enlât"
> (ll. 194-201; "a man's lips speak only as his heart teaches, and when your tongue is insulting, it is the fault of your heart. There are many false and inconstant men in the world who would like to be upright, but their hearts won't let them"—p. 57).

Kâlogrenant here speaks to the linkage between mind/heart and language, and, if he makes no provision for dissembling speech, it is not only because he wishes to see a direct correspondence between Keiî's perfidious heart and his rude words, but also because Kâlogrenant believes strongly in the positive power of words. He is a tale-teller (he has a story to recount but also he can tell tales on himself when necessary) and a man who is aware that words have more than surface meaning. Yet for a moment he is put off by Keiî, to whom he makes the following comparison, as Hartmann uses one of his characteristically homey nature allusions:

> "der humbel der sol stechen,
> ouch ist reht daz der mist
> stinke swâ der ist,
> der hornûz sol diezen"
> (ll. 206-9; "bumblebees sting, hornets buzz, and dung stinks wherever it is"—p. 57).[12]

For a moment Kâlogrenant does not wish to tell his tale. Is he perhaps "stung" by Keiî's mocking praise of his courtliness? Yet the Queen's request, which is actually an order ("'ez ist mîn bete und mîn gebot'"—l. 238; "'it is my wish and my will'"—p. 58) works to change his mind.

Thus, *Iwein* has begun with a verbal set-to between Keiî and Kâlogrenant, with auxiliary skirmishes between the Queen and Keiî. The argument that precedes Kâlogrenant's story[13] has done more than besmirch Keiî's character and reveal Arthur's court to be populated by bickering, sulky knights; dispute is established as a theme in the work. And Kâlogrenant's admonitory and clearly biblically-inspired injunction to listen well to his story serves as a preface to that story, a tale which itself presents two means of dealing with strife. The reader, if he/she takes seriously Kâlogrenant's admonition to listen closely, can see in the subsequent examples of the herdsman and the battling oxen (ll. 471ff.; p. 60) and the storm-making spring (ll. 568ff.; pp. 62-3) two distinct ways to settle strife, if he will but

>". . . merken unde dagen.
>maniger biuten diu ôren dar:
>ern nemes ouch mit dem herzen war,
>sone wirt im niht wan der dôz,
>und ist der schade alze grôz:
>wan si verliesent beide ir arbeit,
>der dâ hoeret und der dâ seit"
>   (ll. 250-6; ". . . keep still and pay attention.
>Some lend their ears, but if they do not understand
>with their hearts, it is only sound. And that is too
>bad, for both he who speaks and those who hear are
>merely wasting time"—p. 58).

Kâlogrenant's story functions as a type of parable.[14] The ears serve as a conduit to the heart of the listener. Drawing upon the function of parables for the Christian believer,[15] if correctly received, the parable/tale enters the listener's mind, and it fulfills its didactic purpose by affecting that mind in a positive way and leading it to understanding.[16] Meaning is embedded in the parable, meaning that is intelligible to those who possess the necessary understanding.

It is important to note that it is not only the reader who learns of Kâlogrenant's adventure for the first time (in that this is the first of several repetitons of the storm-making spring adventures),[17] but also Iwein. Iwein's reception of the tale demonstrates how the mind comes to shape what it perceives.[18] Kâlogrenant's story is a tale that Iwein mulls over in his head and even goes so far as to repeat in encapsulated form in his inner monologue, thus transforming the recounted event into contemplation of the event:

>"wand ich sol in disen drîn tagen
>des endes varn, und niemen sagen,

> in den walt ze Breziljân,
> suochen unz ich vunden hân
> den stîc den Kâlogrenant
> sô engen und sô rûhen vant.
> und dâ nâch sol ich schouwen
> die schoenen juncfrouwen,
> des êrbaeren wirtes kint,
> diu beidiu alsô hövesch sint.
> so gesihe ich, swenne ich scheide dan,
> den vil ungetânen man
> der dâ pfliget der tiere.
> dar nâch sô sihe ich schiere
> den stein und den brunnen:
> des müeze sî mir gunnen
> daz ich in eine begieze,
> ich entgeltes ode genieze"
> (ll. 923-40; "because I shall set out secretly within three days and search the forest of Breziljan until I find the narrow, overgrown path which Kalogrenant came upon. And then I shall see the beautiful girl and her father, the noble lord of the castle, both of whom are so courtly. When I leave there, I shall see the ugly man who takes care of the animals and, soon afterward, the stone and the spring. They cannot stop me from sprinkling it by myself, whether, for pain or pleasure"—p. 66).

The imagination rapidly traverses the verbal landscape detailed in Kâlogrenant's story, and, before Iwein undertakes his imagined and soon to be real adventure,[19] he, in effect, walks himself mentally over the terrain that Kâlogrenant has travelled on horseback. The thought fills his mind to the point that he becomes obsessed by it and resolves to act upon it—and to act upon it in such a manner that the outcome will differ from that experienced by Kâlogrenant.

Hartmann clearly shows which aspect of Kâlogrenant's story appeals to Iwein when he describes Iwein's actual adventure, for he devotes few lines (ll. 947-88; p. 66) to Iwein's encounter with the giant herdsman, whereas he describes Kâlogrenant's meeting with the same man in great detail (ll. 398-564; pp. 60-2). This distinction between Iwein's interests and those of Kâlogrenant comes in part from the former's fascination with fighting and the latter's more evident skill at tale-telling. The battle at the fountain, however, which lasted over ll. 565-722 in Kâlogrenant's account, receives considerable attention in Iwein's re-enactment of Kälogrenant's adventure and, because Iwein's physical prowess exceeds that of Kâlogrenant, is significantly extended beyond the confines of the fountain area into the very castle of the opponent (ll. 989ff.; p. 68).

Iwein's mental progress, however, lags behind that of Kâlogrenant, who has learned a lesson from his encounter that Iwein cannot learn from the mere hearing of it. To see the potential for learning in this lesson that Kâlogrenant gives to the court and that Iwein persists in learning not second-hand but rather through the "school of hard knocks" approach, let us examine the possibilities that events within Kâlogrenant's story present to the reader and to Iwein. In the first episode in which the rustic[20] converses with Kâlogrenant, the reader discerns more than mere jollity at the expense of the appearance of another person, whom Kâlogrenant initially fears may be subhuman ("'waz crêatiure bistû?'"—l. 487; "'what sort of creature are you?'"—p. 60), and particularly one of a lower social class. Clearly this "wild man" has mastery of his environment, regardless of what he may "be," and he controls forces—represented by disparate beasts—that could well wreak havoc if unleashed. Similarly, the scene does more than ironically comment on Kâlogrenant's devastating description of knightly âventiure:[21]

>"ich heize ein riter und hân den sin
>daz ich suochende rîte
>einen man der mit mir strîte,
>der gewâfent sî als ich.
>daz prîset in, ersleht er mich:
>gesige aber ich im an,
>so hât man mich vür einen man,
>und wirde werder danne ich sî"
>(ll. 530-7; "I am called a knight, and my purpose is to ride in search of a man who is armed like me and will fight with me. He will gain fame by defeating me, while if I win the victory, I shall be thought a valiant warrior and be esteemed more highly"—p. 61).

The scene focuses on the containment of warring elements held in an enclosure. The area in which the rustic is found forms a type of enclosure with distinct bounds ("ein breitez geriute"—l. 401; "a clearing"—p. 60) set in the midst of the forest, away from people ("âne die liute"—l. 402; "that showed no signs of human habitation"—p. 60). Moreover, the physical bounds of this cleared area are subordinate to the strong mental sense of enclosure effected by the herdsman, and Hartmann expands upon Chrétien when he allows Kâlogrenant to question why the animals do not run off:

>"sage, waz mac in gewerren
>dîn meisterschaft und dîn huote,
>sine loufen nâch ir muote
>ze walde und ze gefilde?
>wan ich sihe wol, sî sint wilde,
>sine erkennent man noch sîn gebot.
>ichn wânde niht daz âne got

> der gewalt ieman töhte
> dâr sî betwingen möhte
> âne sloz und âne bant"
>
> (ll. 496-505; "But tell me, how do your oversight and mastery prevent them from running off into the forest and field whenever they wish? For they are, after all, wild beasts, which are subject neither to man nor to his command. I wouldn't have thought that anyone but God Himself had the power to control them without chains or fetters"—p. 61).

Despite the strife of the animals, the herdsman maintains control over his beasts and presents such a demeanor that Kâlogrenant, in search of adventure (read: strife, because of ll. 503ff.; p. 61),[22] has no desire to join battle with him. Clearly, adventure seems to mean fighting not only with someone similarly armed but with someone against whom one has a fair chance of winning. Kâlogrenant has clearly weighed his chances in a fight with the giant herdsman, and physical battle is not an option. The two exchange words but not blows, and the Arthurian knight leaves the herdsman's territory unharmed, with a somewhat baffled herdsman wondering why anyone would want to seek such an adventure. He has obviously witnessed the same scene many times before, but its constant re-enactment nevertheless makes no sense. For each person, coming to wisdom is an individual journey, and the herdsman charts his itinerary in a clearing bounded by his mind, while the knights who pass through his territory and use him as a human signpost must chart their own courses, regardless of what wisdom the herdsman may offer them.

Kâlogrenant next proceeds to the charmed territory of the storm-making spring, which is a type of enclosure set off by itself: the spectacular storm is confined to a restricted area, a fact that the townspeople in that region later make clear in their contention that there are many wretched places in the world but no houses built at a worse spot (ll. 7812-5; pp. 145-6). Here, however, Kâlogrenant is the intruder who is rapidly dispatched by the knight controlling the area, and who is banished from that enclosure and from the mind of the defender. This scene is linked, through shared language, with the Mâbonagrîn episode in *Erec*. It is not merely that both the storm-making spring and the "boumgarten" ("orchard") are magical enclosures presided over by powerful men with beautiful wives, but also that both defenders of these enclosures have unusually loud voices. In *Iwein*, the audience is told concerning Ascalôn: "sîn stimme lûte sam ein horn" (l. 701; "his voice rang out like a horn"—p. 63), whereas in *Erec*, Mâbonagrîn's approach is similar:

> nû gehôrte er eine stimme
> starc unde grimme,
> diu lûte sam ein horn dôz

(ll. 8992-4; he heard a loud, fierce voice that sounded like a horn—p. 133).

But most significant is Mâbonagrîn's characterization of the orchard and Kâlogrenant's assessment of the fountain area as "daz ander paradîse" (*Erec*, l. 9542; "a second Garden of Eden"—p. 139; *Iwein*, l. 687; p. 63). The reader must ask why these episodes are so linked, why the one occurs at the romance's end and the other at the outset, and why Hartmann repeats and links significant details. It seems to me that Hartmann's repetition and linkage stem less from linguistic "givens" such as frozen phrases and descriptions but rather from an awareness of scenes in his own works that were written earlier. First, there is the sense that this linkage demonstrates contrast, so that *Erec's* protagonist defeats Mâbonagrîn and does not become just another head on a stake in Mâbonagrîn's outdoor trophy room, while Kâlogrenant in fact does go down to defeat. Yet, how can the contrast remain when Iwein succeeds in conquering the Knight of the Fountain and usurping his place? But it must be countered that the Joy of the Court episode is, for Erec, the culminating adventure, the one when he meets and defeats an opponent much like his unregenerate self. If Iwein *starts* with such a battle, in which he wins a woman and becomes attached to the land, as the new Knight of the Fountain, then it is as if Iwein puts himself in a position not unlike that to which Mâbonagrîn had pledged himself. And Mâbonagrîn is, at the end of *Erec*, ready to leave the enchanted boundaries of his "ander paradîse" (l. 9542). With Iwein, departure from this paradise comes precisely eighty opponents earlier than Mâbonagrîn's (Mâbonagrîn had eighty-one encounters, but Iwein only one, with Keiî, in Iwein's role as protector of the Fountain). Iwein will return to "paradîse," but it will not be until many days and many adventures have passed, and it may be assumed that Mâbonagrîn, given a romance of his own—which he is not—might travel an arduous road that leads back, in romance fashion, to his origins. We can only speculate about his story: it is one of the significant things that is "left out" in romances, because the focus is necessarily on the protagonist. Others' stories are just that—stories told on lazy afternoons or histories told after defeat.

Because, in this last work of Hartmann, Iwein's story is enacted on center stage, the reader learns his reaction when Kâlogrenant tells of what occurred to him. When Iwein responds to the account of the adventure that is ultimately to work such changes on him, he replies impetuously, much as Erec did. He is the first of the assembled knights and Queen to speak:

> er sprach "neve Kâlogrenant,
> ez richet von rehte mîn hant
> swaz dir lasters ist geschehen.
> ich wil ouch varn den brunnen sehen,
> und waz wunders dâ sî"

(ll. 805-9; "Cousin Kalogrenant, I, too, want to go and see the spring and its wonders, and my hand shall avenge you"—p. 64).

This statement provokes yet another outburst from Keiî, an oddly prophetic one this time, for the seneschal, after having attributed Iwein's desire to avenge Kâlogrenant to "one mug of wine" (l. 818; p. 64), urges:

> "slâfet ein lützel dar nâch.
> troume iu danne iht swâre,
> sô sult irs iu zewâre
> nemen eine mâze,
> ode vart iuwer strâze
> mit guotem heile"
> (ll. 828-833; "Sleep on it a little, and if you have a bad dream, you can be more restrained. If not, go your way with God's blessing"—pp. 64-5).

Iwein will sleep the sleep of madness ("'hân ich geslâfen unze her?'"—l. 3510; "'have I been sleeping until now?'"—p. 97), will dream ("'mir hât getroumet'"—l. 3517; "'I dreamed'"—p. 97), and will attain *mâze* ("measure") only after having travelled many a bewildering path. At this point in the narrative, however, Iwein only has access to Kâlogrenant's verbal account of his adventure and reacts to it in a characteristically impulsive fashion. He is faced with two possibilities of action, both of which detail methods of dealing with conflict (with respect to the herdsman, that of not entering into conflict at all, and with respect to the Knight of the Fountain, that of driving the intruder from his territory), and Iwein finds the latter possibility more to his liking, for he devotes only two lines (ll. 934-5; p. 66) in his mental itinerary to the herdsman.

One notes in this choice an apt characterization of Iwein's mind during the first part of the romance. His mind is a vessel that cannot long hold two disparate thoughts without a struggle that ejects one of them. What is particularly damning of Iwein's mental abilities in the earlier part of the work (before the winning of Laudîne) is the fact that Hartmann uses verbs to connote thinking only three times with reference to Iwein, and each time it is clear that it is either the thought of battle that has filled and taken possession of his mind: "'desn wirt nû niemen zuo gedâht /unz ichz hân volbrâht'" (ll. 941-2; "'No one will hear of this until I have done it'"—p. 66); "dô gedâht her Iwein, ob er in niht erslüege ode vienge" (ll. 1062-3; "It then occurred to Sir Iwein that, if he did not capture or slay him . . . ."—p. 67), or the startling consequences of being trapped after that battle ("nu gedâhter was im töhte"—l. 1148; "now [he] began to wonder what should be done"—p. 68). There is no prior contemplation of possible outcomes or even of the wisdom of joining battle in the first place. Iwein is no mental midget, but he is not one

at this point who can weigh possibilities and live with both of them
or even choose wisely between them. Given the possibility of
controlled dispute (the example set by the herdsman) or a dispute in
which one party triumphs over another (the conflict at the spring),
Iwein opts for the latter. In fact, the prospect of the latter drives
the former from his mind, and the herdsman becomes not an example,
as he was in Kâlogrenant's parabolic account, but a way-station on
the road to a more important adventure. Iwein fixes upon the idea
that has filled his mind. He finds those others who would act upon
his impulse definite irritations, particularly when Arthur swears
that he will visit the spring (l. 906; p. 65). At this time the
narrator comments on Iwein's state of mind:

> ez was dem hern Iwein ungemach,
> wand er sich hâte an genomen
> daz er dar eine wolde komen
> (ll. 908-10; Sir Iwein was displeased, as he
> had decided to go alone—p. 65).

Like Erec, he makes plans to leave the court under false pretenses,
telling neither knights nor the king (l. 924; p. 66) of his intent, and
the speed with which he hastens to his adventure is evident in the
few lines that are devoted to his progress to the fountain area. The
subsequent battle reflects the haste of Iwein's departure, as it is
completed with great rapidity. Iwein's overeagerness is
demonstrated, moreover, in the fact that he drives his opponent from
the battle arena and into his adversary's castle. He takes possession
of the fountain area and then, as an intruder in yet another enclosure
(the castle), appropriates it and the lady of the castle as well. The
manner in which Iwein comes to be Lord of the Fountain proves
significant, since it entails essentially two battles that must be won:
the actual strife at the spring, and the striving for Laudîne's
affection. In this matter Iwein has received considerably more than
he bargained for,[23] since Kâlogrenant's tale could not have prepared
him for the consequences of the defeat of Ascalôn. As far as Iwein
can be expected to reason (although there is no indication that he
even sees as a possibility *not* going out to avenge Kâlogrenant's
disgrace), the fountain affair is an opportunity for battle rather
much like any other opportunity the world of Arthurian romance
affords, except with some unsurpassed special effects in the way of
violent weather and unusual birdsong. What Iwein finds, however,
is a situation in which winning a physical battle is a mere prelude to
the task which will then face him: that of changing the mind of a
woman reported to be "unbekêriges muotes" (l. 1997; "of obdurate
mind"—my translation). Initially upon entering Ascalôn's castle,
Iwein's dilemma appears to revolve around the problem of escaping,
as he is, significantly, caught between two portals. The intruder, he
is now captive, and his thoughts are only of how to escape:

> dô suochter wider unde vür
> und envant venster noch tür
> dâ er ûz möhte.
> nu gedâhter waz im töhte
> (ll. 1145-8; Iwein looked all around without finding either window or door from which to escape, and then began to wonder what should be done—p. 68).

What is curious is the fact that Iwein fails to see both the door by which Lûnete enters and the window that she later opens. This oversight lends credence to the concept of enclosure as mind, for Lûnete's entrance is virtually like a thought popping into Iwein's mind, and her opening of a door and a window accordingly bears perceptual implications.

Iwein's first sight of Laudîne emphasizes her attractiveness: "daz er nie wîbes lîp / also schoenen gesach" (ll. 1308-9; "the most beautiful woman he had ever seen"—p. 70). Later, the narrator notes:

> swâ ir der lîp blôzen schein,
> da ersach sî der herre Iwein;
> da was ir hâr und ir lîch
> sô gar dem wunsche glîch
> daz im ir minne
> verkêrte die sinne,
> daz er sîn selbes gar vergaz
> (ll. 1331-7; Sir Iwein caught glimpses of her bare form, and her hair and body were so beautiful that love robbed him of reason, to the point that he quite forgot himself —p. 71).

The passage not only recalls the transformation undergone by Heinrich when he sees the naked maiden and changes his mind, but also looks back to a more involved passage in *Erec* (ll. 3691-3721; pp. 72-3), where the lecherous count is overpowered by "diu kreftige minne" (l. 3692; "Mighty Love"—p. 72), which "robbed him of his reason" (l. 3693; p. 72). In Iwein's case, the sight of Laudîne instills in him an inclination that allows him to disregard his dangerous situation, and he nearly runs to the grief-stricken widow. Lûnete's intervention paints Iwein's proposed course of action in terms of thought and wisdom/folly, once again stressing aspects of mind: "'wes was iu gedâht? / waere iuwer gedanc volbrâht'" (ll. 1493-4; "Where did you get such an idea"—p. 73); "'swes sin aber sô stât'" (l. 1502; "he whose mind is such"—p. 73); "'sînen muot'" (l. 1505; [here] "every idle thought"—p. 73); "'gedenket ir deheiner tumpheit / der muot sî gar hin geleit'" (ll. 1507-8; "If some folly occurs to you, put it aside"—p. 73); "'hât ab ir deheinen wîsen muot'" (l. 1509; "but if you have a clever idea"—p. 73);   "'verdenket'" (l. 1517;   "get suspicious"—p. 73); and:

> "er ist ein vil *wîser* man
> der *tumben gedanc verdenken* kan
> mit *wîslîcher* tât"
>   (ll. 1499-1501, my italics; "It is a wise man who can put an end to foolish whims with sensible deeds"—pp. 72-3).[24]

The effect is much stronger than in the related scene in *Der arme Heinrich*, where the protagonist tries gently to dissuade the maiden from what he feels is rash action, but the basic situation is nevertheless the same: often one does not realize the consequences of acting upon the first thought that occurs.

Another thought comes to Iwein's mind at this point, and a conflict typical to the work begins:

> swie im sîne sinne
> von der kraft der minne
> vil sêre waeren überladen,
> doch gedâht er an einen schaden,
> daz er niht überwunde
> den spot den er vunde,
> sô er sînen gelingen
> mit deheinen schînlîchen dingen
> ze hove erziugen möhte,
> waz im danne töhte
> elliu sîn arbeit
> er vorhte eine schalkheit:
> er weste wol daz Keiî
> in niemer gelieze vrî
> vor spotte und vor leide.
> dise sorgen beide
> die tâten im gelîche wê
>   (ll. 1519-35; Although the power of love had captured his mind, he still remembered one misfortune: that he could not disarm the mockery he would encounter at court when he could not produce any visible proof of his success and that, therefore, all his trouble would be for nothing. He was afraid of the ill nature of Keii, who, he knew, would never spare him scorn and spite. These two cares brought him like pain at first —p. 73).

This duality of mind subsequently occurs in the pairs of oppositions that crowd Iwein's thoughts (love and mortal hatred—ll. 1612, 1613 and p. 74; happiness and trouble—l. 1692 and p. 75; joyfulness and distress—l. 1696 and p. 75). These are not merely conventionalities, like the *liep/leit* ("love"/"pain"/"distress") juxtaposition so common in Middle High German, but are also basic formulations of how Iwein's mind works, for, given these dualities, Iwein's mind will strive to reduce the two things to one ("der zweier einez tuo"—l. 1650; "one of two things"—p. 74). Accordingly, thoughts of Keiî's scorn, which earlier motivated Iwein to give chase to Ascalôn, are relinquished. Hartmann succinctly notes: "vrou Minne nam die obern hant" (l. 1537; "Lady Love got the upper hand"—p. 73). Iwein's mind is made up, and the matters which once loomed so large (his concern that he have a battle token to confound Keiî,[25] and his worry over his escape from confinement) retreat into insignificance as that conflict is resolved by the thought of the woman taking precedence. The thought of her fills his mind as the sight of her delights his eyes.[26]

With respect to winning Laudîne, Hartmann maintains his interest in conflict within the enclosure of the mind, conflict caused by the introduction of a foreign element (in Laudîne's case, the thought of the man soon to be her next husband) into one's consciousness. This foreign element quickly overcomes the resistance it meets and controls the mind.[27] In this respect Laudîne is very much like Iwein—but one indication that the two are suited for each other.[28] They both approach conflict and strife in the same manner; given a conflict, one side triumphs and the other vanishes. Moreover, both are described in terms of duality of mind, but in a slightly different fashion ("zorn unde drô"—l. 2001; "anger and threats"—p. 79; "schande unde schaden"—l. 2029; "shame and harm"—p. 79). Over and above the similarities, however, there are significant differences between the mind of the woman and the mind of the man. Hartmann draws a noteworthy distinction between the sexes with respect to the facility with which women can change their minds. Hartmann's many remarks concerning women, statements that the modern reader would certainly consider disparaging, are not intended to be so. Rather, they appear surprisingly positive given the context of *Iwein*. Although women are branded as mentally fickle at the outset of one of Hartmann's commentaries, the poet staunchly defends their ability to change their mind by the end of the passage:

>swie sî ir die wârheit
>ze rehte hâte underseit
>und sî sich des wol verstuont,
>doch tete sî sam diu wîp tuont:
>sî widerredent durch ir muot
>daz sî doch ofte dunket guot.
>daz sî so dicke brechent
>diu dinc diu sî versprechent,
>da schiltet si vil maneger mite:
>do dunket ez mich ein guot site.
>er missetuot, der daz seit,
>ez mache ir unstaetekeit:
>ich weiz baz wâ vonz geschiht

> daz man sî alsô dicke siht
> in wankelem gemüete
> ez kumet von ir güete.
> man mac sus übel gemüete
> bekêren wol ze güete
> unde niht von güte
> bringen ze übelem gemüete.
> diu wandelunge diu ist guot:
> ir deheiniu ouch anders niht entuot.
> swer in danne unstaete giht,
> des volgaere enbin ich niht:
> ich wil in niuwan guotes jehen.
> allez guot müez in geschehen
> (ll. 1863-1888[29]; When the lady heard this clear statement of the facts and saw it to be such, she still did as women do: their feelings often make them oppose that which they really think best. A lot of people blame them because many times they do things which before they had rejected, but it seems to me a good custom. He who says it is because they are fickle is wrong. I know why they so often waver back and forth: it comes from their goodness. One can therefore change a false notion of theirs to a right one, but not a right one to a false. Such changes of mind are good and no woman have any other. I do not agree with him who says they are inconstant and I speak only well of them. May everything good come to them! —p. 77).

It may be hazarded, on the basis of statements about femininity in the work,[30] that a woman's mind is virtually the only arena for conflict over which she can assuredly exercise power. Words, not arms, are her weapons.[31] The issue of femininity repeatedly arises in the arguments between women and in their inner monologues. Lûnete repeatedly cites femininity as the manifestation of Laudîne's lack of power ("'ez ist wîplich daz ir claget'"—l. 1800; "'ir sprechet eht als ein wîp'"—l. 1921; "'ir sît ein wîp'"—l. 1955; "'You lament as a woman should'"—p. 76; "'You talk just like a woman'"—p. 78; "'Even though you are a woman'"—p. 78), so often that Laudîne refers to her own actions as "'harte unwîplich'" (l. 2299; "'most unwomanly'"—p. 83) and "'der wîbe site'" (l. 2329; "'women's custom'"—p. 83) at those times when she exerts power over Iwein. Similarly, at the end of the work, when Lûnete demurs at advising Laudîne, there is a sense that women wield considerable power:

> si sprach "vrouwe, ir hât den rât
> der iu wol baz ze staten stât.
> ich bin ein wîp, naem ich mich an
> ze râtenne als ein wîser man,

sô waer ich tumber danne ein kint"
(ll. 7849-53; "Lady," said the girl, "you surely have an adviser who is better suited. I am only a woman and would be more foolish than a child if I presumed to give advice like a wise man"—p. 146).

Lûnete, "diu wîse maget" (l. 1758; "the clever girl"—p. 76) who possesses "vil guoten witzen" (1. 2721; "with her cleverness"—p. 88), well knows that her function is precisely that of an advice-giver, and her advice is taken nearly every time she offers it. Women may not be able to effect change on the battlefield, but they get what they want by other means. They may have to press charges, as in the case of the younger sister at the end of the work, or they may have to rely on men to fight battles for them,[32] but they quite clearly know how to manipulate others to achieve their ends.

Women have control over more than their own minds in another sense, for they are able to change profoundly the minds of others and to change them toward the good, an ability of which Hartmann approves. Love is the means by which women can transform men's minds ("minne / verkêrten die sinne"—ll. 1335-6; "Love robbed him of reason"—p. 71), and the change of mind is positive. For example, the Arthurian court laments concerning Iwein's fortunes:

> swie manhaft er doch waere
> und swie unwandelbaere
> an lîbe unde an sinne,
> doch meister vrou Minne
> daz im ein krankez wîp
> verkêrte sinne unde lîp.
> der ie ein rehter adamas
> riterlicher tugende was,
> der lief nû harte balde
> ein tôre in dem walde
> (ll. 3252-60; He was a proven, fearless warrior, but as brave as he was and as steadfast in body and spirit, still Lady Love enabled a frail woman to turn both upside down, for he who had been a diamond of knightly virtue was now rushing wildly about in the forest, a fool—p. 94).

But when one recalls that it is the Arthurian court[33] that has led Iwein away from Laudîne, the truth of Iwein's condition becomes questionable. When the positive effects of Iwein's madness can be assessed, one sees that Laudîne's ability to affect Iwein's mind is beneficial rather than detrimental. Woman has the ability to bring order as well as chaos to man's mind, and in *Iwein* the arena of mind is the enclosure in which she can fight and win her battles.

In this process of causing a man's mind to dwell on thoughts of love and a woman, Lûnete plays a pivotal role,[34] for she manipulates the minds of her lady and soon-to-be lord and also embodies Iwein's and Laudîne's thoughts of each other as the love affair develops. Laudîne has entered Iwein's mind, and he hers, and Lûnete charts the process whereby each mind is changed concerning the other (ll. 2101-3; p. 80). Lûnete is a vehicle, a go-between who plants seeds in the lovers' minds by talking to them, and is the one who repeatedly tells the one what is on the other's mind. Her initial success in this role is signalled by Laudîne's acceptance of Iwein (l. 2333; p. 83) and by the court's equally surprising reception (ll. 2371ff.; p. 84) of the man who had not only murdered Ascalôn but had also violated the sanctuary of the castle. That the court is able to do this depends directly upon a quality of mind that the members of the court share with their lady and her new lord: they can easily forget and can let one thing (or man) slip out of mind and allow another to enter to take its place. As Hartmann notes as the wedding is celebrated: "des tôten ist vergezzen" (l. 2435; "the dead man was forgotten"—p. 85). The court and its liegemen behave, indeed, as if Ascalôn had never existed.

The process whereby the memory of Ascalôn is driven from the minds of Laudîne and her courtiers is tightly bound up in the concept of mind as enclosure for strife, and this in turn is linked to the storm-making spring, so that the mental and physical landscapes converge in the person of Laudîne. Hartmann explicitly links the land with Laudîne. Iwein is given "vrouwen und lant" (l. 2420; "both lady and land"—p. 84), and Gâwein thrice describes Iwein's achievement as having won "'eine künegîn und ein lant'" (l. 2880; "'a beautiful wife, a rich land'"—p. 88), "'ein schoene wîp / ein rîchez lant'" (ll. 2747-8; "'a beautiful woman and a land'"—p. 89), and "'ein schoene wîp und ein lant'" (l. 2782; "'a beautiful woman and a land'"—p. 89). Iwein himself describes his battle prize as "'ein vrouwen und ein rîchez lant'" (l. 3528; "'a rich land and a wife'"—p. 97).[35] Since the person of Laudîne is linked with the territory, one may examine the symbolic implications of the winning of the woman/land. For Laudîne, Iwein can be seen not only as a new challenger for the possession of the storm-making spring but also as a new thought appearing on the horizon of her mind, a thought that enters the mind (the area of the spring) and promptly creates chaos. The thought (read: Ascalôn) that had previously occupied the mind enters into contention with the intruding thought but is overcome and driven out. In the process, Laudîne, once "unbekêriges muotes" (l. 1997; "[Lunete] could not change the lady's mind"— p. 79; lit.: "of unchangeable, obdurate mind"), changes her mind. Lûnete, manifestation of the thought of Iwein, states succinctly:

"ez dunket mich guot
und gan iu wol daz ir den muot
so schone hât verkêret"

> (ll. 2101-3; "I think it is a good idea," said the
> girl, "and I am glad for your sake that you have had
> so happy a change of mind"—p. 80).

After much consideration, Laudîne has given in to Lûnete's reasoning,[36] which is cleverly grounded in the outcome of physical conflict:

> "nû erteilet mir (ir sît ein wîp),
> swâ swêne vehtent umbe den lîp,
> weder tiurre sî, der dâ gesige
> oder der dâ siglos gelige"
> (ll. 1955-8; "Even though you are a woman, you
> can decide this: when two men engage in mortal
> combat, who is the best warrior, the victor or he who
> lies defeated on the field?"—p. 78).

Indeed, the result of the strife at the spring has already decided the mental outcome. Iwein has gained a land through armed conflict; he has gained Laudîne.

Moreover, through details of language, Hartmann makes a telling point in this matter of the man gaining the woman and the land. One recalls that Iwein's first speech after Kâlogrenant's tale was one of intent: "'ich wil ouch varn den brunnen sehen'" (l. 808; "I, too, want to go and see the spring'"—p. 64). This matter of intent is significantly picked up in Laudîne's and Iwein's subsequent interchange: "'swie ir welt, also wil ich / welt ir allez daz ich wil'" (ll. 2290-1, my italics; "'Your will shall be my will'"—p. 83). It is sounded again in a pun when Laudîne exults after the wedding and Arthur's arrival at her court: "si gedâhte: 'ich hân wol gewelt'" (l. 2682; "'I have chosen well,' she thought"—p. 88), where the overt, correct meaning of "choice" still allows for the echo of another word with similar form: "wellen" in the sense of "wollen" is evoked as well as the primary meaning of the verb "weln/wellen" ("to choose"). This shared sense of will, of intent, and of wanting, coupled with Hartmann's reference to "ein ros daz willeclîchen gat" (l. 2395; "however eager a horse may be"—p. 84) and the admission that Laudîne "wolt in doch genomen hân" (l. 2402; "she would have taken him anyway"—p. 84), even if her courtiers had objected, makes clear that will, desire, and sensuality play large roles in Iwein's and Laudîne's union (l. 2339; p. 83). Iwein repeatedly talks of the "advice" his heart and eyes gave him in making his decision (forms of "râten" appear in ll. 2348, 2349, 2352, 2353, 2354; pp. 83-4), yet this seeming emphasis on rationality is illusory on her "schoene und anders niht" (l. 2355; "no[thing] other than your beauty"—p. 84). Had Iwein been able to think rationally, he might have reasoned that union with this woman is perhaps not in his immediate best interest, given his appetite for adventure.

Iwein does not consciously know that he has acted precipitously in marrying, but his receptivity to other possibilities proves to be telling. At this point he is not prepared to let the marriage bed be his only battleground, as indicated by the accessibility of his mind to Gâwein's persuasive, enticing reasoning. Hartmann couches Gâwein's argument in the dual language of physical significance/figurative implication. "'Kêrt ez niht allez an gemach'" (1. 2791; "'Don't turn wholly to a life of ease'"—p. 89), urges Gâwein, and ease harks back to the marriage chamber (Lexer: "gemach" = "Ruhe"—"ease"—as well as "Zimmer"—"room"). Reference is made to Erec, "der sich ouch alsô manigen tac / durch vrouwen Enîten verlac" (ll. 2793-4; "who was idle for a long time because of Lady Enite"— p. 89). Iwein is urged to consider ("'dâ gedenket an'"—l. 2884; "'think of this'"— p. 90), and the uncontrolled strife of the mind is seen to begin again, as the thought of adventure takes precedence over the thought of a woman. It is not farfetched that Gâwein's long speech to Iwein (ll. 2770-2912; pp. 89-90) actually mirrors Iwein's own attitude toward the conflict between fulfilling his knightly duties and being Laudîne's spouse.[37] By characterizing Laudîne in Gâwein's words as "'ein wîp die man hat erkant / in alsô staetem muote'" (ll. 2890-1; "'a wife who has shown herself to be so steadfast'"—p. 90), Hartmann seems to be playing upon what is at once a false perception. Laudîne has, in fact, only recently changed her mind to accept Iwein, and she has always only been "steadfast" to the "man of the moment"—as well as a fundamentally true assessment and a foreshadowing of Laudîne's character for the rest of the romance. Once she has changed her mind in favor of Iwein, she will not be able to change it again. She has regrets, as evidenced in her comment after Iwein has received her permission (by getting her to promise to grant him what he wants *before* he tells her what that wish is—ll. 2916-8; p. 90) to go "turnieren" ("journey to tournaments"—p. 90): "si sprach 'daz sold ich ê bewarn'" (l. 2922; "'I shouldn't have been so hasty,' she said"— p. 90). Yet she recognizes the hold this man has over her (l. 2947; p. 91) and sends him off with an admonition to return to her in a year and with a ring that guarantees its wearer "'senften muot'" (l. 2954; "'content'"—p. 91).

After Iwein departs to ride "the tournament circuit,"[38] no new thought (man) replaces him in Laudîne's mind. Iwein forgets but Laudîne does not, although she does attempt to drive her husband from her mind. That she is not successful is reinforced by the fact that no new man (thought) comes to disturb the spring in Iwein's absence. Laudîne is forced to engage in a period of recollection and remembrance, which one can expect to be extremely difficult for her, since we have primarily seen her as being adept at forgetting and not at remembering. Iwein, too, demonstrates a certain ability for selective forgetting and for using battles as a way to forget, to banish troublesome thoughts. Before we turn to his ultimate inability to forget Laudîne, let us briefly consider his reason for coming to the fountain in the first place and his actions there, for they will show

how the fountain changes meaning for him over the course of the romance, as it keeps pace with changes in his mind. Initially Iwein pays lip service to the idea that he wishes to go to the fountain to avenge the disservice done to his kinsman (ll. 805-7; p. 64), but he adds: "'ich wil ouch varn den brunnen sehen, / und waz wunders da sî'" (ll. 808-9; "'I, too, want to go and see the spring and its wonders'"—p. 64), and one senses that self-interest plays a role.[39] After Keiî's sarcastic rejoinder to Iwein, a third element enters into play, which proves to be the overriding factor in Iwein's motivations: he wants to revenge himself upon Keiî and states: "'ouch enhebet er niht den strît / der den êrsten slac gît'" (ll. 871-2; "'Moreover, the man who strikes out does not start a dispute if the other lets it go'"—p. 65).

After Iwein has won the fountain area for his own, Hartmann shows him facing Keiî in that very enclosure and defeating him soundly. It is as if Keiî's words have penetrated Iwein's mind more than Kâlogrenant's have touched him, and Iwein works to drive Keiî out of the enclosure of his mind (which is now synonymous with the fountain area, since he has won it). It is noteworthy that Keiî henceforth causes no more problems for Iwein. Having vanquished him in battle, Iwein has promptly banished him from his mind. Iwein, however, leaves the area of the fountain and, once it is out of sight, it is, in effect, out of his mind.[40] Lest this assessment be branded a modern formulation, it is important to note that a Middle High German proverb to that effect existed, and reference to it is twice made in *Das (zweite) Büchlein*, which was for a time ascribed to Hartmann. In the first instance the narrator refers to "uz ougen uz muote" (l. 673; "out of sight, out of mind"), and then subsequently notes: "der alte spruch der entouc an mir, / daz uz ougen daz uz muote" (ll. 722-3; "the old proverb that was not valid with respect to me, 'out of sight, out of mind'"). The proverb's import is more than valid in Iwein's case. He does not remember the spring's defence or the woman who is thus to be protected; indeed, Hartmann does not show Iwein *remembering* anything while he is occupied with tournaments. Hartmann fills the year of Iwein's camping out with Gâwein in any number of places where jousting could occur (l. 3067; p. 92) with very little mention of Iwein. Rather, there is a lengthy and pointed interchange between "Hartman" and "vrou Minne," followed by commentary (ll. 2971-3028; pp. 91-2), and then a paean to Gâwein (ll. 3029-38; p. 92) that is succeeded by a brief account of Iwein's activities with his friend and jousting companion (ll. 3039-81; p. 92). Iwein has no reported thoughts.[42] In fact, to highlight Iwein's mental state, in which Laudîne is shown to have vanished from his mind, Hartmann points out that his hero "der jârzal vergaz" (l. 3055; "he forgot about the deadline"—p. 92), and then shortly thereafter allows Iwein to have his first thought in several hundred lines: "er gedâhte, daz twelen waer ze lanc, / daz er von sînem wîbe tete" (ll. 3084-5; "he had been away from his wife for a long time"— p. 92). This thought is "ein[] senede[r] gedanc" (l. 3083; "love's desire"—p.

92; lit.: "a longing thought"), which harks back to when Iwein hid his distress upon leaving Laudîne ("daz senen bedaht her Iwein / als er dô beste kunde"—ll. 2962-3; "Sir Iwein concealed his pain as best he could"—p. 91) and looks forward to the proverb voiced after the maiden has tipped the salve box into the stream:

> niemen hâbe seneden muot
> umbe ein verlorenez guot
> des man niht wider müge hân
>   (ll. 3691-3; It's useless to grieve over lost goods which can't be regained—p. 99).

This proverb is applicable as well to Iwein, who fears that he will never regain Laudîne's favor. Iwein's sudden thought comes as a surprise to both the audience and the protagonist. It strikes him speechless: "daz er sîn selbes vergaz / und allez swîgende saz" (ll. 3091-2; "he sat silently, like a fool"—p. 92; lit.: "that he forgot himself and sat silently").[43]

So intertwined are the mental and physical landscapes that Iwein's thought is immediately reinforced by the appearance of a reproachful Lûnete, the corporeal representation of Laudîne's thought of Iwein and Iwein's sudden remembrance of Laudîne. Laudîne, in the guise of Lûnete, is the thought that will return again and again to Iwein's mind. Significantly, Lûnete does not upbraid him on this occasion for his forgetfulness; she has no need of doing so, for her very presence signals his remembrance of his obligations. She does, however, chide him for his thoughts toward her: "'Wan gedâht ir doch dar an / waz ich iu gedienet hân?'" (ll. 3140-1; "'Why didn't you at least remember what I did for you?'"—p. 93), but the simple fact is that Iwein has not *thought* at all. She takes back his ring, and with it his false sense of good fortune and content (l. 2954; p. 91), bows quickly to the king, and is gone as quickly as she appeared.

Iwein's immediate response to Lûnete's reproach is self-loathing (ll. 3225-6; p. 94)[44] and madness, which is described in terms of a conflict in the mind ("daz im in daz hirne schôz / ein zorn und ein tobesuht"—ll. 3232-3; "rage and madness seized his brain"—p. 94), succeeded by an absence of thought (ll. 3399ff.; pp. 94-5). His only concern is with his physical sustenance ("in ist niht mêre witze kunt / niuwan diu eine umbe den munt"—ll . 3269-70; "he lacks wits except to attend to the needs of his mouth"—my translation), and he reverts to a primitive state. In fact, Hartmann shows how the inner man works upon the outer man when he describes Iwein's condition in terms of mind and body: "er lief nû nacket beider / der sinne und der cleider" (ll. 3359-60; lit: "he ran off, naked of both senses and clothes"—my translation).[45]

Naked, of both clothes and sensibility, Iwein manages to provide himself with bow and arrows, with which he kills such game as he can find. He encounters a hermit, who strikes a bargain with him: he provides Iwein with bread and water, and, because "der tôre und diu kint / vil lîhte ze wenenne sint" (ll. 3321-2; "children and fools adapt themselves easily"—p. 95), Iwein responds with "ein tier" (l. 3326; here: "a deer"—p. 95) heaved up against the hermit's door. The hermit is obviously a man of "bedâhter sich" ("sensibility") (l. 3300; "At last he thought of something"—p. 95), while Iwein at this stage is not a thinking being. He is called "der unwîse" (l. 3345; lit.: "the un-wise one"), "der edel tôre" (l. 3347; "the noble madman"—p. 95) who was once but is no longer "hövesch unde wîse" (l. 3356; "clever and courtly"—p. 95). He is sane enough that he can feed himself, but he does nothing more than hunt, eat, and sleep. Indeed, he is found (l. 3362; p. 95) and recognized (ll. 3376, 3381; p. 96) by three ladies while he sleeps in the forest (ll. 3438, 3459; pp. 95-6), an apt physical description of his mental state. Diagnosed to be suffering from a "suht" (l. 3420; "sickness"—p. 96), in particular a "hirnsühte" (l. 3427; "a brain ailment"—p. 96), he is cured by judicious, if over-eager, application of salve prepared by none other than Feimorgan (ll. 3423-4; p. 96), who, it will be recalled, fashioned the plaster for Erec when he spent an unwilling night at Arthur's peripatetic court. What is worth noting is that the salve box is totally emptied (l. 3480; p. 97) so that it, as vessel and enclosure, is poured out in order that Iwein's mind might once again be filled.

Moreover, the rapidity of Iwein's recovery builds on the concept that Hartmann has previously explored in *Der arme Heinrich*. A cure does not occur instantaneously. Iwein's return to his former status is effected in stages. The restoration of his body, accomplished in the scene in which Iwein is anointed and provided with new clothes, is followed by the restoration of the mind, brought about in a long lament (ll. 3509ff.; pp. 97f.) that is pure recollection and consideration,[47] both of which are activities that Iwein has not cultivated in the past. Iwein's assumption of the new clothes is capped by the use of the term "bedahte" (l. 3595; "covered"—p. 98). At this point I should also like to note that the word "bedahte" also deserved consideration in the scene in which Kâlogrenant arrives at the fountain. When Kâlogrenant enters the fountain area and pours water from a vessel onto the rock, a storm is produced that strips the linden tree of its leaves. There is a subsequent period of calm, during which the birds return: "ez wart von ir gevidere / diu linde anderstunt bedaht" (ll. 680-1; "their feathers again covering the linden"—p. 63). The linkage to the madness/restoration of the mind sequence is implicit, for in both instances conflict results in a stripping away of the exterior (leaves, clothes) and an ultimate re-covering of the exterior (birds, new clothes). The linden and Iwein recover, and this is signalled by the fact that they are re-covered.

Iwein does begin to "put on" understanding as if a new garment, so that references to "dâhte," "bedâhte," and "muot" begin to appear, and often with respect to battles and conflicts.[48] Described as "hövesch, biderbe und wîs" (l. 3752; "brave, courtly, and wise"—p. 99), Iwein first dispatches Count Aliers and then considerately spurns the offer of the lady of Narisôn, whose mind is set on him ("wand an in stuont al ir muot"—l. 3807; "because she was in love with him"—p. 100), but his mind is turned to the forest path, so that, as soon as he can, he looks for "the first road he found" (l. 3826; p. 100). Moreover, he begins to think before he acts. In the clearing (l. 3837; p. 100) where the lion and the dragon fight, Hartmann depicts Iwein reflecting ("und bedahte sich daz er wolde / helfen dem edelen tiere"—ll. 3848-9; "decided to aid the noble beast"—p. 101), dismounting, and then aiding the lion. Hartmann then describes Iwein: "doch dâht er als ein vrum man" (l. 3861; "as a brave man"—p. 101), and the lion, earlier the underdog in the fight (ll. 3841-5; p. 101), triumphs with Iwein's aid. Iwein has thus weighed the possibilities and benefited accordingly from this consideration.

Along with his newfound circumspection with regard to battle and strife[49] comes a renewed memory of his wife, and the fountain thus appears precisely when he needs it:

> dô truoc in diu geschiht
> (wande ern versach sichs niht)
> vil rehte an sîner vrouwen lant,
> dâ er den selben brunnen vant,
> von dem im was geschehen,
> als ich iu ê hân verjehen,
> grôz heil und michel ungemach.
> als er die linden drobe sach,
> und dô im dâ zuo vor schein
> diu kapelle und der stein,
> dô wart sîn herze des ermant
> wie er sîn êre und sîn lant
> haete verlorn und sîn wîp.
> des wart sô riuwec sîn lîp
> von jâmer wart im alsô wê,
> daz er vil nâch als ê
> von sînem sinne was komen
> (ll. 3923-39; As fate quite unexpectedly led him straight to his lady's country, where he found the same spring which—as I have already told you—brought him both great happiness and bitter sorrow. When he saw the linden above it and when the chapel and the stone appeared before him, his heart was reminded of how he had lost honor, land, and wife. He became so sad and tormented by grief that he almost lost his mind again—pp. 101-2).

Iwein very nearly loses his mind again—and the lion, in what must be one of the most truly comic/serious scenes in Middle High German literature, contemplates suicide, overcome by leonine mental distress (l. 3950; p. 102)—and recovers himself in time to stop the lion from killing himself. Iwein muses on the loyal action of the lion and comes to the conclusion that its behavior should be emblematic for his future actions:

> "ich solt es ouch selbe buoze enpfân
> (nu gît mir doch des bilde
> dirre lewe wilde,
> daz er von herzeleide sich
> wolde erstechen umbe mich,
> daz rehtiu triuwe nâhen gât),
> sît mir mîn selbes missetât
> mînen vrouwen hulde,
> und dehein ir schulde,
> ân aller slahte nôt verlôs,
> und weinen vür daz lachen kôs"
> (ll. 4000-10; "Since I have done this to myself—since it was my own misdeed and no fault of hers that caused me quite needlessly to lose the affection of my lady and to exchange laughter for tears—I should be punished for it. The wild lion who wanted to kill himself because of grief for me has shown me that true loyalty is no small thing"—p. 102).

And thought of Laudîne immediately produces that emissary of Laudîne's mind, Lûnete. Judging by Lûnete's imprisonment and the collective unrest in the court, Laudîne's mind has run a good deal on Iwein's absence, and Lûnete has been perceived by her mistress as reminding her of Iwein more than she cares to be reminded of him. Lûnete and Iwein engage in an odd bit of one-upmanship over who has suffered the most, until Iwein concedes that Lûnete is in worse straits than he is and abandons the argument (l. 4075; p. 103). Her lament is characterized by her fear that she is lost ("'ich armiu verlorne'"—l. 4139; "'forsaken'"—p. 104; "'ich hân mich selben verlorn'"—l. 4145; "'unfortunately, that's what I did'"—p. 104) and by her certainty that Iwein or Gâwein would help her, if either knew of her predicament (l. 4095; p. 103). Iwein's immediate query, "'welhen Iwein meinet ir'" (l. 4179; "'Which Iwein do you mean?'"—p. 104) is neither teasing nor deliberately retarding but rather straightforward and ironic at the same time. There *is* more than one Iwein in Arthur's realm,[50] and Iwein himself can be said to have gone through an identity crisis, so that the Iwein at the outset of the romance is not the same person as Iwein at its conclusion. Iwein agrees to help Lûnete, yet the motivation he offers for his aid leaves Lûnete little hope that she will survive her ordeal. Iwein, in effect, intends to die in the process of defeating Lûnete's enemies,[51] as he feels that he has forever lost Laudîne's favor (l. 4216; p. 105). He repeatedly voices this contention (ll. 4235, 4237, 4258; pp. 104-5), to the point that the reader feels the uneasiness that must certainly be afflicting Lûnete, for she is next seen to be nervously chattering about the absent Gawein:

> si sprach "haet ich den vunden,
> sô haet ich überwunden
> mîne sorgen zehant"
> (ll. 4285-7; "My worries would have been over at once. That I didn't find him . . ."—p. 106).

Implicitly, had the absent Gâwein been at Arthur's court—he was giving chase to the knight to whom Arthur had foolishly entrusted the Queen—she would rather have had his hearty aid and flattery than Iwein's morose vows to die in the process of vindicating her. She voices her fears obliquely in a speech that is deliberately reminiscent of Enîte's "'wir wegen ungelîche'" speech (ll. 3173ff. pp. 66ff.) in *Erec*:

> sî sprach "lieber herre,
> sô stüende iuch alze verre
> enwâge ein alsô vorder lîp
> umb ein alsus armez wîp.
> mir waere der rede gar ze vil,
> und wizzet daz ich iemer wil
> den willen vür die werc hân,
> ir sult der rede sîn erlân.
> iuwer leben ist nützer danne daz mîn.
> und möht ez ein wâge sîn,
> sô getorst ich sin wol biten:
> diz ist gar wider den siten
> daz einer kempfe drî man.
> diu liute habent sich joch dar an
> daz zwêne sîn eines her.
> sô waere diz gar âne wer.
> verlürt ir durch mich den lîp,
> sone wart nie dehein armez wîp
> so unsaelec als ich,
> und dannoch slüegen sî ouch mich.
> so ist bezzer mîn verderben
> danne ob wir beidiu sterben"
> (ll. 4315-36; "Dear sir," she answered, "it would be a mistake to risk so worthy a life for such a poor woman; this is too much for me to ask. I'll accept the intent in place of the deed and release you from your promise, for your life is of more use than mine. People claim that even two are too many, so this would be no contest at all. If you were to lose your life, then they would kill me also. It is better for me to perish alone than for us both to die"—p. 106).

For a moment, the outcome weighs in the balance (and the proximity of "'enwâge ich'"—l. 4317 ("'to risk'"—p. 106; and "'eine wage'"—l. 4324; "'equal'"—p. 106 reinforce this impression), and the reader hears Lûnete suggest: "'so ist bezzer mîn verderben / danne ob wir beidiu sterben'" (ll. 4335-6; "'It is better for me to perish alone than for us both to die'"—p. 106). Lûnete, in effect, is persuading Iwein toward living, rather than dying, and she is doing it, even in her desperate circumstances (although, why doesn't Iwein simply free her from her prison?) because she trusts her ability to give advice and influence outcomes. Accordingly, by the end of Iwein's meeting with Lûnete, the scales tip toward life rather than death, with Iwein speaking of slaying her enemies rather than killing himself.

Hard upon Iwein's promise to Lûnete follows a closely timed[52] series of adventures in which Iwein each time enters an enclosure/castle/battle arena and delivers those within, but fights, as critics have noted, for the right instead of the wrong reasons.[53] Iwein's saving of Lûnete involves a return to the spring area and a glimpse of Laudîne, but he goes unrecognized (ll. 5451ff.; p. 119)[54] and is even approached by Laudîne and invited to stay with her:

> sî sprach "lieber herre,
> durch got belîbet hie mit mir,
> wand ich weiz wol daz ir
> und iuwer leu sît starke wunt.
> lât mich iuch machen gesunt"
>   (ll. 5460-5465; "For God's sake, dear sir, stay
> here with me so that I can take care of you until you
> are well. I know that both you and your lion are
> badly wounded"—pp. 119-20).

Iwein spurns this "doctoring," whereas in the past he was quite open to Love's "arzâte" (ll. 1553, 1555; "doctor"—p. 73), because the time is not right for him to return to her; he feels the need to perform more deeds to erase his feeling of unworthiness. Laudîne reluctantly lets him depart, closing her remarks to him with a sentiment that is prophetic:

> "so ergib ich iuch in gotes segen:
> der kan iuwer baz gepflegen
> und ruoche iu durch sine güete
> iuwer swaerez ungemüete
> vil schiere verkêren
> ze vreuden und ze êren"
>   (ll. 5535-40; "Since you won't accept my aid, I
> commend you to God, Who can care for you better
> than I. May He in His kindness soon transform your
> sorrow to happiness and honor"—p. 120).

Hartmann's reason for bringing Iwein back to the enchanted spring area, over and above Chrétien's example, would seem to be two-fold. First of all, Iwein's very presence demonstrates that he is still on Laudîne's mind even though she is unaware of it on a conscious level. Second, Hartmann allows Iwein to go unrecognized because, while Iwein is changed physically, he is altered spiritually to the point that he is not the same man. His final return to the spring area and to recognition can only occur after two more significant adventures (the freeing of the three hundred women and the duel with Gâwein) are played out. In the first adventure, Iwein finds himself trapped in the castle with the three hundred captured women who are forced to labor in dreadful working conditions; he succeeds in freeing them, as well as in escaping the host's desire that he marry his daughter.

Iwein *is* tempted by the host's daughter, who comes with "lant" (l. 6609; "land"—p. 132), for she is said to be nearly as beautiful as his wife:

> ern erkunte sît noch ê
> âne sîn selbes wîp
> nie süezer rede noch schoenern lîp
> (ll. 6514-6; Except for his wife, he had never met a woman before or later who was as lovely or spoke with such charm—p. 131).

Her characterization draws not only from that of Mâbonagrîn's wife in *Erec*, as she, too, is "in dem boumgarten" (l. 6491; "in the park"—p. 131), but also from that of the girl in Kâlogrenant's idyll at the outset of the romance, as both have the requisite "jugent" and "tugent" (ll. 339-40; "great beauty and every virtue"—p. 59; literally: "youth" and "virtue") as they lead the men "an daz schoeneste gras" (ll. 334, 6490; "the finest lawn"—p. 59; "the finest turf"—p. 131). That the temptation is sexual is underscored by the narrator's comment that Iwein did not sleep with the girl:

> swer daz nu vür ein wunder
> im selbem saget
> daz im ein unsippiu maget
> nahtes alsô nâhen lac
> mit der er anders niht enpflac,
> dern weiz niht daz ein biderbe man
> sich alles des enthalten kan
> des er sich enthalten wil
> (ll. 6574-81; Whoever thinks it strange that a girl not of kin should sleep so near the knight without his touching her is not aware that an upright man can deny himself everything he should—p. 132).

They stay "besunder" (l. 6573; "separate"—p. 132) in their beds, and the internal allusion to *Grêgôrius* is made even stronger by the fact that Iwein does not sleep with even "ein unsippiu maget" (l. 6576; "a girl not of kin"—p. 132), whereas the brother in *Grêgôrius* commits a sin that other men are warned of:

> nû sî gewarnet dar an
> ein iegelîche man
> daz er swester und niftel si
> niht ze heimlîche bî
>   (ll. 415-8;
> Let their example serve to warn
> Every man of woman born
> Against his growing intimate
> With female kin beyond what's fit—p. 45).

In *Iwein* such emphasis is placed on the fact that the two slept apart despite mutual attraction that Iwein's subsequent words sound hollow: "'ichn ger iuwer tohter niht'" (l. 6630; "'I don't want your daughter'"—p. 133). He quite obviously does desire her, but he is mindful of "mâze" (ll. 6629, 6633; p. 133) and of his wife (l. 6804; p. 134). He does not feel obligated to marry the girl just because she is part and parcel of the adventure. The old Iwein, it should be recalled, fought himself into and out of a similar situation when he first won Laudîne. By the end of the romance Iwein has come to an understanding that love entails more than just gathering up women as the spoils for battle.[55]

In the subsequent protracted duel with Gâwein,[56] moreover, Iwein learns a more significant lesson concerning fighting. He and Gâwein have ridden "in einen rinc" (l. 6907; "into the ring"—p. 136) and fight manfully in what is essentially a needless conflict. Clearly the right is on the side of the younger sister, and if Arthur had been exercising his kingly judgment wisely he would never have let the matter escalate to the point that it has, but would simply have commanded the older sister to share her inheritance, and that would have been the end of the matter.[57] Arthur is to be commended for leading the older daughter to recognize her wrong, which he accomplishes through her involuntary response, "'ich bin hie'" (l. 7660; "'Here I am'"—p. 144), to his request for the whereabouts of the woman

> "diu ir swester hât versaget
> niuwan durch ir übermuot
> ir erbteil und daz guot
> daz in ir vater beiden lie?"
>   (ll. 7656-9; "who through arrogance alone,
> refused to give a sister her portion of the inheritance
> which their father left to both?"— p. 144).

This comes about, however, only after Iwein and Gâwein have come to terms and have refused to continue the fight. Their enmity is overcome by their love for each other. During the battle "vrou Minne" ("Lady Love") pauses to tell Hartmann how it is possible that "'minne unde haz / alsô besitzen ein vaz'" (ll. 7017-8; "'are living in one vessel'"—p. 137):

> "Nû wil ich iu bescheiden daz,
> wie herzminne und bitter daz
> ein vil engez vaz besaz.
> ir herze ist ein gnuoc engez vaz:
> dâ wonte ensament inne
> haz unde minne"
> (ll. 7041-6; "I'll explain how earnest love and bitter hate remained in a narrow vessel. Each of their hearts was quite narrow and yet hate and love dwelt there together"—p. 137).[58]

She goes on to state that it is "'diu unkünde'" (l. 7055; "'ignorance'"—p. 137) that brings about such results.[59] Gâwein and Iwein quite literally do not recognize each other.[60] Recognition ends their conflict, and with recognition come disparate emotions: regret at having done each other harm and joy at having not done more harm. Iwein is not likely to forget what that conflict has taught him.

The message must be understood in terms of mind, although the mental transformation is cued, as it is throughout the romance, by physical occurrences. For this reason Hartmann places the protracted battle between Iwein and Gâwein just before Iwein's reconciliation with Laudîne. The poet notes concerning the opponents:

> diu unkünde was diu want
> diu ir herze underbant,
> daz si die gevriunt von herzen sint,
> macht mit gesehenden ougen blint
> (ll. 7055-8; Ignorance was the wall which divided their hearts so that their seeing eyes were blind although they were good friends—p. 137).

Here Hartmann echoes themes he has developed throughout the romance with respect to faulty perception. One recalls that the courtiers in Ascalôn's castle cannot see and maneuver accordingly, as Lûnete had predicted. These are men who, when confronted with a presence they cannot identify in their castle/enclosure, attempt to destroy it. Similarly, Iwein's mind/heart will later serve as an arena into which love will enter and will not be recognized fully for what it is and what it entails. Recognition, on Hartmann's account, involves two things, and while one is clearly physical (the sighting of a familiar figure through the agency of the eyes), the other is certainly mental: one can be "mit gesehenden ougen blint" ("their seeing eyes were blind") when one does not exercise mental reflection upon what one knows. Thus recognition entails more than just the perceptions of sense organs. It involves *re-cognition* and the exercising of mind. Iwein and Gâwein have eyes, but they cannot recognize each other, not merely because armor and the nighttime obscure vision, also because they at the moment are like those whom Kâlogrenant earlier scorns for offering their ears but not their hearts to his tale. So much unrecognition and so many conflicts go on in the work precisely because the mind does not reflect upon its own contents or upon the past and contemplated future actions of the body. Instead, rash action is consistently taken, and Iwein and Laudîne both exchange hearts without truly understanding the contents of their own hearts and minds. Over the course of the romance, then, the hero and his wife are both brought, through strife, to change and, then, to know their own minds. Iwein is brought back to the fountain area again and again so that he will remember that Laudîne is as much and, indeed, a more important part of his existence than Arthurian *âventiure*; the physical return to the spring will trigger the mental recollection that is so important to his spiritual progress.

Iwein thus becomes a man for whom the past has meaning; its lessons are given in order that man may recollect and reflect upon them and, hopefully, profit from them. Iwein must, in effect, lose his mind in order to have it restored to him, for while he had his mind he did not profit from recollection. Regaining his mind is tantamount to sudden apprehension of its contents, just as Laudîne's jolting realization that the "riter mittem lewen" ("the knight with the lion") and her husband are identical is tantamount to understanding what kind of man her husband is: a man who through adversity can change his mind. It is only fitting that Laudîne, too, undergoes a change of heart at the work's end (ll. 8122ff.; p. 149),[62] when she accepts Iwein, and that the mind of Lûnete has brought about reconciliation (ll. 8151-5; p. 149), for Hartmann's intent in *Iwein* is to show how the exterior word of strife can work changes on the interior landscape of the heart and mind.

As the final work of the series, *Iwein* builds consciously on language, scenes, themes, and lessons presented in the earlier poems. The concern with mind, expressed variously in the other poems, becomes paramount, so that the entire outside world comes to reflect mental processes. And the smaller movements of the poem, such as Iwein's sickness, his repeated return to the fountain area, his mental debates, and his chain of adventures, look back to Heinrich's illness, Grêgôrius' homing instinct for his mother, the heart's and body's wranglings in *Die Klage*, and Erec's progressional adventures. *Iwein*, it seems, draws its darker tones from the other poems and deepens them. Keiî's slyness and consternation in *Erec* are transformed into vitriol and humiliation in Iwein. The killing of robbers in self-defense in *Erec* escalates to the murder of the defender of the Fountain in *Iwein*. Self-imposed penance and contemplation in

Grêgôrius give way to involuntary madness and animal behavior in *Iwein*. Loyalty and concern in *Erec*, always on Enîte's part and eventually on Erec's, are replaced by forgetfulness and omission on Iwein's part. Reconciliation and reunification of the lovers in *Erec* are effected seemingly in name only in *Iwein*, where the woman who twice notes her husband's disregard of her ("'der ûf mich dehein ahte enhât'"—l. 8081; "'der nie dehein ahte ûf mich gewan'"—l. 8088; "'someone who cares nothing about me'"; "'a man who had no regard for me'"—p. 148) takes him back because she has said she would, and breaking one's word is unthinkable for her ("'ich hân es gesworn'"—l. 8114; "'I took an oath'"—p. 149) as it is for Arthur.

Iwein's conclusion comes so rapidly on the heels of Iwein's and Laudîne's reconciliation that it is almost as if Hartmann did not know where to take the story from there. He disclaims knowledge of the pair's future existence on the grounds that his source did not provide him with that information:

> ez was guot leben waenlich hie,
> ichn weiz aber waz ode wie
> in sît geschaehe beiden.
> ezn wart mir niht bescheiden
> von dem ich die rede habe
> (ll. 8160-3; One may suppose that a joyous life began at this court, but I don't know for certain what happened from this time on, since he from whom I got the story didn't say—p. 149).

But the very paucity of information is revealing in a poet who finds the leisure to elaborate on Enîte's saddle and the poem's many involved battle encounters, for example, and who expands the number of lines in his Arthurian romances over and above the number Chrétien employs. The haste with which Hartmann backs off from describing the "manige süeze zît" (l. 8147; "a joyous life"—p. 149) that the two might have, "lât diu got alten" (l. 8146; "when God lets them grow old"—p. 149), and the earlier noted repetition of "waenlich" (ll. 8148, 8159; "may suppose"—p. 149) place Hartmann's sense of the stability of this pair of lovers on shaky ground.[64] Iwein has certainly learned lessons in his series of adventures, but the fact remains that he returns to a woman who is inextricably linked (in her own and in other's eyes) with her land, and her land *is* the fountain area, the storm-making spring. It may be hopeful that the fountain area was not disrupted in Iwein's absence and that it is Iwein's return—and not the arrival of another knight—that sets off the storm again, but Laudîne is in a way of being tied to the spring and its custom in the sense that Mâbonagrîn is bound to his charmed orchard and its grisly tradition. Arthurian romance being what it is, Laudîne cannot be freed of her responsibility—she cannot "'var. . . ûz'" (l. 9589; "'I'll go out and travel'"—p. 140) as can Mâbonagrîn—and it may be that Hartmann senses that problem. Hartmann's other heroines have been quite able to move freely about the landscape—the maiden journeys to Salerno, Grêgôrius' mother/wife pilgrimages to Rome, Enîte ranges far and wide in the forest, and the host of other female emissaries like Lûnete and the various damsels in distress are quite mobile—and only Laudîne, Mâbonagrîn's wife (of her own volition) and the, respectively, eighty widows and three hundred ladies in *Erec* and *Iwein* (held against their wills), are frozen in space. The captive ladies are freed and regain their mobility, Mâbonagrîn is released from his obligation, but one senses that there are hard times ahead for his wife, who reveals not only her jealousy of other woman but also the mental obduracy of forcing her will on her husband. But, since she is a minor character in the work and it is a work in which Mâbonagrîn appears as only a secondary character, Hartmann can gloss over her situation with a few well-meaning platitudes. In *Iwein*, though, Laudîne is a major character—and the first and only major character that has been identified so strongly with land—and the situation is not that easy to remedy. The best way out, given the conventions under which Hartmann operates, is to end the story then and there, and to leave the reader to speculate as to the final outcome.

SUMMARY

Mind as the informing principle in Hartmann's works manifests itself variously in each of the poems, binding together imagination, evaluation, rationalization, and memory. Mind, on Hartmann's account, becomes the filter through which characters sift perceptions, as well as the arena for internal debates, the receptacle (along with the heart) of joyful and stormy emotions, and the seat of contemplation. On the one hand, mind functions in terms of time, so that all of Hartmann's heroes' minds are fundamentally altered as a result of their experiences; mind reaches backward in time through memory and forward in fantasy. Grêgôrius' mind is a prime example of this faculty, for he both reflects on his origins and daydreams about prospective feats of knightly prowess. Yet, on the other hand, Hartmann conceives of mind in spatial terms, and *Iwein* exists as his most sophisticated working-out of that thesis: the mental world in the poem is cued to the physical world in a more carefully realized manner than in *Erec*.

Overwhelmingly, mind, as Hartmann understands it, is verbal. It is keyed to words not only in the characters' inner and outer ruminations, but also in Hartmann's faith in language's ability to communicate meaning to an audience (as evidenced in his reliance on parable, proverb, and authorial intrusion) and to God (through prayer and contemplation as much as through penitent actions). The poems themselves serve as products of mind that examine mind, and they speak to mind's limitations (human incomprehension of the workings of the divine mind, which is clearly not linear and successive in the way in which human minds often operate) as well as to mind's potential for growth and change. Hartmann's is a lively intelligence, and he continually challenges the reader with his mind-games, not only in the sense that his poems prove to be puzzles to be worked out, but also in the sense that he gives the reader access to minds in action, as, for example, in the heart-body debates and in the sportive interchanges between "Hartman" and "vrouw Minne." The reader is kept on his/her toes to sort out the meaning in the narratives, to react to them with certain and predicted expectations, and to reflect upon them. So verbally conscious, in fact, is Hartmann that mind becomes word over time and space and, accordingly, stands to Word in the precise hierarchical relationship that the human mind stands to the Divine mind. Hartmann's heroes are most silent and the narrative most perfunctory at those times when the divine mind is cleansing (in *Iwein*) or healing (in *Grêgôrius* and in *Der arme Heinrich*) a human mind. The word bows to the Word.

Finally, mind is for Hartmann a process of fragmentation and unification. The verbal debate of *Die Klage*, where heart and body finally form halves of one entity, is succeeded by *Erec*, where a man and woman are seen to be one being. This is followed by *Grêgôrius* (in which the union of mother/wife and son/husband is broken and reformed twice) and by *Der arme Heinrich* (in which the maiden at Heinrich's feet orients him, he "sees" correctly, and they wed). Only in *Iwein* does the fragmentation remain close to the surface narrative at the work's end, and in the completion of *Iwein* Hartmann comes full circle, alluding to his other works through plot, thematics, language, and message, and ends his creative cycle where he began it, with an undercurrent of unresolved dispute.

EDITIONS AND TRANSLATIONS

Line numbers in parentheses refer to the following editions: 1) Hartmann von Aue, *Die Klage, Das (zweite) Büchlein aus dem Ambraser Heldenbuch*, ed. Herta Zutt (Berlin: Walter de Gruyter, 1968); 2) Hartmann von Aue, *Erec, Iwein: Text, Nacherzählung, Worterklärung*, ed. Ernst Schwarz (Darmstadt: Wissenschaftliche Buchgesellschaft, 1967); 3) Hartmann von Aue, *Gregorius, Der arme Heinrich: Text, Nacherzählung, Worterklärung*, ed. Ernst Schwarz (Darmstadt: Wissenschaftliche Buchgesellschaft, 1967); 4) *Des Minnesangs Frühling*, ed. Carl von Kraus, 35th ed. (Stuttgart: S. Hirzel, 1970). The Wissenschaftliche Buchgesellschaft editions, it should be noted, are faithful to the standard editions, with very minor emendations, so that *Grêgôrius* depends upon Bech/Neumann, *Der arme Heinrich* on Wolff's Altdeutsche Textbibliothek edition, *Erec* on Leitmann/Wollf's ATB edition, and *Iwein* on Benecke/Lachmann/Wolff. In citing passages from the texts, I will observe the conventions regarding long vowels that the editors have chosen (Schwarz's and von Kraus's editions indicate long vowels, while Zutt's does not), and I will mark long vowels in the names of characters as they appear in my readings of Hartmann's works. Citations from secondary literature will reflect whether or not those critics employ long marks. I will employ quotation marks when citing Middle High German passages in the text proper, and I will use single quotes within those passages to indicate direct speech. Set-off quotes will employ quotes only for direct speech. Individual Middle High German words will be italicized when they are used as general terms. Translations into English are provided following the Middle High German passages. For *Die Klage* I use the unpublished translation done by Rolph Hornung (Ph.D., Rice University); for *Erec* that of J.W. Thomas (Lincoln: University of Nebraska Press, 1982); for *Grêgôrius* that of Sheema Bühne (New York: Ungar, 1966); for *Der arme Heinrich* that of J.W. Thomas (in *The Best Novellas of Medieval Germany* (Columbia: Camden House, 1984); and for *Iwein* that of J.W. Thomas (Lincoln: University of Nebraska Press, 1979). I have consulted the translation of *Erec* by Michael Resler (Philadelphia: University of Pennsylvania Press, 1987).

SECONDARY LITERATURE CONSULTED

Anderson, Philip. "Court and Anti-Court in Hartmann von Aue's *Der arme Heinrich*." *New German Studies*, 7 (1979), 169-87.

Andersson, Björn. "*Der arme Heinrich*: Zum Elan der Spannung einer Dichtung des Mittelalters." *Studia Neophilologica*, 52 (1980), 337-51.

Andersson, Theodore M. *Early Epic Scenery: Homer, Virgil, and the Medieval Legacy.* Ithaca: Cornell University Press, 1976.

Artin, Tom. *The Allegory of Adventure: Reading Chrétien's Erec and Yvain.* Lewisburg, Pennsylvania: Bucknell University Press, 1974.

Asher, John Alexander. "Hartmann and Gottfried: Master and Pupil." *Journal of the Australasian Universities Languages and Literatures Association,* 16 (1961), 134-44.

Attwater, Donald. *The Dictionary of Saints.* Baltimore: Penguin, 1965.

Auerbach, Erich. "The Knight Sets Forth." In: *Mimesis: The Representation of Reality in Western Literature.* Trans. Willards R. Trask. Princeton: Princeton University Press, 1953.

Bang, Carol K. "Emotions and Attitudes in Chrétien de Troyes' *Erec et Enide* and Hartmann von Aue's *Erec der wunderaere.*" *Publications of the Modern Language Association,* 57 (1942), 297-326.

Batts, Michael S. "Hartmann's *humanitas*: A New Look at *Iwein.*" In: *Germanic Studies in Honor of Edward Henry Sehrt.* Ed. Frithjof Andersen Raven, Wolfram K. Legner, and James Cecil King. Miami Linguistic Series, 1. Coral Gables, Florida: Universit of Miami Press, 1968. 37-52.

Bayer, Hans. "'Bî den liuten ist so guot': Die *meine* des *Erec* Hartmanns von Aue." *Euphorion,* 73 (1979), 272-85.

Benecke, Georg Friedrich, Wilhelm Müller, und Friedrich Zarncke. *Mittelhochdeutsches Wörterbuch,* 3 vols. Leipzig: S. Hirzel, 1861.

Bennholdt-Thomsen, Anke. "Die allegorischen *kleit* im *Gregorius*-Prolog." *Euphorion,* 56 (1962), 174-84.

Berger, Joachim. "Der Aufbau von Hartmanns *Iwein.*" *Amsterdamer Beträge zur älteren Germanistik,* 8 (1975), 33-57.

Bettelheim, Bruno. *The Uses of Enchantment: The Meaning and Importance of Fairy Tales.* New York: Knopf, 1977.

Blamires, David. "Fairytale Analogues to *Der arme Heinrich.*" In: *Hartmann von Aue: Changing Perspectives.* Ed. Timothy McFarland and Silvia Ranawake. Göppingen: Kümmerle, 1988. 187-98.

Blosen, Hans. "Hartmanns *Erec* als eifersüchtiger Ehemann: Nachtragnotiz zu meinem Aufsatz: Noch einmal: Zu Enites Schuld in Hartmanns *Erec*," *Orbis Litterarum,* 31 (1976), 81-109.

Blosen, Hans. "Noch einmal: Zu Enites Schuld in Hartmanns *Erec*: Mit Ausblicken auf Chrétiens Roman und das *Mabinogi* von *Gereint.*" *Orbis Litterarum,* 31 (1976), 81-109.

Boggs, Roy Amos. "Hartmann's *Erec.*" In: *Innovation in Medieval Literature: Essays to the Memory of Alan Markman.* Ed. Douglas Radcliff-Umstead. Pittsburgh: University of Pittsburgh Press, 1971. 49-62.

_____. Hartmann von Aue: Lemmatisierte Konkordanz zur
   Gesamtwerk. 2 Vols. Indices zur deutschen Literatur, 12/13.
   Nendeln: KTO Press, 1979.
Boon, Pieter. "Die Ehe des Armen Heinrich: eine Mésalliance?"
   Neophilologus, 66 (1982), 92-101.
Borck, Karl Heinz. "'Nû ist si vrî als ich dâ bin': Bemerkungen zu
   Hartmanns Armen Heinrich." In: Medium aevum deutsch:
   Beiträge zur deutschen Literatur des hohen und späten
   Mittelalters: Festschrift für Kurt Ruh zum 65. Geburtstag. Ed.
   Dietrich Huschenbett. Tübingen: Max Niemeyer, 1979. 37-50.
Bossy, M.A. "Medieval Debates of Body and Soul." Comparative
   Literature, 28 (1976), 144-63.
Brody, Saul Nathaniel. The Disease of the Soul: Leprosy in
   Medieval Literature. Ithaca: Cornell University Press, 1974.
Buck, Timothy. "Heinrich's Metanoia: Intention and Practice in Der
   arme Heinrich." Modern Language Review, 60 (1965), 391-4.
_____. "Hartmann's reine maget." German Life and Letters, 18
   (1964-65), 169-76.
Carne, Eva-Maria. Frauengestalten bei Hartmann von Aue: Ihre
   Bedeutung im Aufbau und Gehalt der Epen. Marburger Beiträge
   zur Germanistik, 31. Marburg: N.G. Elwert, 1970.
Cirlot, J.E. A Dictionary of Symbols. Trans. Jack Sage. New York:
   Philosophical Library, 1962.
Clark, S.L. "Changing One's Mind: Arenas of Conflict and
   Resolution in Hartmann's Iwein." Euphorion, 73 (1979), 286-303.
_____. "'Ein schoenez bilde': Walther von der Vogelweide
   and The Idea of Image." From Symbol to Mimesis: The
   Generation of Walther von der Vogelweide. Ed. Franz H.
   Bäuml. Göppinger Arbeiten zur Germanistik. Göppingen:
   Kümmerle, 1984.
_____. "Hartmann's Erec: Language, Perception, and
   Transformation." Germanic Review, 56 (1981), 81-94.
_____. "'Ze glîcher wîs': Mechthild von Magdeburg and
   the Concept of Likeness." In: The World of Medieval Women:
   Creativity, Influence, and Imagination. Ed. Constance H.
   Berman, Charles W. Connell, and Judith Rice Rothschild.
   Morgantown: West Virginia University Press, 1985. 41-50.
Clark, S.L., and Julian N. Wasserman. "Conflict and Resolution:
   Implications of Enclosure in Chrétien's Yvain." Essays in
   Literature, 8 (1981), 63-72.
_____. "Constance as Romance and Folk Heroine in
   Chaucer's Man of Law's Tale." Rice University Studies, 64
   (1978), 13-24.
_____. "Language, Silence, and Wisdom in Chrétien's Erec
   et Enide." The Michigan Academician, 9,iii (1977), 285-98.
Clifton-Everest, J.M. "Christian Allegory in Hartmann's Iwein."
   Germanic Review, 48 (1973), 247-59.
Combridge, Rosemary. "The Uses of Biblical and Other Learned
   Symbolism in the Narrative Works of Hartmann von Aue." In:

Hartmann von Aue: Changing Perspectives. Ed. Timothy McFarland and Silvia Ranawake. Göppingen: Kümmerle, 1988. Pp. 271-84.

Cormeau, Christoph. *Hartmanns von der Aue Armer Heinrich und Gregorius: Studien zur Interpretation mit dem Blick auf die Theologie zur Zeit Hartmanns.* Münchener Texte und Untersuchungen zur deutschen Literatur des Mittelalters, 15. Munich: Beck, 1966.

Cornelius, Roberta R. *The Figurative Castle: A Study in the Medieval Allegory of the Edifice with Especial Reference to Religious Writings.* Diss. Bryn Mawr, 1930.

Cramer, Thomas. "*Saelde* und *êre* in Hartmanns *Iwein.*" *Euphorion,* 60 (1966), 30-47.

_____. "Soziale Motivation in der Schuld-Sühne Problematik von Hartmanns *Erec.*" *Euphorion,* 66 (1972), 97-112.

Deitmaring, Sister Ursula. "Die Bedeutung von Rechts und Links in den theologischen und literarischen Texten bis um 1200." *Zeitschrift für deutsches Altertum,* 98 (1969), 265-92.

Dickerson, Harold D. "Hartmann's *Gregorius*: An Alternate Reading." In: *Wege der Worte: Festschrift für Wolfram Fleischhauer: anlässlich seines 65. Geburtstags und des 40. Jahres seines Wirkens als Professor der deutschen Philologie an der Ohio State University mit Beiträgen von Freunden, Kollegen und Schülern.* Cologne: Böhlau, 1978. 178-88.

Dittmann, Wolfgang. "'Dune hâst niht wâr, Hartmann!' Zum Begriff der *wârheit* in Hartmanns *Iwein.*" In: *Festgabe für Ullrich Pretzel.* Ed. Werner Simon, Wolfgang Bachofen, und Wolfgang Dittmann. Berlin: Erich Schmidt, 1963. 150-61.

Dodd, C.H. *The Parables of the Kingdom.* New York, 1961.

Dorn, Erhard. *Der sündige Heilige in der Legende des Mittelalters.* Medium Aevum, 10. Munich: Fink, 1967.

Ehrismann, Otfrid. "Enite: Handlungsbegründungen in Hartmanns von Aue *Erec.*" *Zeitschrift für deutsche Philologie,* 98 (1979), 321-44.

Eliade, Mircea. *The Rites and Symbols of Initiation: The Mysteries of Birth and Rebirth.* New York: Harper, 1965.

Endres, Rolf. "Der Prolog von Hartmanns *Iwein.*" *Deutsche Vierteljahrsschrift für Literaturwissenschaft und Geistesgeschichte,* 40 (1966), 509-37.

_____. "Die Bedeutung von *güete* und die Diesseitigkeit der Artusromane Hartmanns." *Deutsche Vierteljahrsschrift für Literaturwissenschaft und Geisteswissenschaft,* 44 (1970), 595-612.

_____. "Heinrichs *hôchvart.*" *Euphorion,* 61 (1967), 267-94.

Erben, Johannes. "Zu Hartmanns *Iwein.*" *Zeitschrift für deutsche Philologie,* 87 (1968), 344-59.

Erickson, Carolly. *The Medieval Vision: Essays in History and Perception.* New York: Oxford University Press, 1976.

Ernst, Ulrich. "Der Antagonismus von *vita carnalis* und *vita spiritualis* im *Gregorius* Hartmanns von Aue: Versuch einer

Werkdeutung im Horizont der patristischen und monastischen Tradition." *Euphorion*, 72 (1978), 160-226.

_____ . "Der Antagonismus von *vita carnalis* und *vita spiritualis* im *Gregorius* Hartmanns von Aue: Versuch einer Werkdeutung im Horizont der patristischen und monastischen Tradition, Teil 2." *Euphorion*, 73 (1979), 1-105.

Eroms, Hans-Werner. *'vreude' bei Hartmann von Aue*. Medium Aevum, 20. Munich: Fink, 1970.

Ertzdorff, Xenja von. "Spiel der Interpretation: Der Erzähler in Hartmanns *Iwein*." In: *Festgabe für Friedrich Maurer*. Ed. Werner Besch, Siegfried Grosse, und Heinz Rupp. Düsseldorf: Schwann, 1968. 135-57.

Fechter, Werner. "Absalon als Vergleichs- und Beispielfigur im mittelhochdeutschen Schrifttum." *PBB*, 83 (1961-2), 302-16.

_____ . "Über den *Armen Heinrich* Hartmanns von Aue." *Euphorion*, 49 (1955), 1-28.

Fierz-Monnier, Antoinette. *Initiation und Wandlung: Zur Geschichte des altfranzösischen Romans im zwölften Jahrhundert von Chrétien de Troyes zu Renaut de Beaujeu*. Studiorium Romanicorum Collectio Turicensis, 5. Bern: Francke, 1951.

Fisher, Rodney. "Erecs Schuld und Enitens Unschuld bei Hartmann." *Euphorion*, 69 (1975), 160-74.

Freytag, Wiebke. "Zu Hartmanns Methode der Adaption im *Erec*." *Euphorion*, 72 (1978), 227-39.

Gaier, Ulrich. "Sebastian Brant's *Narrenschiff* and the Humanists." *Publications of the Modern Language Association*, 83 (1968), 266-70.

Gellinek, Christian J. "Iwein's Duel and Laudine's Marriage." In: *The Epic in Medieval Society: Aesthetic and Moral Values*. Ed. Harald Scholler. Tübingen: Niemeyer, 1977. 26-39.

_____ . "Zu Hartmann von Aues Herzenstausch." *Amsterdamer Beiträge zur älteren Germanistik*, 6 (1974), 133-42.

Gewehr, Wolf. *Hartmanns Klage-Büchlein im Lichte der Frühscholastik*. Göppinger Arbeiten zur Germanistik, 167. Göppingen: Kümmerle, 1975.

Gilbert, Leon J. "Symmetrical Composition in Hartmann's 'froun Lûneten rât.'" *Modern Language Notes*, 83 (1968), 430-4.

Gilbert, Sandra M., and Susan Gubar. *The Madwoman in the Attic: The Woman Writer and the Nineteenth-Century Literary Imagination*. New Haven: Yale University Press, 1979.

Gillespie, George T. *A Catalogue of Persons Named in German Heroic Literature (700-1600) Including Named Animals and Objects and Ethnic Names*. Oxford: Oxford University Press, 1973.

_____ . "Real and Ideal Images of Knightly Endeavour and Love in the Works of Hartmann von Aue." In: *Hartmann von Aue: Changing Perspectives*. Ed. Timothy McFarland and Silvia Ranawake. Göppingen: Kümmerle, 1988. 253-270.

Goebel, Dieter K. *Untersuchungen zu Aufbau und Schuldproblem in Hartmanns Gregorius.* Philologische Studien und Quellen, 78. Berlin: Erich Schmidt, 1974.

Goebel, Ulrich. "Concerning the Promotion of Hartmann's *Erec.*" *Semasia,* 2 (1975), 75-81.

Goheen, Jutta. "'Bistuz Iwein, oder wer?' Hartmanns letztes Epos als Spätwerk." *Amsterdamer Beiträge zur älteren Germanistik,* 7 (1974), 47-83.

Gössmann, Elisabeth. "Typus der Heilsgeschichte oder Opfer morbider Gesellschaftsordnung? Ein Forschungsbericht zum Schuldproblem in Hartmanns *Gregorius.*" *Euphorion,* 68 (1974), 42-80.

Grandin, Larry Robert. "*Guot, güete, unguot, guottât*: A Word Study in Hartmann's *Gregorius.*" *Modern Language Notes,* 88 (1973), 927-46.

Green, D.H. "Hartmann's Ironic Praise of Erec." *Modern Language Review,* 70 (1975), 795-807.

_____. "On the Primary Reception of Narrative Literature in Medieval Germany." *Forum for Modern Language Studies,* 20 (1984), 289-308.

Gross, Hedwig. *Hartmanns Büchlein.* Diss., Bonn, 1936.

Grosse, Siegfried. "Beginn und Ende der erzählenden Dichtungen von Hartmann von Aue." In: *Hartmann von Aue.* Ed. Hugo Kuhn and Christoph Cormeau. Wege der Forschung, 359. Darmstadt: Wissenschaftliche Buchgesellschaft, 1973. 172-94.

_____. "'Wis den wisen gerne bi!' Die höfischen Lehren in Hartmanns *Gregorius* und Wolframs *Parzival.*" *Der Deutschunterricht,* 14,vi (1962), 52-66.

Gruenter, Rainer. "Zum Problem der Landschaftsdarstellung im höfischen Versroman." *Euphorion,* 56 (1962), 248-78.

Hahn, Ingrid. "Hartmanns *Büchlein*-Zitat im *Gregorius.*" In: *Sagen mit Sinne: Festschrift für Marie-Luise Dittrich zum 65. Geburtstag.* Göppingen: Alfred Kümmerle, 1976. 95-108.

Harms, Wolfgang. *Homo viator in bivio: Studien zur Bildlichkeit des Weges.* Medium Aevum, 21. Munich: Fink, 1970.

_____. *Der Kampf mit dem Freund oder Verwandten in der deutschen Literatur bus um 1300.* Munich: Eidos, 1963.

Hart, Thomas Elwood. "The Structure of *Iwein* and Tectonic Research: What Evidence, Which Methods?" *Colloquia Germanica,* 10 (1976-7), 97-120.

Hatto, Arthur Thomas. "'Der aventiure meine' in Hartmann's *Iwein.*" In: *Medieval German Studies Presented to Frederick Norman.* London: University of London Institute of Germanic Studies, 1965. 94-103.

_____. "Enid's Best Dress. A Contribution to the Understanding of Chrétien's and Hartmann's *Erec* and the Welsh *Gereint.*" *Euphorion,* 54 (1960), 437-41.

Heine, Thomas. "Shifting Perspectives: The Narrative Strategy in Hartmann's *Erec.*" *Orbis Litterarum,* 36 (1981), 95-115.

Heinen, Hubert. "Irony and Confession in Hartmann's 'Sît ich den sumer' (*MF* 205,1). *Monatshefte*, 80 (198), 416-28.

———. "'Mit gemache lân': A Crux in Hartmann's 'Maniger grüezet mich alsô' (*MF* 216, 29)." In: *Studies in Medieval Culture* (1978), 85-110.

———. "The Concepts *hof, hövesch,* and the Like in Hartmann's *Iwein*. In: *The Medieval Court in Europe*. Ed. Edward R. Haymes. Houston German Studies, 6. Munich: Fink, 1986.

———. "The World and Worldiness in Hartmann von Aue's *Der arme Heinrich*." In: *Languages and Cultures: Studies in Honor of Edgar C. Polomé*. Berlin, New York, Amsterdam: Mouton de Gruyter, 1988. 260-8.

Henne, Hermann. *Herrschaftsstruktur, historischer Prozeß und epische Handlung: Sozialgeschichtliche Untersuchungen zum Gregorius and Armen Heinrich*. Göppinger Germanistische Arbeiten, 340. Göppingen: Kümmerle, 1982.

Herlem-Prey, Brigitte. "Neues zur Quelle von Hartmanns *Gregorius*." *Zeitschrift für deutsche Philologie*, 97 (1978), 414-26.

Höhler, Gertrud. "Der Kampf im Garten. Studien zur Brandigan Episode in Hartmanns *Erec*." *Euphorion*, 68 (1974), 371-419.

Hruby, Antonín. "Moralphilosophie und Moraltheologie in Hartmanns *Erec*." In: *The Epic in Medieval Society: Aesthetic and Moral Values*. Ed. Harold Scholler. Tübingen: Niemeyer, 1977. 193-213.

———. "Die Problemstellung in Chrétiens und Hartmanns *Erec*." *Deutsche Vierteljahrsschrift für Literaturwissenschaft und Geistesgeschichte*, 38 (1964), 337-60.

Huby, Michel. "L'approfondissement psychologique dans *Erec* de Hartmann." *Etudes germaniques*, 34 (1979), 13-26.

———. "La 'faute' d'Iwein." *Etudes germaniques*, 34 (1979), 129-40.

Hunter, J.A. "'Sam Jôben den rîchen': Hartmann's *Der arme Heinrich* and the *Book of Job*." *Modern Language Review*, 68 (1973), 358-66.

Jackson, Timothy R. "Paradoxes of Person: Hartmann Von Aue's Use of the *Contradictio in Adiecto*." In: *Hartmann von Aue: Changing Perspectives*. Ed. Timothy McFarland and Silvia Ranawake. Göppingen: Kümmerle, 1988. 285-311.

Jackson, W.H. "Some Observations on the Status of the Narrator in Hartmann von Aue's *Erec* and *Iwein*." *Forum for Modern Language Studies*, 6 (1970), 65-82.

———. "The Tournament in the Works of Hartmann von Aue: Motifs, Style, Functions." In: *Hartmann von Aue: Changing Perspectives*. Ed. Timothy McFarland and Silvia Ranawake. Göppingen: Kümmerle, 1988. 233-252.

Jones, Martin H. "Changing Perspectives on the Maiden in *Der arme Heinrich*." In: *Hartmann von Aue: Changing Perspectives*. Ed.

Timothy McFarland and Silvia Ranawake. Göppingen: Kümmerle, 1988. 211-31.
Kaiser, Gert. "*Iwein* oder *Laudine*." *Zeitschrift für deutsche Philologie*, 99 (1980), 20-8.
_____. *Textauslegung und gesellschaftliche Selbstdeutung: Die Artusromane Hartmanns von Aue*. 2nd ed. Wiesbaden: Akademie, 1978.
Kalinke, Marianne. "*Vorhte* in Hartmann's *Erec*." *Amsterdamer Beiträge zur älteren Germanistik*, 11 (1976), 67-80.
Keller, Thomas. "Iwein and the Lion." *Amsterdamer Beiträge zur älteren Germanistik*, 15 (1980), 59-75.
_____. "MF 205,1: 'Sit ich den sumer truoc' as Microcosm of *Iwein* of Hartmann von Aue." *Germanic Notes*, 11 (1980), 5-7.
Kelly, T.D. and John Irwin. "The Meaning of *Cleanness*: Parable as Effective Sign." *Mediaeval Studies*, 35 (1973), 232-60.
Kern, Peter. "Der Roman und seine Rezeption als Gegenstand des Romans: Beobachtungen zum Eingangsteil von Hartmanns *Iwein*." *Wirkendes Wort*, 23 (1973), 246-52.
_____. "Interpretation der Erzählung durch Erzählung: Zur Bedeutung der Wiederholung, Variation und Umkehrung in Hartmanns *Iwein*." *Zeitschrift für deutsche Philologie*, 92 (1973), 338-59.
King, K.C. "The Mother's Guilt in Hartmann's *Gregorius*." In: *Medieval German Studies Presented to Friedrich Norman*. London: University of London Institute of Germanic Studies, 1965. 84-93.
_____. "Zur Frage der Schuld in Hartmanns *Gregorius*." *Euphorion*, 57 (1963), 44-66.
Knapp, F.P. "Enites Totenklage und Selbstmordversuch in Hartmanns *Erec*: Eine quellenkritische Analyse." *Germanisch-romanische Monatsschrift*, 26 (1976), 83-90.
_____. "Hartmann von Aue und die Tradition der platonischen Anthropologie im Mittelalter." *Deutsche Vierteljahrsschrift für Literaturwissenschaft und Geistesgeschichte*, 46 (1972), 213-47.
Kraft, Karl-Friedrich O. *Iweins Triuwe: Zu Ethos und Form der Aventiurenfolge in Hartmanns 'Iwein': Eine Interpretation*. Amsterdamer Publikationen zur Sprache und Literatur, 42. Amsterdam: Rodopi, 1979.
Kramer, Hans-Peter. *Erzählbemerkung und Erzälerkommentare in Chrestiens und Hartmanns Erec und Iwein*. Göppinger Arbeiten zur Germanistik, 35. Göppingen: Kümmerle, 1971.
Kuhn, Hugo. *Dichtung und Welt im Mittelalter*. Stuttgart: Metzler, 1959.
_____. "Hartmann von Aue als Dichter." *Der Deutschunterricht*, 5,ii (1953), 11- 27.
Kunz, George Frederick. *The Curious Lore of Precious Stones*. New York: Dover, 1971.

Kuttner, Ursula. *Das Erzählen des Erzählten: Eine Studie zum Stil in Hartmanns Erec und Iwein.* Bonn: Bouvier, 1978.
Le Sage, D. "'Ane zuht' or 'âne schulde'? The Question of Iwein's Guilt." *Modern Language Review*, 77 (1982), 100-13.
Lewis, Gertrud Jaron. "'Daz häzliche spil' im *Iwein*: Ein Beispiel der Erzählkunst Hartmanns von Aue." *Seminar*, 9 (1973), 97-108.
Lewis, Robert E. *Symbolism im Hartmann's Iwein.* Göppinger Arbeiten zur Germanistik, 154. Göppingen: Kümmerle, 1975.
Lexer, Matthias. *Mittelhochdeutsches Handwörterbuch.* Leipzig: S. Hirzel, 1872.
Linke, Hansjürgen. *Epische Struktur in der Dichtung Hartmanns von Aue: Untersuchungen zur Formkritik, Werkstruktur und Vortragsgliederung.* Munich: Fink, 1968.
Lofmark, Carl. "The Advisor's Guilt in Courtly Literature." *German Life and Letters*, 24 (1970-1), 3-13.
Lorenz, Bernd. "Bemerkungen zum Motiv der 'Zwei Wege' in Hartmanns *Gregorius*." *Euphorion*, 71 (1977), 92-6.
Margetts, John. "Gefühlsumschwung im *Iwein*: *minne unde haz, luf* and envy." In *Grossbrittanien und Deutschland: Festschrift John W.P. Bourke.* Munich: Wilhelm Goldmann, 1974. 452-60.
_____. "Observations on the Representation of Female Attractiveness in the Works of Hartmann von Aue with Special Reference to *Der Arme Heinrich*." In: *Hartmann von Aue: Changing Perspectives.* Ed. Timothy McFarland and Silvia Ranawake. Göppingen: Kümmerle, 1988. 199-210.
Markey, T.L. "The *Ex Lege* Rite of Passage in Hartmann's *Iwein*." *Colloquia Germanica*, 11 (1978), 97-110.
Masser, Achim. *Bibel- und Legendenepik des deutschen Mittelalters.* Grundlagen der Germanistik, 19. Berlin: Erich Schmidt, 1976.
Mayer, Hartwig. "*Topoi* des Verschweigens und der Kürzung im höfischen Epos." In: *Getempert und gemischet: Festschrift Wolfgang Mohr.* Göppingen: Kümmerle, 1972. 231-49.
McCann, W.J. "Gregorius's Interview with the Abbott: A Comparative Study." *Modern Language Review*, 73 (1978), 82-95.
McDonald, William C. "The Maiden in Hartmann's *Armen Heinrich*: Enite *redux*?" *Deutsche Vierteljahrsschrift für Literaturwissenschaft und Geistesgeschichte*, 53 (1979), 34-48.
McFarland, Timothy. "Narrative Structure and the Renewal of the Hero's Identity in *Iwein*." In: *Hartmann von Aue: Changing Perspectives.* Ed. Timothy McFarland and Silvia Ranawake. Göppingen: Kümmerle, 1988. 129-58.
McKenzie, Donald A. "Hartmann's *Der arme Heinrich*: Some Explications and a Theory." *Modern Language Quarterly*, 11 (1950), 472-5.
McMahon, James V. "Enite's Relatives: The Girl in the Garden." *Modern Language Notes*, 85 (1970), 367-72.
Meng, Armin. *Vom Sinn des ritterlichen Abenteuers bei Hartmann von Aue.* Zürich: Juris, 1967.

Mertens, Volker. "'*Factus est per clericum miles cythereus*': Überlegungen zu Entstehungs- und Wirkungsbedingungen von Hartmanns *Klage-Büchlein*. In: *Hartmann von Aue: Changing Perspectives*. Ed. Timothy McFarland and Silvia Ranawake. Göppingen: Kümmerle, 1988.1-20.

──────────. *Gregorius Eremita: Eine Lebensform des Adels bei Hartmann von Aue in ihrer Problematik und ihrer Wandlung bei der Rezeption*. Zürich: Artemis, 1978.

──────────. "*Imitatio Arthuri*: Zum Prolog von Hartmanns *Iwein*." *Zeitschrift für deutsches Altertum*, 106 (1977), 350-8.

──────────. *Laudine: Soziale Problematik im Iwein Hartmanns von Aue*. Beihefte zur Zeitschrift für deutsche Philologie, 3. Berlin: Erich Schmidt, 1978.

Milnes, Humphrey. "The Play of Opposites in *Iwein*." *German Life and Letters*, 14 (1960), 241-56.

Mohr, Wolfgang. "Iweins Wahnsinn: Die Aventiure und ihr 'Sinn.'" *Zeitschrift für deutsches Altertum*, 100 (1971), 73-94.

Moser, Hugo. "Hartmanns *Armer Heinrich*—eine Mirakelerzählung." In: *Gedenkschrift für Jost Trier*. Ed. Helmut Becker und Hans Schwarz. Cologne: Böhlau, 1975.

Mowatt, D.G. "Irony in Hartmann's *Iwein*." In: *Deutung und Bedeutung: Studies in German and Comparative Literature Presented to Karl-Werner Maurer*. Ed. Brigitte Schludermann, Victor G. Doerksen, Robert J. Glendinning, and Evelyn Sherabon Firchow. The Hague: Mouton, 1973. 34-53.

──────────. "Tristan's Mothers and Iwein's Daughters." *German Life and Letters*, 23 (1969-70), 18-31.

Murdoch, Brian. "The Garments of Paradise: A Note on the *Wiener Genesis* and the *Anegenge*." *Euphorion*, 61 (1967), 375-82.

──────────. "Hartmann's *Gregorius* and the Quest of Life." *New German Studies*, 6 (1978), 79-100.

Nagel, Bert. *Staufische Klassik: Deutsche Dichtung um 1200*. Heidelberg: Lothar Stiehm, 1977.

Nelson, Deborah H. "Enide: *Amie* or *Femme*." *Romance Notes*, 21,iii (1981), 1-6.

Ohly, Friedrich. "Vom geistigen Sinn des Wortes im Mittelalters." *Zeitschrift für deutsches Altertum*, 89 (1959), 1-23.

Pearce, L. "Relationships in Hartmann's *Iwein*." *Seminar*, 6 (1970), 15-30.

Palmer, Nigel F. "Poverty and Mockery in Hartmann's *Erec*, v. 525ff.: A Study of the Psychology and Aesthetics of Middle High German Romance." In: *Hartmann von Aue: Changing Perspectives*. Ed. Timothy McFarland and Silvia Ranawake. Göppingen: Kümmerle, 1988. 65-92.

Peil, Dietmar. *Die Gebärde bei Chrétien, Hartmann und Wolfram: Erec-Iwein-Parzifal*. Medium Aevum, 28. Munich: Fink, 1975.

Pérennec, René. "Adaption et Société: L'adaption par Hartmann d'Aue du roman de Chrétien des Troyes *Erec et Enide*." *Etudes germaniques*, 28 (1973), 289-303.

Peters, Ursula. "Artusroman und Fürstenhof: Darstellung und Kritik neuerer sozialgeschichtlicher Untersuchungen zu Hartmanns *Erec*." *Euphorion*, 69 (1975), 175-96.
Pickering, F.P. "The 'Fortune' of Hartmann's *Erec*." *German Life and Letters*, 30 (1977), 94-109.
Picozzi, Rosemary. "Allegory and Symbol in Hartmann's *Gregorius*." In: *Essays on German Literature in Honour of G. Joyce Hallamore*. Ed. Michael Batts and Marketa G. Stankiewicz. Toronto: University of Toronto Press, 1968. 19-33.
Polsakiewicz, Roman. "Zur Chronologie der epischen Werke Hartmanns von Aue." *Euphorion*, 71 (1977), 82-91.
Priesach, Theodor. "Laudine's Dilemma." In: *Sagen mit Sinne: Festschrift für Marie-Luise Dittrich um 65. Geburtstag*. Göppingen: Kümmerle, 1976. 109-32.
Pütz, Horst Peter. "Artus-Kritik in Hartmanns *Iwein*." *Germanisch-romanische Monatsschrift*, 53 (1972), 193-7.
Ranawake, Silvia. "Erec's *verligen* and the Sin of Sloth." In: *Hartmann von Aue: Changing Perspectives*. Ed. Timothy McFarland and Silvia Ranawake. Göppingen: Kümmerle, 1988. 93-116.
Reinitzer, Heimo. "Über Beispielfiguren im *Erec*." *Deutsche Vierteljahrsschrift für Literaturwissenschaft und Geistesgeschichte*, 50 (1976), 597-639.
Renoir, Alain. "Descriptive Technique in *Sir Gawain and the Green Knight*." *Orbis Litterarum*, 13 (1958), 126-32.
Reusner, Ernst von. "*Iwein*." *Deutsche Vierteljahrsschrift für Literaturwissenschaft und Geistesgeschichte*, 46 (1972), 494-512.
Robertshaw, Alan. "Ambiguity and Morality in *Iwein*." In: *Hartmann von Aue: Changing Perspectives*. Ed. Timothy McFarland and Silvia Ranawake. Göppingen: Kümmerle, 1988. 117-28.
Robertson, D.W., Jr. *A Preface to Chaucer: Studies in Medieval Perspectives*. Princeton: Princeton University Press, 1963.
Rose, Ernst. "Problems of Medieval Psychology as Presented in the 'klein gemahel' of *Heinrich the Unfortunate*." *Germanic Review*, 22 (1947), 182-7.
Ruh, Kurt. "Hartmanns *Armer Heinrich*. Erzählmodell und theologische Implikation." In: *Mediaevalia litteraria: Festschrift Helmut de Boor*. Ed. Ursula Hennig and Herbert Kolb. Munich: Beck, 1971.
_____. *Höfische Epik des deutschen Mittelalters*. Grundlagen der Germanistik, 7. Berlin: Erich Schmidt, 1967.
_____. "Zur Interpretation von Hartmanns *Iwein*." In: *Philologia Deutsch: Festschrift W. Henzen*. Ed. Werner Kohlschmidt and Paul Zinsli. Bern: Francke, 1965.
Sacker, Hugh. "An Interpretation of Hartmann's *Iwein*." *Germanic Review*, 36 (1961), 5-26.
Salmon, Paul. "'Ane zuht': Hartmann von Aue's Criticism of *Iwein*." *Modern Language Review*, 69 (1974), 556-61.

_____. "The Underrated Lyrics of Hartmann von Aue." *Modern Language Review*, 66 (1971), 810-25.

_____. "The Wild Man in *Iwein* and Medieval Descriptive Technique." *Modern Language Review*, 56 (1961), 520-8.

Sayce, Olive. "Romance Elements in the Lyrics of Hartmann von Aue." In: *Hartmann von Aue: Changing Perspectives*. Ed. Timothy McFarland and Silvia Ranawake. Göppingen: Kümmerle, 1988. 53-64.

Schirokauer, Arno. "Zur Interpretation des *Armen Heinrich*." *Zeitschrift fü deutsches Altertum*, 83 (1951-2), 59-78.

Scholler, Harald. "'Wâ sint diu werc, die rede hoere ich wol': Ein Beitrag zur Interpretation von Hartmanns *Iwein*. In: *Husbanding the Golden Grain: Studies in Honor of Henry W. Nordmeyer*. Ed. Luanne T. Frank and Emory E. George. Ann Arbor: University of Michigan Press, 1973. 295-320.

Schröder, Joachim. *Zur Darstellung und Funktion der Schauplätze in den Artusromanen Hartmanns von Aue*. Göppinger Arbeiten zur Germanistik, 61. Göppingen: Alfred Kümmerle, 1972.

Schröder, Werner. "*Der arme Heinrich* Hartmanns von Aue im Lichte einer neuen Quelle." In: *Festschrift für Karl Bischoff zum 70. Geburtstag*. Ed. Günter Bellmann, Günter Eifler, and Wolfgang Kleiber. Cologne: Böhlau, 1975. 308-27.

Schupp, Volker. "Kritische Anmerkungen zur Rezeption des deutschen Artusromancen anhand von Hartmanns *Iwein*: Theorie--Text--Bildmaterial." *Frühmittelalterliche Studien*, 9 (1975), 405-42.

Schusky, Renate. "Lunete—eine 'kupplerische Dienerin'?" *Euphorion*, 71 (1977), 18-46.

Schwarz, Werner. "Free Will in Hartmann's *Gregorius*." *PBB*, 89 (1967), 129-50.

Schweikle, Günther. "Zum *Iwein* Hartmanns von Aue: Strukturale Korrepondenzen und Oppositionen." In: *Probleme des Erzählens in der Weltliteratur: Festschrift für Käte Hamburger zum 75. Geburtstag am 21. September 1971*. Ed. Fritz Martini. Stuttgart: Ernst Klett, 1971. 1-21.

Schwietering, Julius. "The Origins of the Medieval Humility Formula." *Publications of the Modern Language Association*, 69 (1954), 1279-91.

Seiffert, Leslie. "Hartmann von Aue and his Lyric Poetry." *Oxford German Studies*, 3 (1968), 1-29.

_____. "On the Language of Sovereignty, Deference and Solidarity: The Surrender of the Accusing Lover in Hartmann's *Klage*." In: *Hartmann von Aue: Changing Perspectives*. Ed. Timothy McFarland and Silvia Ranawake. Göppingen: Kümmerle, 1988. 21-52.

_____. "The Maiden's Heart: Legend and Fairy-Tale in Hartmann's *Der arme Heinrich*." *Deutsche Vierteljahrsschrift für Literaturwissenschaft und Geistesgeschichte*, 37 (1963), 384-405.

Selbmann, Rolf. "Strukturschema und Operatoren in Hartmanns *Iwein*." *Deutsche Vierteljahrsschrift für Literaturwissenschaft und Geistesgeschichte*, 50 (1976), 60-83.
Siefken, Hinrich. "'Der saelden strâze': Zum Motiv der zwei Wege bei Hartmann von Aue." *Euphorion*, 61 (1967), 1-21.
Siegfried, Hans. "Der Schuldbegriff im *Gregorius* und im *Armen Heinrich* Hartmanns von Aue." *Euphorion*, 65 (1971), 162-82.
Snow, Ann. "Heinrich and Mark: Two Medieval Voyeurs." *Euphorion*, 66 (1972), 113-27.
Sparnaay, Hendricus. "Brauchen wir ein neues Hartmann-Bild?" *Deutsche Vierteljahrsschrift für Literaturwissenschaft und Geistesgeschichte*, 39 (1965), 639-49.
_____. "Hartmanns *Iwein*." In: *Zur Sprache und Literatur des Mittelalters*. Groningen: J.B. Wolters, 1961. 216-30.
_____. "'Mîn her Salatîn.'" *Germanisch-romanische Monatsschrift*, 22 (1934), 477-9.
Swinburne, Hilda. "The Miracle in *Der arme Heinrich*." *German Life and Letters*, 22 (1969), 205-9.
_____. "Some Comments on the Language of *Der arme Heinrich*." *German Life and Letters*, 24 (1971), 303-15.
Tar, Anne Marie. *Die Funktion der Hauptzofen in Yvain, Iwein, und Tristan*. M.A. Thesis, Rice, 1982.
Tax, Petrus. "Der *Erek* Hartmanns von Aue. Ein Antitypus zu der *Eneit* Heinrichs von Veldecke?" In: *Festschrift Helen Adolf*. Ed. Sheema Z. Bühne, James L. Hodge, and Lucille B. Pinto. New York: Ungar, 1968. 47-62.
_____. "Studien zum Symbolischen in Hartmanns *Erec*: Erecs ritterliche Erhöhung." *Wirkendes Wort*, 13 (1963), 277-88.
_____. "Studien zum Symbolischen in Hartmanns *Erec*: Enites Pferd." *Zeitschrift für deutsche Philologie*, 82 (1963), 29-44.
Thoran, Barbara. "'Diu ir man verrâten hât.' Zum Problem von Enites Schuld im *Erec* Hartmanns von Aue." *Wirkendes Wort*, 5 (1975), 255-68.
Thum, Bernd. *Aufbruch und Verweigerung: Literatur und Geschichte am Oberrhein im hohen Mittelalter*. Waldkirch im Breisgau: Waldkircher Verlagsgesellschaft, 1980.
Tobin, Frank J. *Gregorius and Der arme Heinrich: Hartmann's Dualistic and Gradualistic Views of Reality*. Stanford German Studies, 3. Bern: Lang, 1973.
_____. "Hartmann's *Erec*: The Perils of Young Love." *Seminar*, 14 (1978), 1-14.
Tonomura, Naohiko. "Zur Schuldfrage im *Gregorius* Hartmanns von Aue." *Wirkendes Wort*, 18 (1968), 1-17.
Valk, Melvin. *Word-Index to Gottfried's Tristan*. Madison, Wisconsin: University of Wisconsin Press, 1958.
van Stockum, T.C. "Eine *crux philologorum*: Die prognostisch-therapeutische Formel in *Armen Heinrich* des Hartmann von Ouwe." *Neophilologus*, 48 (1964), 146-50.

Wapnewski, Peter. "Der *Gregorius* in Hartmanns Werk." *Zeitschrift für deutsche Philologie*, 80 (1961), 225-52.

_____. *Hartmann von Aue*. 4th ed. Sammlung Metzler, 17. Stuttgart: Metzler, 1969.

_____. "Poor Henry—Poor Job: A Contribution to the Discussion of Hartmann's von Aue so-called Conversion to an Anti-Courtly Attitude." In: *The Epic in Medieval Society: Aesthetic and Moral Values*. Ed. Harald Scholler. Tübingen: Niemeyer, 1977. 214-25.

Wehrli, Max. "Iwein's Erwachen." In: *Formen mittelalterlicher Erzählung: Aufsätze*. Zürich: Atlantis, 1969. 177-93.

Wells, D.A. "Gesture in Hartmann's *Gregorius*." In: *Hartmann von Aue: Changing Perspectives*. Ed. Timothy McFarland and Silvia Ranawake. Göppingen: Kümmerle, 1988.

_____. "The Medieval Nebuchadnezzar: The Exegetical Tradition of *Daniel IV* and its Significance for the Ywain Romances and for German Vernacular Literature." *Frühmittelalterliche Studien*, 16 (1982), 380-432. 159-86.

Werbow, Stanley Newman. "Queen Guinevere as a Pedagogue: Pronominal Reference and Literary Composition in Hartmann's *Iwein*." *Modern Language Notes*, 80 (1965), 441-8.

Wheeler, J.A. "Hartmann's *Iwein* and Chrétien's *Yvain* as Seen by the Critics." *Journal of the Australasian Universities Language and Literature Association*, 2 (1954), 49-56.

Whitehead, F. "Yvain's Wooing." In: *Medieval Miscellany Presented to Eugène Vinaver*. Manchester: Manchester University Press, 1965. 321-36.

Wiehl, Peter. "Zur Komposition des *Erec* Hartmanns von Aue." *Wirkendes Wort*, 22 (1972), 89-107.

Willson, H.B. "A 'New Order' in Hartmann's *Gregorius* and *Der arme Heinrich*." *Nottingham Mediaeval Studies*, 18 (1974), 3-16.

_____. "*Amor inordinata* in Hartmann's *Gregorius*." *Speculum*, 41 (1966), 86-104.

_____. "*Der arme Heinrich's* 'Confession' and Guilt." *Journal of English and Germanic Philology*, 78 (1939), 469-84.

_____. "Hartmann's *Gregorius* and the Parable of the Good Samaritan." *Modern Language Review*, 54 (1959), 194-203.

_____. "*Inordinatio* in the Marriage of the Hero in Hartmann's *Iwein*." *Modern Philology*, 68 (1970-71), 242-53.

_____. "Kalogrenant's Curiosity in Hartmann's *Iwein*." *German Life and Letters*, 21 (1968), 287-96.

_____. "Love and Charity in Hartmann's *Iwein*." *Modern Language Review*, 57 (1962), 216-27.

_____. "'Marriageable' in *Der arme Heinrich*." *Modern Philology*, 64 (1966-67), 95-102.

_____. "New Light on *Der arme Heinrich* from Variant Readings." *Modern Language Review*, 74 (1979), 335-40.

_____. "*Ordo* in the Portrayal of the Maid in *Der arme Heinrich*." *Germanic Review*, 44 (1969), 83-94.

_____. "The Role of Keii in Hartmann's *Iwein*." *Medium Aevum*, 30 (1961), 145-58.

_____. "Sin and Redemption in Hartmann's *Erec*." *Germanic Review*, 33 (1958), 5-14.

_____. "Symbol and Reality in *Der arme Heinrich*." *Modern Language Review*, 53 (1958), 526-36.

_____. "*Triuwe* and *untriuwe* in Hartmann's *Erec*." *German Quarterly*, 43 (1970), 5-23.

Wisniewski, Roswitha. "Hartmanns *Klage-Büchlein*." *Euphorion*, 57 (1963), 341-69.

Zuntz, Günther. "Ödipus und Gregorius: Tragödie und Legende." In: *Hartmann von Aue*. Wege der Forschung, 359. Darmstadt: Wissenschaftliche Buchgesellschaft, 1973. 87-107.

Zutt, Herta. "Die formale Struktur von Hartmanns *Klage*." *Zeitschrift für deutsche Philologie*, 87 (1968), 359-72.

NOTES

INTRODUCTION

1. Line numbers in parentheses refer to the editions cited in EDITIONS AND TRANSLATIONS.

2. There has been a tendency to separate the "courtly" works (*Erec* and *Iwein*) from the "religious poems (*Grêgôrius* and *Der arme Heinrich*). In fact, H.B. Willson, "A 'New Order' in Hartmann's *Grêgorîus* and *Der arme Heinrich*," *Nottingham Mediaeval Studies*, 18 (1974), 3-4, advances the argument that the religious poems are a type of expiation, an "atonement for Hartmann's earlier concern with poetry in which *der werlde lôn* was too favorably presented. Both appear to have been written when the poet was in the mood of contrition and genuinely feared for the salvation of his soul." Willson here verges on biographical criticism, the pitfalls of which are noted by Leslie Seiffert, "Hartmann von Aue and his Lyric Poetry," *Oxford German Studies*, 3 (1968), 4:
> In the first place, each philological clue may, by simple extrapolation of its internal terms of reference, lead to a different type of poet's *vita*.

3. Antonín Hruby, "Moralphilosophie und Moraltheologie in Hartmanns Erec," in *The Epic in Medieval Society: Aesthetic and Moral Values*, ed. Harald Scholler (Tübingen: Niemeyer, 1977), p. 194, speaks of "Hartmanns Klarheit." And John Alexander Asher, "Hartmann and Gottfried: Master and Pupil?" *Journal of the Australasian Universities Language and Literature Association*, 16 (1961), 140, notes "the simplicity of Hartmann's style." Seiffert, p. 1, contends that Hartmann's lyric poems have similarly suffered in critical evaluation and have been "relegated, if not explicitly, then at least in intention to the category of *juvenalia*." Hubert Heinen has recently published on Hartmann's lyrics. See "Irony and Confession in 'Sît ich den sumer' (*MF* 205,1)," *Monatshefte*, 80 (1988), 416-28; and "'Mit gemache lân': A *Crux* in Hartmann's 'Maniger grüezet mich alsô' (*MF* 216,29)," *Studies in Medieval Culture*, ed. John R. Sommerfeldt and Thomas H. Seiler (Kalamazoo, Michigan: The Medieval Institute, 1978), pp. 85-110.

4. I have earlier examined this fascination with mind in two articles that form the nucleus for this study's second and final chapters. See S.L. Clark, "Changing One's Mind: Arenas of Conflict and Resolution in Hartmann's *Iwein*," *Euphorion*, 73 (1979), 286-303, and S.L. Clark, "Hartmann's *Erec*: Language, Perception, and Transformation," *Germanic Review*, 56 (1981), 81-94.

5. In referring to Hartmann's audience as "the reader," I do not disregard oral tradition or performance but, first of all, employ a term of convenience that adapts to Hartmann's modern audience, and, secondly, indicate my mindfulness of Hartmann's awareness of a reading public.

6. Ulrich Ernst, "Der Antagonismus von *vita carnalis* und *vita spiritualis* im *Gregorius* Hartmanns von Aue: Versuch einer Werkdeutung im Horizont der patristischen und monastischen Tradition, Teil 2," *Euphorion*, 73 (1979), 1, notes Hartmann's use of "spirituelle Topographie." Other critics, among them Bernd Lorenz, "Bemerkungen zum Motiv der 'zwei wege' in Hartmanns *Gregorius*," *Euphorion*, 71 (1977), 92-6, have noted Hartmann's use of landscape in his moral commentary.

7. See Erich Auerbach, "The Knight Sets Forth," in *Mimesis: The Representation of Reality in Western Literature*, trans. Willard R. Trask (Princeton: Princeton University Press, 1953), pp. 128-9, where he discusses the moral significance of directions. See also Sister Ursula Deitmaring, "Die Bedeutung von Rechts und Links in theologischen und literarischen Texten bis um 1200," *Zeitschrift für deutsches Altertum*, 98 (1969), 265-92.

8. For the critic there is considerable fascination in what poets put in and leave out of their descriptions of landscape and physical surroundings. See Theodore M. Andersson, *Early Epic Scenery: Homer, Virgil, and the Medieval Legacy* (Ithaca: Cornell University Press, 1967), for a well-reasoned and provocative study of the evolution of spatial description in which he examines Homer's technique ("Homer's method is to provide the reader with a large, blank canvas, on which, as time goes on, he enters a few items here and there, more or less at random"—p. 23), Virgil's method ("the outlining of a scene before it is narrated, the view from alternating distances, visualization through the use of various lines and shapes, animation through sight, sound, and motion, the abundant use of contrast, revelation in the eye of a beholder, and the application of complementary perspective"—p. 75), and the subsequent medieval tradition in which perspectives begin to vanish (pp. 160ff.) and models are diluted (p. 162) so that "the romance makes everything explicit, but, for all its directness, it tells us less than the original" (p. 167). Andersson looks ahead, in the final analysis, toward a "definition of romance, in this case through the study of scenic reductions. Once more it should be apparent that whatever romance is, it is not epic." He does not undertake a complete definition of romance or even an exhaustive analysis of spatial elements that might contribute to this definition, but he provides valuable critical tools for other scholars in other disciplines in pointing out how sound, light, and space serve as "focusing qualities" (p. 68) and in demonstrating how "sometimes the dwelling upon detail appears to transport us into a recalibrated time frame" (p. 31). Andersson gives the student of narrative technique a good working model to observe.

9. Seeking counsel was the norm, rather than the exception, in medieval society, but Hartmann's characters often offer it unsolicited.

10. At the risk of being labelled reductive by resorting to word-counting, I nevertheless find telling the lesser incidence of "mind-terms" in, for example, Gottfried's Tristan. See Melvin E. Valk, *A Word Index to Gottfried's Tristan* (Madison: University of Wisconsin Press, 1958), who cites 210 entries for *wissen* and related forms, 31 for *denken*, 1 for *erdenken*, 17 for *gedenken*, 140 for *sin*, 236 for *muot*, 12 for *tump*, 114 for *wîs*, and 81 for *gedanc* and its derivatives. Despite this high number of entries for over nearly 20,000 lines of Gottfried's poem, Hartmann produces a far greater total of instances for the above words and derivatives. See Roy A. Boggs, *Hartmann von Aue: Lemmatisierte Konkordanz um Gesamtwerk*, 2 vol., Indices zur deutschen Literatur, 12/13 (Nendeln: KTO Press, 1979).

11. My purpose, then, is not to determine the extent of Hartmann's possible debt to Augustine, to Hugh of St. Victor, or to scholastic philosophy in general. Other scholars have considered this subject at length and have arrived at valuable conclusions. For example, K. Dieter Goebel, *Untersuchungen zu Aufbau und Schuldproblem in Hartmanns Gregorius*, Philologische Studien und Quellen, 78 (Berlin: Erich Schmidt, 1974), p. 122, discusses how scholarly opinions are split over whether the second incest scene in *Grêgôrius* is sin, and the split occurs along the lines of whether Hartmann knew scholastic theory or not. So little, in fact, is known about Hartmann (see Resler, pp. 11-15) and the exact sources of his thought that it cannot be definitively determined whether or not he consciously based his concept of mind on other established views. Wolf Gewehr, *Hartmanns Klage-Büchlein im Lichte der Frühscholastik*, Göppinger Arbeiten zur Germanistik, 167 (Göppingen: Kümmerle, 1975), is fairly typical of the critics who adhere to the view that Hartmann was familiar with early scholastic teachings. These scholars' findings are useful in examining those mind-related problems that Hartmann poses in his themes, his relationship as a poet to the reader, and in his choice of language, but I prefer to work with the "presence" of mind-terms in the texts and the patterns they create within and between the poems, rather than with the "absent" elements that are putative sources. To be sure, it could be argued that a study of Hartmann and mind cannot be convincing unless the writer works his or her way through the *Patrologia latina* with an eye for references to *mens, cogitare*, and the like. While this methodology has many proponents—I feel uneasy with it in dealing with Hartmann. In the final analysis, we are told by Hartmann that he has read many books ("er nam im manige schouwe / an mislîchen buochen"—*Der arme Heinrich*, ll. 6-7), but we do not know what books they were, other than the Old French sources that he drew upon for *Erec, Iwein*, and *Grêgôrius*. Were we to speculate upon his reading list, we might be as surprised as the abbot in *Grêgôrius* is

when he discovers that his pupil has not only ingested theology and grammar but has secretly also feasted on popular chivalric works. "The Foreward," *Hartmann von Aue: Changing Perspectives*, ed. Timothy McFarland and Silvia Ranawake, Göppinger Germanistische Arbeiten, 486 (Göppingen: Kümmerle, 1988) also notes the lack of biographical details but the strong presence of this poet and his *persona* as both *miles* and *clericus* (p. ix).

12. Peter Wapnewski, *Hartmann von Aue*, 4th ed., Sammlung Metzler, 17 (Stuttgart: Metzler, 1969), p. 16, sets forth a generally agreed upon chronology of Hartmann's works.

13. I use here the title of a work that has meant much to me in my understanding of individuality and gender. See Carol Gilligan, *In a Different Voice: Psychological Theory and Women's Development* (Cambridge: Harvard University Press, 1982).

CHAPTER 1. DIE KLAGE

1. Hedwig Gross, *Hartmanns Büchlein* (Diss., Bonn, 1936), who holds that "*Das Büchlein* ist ein Gespräch des jungen Hartmann mit sich selbst, ein Gespräch zwischen Herz und Leib, also ein Selbstgespräch in der dramatischen Einkleidung einer Allegorie, in welchem das Verhältnis der beiden Partner zueinander von vornherein klar ist" (p. 5), also takes the view that the heart possesses the functions of mind: "Legen wir das augustinische Seelenschema zugrunde, wonach die Seele a) *vivificatio*, Lebensgeist, b) *mens*, intellective Wesenheit ist, welche letztere sich wieder in die drei Seelenvermögen: *memoria, intellectus, voluntas* spaltet, so ist klar, dass das Herz im *Büchlein* auf das Ganze gesehen die Funktionen der *mens* hat" (p. 10). I will, however, argue that both heart and body exhibit functions of mind. Good background material for the debate genre can be found in M.A. Bossy, "Medieval Debates of Body and Soul," *Comparative Literature*, 28 (1976), 144-63.

2. See Herta Zutt, "Die formale Struktur von Hartmanns *Klage*," *Zeitschrift für deutsche Philologie*, 87 (1968), 359-72, for a fine article on the work's numerical structure gleaned through manuscript initials.

3. Interestingly, the plight he finds himself in is so dire that he, like Erec, who flees society, later voices his estrangement from his fellow men through the statement:

"Mir wirt aber sus so we
daz ich bi den liuten me
nicht beliben getar"
(ll. 377-9; "I was in such pain that I did not dare to remain around other people").

4. Roswitha Wisniewski, "Hartmanns *Klage-Büchlein*," *Euphorion*, 57 (1963), 355, notes the alternation of "Anklage" and "Wehklage" in the poem. See also Volker Mertens, "'*Factus est per clericum miles cythereus*': Überlegungen zu Enstehungs-und Wirkungsbedingungen von Hartmanns *Klage-Büchlein*," in *Hartmann von Aue: Changing Perspectives*, ed. Timothy McFarland and Silvia Ranawake, Göppinger Arbeiten zur Germanistik, 486 (Göppingen: Kümmerle, 1988), pp. 1-19. Mertens points out (p. 7) that the audience deals here not with soul and body but rather heart and body.

5. Gross, p. 15, views the heart as an "erkennendes und ratendes Organ."

6. See Heinen, *Monatshefte*, and *Studies in Medieval Culture*.

7. Thomas L. Keller, "*MF* 205,1: 'Sit ich den sumer truoc' as a Microcosm of the *Iwein* of Hartmann von Aue," *Germanic Notes*, 11 (1980), 5, comments:
> One day, however, he suddenly realizes that he has remained away too long and is overcome by remorse. Lunete then arrives and delivers a speech before King Arthur and his court condemning Iwein. It is at this point that MF 205,1 could be appropriately inserted thematically into the story as Iwein's lament.

8. Particularly striking is the phrase "mîn selbes vîent" (*MF* 205,11), which appears in l. 1452 of *Die Klage*.

9. Wapnewski, p. 42.

10. Wapnewski, p. 40.

11. Moreover, *Die Klage* will be seen to be related to *Erec* in terms of its frequent mention of constancy (Enîte, in her *triuwe*, is constant), wounded feelings (Erec specializes in them), cowardice (Guivreiz will underestimate Erec), advice-giving, and knowledge.

CHAPTER TWO: EREC

1. Peter Wiehl, "Zur Komposition des *Erec* Hartmanns von Aue," *Wirkendes Wort*, 22 (1972), 89-107, does an impressive piece of work in his study of how *Erec* is structured with respect to numerical composition. Hansjürgen Linke, *Epische Strukturen in der Dichtung Hartmanns von Aue: Untersuchungen zur Formkritik, Werkstruktur und Vortragsgliederung* (Munich: Fink, 1968), pays scrupulous attention to the manuscript tradition in his examination of structure in Hartmann's works.

2. See Ulrich Gaier, "Sebastian Brant's *Narrenschiff* and the Humanists," *Publications of the MModern Language Association*, 83 (1968), 266-70.

3. This rhyme-pair surfaces in ll. 1230-1 and ll. 3829-30.

4. Several critics have examined Hartmann's narrative intrusions, among them: Wolfgang Dittmann, "'Dûne hâst niht wâr, Hartmann!' Zum Begriff der '*wârheit*' in Hartmanns *Iwein*," in

Festgabe für Ulrich Pretzel, ed. Werner Simon, Wolfgang Bachofer, and Wolfgang Dittmann (Berlin: Erich Schmidt, 1963), who notes, p. 155: "Hartmann deutet nicht aus der Handlung heraus, sondern interpretiert neben der Handlung"; Xenja von Ertzdorff, "Spiel der Interpretation: Der Erzähler in Hartmanns *Iwein*," in *Festgabe für Friedrich Maurer*, ed. Werner Besch, Siegfried Grosse, and Heinz Rupp (Düsseldorf: Schwan, 1968), pp. 135-7; Hans-Peter Kramer, *Erzählbemerkung und Erzählerkommentare in Chrestiens und Hartmanns Erec und Iwein*, Göppinger Arbeiten zur Germanistik, 35 (Göppingen: Kümmerle, 1971).

5. He also notes that both men's voices were altered because of the stress of battle: "und des kampfes grimme / verwandelt ir stimme" (ll. 7519-20). This vocal aspect is important, as good perceivers are usually able to recognize each other in this manner. For example, Guivreiz stops his attack on Erec when he realizes that the woman appealing to him is in fact Enîte: "Guivreiz vrouwen Enîten / bî der stimme erkande" (ll. 6958-9). Moreover, Keiî determines Erec's identity on the basis of his voice:
"er enwolde sich nicht nennen.
sîne stimme hôrte ich,
wan er jach vil wider mich:
als ichz dar an kiesen mac,
sôst ez Erec fil de roi Lac"
(ll. 4853; "He wouldn't give his name. But I heard his voice—indeed he said a lot to me—and I would judge by it that he is Erec the son of King Lac"—p. 87).

6. D.G. Mowatt, "Irony in Hartmann's *Iwein*," in *Deutung und Bedeutung: Studies in German and Comparative Literature Presented to Karl-Werner Maurer*, ed. Brigitte Schluderman, Victor G. Doerksen, Robert J. Glendinning, and Evelyn Sherabon Firchow (The Hague: Mouton, 1973), p. 39, supports this literalist response: "a good knight wears armour and helmet even when the inevitable impairment in hearing and vision endangers his life."

7. My colleague, Hubert Heinen, has quite sensibly pointed out that it is a good deal easier to be aware of someone if you are in fact looking out for him (Erec's pursuers seeking him or bandits on the lookout for booty) than it is to be aware of enemies that may or may not be present (Erec in a more or less deserted forest). Heinen's point is well taken, but I would add that the extreme one-sidedness of Hartmann's portrayal earlier in the romance suggests not a justification of Erec's unawareness but rather a calling to attention of a character flaw. One would think that because Erec rode forth to seek adventure, his senses would be tuned to situations that might provide adventure, yet this is not the case in the early part of this romance, for Erec, with Enîte as bait, simply stumbles into situations. Adventure, by etymology and tradition, is supposed to be something that "comes" to the knight. Yet one would expect Erec, so eager to

find it in his flight from the safety of his castle, to meet it at least half-way.

8. Although he treats another work, Hugh Sacker, "An Interpretation of Hartmann's *Iwein*," *Germanic Review*, 36 (1961), p. 6, makes a perceptive comment that can here be applied to the relationship between Hartmann's disclaimer in *Erec* (ll. 4150-9) and the narrative events that surround it:

> One must admittedly assume that the meaning of a work is not necessarily adequately expressed in the statements of the narrator, but that the events themselves furnish as important a guide to the meaning as do the narrator's comments.

In *Erec*, the narrator's intrusion has the effect of making the reader look carefully at the events that inspired the authorial gloss: would an unarmed Erec perceive danger threatening his wife, or is Erec's physical unaccountability a commentary on his mental readiness?

9. Commenting upon the effect of Erec's and Enîte's preoccupation with each other at this point in the romance, Kurt Ruh, *Höfische Epik des deutschen Mittelalters, Grundlagen der Germanistik*, 7 (Berlin: Erich Schmidt, 1967), p. 123, notes: "Das ist ein für die Umwelt peinlicher Flitterwochenzustand ohne Ende."

10. Ruh, pp. 127f., provides a meticulous catalogue of the consequence of this *gemach*, for he notes (p. 127), "Das erste Thema des Auszugs ist *ungemach*," and then cites the series of words indicating unpleasantness that Hartmann selects to underscore the contrast between the *gemach* of the past and the *ungemach* of the present.

11. That Enîte perceives him as both husband and lover is apparent in the following exchange between her and Oringles: "'was er, iuwer âmîs oder iuwer man?' / 'beide, herre'" (ll. 6172-3). For a perceptive article that treats this formulation in Chrétien's *Erec et Enide*, see Deborah Nelson, "Enide: *Amie* or *Femme*?" *Romance Notes*, 21,iii (1981), 1-6, who contends in her abstract:

> Most critics define the unifying theme of *Erec et Enide* in terms of an evaluation of Erec's character and experiences and consider Enide merely as an extension of her husband's personality. . . In fact, Enide emerges as the focal point as the plot develops around the dramatic changes in her status. Her transition from *pucelle* to *amie* occurs in a traditional fashion, but surprisingly her role as *amie* does not terminate with her marriage and assumption of the duties and responsibilities of *femme*. Unlike the situation in Marie de France's Elidus, where *amie* and *femme* are neatly divided between Guildeluec and Guilliadun, Enide must undergo severe testing at the hands of her husband, which she surmounts paradoxically through disobedience. The freeing of Mabonagrain in the *Joie de la Cour* episode proves the

final blow in the destruction of the *amie* in Enide and the confirmation of the *femme*, making her then eligible to become *reine*. The tears shed by the *demoiselle* at the release of her lover reflect the which is now finished forever.

12. Marianne Kalinke, "*Vorhte* in Hartmanns *Erec*," *Amsterdamer Beiträge zur älteren Germanistik*, 11 (1976), 74, points out that "Erec's *verligen* is a consequence and combination of Enite's silence and his own mistaken belief that honor, once attained, need not be reconfirmed."

13. See Georg Friedrich Benecke, Wilhelm Müller, and Friedrich Zarncke, *Mittelhochdeutsches Wörterbuch*, Vol. 3 (Leipzig: S. Hirzel, 1861), pp. 757-8, meaning 2: *wîselos* = "unverständig." *wîselos*, meaning both lacking direction and lacking wisdom/understanding, indicates to the reader that, for Hartmann, sure movement in a threatening landscape is only possible when the protagonist acts wisely. Direction, then, operates in a spiritual as well as a physical dimension: he who knows where to go so that he can lead others (*wîsen*) is truly wise (*wîs*). One should also note that Hartmann employs the term *wîseloser rât* (l. 1582) in *Die Klage*, which lends strength to this reading.

14. H.B. Willson, "*Triuwe* and *untriuwe* in Hartmann's *Erec*," *German Quarterly*, 43 (1970), 6, contends that Enîte displays "a higher order of *triuwe*" in disobeying Erec. Hans Blosen, "Noch einmal: Zu Enîtes Schuld in Hartmanns *Erec*: Mit Ausblicken auf Chrétiens Roman und das *Mabinogi* von *Gereint*," *Orbis Litterarum*, 31 (1976), 98-102, investigates the employment of the term *treu* and other related words in *Erec*.

15. Hugo Kuhn, *Dichtung und Welt im Mittelalter* (Stuttgart: Metzler, 1959), pp. 147-8, draws a useful distinction in this regard between the adventures of the first part of the romance ("alle Episoden des ersten Teils sind 'Zufälle'") and those of the second part: "Im zweiten Teil bestimmt Erec selbst die Reise." Yet what I see is less a conscious exercising of Erec's volition than a poetic purpose that orders all adventures in a sequence according to how Erec can best survive and learn from them: all contain virtually the same components, arranged among different incidents, so that the testing of Erec consists not of one climactic adventure—akin to, for example, to Roland's rearguard action with the Saracens—but rather a series of related adventures, whereby he is given the option to make the same mistake repeatedly until he masters the skill that enables him to perform wisely and well.

16. I will show that Hartmann's romance speaks for the gradual development of the hero, rather than for the blanket statement of Michel Huby, "L'approfondissement psychologique dans *Erec* de Hartmann," *Etudes germaniques*, 22 (1967), 23: "Le Moyen Age ne connaît pas l'évolution lente, le déploiement progressif d'une personalité comme nous la rencontrons chez les poètes moderns, dans

'Wilhelm Meister' par exemple. Le Moyen Age ne connaît pas le Werden notion éminemment moderne . . . ."

17. Hinrich Siefken, "'Der saelden straze.' Zum Motiv der zwei Wege bei Hartmann von Aue," *Euphorion*, 61 (1967), 2, employs the term "Bedeutungsgeographie," an apt description for Hartmann's interwoven mental and physical landscapes.

18. Erec exhibits an eagerness to undertake the adventure of following the threesome, and, we later learn that this opportunity is really his first occasion to prove himself to the Arthurian court, to which he, as is the case with many other young knights, is attached. Taking this situation from a more socio-historical perspective, Bernd Thum, *Aufbruch und Verweigerung: Literatur und Geschichte zum Oberrhein im hohen Mittelalter* (Waldkirch im Breisgau: Waldkircher Verlagsgesellschaft, 1980), p. 157, sees in Hartmann's *Erec* the problem common to young sons, "die in fremde Dienste treten mussten oder wollten."

19. Erec, however, is rash only a little later in the romance, as noted by Roy Amos Boggs, "Hartmann's *Erec*," in *Innovation in Medieval Literature: Essays to the Memory of Alan Markman*, ed. Douglas Radcliff-Umstead (Pittsburgh: University of Pittsburgh Press, 1971), p. 54: "Erec's complete disregard for his own safety (*ungewarheit*) during the post-wedding tournament also evidences a certain amount of youthful brashness."

20. Barbara Thoran, "'Diu ir man verrâten hât'—Zum Problem von Enîtes Schuld im *Erec* Hartmanns von Aue,'" *Wirkendes Wort*, 25 (1975), 256, comments upon Enîte's taciturnity in the first 2923 lines: "Der sonst so dialogfreudige Hartmann lässt sie nur vier Worte sprechen."

21. Boggs, p. 49, notes Erec's "outdated arms" during the Imâin episode: "the outdated arms merely underscore the deplorable condition in which Erec finds himself. But he clearly knows how to use them."

22. This passage, and others, have caused Tobin, p. 3, to comment that Enîte is "shy and childlike in public."

23. See Matthias Lexer, *Mittelhochdeutsches Handwörterbuch* (Leipzig: S. Hirzel, 1872), Vol. 1, pp. 1930-1.

24. For the horse as a "commonplace figure for the flesh," see Tom Artin, *The Allegory of Adventure: Reading Chrétien's Erec and Yvain* (Lewisburg: Bucknell University Press, 1974), p. 79. Enîte's particular association with one horse is explored by Petrus W. Tax, "Studien zum Symbolischen in Hartmanns *Erec*: Enites Pferd," *Zeitschrift für deutsche Philologie*, 82 (1963), 29-44.

25. The term *gelpfer rubîn* appears in Iwein, l. 625, and is one of the many linguistic parallels that work to link the romances thematically.

26. Enîte's beauty, it should be recalled, is such that it has an extraordinary effect on the members of the Arthurian court: "so daz si ir selber vergâzen" (l. 1739; "forgetting themselves"—p. 50). This is very much like Iwein's reaction at seeing Laudîne for the first

time: "daz er sîn selbes gar vergaz" (l. 1337; "he quite forgot himself"—p. 71). However, where Laudîne and her court can easily forget the former ruler, Ascalôn ("des tôten ist vergezzen"—l. 2435; "the dead man was forgotten"—p. 85), Enîte cannot let Erec slip from her mind: "nû enmohte si aber nicht vergezzen / ir lieben gesellen" (ll. 6435-6; "Enite could not forget her dear husband"—p. 104).

27. Concerning Erec's attitude to Enîte, Eva-Maria Carne, *Frauengestalten bei Hartmann von Aue: Ihre Bedeutung im Aufbau und Gehalt der Epen*, Marburger Beiträge zur Germanistik, 31 (Marburg: N.G. Elwert, 1970), calls attention to the "Geringschätzung der Frau" (p. 2) in the culture of the Jews and the Romans, an attitude later enlarged upon by the Church Fathers, so that woman was viewed as "blosses Objekt" (p. 2). She goes on to explain Erec's attitude in these terms: "Die Frau ist für Erec noch Nebensache. Sie ist kein 'Du', sondern ein 'Es', das ihm für die ritterliche Lebensform notwendig ist" (p. 35).

28. In *Die Klage*, l. 98, we find the bafflement ("'ichne weiz wes si mir niht ist guot'"; "'I don't know why she isn't good to me'") that Erec must experience in his first stunned apprehension of Enîte's speech, as well as his subsequent railing as she continues to defy him by warning him of dangers.

29. Thoran, p. 257, notes that during ll. 2923-7111 Enîte is "als fühlende, denkende, und handelnde Person im Vordergrund" but does not draw the connection that Erec is here virtually dumb and mentally vacant.

30. Thomas Cramer, "Soziale Motivation in der Schuld-Sühne-Problematik von Hartmanns *Erec*," *Euphorion*, 66 (1972), 109, sees in Enîte's directional ability a reflection of social status: "Enite ist Erec gleichrangig, und nicht zufällig kann sie ihm jetzt den richtigen Weg durch das Land weisen, das er nicht kennt." I would argue that social status may have something to do with Enîte's abilities to extricate Erec from difficult situations but that the crucial factor is her heightened perceptivity at those times when his is suppressed.

31. For a representative as well as comprehensive statement of recent scholarship's assessment of Hartmann's debt to Chrétien, see Wiebke Freytag, "Zu Hartmanns Methode der Adaption im *Erec*," *Euphorion*, 72 (1978), 227-39. Freytag first sees two major tendencies typified by Huby (who views Hartmann as "der getreue Übersetzer Chrétiens") and by R. Pérennec, "Adaption et societé: l'adaption par Hartmann d'Aue du roman de Chrétien de Troyes, *Erec et Enide*," *Etudes germaniques*, 28 (1973), 289-303, who takes the view that Hartmann had to adapt North French social structures to a mode comprehensible to the German nobility. Freytag's own contention is that Hartmann develops "eine moralisch-religiöse Einsicht" (p. 239) over and above that of Chrétien. Carol K. Bang, "Emotions and Attitudes in Chrétien de Troyes' *Erec et Enide* and Hartmann von Aue's *Erec der wunderaere*," *Publications of the Modern Language Association*, 57 (1942), 304, points out how "in episode after episode

how the emotions of joy and pride in Chrétien become transformed by Hartmann's ethical, religious, and pedagogical conceptions."

32. The narrative perspective has been solidly with Erec until this point, and then it suddenly shifts, so that Erec's thoughts will become closed to the reader. Thomas Heine, "Shifting Perspectives: The Narrative Strategy in Hartmann's *Erec*," *Orbis Litterarum*, 36 (1981), 95-115, corroborates some of the argument in the reading of *Erec* that I advance in this chapter and in "Language, Perception, and Transformation," *Germanic Review*, 56 (1981), 81-94. Heine, p. 95, takes note of

> related changes in the protagonist and in the narrative perspective. Initially, the narrator's use of psycho-narration and commentary provides access to Erec's inner qualities and reflections; the reader's familiarity with the protagonist in the opening episodes parallels the latter's unproblematic relationship with society. When Erec becomes estranged from his court and Enite, the narrator's stance shifts accordingly. During the Probefahrt, the prevailing mode of narration, reportage, reveals not more about Erec's state of mind than does Erec himself. As a result, Erec's behavior in this section remains so much of a mystery to the reader as to the other characters in the story. As Erec overcomes his isolation in the final episodes, both the protagonist and the narrator provide insight into the source of Erec's problem: the narrator penetrates Erec's exterior, while the protagonist becomes more talkative and willing to discuss the nature of his difficulties. And yet the lesson to be learned from Erec's experiences becomes explicit only when he himself expresses it to Mabonagrin. Thus Hartmann places us in a situation analogous to that of his protagonist: Erec's insights become our insights. Like Erec, we proceed from ignorance to a new understanding of the knight's proper relationship to society.

Heine notes Erec's early "prudent restraint" and "his openness and sociability" (p. 97), then his "emotional volatility" during the Probefahrt (p. 100), and finally examines elements of "his new relationship with society" (p. 113).

33. See Werner Fechter, "Absalon als Vergleichs- und Beispielfigur im mittelhochdeutschen Schrifttum," *PBB*, 83 (1961-2), 302-16. In addition, Green notes (p. 799) that Absalom, held to be a paragon of beauty, also killed his half-brother and rebelled against his father. Moreover, the reference to Solomon is complicated as well. "By means of what is revealed as an unjustified comparison with Solomon's ideal wisdom Hartmann points up the restricted nature of Erec's *wîsheit* (p. 802). Finally, with respect to the

comparison to Alexander, Green notes (p. 803) that "It is part of Hartmann's ironic technique to reveal this falling-short to us by an apparent praise of his hero at this premature stage." Green asserts that

> There is something forced about this eulogy, as if Hartmann had found it difficult to find a positive point to make, since the context into which this praise of a detail is inserted is hardly flattering to Erec (p. 799).

34. Carne, p. 89, points out concerning Erec's uxoriousness that "seine Ich-Befangenheit macht ihn blind und taub für die Umwelt."

35. Artin, p. 83, sees religious implications in Erec's earlier refusal to clothe Enide: "clothes are, on the one hand, the sign of the Fall. Thus, the finest gown the count might give Enide would represent only more pointedly the corruption that Erec has sacramentally overcome."

36. A.T. Hatto, "Enid's Best Dress: A Contribution to the Understanding of Chrétien's and Hartmann's *Erec* and the Welsh *Gereint*," *Euphorion*, 54 (1960), 438, notes "a close symbolical connexion between a woman's dress and her conjugal fidelity" and suggests that Gereint's intent is to shame his wife, "for to parade a woman in an old, cut, tattered or coarse dress was to parade her as an adultress or faithless woman, in fiction and in fact."

37. Rodney Fisher, "Erecs Schuld und Enitens Unschuld bei Hartmann," *Euphorion*, 69 (1975), 168, remarks in a related context that all of Erec's opponents value Enîte, although Erec himself does not appear to.

38. F.P. Knapp, "Enites Totenklage und Selbstmordversuch in Hartmanns *Erec*: eine quellenkritische Analyse," *Germanisch-romanische Monatsschrift*, 26 (9176), 83-90, in examining Enîte's monologue, breaks her speech into ten motifs, only three of which appear in Chrétien's version of the tale.

39. Artin, p. 104, points out concerning Erec's attitude that "when he prohibits Enide to speak to him, even to warn him of danger to his life, he is like a man who wishes to pass through the dangers of this world without the benefit of his senses."

40. Wapnewski, p. 66, views *Iwein* "als Gegenstück" of *Erec*.

41. Kâlogrenant's message, as Artin points out in a discussion of Chrétien's *Yvain* (pp. 39-40), is in the form of a parable. Those who have ears and can hear will gain the full benefit of the spiritual message.

42. D.W. Robertson, Jr., *A Preface to Chaucer: Studies in Medieval Perspectives* (Princeton: Princeton University Press, 1963), p. 74.

43. Knapp, p. 85, in addition to seeing parallels between the tale of Erec and Enîte and that of Pyramus and Thisbe, also sees the statement "'ein man und ein wîp / suln wesen ein lîp'" (ll. 5826-7; "'a man and his wife should be one body'"—pp. 97-8) as a paraphrase of the *Vulgate Genesis 2:24* ("*erunt duo in carne una*").

44. Ruh, p. 110, sensibly notes concerning the possibility of interpreting Hartmann on several levels: "Die damit zugesprochene Möglichkeit einer Mehrdeutigkeit braucht uns nicht zu beunruhigen."

45. In a related vein, Tobin writes of "how intricate are the bonds which hold [Erec and Enîte] together and how mutually dependent they are for their very existence" (p. 8).

46. A representative example of this tendency can be found in Wolfgang Harms, *Der Kampf mit dem Freund oder Verwandten in der deutschen Literatur bis um 1300* (Munich: Eidos, 1963), p. 122.

47. Fisher, p. 174, notes Erec's "autoritäre Behandlung" of Enîte.

48. It is worthy of note that Enîte herself earlier speaks of her *armuot* as a thing of the past, for she refers to Erec as "'der mich von grôzer armuot / ze vrouwen schuof über michel guot'" (ll. 3362-3; "'who raised me from poverty to be mistress of such great wealth'"— p. 69). See Nigel F. Palmer, "Poverty and Mockery in Hartmann's *Erec*, v. 525ff.: A Study of the Psychology and Aesthetics of Middle High German Romance." In: *Hartmann von Aue: Changing Perspectives*, Göppinger Arbeiten zur Germanistik, 486 (Göppingen: Kümmerle, 1988), pp. 65-92.

49. Tobin, p. 11, comments: "However, her fabrications do seem to contain some hidden truths about the ambiguity of her position."

50. Tobin, p. 12, has argued that the protagonist is a man "who has shown no great ability to think through and beyond the clichés around him," and this would seem to be a fairly accurate evaluation of the protagonist for the greater part of the romance.

51. Carne, p. 93, notes in this respect: "Der nächste Gegner Erecs sieht Enites Schönheit nicht mit den Augen der Begehrlichkeit wie die Vorigen. Für Guivreiz ist sie also Begleiterin des Ritters ein Beweis für dessen Wert (ll. 4332-5)."

52. Hans Bayer, "'Bî den liuten ist sô guot': Die meine des *Erec* Hartmanns von Aue," *Euphorion*, 73 (1979), 274, comments: "Der in seiner Ehre verletzte Erec zeigt sich in jeder Hinsicht als ein 'Gefäss des Zorns.'"

53. The phrase "hügete ûf die vart" ("think of . . . his journey"—p. 91; "wanted to start out again"—p. 113) appears in ll. 5249 and 7239. Erec is thinking, but his thoughts are on travel rather than on any particular person or moral issue.

54. Rosemary Picozzi, "Allegory and Symbol in Hartmann's *Gregorius*," in *Essays on German Literature in Honor of G. Joyce Hallamore*, ed. Michael S. Batts and Marketa G. Stankiewicz (Toronto: University of Toronto Press, 1968), p. 19, comments concerning Erec's injury:

> The hero receives a wound in the side, the healing of which proceeds as the rift between himself and Enite gradually heals. At first the wound fails to heal and reopens prior to his reunion with her; it is only

finally healed once his marriage has been truly mended.

55. Erec has a similar fear that humans will hear him and do him harm (l.4236; p. 79), but "vergebene was doch der gedanc / wan ez nieman vernam" (ll. 4239-40; "However, his anxiety was needless since no one heard of the matter [until he was well out of the forest]"—p. 79).

56. Cramer, p. 111, notes that, according to legal precedent, Mâbonagrîn's wife is underage.

57. The relationship of Mâbonagrîn and his wife to Erec and Enîte has been variously examined by many scholars, among them Marianne Wünsch, "Allegorie und Sinnstruktur in *Erec* und *Tristan*," *Deutsche Vierteljahrsschrift für Literaturwissenschaft und Geistesgeschichte*, 46 (1972), 516, who sees the Joie de la cort episode "als Interpretaton und verkürztes Modell von Erecs Handlungsweg"; Artin, p. 119, who comes to the conclusion that the "*Joie de la cort* is figuratively the image of the spiritual condition that was Erec's quest first to flee, but then to confront and overcome. It is the image of the willing enslavement of reason to the whims of passion"; Hans Werner Eroms, *'vreude' bei Hartmann von Aue*, Medium Aevum, 20 (Munich: Fink, 1970), p. 65, who believes that "alles, was Mâbonagrîn und seine Geliebte betrifft, lässt sich auch von Erecs und Enîtes Aufenthalt in Karnant sagen"; and Thoran, p. 263, who makes short work of any "parallels" between the two situations:

> Die parallelen zwischen den beiden paaren Erec-Enîte in Karnant und Mâbonagrîn und seiner geliebten im baumgarten sind gering, die gegensätze gross. Durch Mâbonagrîn war dem hof 'benomen / elliu sin wünne gar / und was et schoener vreuden bar' (10503f). Auch von Erec's hof heisst es, dass er 'aller freuden bar' sei (2989). Soweit die parallelen.

58. I have treated the concept of *bilde* in "'Ein schoenez bilde': Walther von der Vogelweide and the Idea of Image," *From Symbol to Mimesis: The Generation of Walther von der Vogelweide*, ed. Franz H. Bäuml, Göppinger Arbeiten zur Germanistik (Göppingen: Kümmerle, 1984).

59. In essence, because she is perceived as an image, people make an image of her and then are later startled when it does not congrue with reality. For example, Antoinette Fierz-Monnier, *Initiation und Wandlung: Zur Geschichte des altfranzösischen Romans im zwölften Jahrhundert von Chrétien de Troyes zu Renaut de Beaujeu*, Studium Romanicorum Collectiones Turicensis, 5 (Bern: Francke, 1951), p. 30, notes concerning Chrétien's depiction of Erec's reaction to Enide's outburst: "Blitzartig wird es ihm bewusst, dass Enide mit dem Bilde, das er sich von ihr gemacht hat, nicht übereinstimmt."

60. Three, of course, is a number with many positive associations and one that occurs frequently in medieval romance, as a result of its association with the Harrowing of Hell tradition. Internally within Hartmann's works, I link the sheltering "drî

buochen" ("three beeches") with the facilitating "driu krut" ("three herbs") of

61. See George Frederick Kunz, *The Curious Lore of Precious Stones* (New York: Dover, 1971), pp. 162, 168.

62. Heine, p. 110, notes that "just as Erec baffles others by his unusual behavior on the Probefahrt, so now he finds himself confronted by a virtual double whose motives seem equally obscure."

63. Petrus W. Tax, "Studien zum Symbolischen in Hartmanns *Erec*: Eine ritterliche Erhöhung," *Wirkendes Wort*, 13 (1963), 281, remarks concerning this line: "er gehört also durchaus zu den Sapientes."

64. Concerning the phrase "bî den liuten," Kuhn, p. 145, states,
> Wahrhaft vollkommene Minne ist erst die, die nicht sich in geniessendem Besitz abschliesst, sondern in der Welt bewährt und bestätigt! Man muss aus dem verschlossenen Freudegarten heraus, muss in draussen in der Welt als innerlichen Besitz neu ich schenken lassen.

Bayer, p. 284, sees in *Erec* the influence of Waldensian piety, with the result that Erec's "bî den liuten" speech is an indication of his commitment to the *"vita communis,"* "das sozial-aktive Leben." And, looking ahead to *Grêgôrius*, I should like to point out that incest happens away from people, for the brother begins to caress his sister "mê dan vor den liuten" (l. 376; "more than his wont in the eyes of men"—p. 43; literally: "more than when other people were around").

65. Heine, p. 111, adds the following insight concerning Mâbonagrîn's explanation of his situation:
> Mâbonagrîn's claims of innocence are also at odds with his bizarre practice of displaying his trophies, the heads of his victims. For someone who complains of his unpleasant task, he has fulfilled his duty with gruesome thoroughness.

66. See H. Bernard Willson, "Sin and Redemption in Hartmann's *Erec*," *Germanic Review*, 33 (1958), 5-14, especially p. 13:
> Hartmann's poem is a poem of love in the fullest sense. Salvation and self-sacrificial love are inseparable. The highest degree of *caritas* can redeem from sin. It is redemption. . . . The loving grace of God, through Enite, is *caritas*.

67. Carne, p. 128, posits the following situation:
> Auf echt weibliche Weise beginnt sie ein Gespräch über Heimat und Verwandte. Die Verwandtschaft, die sich zwischen beiden herausstellt, ist auch symbolisch zu deuten: Enite versteht es, sich der Fremden menschlich zu nähern, ihr entgegenzukommen und eine Beziehung herzustellen.

Enîte does know how to approach and ingratiate herself with new acquaintances, but Carne is mistaken in limiting interest in origins and kinship to females in Hartmann's works, as many scenes involve males who reveal their lands and noble heritage to each other, as, for example, Koralus and Erec and subsequently Erec and Guivreiz do to each other.

68. I do not find central the argument of Cramer, p. 105, who holds that "Erecs und Enites aventiuren-Fahrt muss die Funktion haben, die beiden Protagonisten sozial gleichzustellen." Moreover F.P. Pickering, "The 'Fortune' of Hartmann's *Erec*," *German Life and Letters*, 30 (1977), 95, makes an unconvincing case that

> Erec is ... successful, not because he is or becomes over the course of his trials a perfect knight with a social conscience, and so deserves his success. He succeeds because he takes his chances, and because he recognizes when the moment has come to risk the gambler's throw, all or nothing.

69. See ll. 38, 41, 47, 126, 218, 360, 422, 459, 586, 659, 703, 1080, 1355, 1423, 1502, 1750, 2672, 2835, 3151, 3617, 3736, 3946, 3983, 3979, 4058, 4075, 4119, 4177, 4293, 4449, 4473, 4475, 4522, 4694, 4743, 4752, 4791, 4824, 4828, 5172, 5222, 5438, 5451, 5844, 5844, 5863, 5939, 6195, 6495, 6529, 6535, 6602, 6612, 6720, 6869, 7056, 7119, 7519, 7803, 7826, 7929, 7948, 7953, 7958, 7985, 7990, 7996, 7998, 8096, 8116, 8160, 8166, 8321, 8371, 8387, 8460, 8520, 8661, 8714, 8748, 8861, 8886, 8948, 9242, 9358, 9371, 9649, 9715, 9795, 9884, 9910

70. I include under the *denken* group *bedenken*, erdenken, and *gedenken*, as well as the noun *gedanc*. See ll. 264, 531, 582, 931, 960, 1094, 1205, 1353, 1806, 1872, 2249, 2254, 2545, 2788, 3004, 3024, 3167, 3353, 3485, 3669, 3672, 3719, 3972, 4030, 4239, 4366, 4412, 462956, 4935, 4998, 5050, 5949, 5999, 6061, 6235, 6355, 6711, 6719, 6735, 7197, 7243, 7757, 7779, 7798, 8120, 8147, 8294, 8350, 9183, 9190, 9194, 9230, 9274, 9491, 9499.

71. See ll. 314, 501, 564, 619, 673, 718, 899, 906, 970, 983, 1057, 1230, 1361, 2104, 2265, 2280, 2730, 2836, 2845, 2925, 3002, 3079, 3148, 3167, 3221, 3702, 3745, 3780, 3828, 3853, 3957, 3960, 3973, 4129, 4140, 4304, 4443, 4646, 4689, 4739, 4755, 5127, 5242, 5291, 5373, 5742, 5777, 5811, 6291, 6395, 7186, 7351, 7374, 7961, 8049, 8119, 8294, 8404, 8436, 8483, 8868, 9101, 9394, 9439, 9446, 9515, 9685, 9702, 9786, 9851, 10091.

72. I include in the group as well words such as *vernemen*, *ahten*, and *verstehen*, as they are used by Hartmann to indicate perceptual recognition. See ll. 66, 245, 470, 472, 644, 1182, 2522, 2571, 3032, 3033, 3050, 3243, 3311, 3327, 3338, 3604, 3613, 3685, 3998, 4412, 4550, 4665, 4908, 5041, 5698, 6201, 6609, 6614, 8049.

73. Adjectival and noun forms are included in this listing. See, for wisdom, ll. 88, 100, 250, 387, 1592, 1595, 2521, 2816, 3439, 4189, 4827, 5232, 5850, 6480, 7443, 7468, 7498, 7511, 7537, 8633, 10085. For folly, see ll. 5448, 5960, 5965, 5966, 6491, 6505, 6519, 6532, 7010, 7012, 7013, 8480, 8702, 9005, 9030, 9044.

74. See ll. 479, 495, 508, 609, 632, 907, 975, 3150, 3371, 3908, 3937, 3981, 4616, 4654, 4993, 7672, 7635, 7974, 8001, 8035, 8402, 8412, 8510, 8582, 8980, 8984, 9826.

75. I also include in a partial listing of this large group the words *wort, klaffen, galm, rede, antwurt, vrâgen,* and their related forms. See ll. 44, 45, 76, 83, 577, 1086, 1452, 1458, 1459, 1895, 2403, 2521, 2713, 2723, 2727, 2737, 2812, 2833, 2844, 3034, 3035, 3041, 3042, 3044, 3047, 3051, 3052, 3093, 3099, 3146, 3147, 3181, 3184, 3185, 3222, 3240, 3374, 3375, 3379, 3421, 3734, 3807, 3816, 3839, 3964, 4300, 4301, 4468, 4509, 4679, 4838, 4839, 4985, 5107, 5224, 5373, 5454, 5455, 5466, 5467, 5824, 6287, 6420, 6458, 6508, 6509, 6510, 6551, 6595, 7007, 7054, 7055, 7454, 7455, 7500, 7501, 7518, 7519, 7592, 7593, 7668, 7830, 7831, 7895, 7992, 7993, 8306, 8307, 8391, 8464, 8465, 8692, 9689, 9736, 9737.

CHAPTER 3. GREGORIUS

1. In this study I will not concentrate on the work's prologue, but I will make occasional reference to it. See Anke Bennholdt-Thomsen, "Die allegorischen *kleit* im *Gregorius*-Prolog," *Euphorion*, 56 (1962), 174-84, for a treatment of ll. 97-143. Bennholdt-Thomsen contends that these lines do more than retell the Good Samaritan story, as she draws parallels both to the Prodigal Son story (Luke 15:11) and to Bede, where spes and terror are interpreted as the meanings of *oleum* and *vinum*.

2. Hartmann's poems contain many advice givers, ranging from Lûnete in *Iwein* to Guivreiz in *Erec*, to the king, the wise old man/advisor, and the abbot in *Grêgôrius*. Carl Lofmark, "The Advisor's Guilt in Courtly Literature," *German Life and Letters*, 24 (1970-1), 7, contends that "the importance of heeding good advice is too deeply rooted in the medieval outlook to apply only as an alibi for kings. It is one of the major virtues of any good man, as Hartmann explains in *Iwein* (ll. 2153ff.)."

3. H.B. Willson, "*Amor inordinata* in Hartmann's *Grêgorîus*," *Speculum*, 41 (1966), 104, states concerning the incest theme: "Hartmann could scarcely have chosen a more effective symbol than incest to underline the perversion represented by inordinate love, whatever may be the form it takes in man separated from God by sin."

4. See Harold D. Dickerson, "Hartmann's *Grêgorîus*: An Alternate Reading," in *Wege der Worte: Festschrift für Wolfgang Fleischhauer: anlässlich seines 65. Geburtstags und des 40. Jahres seines Wirkens als Professor der deutschen Philologie an der Ohio State University mit Beiträgen von Freunden, Kollegen und Schülern* (Cologne: Böhlau, 1978), p. 85, who asserts:

> On a simple level, the ivory tablet serves as a letter of introduction for the young Gregorius. But it is more . . . the point I want to make is that the tablet serves a double function: it both preserves and externalizes the dark circumstances surrounding

Gregorius' birth by transforming them into a material substance which Gregorius can both touch and carry on his person.

5. Tobin, p. 35, appropriately comments: "Thus the incest takes on the characterization of a *felix culpa* because a greater good paradoxically arises out of evil."

6. In speaking of the nature of sin in *Grêgôrius*, Dickerson, p. 179, points out that:

> Though a necessary tool for understanding any medieval work, the theological approach has 'ironically' helped to foster in the minds of many students the false idea that this is the only approach and that Hartmann's works are somehow irrelevant to the problems of our non-theological age. To be sure, Gregorius stems from a time that had an unshakeable belief in God's grace. But this need not preclude the possibility of an alternative, non-theological reading which would focus on the existential dilemma that lies at the heart of the poem.

He further argues that

> In other words, we should address ourselves to the question that Hartmann himself poses: How does one achieve grace in a world so treacherous that an exemplary figure like Gregorius can unknowingly commit no less a crime than incest with his own mother?

Many scholars have concerned themselves with the matter of guilt and sin in Hartmann's works, among them: Hans Siegfried, "Der Schuldbegriff im *Gregorius* und im *Armen Heinrich* Hartmanns von Aue," *Euphorion*, 65 (1971), 162-82; Naohiko Tonomura, "Zur Schuldfrage im *Grêgorîus* Hartmanns von Aue," *Wirkendes Wort*, 18 (1968), 1-17.

7. With respect to the waves and water symbolism, Dickerson, p. 186, offers a valuable insight:

> The sea has a threefold prominence in Gregorius' life: first, when his mother sets him adrift in the tiny casket; second, when he sails from the island monastery; and third, when the fisherman takes him to his rock of atonement. It would do the poem an injustice to simply dismiss the sea as a symbol of life's journey: it is much more. The sea is a self-referential symbol which links together the various stations in Gregorius' life. But as a life symbol it becomes even more convincing when we consider that this unfathomable ocean of life is permeated with evil. Thus it is no accident that the monastery and the rock of atonement, literally the two high points

in Gregorius' religious development, are islands. Both are outposts of good in an ocean of evil.

8. Dickerson, p. 182, makes the following distinction: "Gregorius did not inherit his father's guilt; he was the victim of a diabolical irony and was doomed to repeat the crime of his father."

9. Dickerson, p. 181, comments concerning the concealment of the child: "The implication here is that if their crime can be concealed from society, it will somehow disappear and their honor will remain intact. In other words, without objective proof there was no crime." With respect to the disappearance of the husband/brother, there is valuable insight to be gained from Bruno Bettelheim, *The Uses of Enchantment: The Meaning and Importance of Fairy Tales* (New York: Knopf, 1977), p. 196, who notes how, in fairy tales, the concept of "wishing away" a person is represented by the death of that person, and this is clearly applicable to this situation in *Grêgôrius*, which itself contains a great number of fairy tale resonances, not only the features of the evil stepmother, the "two brothers" theme, the "brother and sister" theme, but also the choice of a "new pope" motif and the Oedipal theme—which is so basic to the interpretation of fairy tales. Palmer, pp. 78ff., discusses fairy tale motifs in *Erec*. See also David Blamires, "Fairytale Analogues to *Der arme Heinrich*," in *Hartmann von Aue: Changing Perspectives*, ed. Timothy McFarland and Silvia Ranawake, Göppinger Arbeiten zur Germanistik, 486 (Göppingen: Kümmerle, 1988), 187-98.

10. The "foundness" of Grêgôrius is not only marked later when he is revealed to be a foundling (ll. 1337, 1399, 1411) but is also stressed continually in the frequent reference to finding things that are associated with Grêgôrius: "und ob sîn vindaere / alsô kristen waere" (ll. 743-4; "And, should the finder wish to be / Truly a Christian"—p. 63); "dâ vunden si eine barke" (l. 781; "They found . . . a bark"—p. 65); "vunden si ûf der vreise / sweben des kindes barke" (ll. 954-5; "Upon the seething sea they found / The infant's little bark afloat"—p. 77); "ir vundene sache" (l. 974; "their find"—p. 77); "wie si ez vunden ûf dem sê" (l. 1028; "how they'd found it out at sea"—p. 81); "und lobete got des vundes" (l. 1049; "he praised God on high / that the infant had been found"—p. 81); "Daz kindelîn si vunden" (l. 1051; "the little child that they had found"—p. 81).

11. Dickerson, p. 186, notes how the casket is "not only watertight but airtight" and sees it as "the first station in Gregorius' long journey where he is hermetically sealed off from the rest of the world."

12. I would also add that this one child, Grêgôrius functions almost like a guilty thought in the mind: the underlying message is that the truth will out.

13. Ingrid Hahn, "Hartmanns *Büchlein*-Zitat im *Gregorius*," in *Sagen mit Sinne: Festschrift für Marie-Luise Dittrich zum 65. Geburtstag* (Göppingen: Alfred Kümmerle, 1976), p. 96, notes that Grêgôrius'

justification for being a knight comes from *Das Büchlein* (ll. 781-4, 738, 743; referred to in this study as *Die Klage*).

14. The consequences of Grêgôrius' rejection of the religious life are explored by K. Dieter Goebel, *Untersuchungen zum Aufbau und Schuldproblem in Hartmanns Gregorius,* Philologische Studien und Quellen, 28 (Berlin: Erich Schmidt, 1974), p. 65, when he notes: "Indem Gregorius sich vom Kloster abwendet, trifft er eine Entscheidung, mit der er sich auf von Gott abwendet." Moreover (p. 66), he sees Grêgôrius' having left the monastery as running parallel to the mother's straying from her vow to love only Christ. Peter Wapnewski, "Der *Gregorius* in Hartmanns Werk," *Zeitschrift für deutsche Philologie*, 80 (1961), 243, comments:

> Gregorius ist aus dem ihm durch Geburt und Schicksal bestimmten *ordo* ausgebrochen. Er handelt dem mütterlichen Gebot zuwider, missachtet den väterlichen Rat des Abtes und fährt in die Welt, in die ihn die *gir* treibt, die *cupiditas*, die—nach Augustin— Folge der menschlichen Ursünde ist, der *superbia*.

15. W.J. McCann, "Gregorius's Interview with the Abbot: A Comparative Study," *Modern Language Review*, 73 (1978), 93, states in this connection that

> Gregorius has simply out-argued the abbot, rather than disproved any of his contentions, and the dispute could be seen as one between the robust, though by no means simple, faith and patience of the abbot and the impatience and dialectic skill of Gregorius.

16. Salmon, p. 815, points out concerning Hartmann's lyric output, that "Hartmann's most striking rhetorical practice is, however, probably his indulgence in word-play," and I contend that this fondness carries over into his longer poems. I too think it likely that Hartmann's sense of language is much more finely honed than has been believed. For articles dealing with the awareness of his scrupulous sense of language, see: Rolf Endres, "Die Bedeutung von güete und die Diesseitigkeit der Artusromane Hartmanns," *Deutsche Vierteljahrsschrift für Literaturwissenschaft und Geistesgeschichte*, 44 (1970), 595-612; and Larry Robert Granlin, "*Guot, güete, unguot, guttât*: A Word Study in Hartmann's Gregorius," *Modern Language Notes*, 88 (1973), 927-46.

17. H.B. Willson, "Hartmann's *Gregorius* and the Parable of the Good Samaritan," *Modern Landguage Review*, 54 (1959), 198, points out that "Gregorius's parents are, like Adam and Eve, of the same flesh and blood." This would lend strength to the argument that Gregorius falls into sin because as a man, as a child of Adam, he simply will sin. Supporting this reading is Armin Meng, *Vom Sinn des ritterlichen Abenteuers bei Hartmann von Aue* (Zürich: Juris, 1967), p. 83.

18. Brian Murdoch, "Hartmann's *Gregorius* and the Quest of Life," *New German Studies*, 6 (1978), notes that Adam is referred to in Middle High German religious poetry as *der ellende* ("the exile," in effect, "the man without a country").

19. K.C. King, "The Mother's Guilt in Hartmann's *Gregorius*," in *Medieval German Studies Presented to Frederick Norman* (London: University of London Institute of Germanic Studies, 1965), pp. 92-3, makes the following point:

> They both act in a way which not only seems justified to them in the circumstances in which they find themselves but which is also in accordance with an acknowledged way of life; nevertheless they both fall into sin, and sin of a particularly heinous nature, namely, incest. Hartmann's purpose is not to criticize the behavior of either mother or son, nor, particularly, the mode of life which could lead such 'good' people into such sin; it is to show that where there is true repentance forgiveness is never impossible.

20. K. Goebel, pp. 92, 93, draws correspondences between the first and second incest scenes in terms of "1) frohes Zusammenleben, 2) Wandlung bei der Frau, 3) Fragen des Mannes: 'waz wirret dir?', 4) Klageszene, 5) in die Klageszene eingeschobener Kommentar des Erzählers, 6) die Frau bemüht sich um 'rât,' 7) Bussanweisung, 8) Scheidung."

21. Carne, p. 113, notes the literalmindedness of the fisher: "Er ist letzten Endes immer der Mensch, der äussere Beweise braucht."

22. Elisabeth Gössmann, "Typus der Heilsgeschichte oder Opfer morbider Gesellschaftsordnung? Ein Forschungsbereicht zum Schuldproblem in Hartmanns *Gregorius*," *Euphorion*, 68 (1974), 43, distinguishes with respect to Grêgôrius' sin and redemption between four schools of interpretation: 1) "theologisierende Interpretationen," 2) "theologische Interpretationen," 3) "literaturwissenschaftliche / philologische Interpretationen," and 4) "sozialgeschichtlich orientierte Interpretationen."

23. Hartmann notes in this connection: "daz tet er mêre umbe ir guot / dan durch sînen milten muot" (ll. 3269-70; "Their wealth caused him to play this part, / And not the kindness of his heart"—p. 205).

24. Bettelheim, p. 53, states that "Except that God is central, many Bible stories can be recognized as very similar to fairy tales," and *Grêgôrius*, if not a Bible story, is sufficiently grounded in religion that we may apply Bettelheim's assertion to it.

25. With respect to the cyclical fashion of the narrative, K. Goebel holds that *Grêgôrius* is more than a saint's legend (p. 9) and exhibits a basic structure of separation and reunion (p. 10). Ulrich Ernst, "Der Antagonismus von *vita carnalis* und *vita spiritualis* im *Gregorius* Hartmanns von Aue: Versuch einer Werkdeutung im

Horizont der patristischen und monastischen Tradition, Teil 2," *Euphorion*, 73 (1979), 97, notes that, at the final return: "Für seine Mutter ist er Kind, Gatte und geistlicher Vater (Papst, Beichtvater), während sie für ihn Kind (Beichtkind), Frau und Mutter ist."

26. Ul*rich Ernst*, "Der Antagonismus von *vita carnalis und vita spiritualis* im *Gregorius* Hartmanns von Aue: Versuch einer Werkdeutung im Horizont der patristischen und monastischen Tradition," *Euphorion*, 72 (1968), 160-226, presents a well-argued and scrupulously documented exposition of the applicability to *Grêgôrius* of the following oppositions: *gloria caelestis* vs. *gloria saecularis*, *vita carnalis* vs. *vita spiritualis*, *civitas Dei* vs. *civitas diaboli*. He also sees a dichotomy between the "hässliche Schönheit" of Grêgôrius at the work's end and the "schöne Hässlichkeit" of the sister at the work's outset (p. 195).

27. Erhard Dorn, *Der sündige Heilige in der Legende des Mittelalters*, Medium Aevum, 10 (Munich: Fink, 1967), p. 18, sees Grêgôrius as "das hervorragende Beispiel einer Sünderheiligen-Legende in deutscher Sprache."

28. *Grêgôrius*, then, demonstrates the medieval romance principle that "you can go back home again"—if you have changed sufficiently—yet illustrates it with surprising economy. Like a mind that returns again and again to a thought not fully worked out, the narrative repeatedly circles back to a meeting of Grêgôrius and his origins/quest/end—that is, his mother/wife/child. Goebel, p. 24, notes the telling difference between Grêgôrius' final meeting with his mother and their earlier incestuous relationship: "Der Hauptunterschied lautet also: Verbindung, die alsbald wieder getrennt wird; Bekenntnis führt zu einer glücklichen und dauernden Vereinigung."

CHAPTER 4. DER ARME HEINRICH

1. Gross, p. 18, notes that "Im *Gregor* handelt es sich um das 'das' der Existenz der Seele, im *a. Heinrich* handelt es sich um das 'wie'."

2. An interesting stylistic feature crops up in the prologue and contributes to the mood of authority that Hartmann consciously creates. "Dâ"-compounds abound ("dar an"—ll. 3, 8, 20; "dâ mite"—ll. 10, 14; and "dar umbe"—l. 18) and work to create the impression of logic, precision in location and argumentation, and ties from the narrator to things in the wider world. All are conventional attributes of authority.

3. And these lines hark back to a similar phrasing at the conclusion of *Grêgôrius*:

> 'Hartman, der sîn arbeit
> an diz liet hât geleit
> gote und iu ze minnen
> der gert dar an gewinnen
> daz ir im lât gevallen

ze lône von in allen
die ez hoeren oder lesen
daz si im bittende wesen
daz im diu saelde geschehe
daz er iuch nach gesehe
in dem himelrîche'

(ll. 3989-99; "Hartmann, who berhymed this tale with effort that it might avail to God's pleasure and to yours, too, desires that there may be due, in reward for what he's done, this reward from everyone, from those who hear and those who read his tale: that each one pray and plead that this good fortune him betide: In Heaven he will see you and abide in that Kingdom without end"—p. 249).

4. Green, p. 796, calls attention to Hartmann's predilection for resorting to "praise on the brink of disaster."

5. J.A. Hunter, "'Sam Jôben den rîchen': Hartmann's *Der arme Heinrich* and the *Book of Job*," *Modern Language Review*, 68 (1973), 363, sees Heinrich and Job (the Job of the Dialogue and not the Job of the Prologue) as having parallel reactions, but he notes (p. 361) that, "In comparison with Job, however, it is abundantly clear that one vital element is lacking, namely fear of the Lord."

6. The allusion to "dem miste" (l. 131; "the dunghill"—p. 24) calls to mind the familiar fable-situation of the Late Middle Ages: the pearl in the dung heap. I am not positing here a connection to fable collections, such as Boner's *Edelsteine*, but am suggesting that *mist* ("manure") works in both instances in a very similar way upon the reader's expectations: it becomes emblematic of both a fall and a promise of arising from that fall. That, in a nutshell, is what *Der arme Heinrich* is all about.

7. With respect to hopes of a cure, Philip Anderson, "Court and Anti-Court in Hartmann von Aue's *Der arme Heinrich*," *New German Studies*, 7 (1969), p. 174, points out that "His aventiuren lead him not to jousts with wicked knights but to symbolic jousts in Montpellier and Salerno, the centres of medical learning, with doctors who 'defeat' him by telling him he cannot be cured." As a leper, he is defeated. With respect to the disease, Kurt Ruh, "Hartmanns '*Armer Heinrich*.' Erzählmodell und theologische Implikation," in *Mediaevalia litteraria: Festschrift Helmut de Boor*, ed. Ursula Hennig and Herbert Kolb (Munich: Beck, 1971), pp. 316ff., discusses medieval legends that treat leprosy and comes to the conclusion that *Der arme Heinrich* presents an integration of two different variants of "Aussatzlegende." For a more encompassing historical treatment of leprosy in the Middle Ages, see Saul Nathaniel Brody, *The Disease of the Soul: Leprosy in Medieval Literature* (Ithaca: Cornell University Press, 1974).

8. The idea of a clearing is important, as shall become apparent in the subsequent chapter's reading of *Iwein*, where clearings function as enclosures for strife, even as the mind holds

contention. The reader knows that a spiritual battle will be joined in Heinrich's clearing. Thum, p. 4-7, speaks in historical terms to the phenomenon of clearing forests.

9. See S.L. Clark and Julian N. Wasserman, "Language, Silence, and Wisdom in Chrétien's *Erec et Enide*," *Michigan Academician*, 9,iii (1977), 289-98, for an exposition of this technique in Chrétien.

10. Ann Snow, "Heinrich and Mark, Two Medieval Voyeurs," *Euphorion*, 66 (1972), 113-27, demonstrates that Heinrich suddenly sees the girl in a new light: as marriageable. Tobin, p. 96, adds that "this seeing through the wall is the real moment of in-sight which leads to [Heinrich's] conversion." See also Martin H. Jones, "Changing Perspectives on the Maiden in *Der arme Heinrich*," in *Hartmann von Aue: Changing Perspectives*, ed. Timothy McFarland and Silvia Ranawake, Göppinger Arbeiten zur Germanistik, 486, pp. 211-31.

11. H.B. Willson, "*Inordinatio* in the Marriage of the Hero in Hartmann's *Iwein*," *Modern Philology*, 68 (1970-71), 252, makes a statement concerning *caritas*, "the supreme Christian virtue," that is applicable as well to *Der arme Heinrich*.

12. William C. McDonald, "The Maiden in Hartmann's *Armen Heinrich*: Enite *redux*?" *Deutsche Vierteljahrsschrift für Literaturwissenschaft und Geistesgeschichte*, 53 (1979), notes the similarity between the two figures, points out that "Both women have an encounter with a cutting edge (Enite with Erec's sword, the 'maget' with the surgeon's knife)" (p. 44) and that each work contains a "foiled death scene" (p. 46).

13. Carne, p. 51, calls attention to the fact that "Auch Mabonagrin entführt seine Geliebte als Elfjährige."

14. J.E. Cirlot, *A Dictionary of Symbols*, trans. Jack Sage (New York: Philosophical Library, 1962), p. 106.

15. To support this hypothesis, I note that Hartmann earlier has the ill-intentioned fisher describe what Grêgôrius' feet should look like, if he were in fact as committed to austerity as he should be (ll. 2917ff.; p. 185). The idea that the feet should reflect man's inner state draws from the function of the foot to keep man upright, and to "stand" in some sense for his soul.

16. Timothy Buck, "Hartmann's 'reine maget,'" *German Life and Letters*, 18 (1964-65), 170, asks:
> Is she genuinely altruistic? Her religious fervour and the manner in which it finds expression are such that we are left wondering whether she is still in fact concerned with her parents and Heinrich or whether she has not come to regard her lord's affliction simply as the means whereby she can achieve her goal of an early salvation.

17. See Sandra M. Gilbert and Susan Gubar, *The Madwoman in the Attic: The Woman Writer and the Nineteenth-Century Literary Imagination* (New Haven: Yale University Press, 1979), pp. 51-64, 69,

71, 72, 74, 76, for a discussion of the link between disease and disease.

18. Ernest Rose, "Problems of Medieval Psychology as Presented in the 'klein gemahel' of *Heinrich the Unfortunate*," *Germanic Review*, 22 (1947), 185, comments upon ll. 700-2: "Such verses use medieval words, but they betray the same sense of confusion which usually seizes a modern girl at her first becoming aware of her senses. Such verses express a kind of inner vertigo in medieval terms, a medieval puberty." Arnold Shirokauer, "Zur Interpretation des *Armen Heinrich*," *Zeitschrift für deutsches Altertum*, 83 (1951-52), 64, takes into account the maiden's age (she is eleven) and notes that Gottfried (*Tristan*, ll. 17136ff.) states concerning the Minnegrotte: "Ich hân die fossiure erkant sît mînen eilif jâren ê." The age of the *maget* in *der arme Heinrich* is also compared to that of Mâbonagrîn's lady and to that of Grêgôrius, who was an excellent *grammaticus* at the time that he was "an sîme einleften jâre" (ll. 1183, 1181; "on reaching his eleventh year"—p. 89). Clearly, eleven years seems to be the age of wisdom: it is a code for knowledge, be it carnal or intellectual.

19. It was earlier noted that the maiden may be flattering her parents by appealing to their sense of vanity at having produced such a beautiful child—and "beautiful" children play such important roles in Hartmann's works and in medieval works in general. It is not far-fetched to suggest that the maiden's description of Christ as "ein vrîer bûman" (l. 775; "a free farmer"—p. 29) can have special self-referential appeal to her father, an earthly ploughman himself ("ein vrîer bûman"—l. 269; a "free farmer"—p. 25).

20. Seiffert jocularly labels her "Hartmann's peasant princess" (p. 7).

21. See Bettelheim, pp. 225ff.

22. Anderson, p. 180, states in this connection: "For the girl, Christ appears as the Heavenly Farmer, Heaven as the Farm-Without-Care."

23. I have argued this point in "The Manipulated Image: Walther von der Vogelweide's 51,13," *Rice University Studies*, 62 (1976), 17-28.

24. Particularly interesting is the maiden's description of how nature can undo in a half day what years of labor have accomplished:

> 'ze dem wil ich mich ziehen
> und solhen bû vliehen
> den der schûr und der hagel sleht
> und der wâc abe tweht,
> mit dem man ringet und ie ranc.
> swaz man daz jâr alsô lanc
> dar ûf garbeiten mac,
> daz verliuset schiere ein halber tac.
> den bû den wil ich lâzen:
> er sî von mir verwâzen'

> (ll. 789-97; "'I want to go there and shun the
> farms that are beaten by thunderstorms and hail and
> washed by the floods with which one has always
> had to contend--where that for which one has
> worked all year can be quickly lost, in half a day. A
> curse on such husbandry! I want to leave it behind
> me'"—p. 29).

Reduced to a bare-bones situation, this is precisely what happens in the fountain area and its environs in Iwein. The reactions of the inhabitants at the destruction wrought by "hagel . . . regen" (l. 659) ranges from Ascalôn's rage,

> 'nu wie sihe ich mînen walt stân!
> den hât ir mir verderbet
> und mîn wilt ersterbet
> und mîn gevügele verjaget'
> (l. 716-9; "'Look at my forest! You have
> destroyed it, killed the animals, and driven away
> the wild fowl'"—p. 63).

to the populace's angry resignation:

> 'vervluochet müezer iemer wesen',
> sprach dâ wîp unde man,
> 'der ie von êrste began
> bûwen hin ze lande'"
> (ll. 7812-5; "'Damned be forever who first
> settled this land!'" cried all the people there'"—p.
> 145).

Violation/implantation/impregnation seem to go hand in hand in Hartmann's works. He knows his symbols well, and one gains in the process a graphic picture of appropriation of territory and women, which are often linked.

    25. Buck, p. 173, argues, and I do not agree with him that
> Even if we accept that Hartmann may have
> possessed insight into the workings of the
> adolescent sub-conscious mind, it is hardly feasible
> that he would have chosen to invalidate the
> carefully-expounded religious motivation of her
> sacrifice and thus parody in grotesque fashion that
> same Christian objective of eternal life which he
> earnestly represents to his audience at the poem's
> close as man's ultimate goal: "den lôn [daz êwige
> rîch] den si dâ nâmen, / des helfe uns got, âmen"
> ("May this at the end be our lot. God help us to gain
> the reward they received"—Buehne, p. 35).

    26. Cast as a good perceiver ("erhôrte"—l. 460; "marhte"—l. 468; "heard," "noted"—p. 26), she is also a thinker who knows the wisdom of her sacrifice.

    27. See Donald Atwater, *The Dictionary of Saints* (Baltimore: Penguin, 1965), pp. 250-1.

    28. Anderson, p. 177, states:

> Hartmann clearly points out that her willingness to sacrifice herself for Heinrich comes from her erotic love. Unable to be married to him in reality, even after three years of their 'play-marriage', she conceives the idea of sacrificing her life for his.

29. K. Goebel, p. 12, notes Hartmann's use of retarding moments in *Grêgôrius*, and I would suggest that the tempo of this scene in *Der arme Heinrich* also draws from this technique.

30. Anderson, pp. 182-3, comments concerning these lines:
> Here we have an 'erotic conversion' such as can be found in *Erec*, *Gregorius*, and *Iwein*. Erec was first attracted to Enite when he saw her in tattered and ragged clothes, with which she was scarcely able to cover herself (*Erec*, ll. 324-38). Gregorius' parents were similarly attracted to each other (*Gregorius*, ll. 323ff.). And Iwein is first ensnared by *minne* when he sees Laudine tearing her clothes in anguish and thereby exposing her body (*Iwein*, ll. 1310ff., 1331-2).

31. The attitude toward sacrifice in *Der arme Heinrich* calls forth echoes of the Old and the New Law, with the cutting out of the heart representing a sacrifice much like Isaac's, and Heinrich's intervention—and giving up hope for a cure, with death a certain result—evoking Christ's self-sacrifice.

32. For an excellent treatment of cinematic technique, see Alain Renoir, "Descriptive Technique in *Sir Gawain and the Green Knight*," *Orbis Litterarum*, 13 (1958), 126-32. Renoir's article opened windows for me as a critic for which I am very grateful.

33. Björn Andersson, "*Der arme Heinrich*: Zum Elan der Spannung einer Dichtung des Mittelalters," *Studia Neophilologica*, 52 (1980), 346, comments on Hartmann's technique of establishing tension: "Es ist eines der ausgeprägtesten Mittel zur Erzeugung von Spannung: die Wette mit der Zeit, ein Geschehen, das der Katastrophe zueilt, und der Held, der es abwenden soll."

34. Schirokauer, p. 63, has noticed another manifestation of this technique in *Der arme Heinrich*:
> Der ganze Absatz *daH*. 295-348 lebt ja von dem dialektischen Spiel mit den Wörtern *kint* und *maget*: 302-3; 330-1 folgen sie unmittelbar aufeinander, bis schliesslich in 341-2 die Wortpaarung in *gemahel*: *maget* gipfelt. Der Sinn dieses Jonglierens ist offenkundig der, die Grenze der Begriffe von Kind und Magd zu verwischen und anzudeuten, dieses Kind sei in seelischer Beziehung, *an witze, eine maget*, womit schon auf eine Bedingung des Arztes von Salerno (v. 224) ansgepielt ist.

35. Werner Fechter, "Über den '*Armen Heinrich*' Hartmanns von Aue," *Euphorion*, 49 (1955), 21, speaks to Hartmann's selectivity of vision in noting that, "Die Jahreszeiten, die das Bild einer Landschaft stark bestimmen, scheinen nicht vorhanden zu sein.

Dagegen spielen Nacht und Morgen eine sinnerhellende Rolle, freilich ohne Mond und Sterne oder die aufgehende Sonne." It is as fascinating to me to see what a writer leaves out as what he/she includes, and the delineating of times of day is particularly noted in *Der arme Heinrich*, while the passage of time over space (for example, the journey to and from Salerno) receives short shrift.

36. But the reader is not given access to the maiden's thoughts, and it is almost as if she fades from the story. Buck, pp. 173-4, notes how the maid in *Der arme Heinrich* recedes from the center of the narrative to become "entirely passive."

37. Rolf Endres, "Heinrichs *hôchvart*," *Euphorion*, 61 (1967), 267-94, gives a good, close reading of the poem and draws on the concept of *superbia* in Bernard of Clairvaux's *De gradibus humilitatis et superbiae*. Endres links Heinrich's condition with that of Adam, whose sin is "der unbewusste Ungehorsam gegen ein ihm unbekanntes Gebot Gottes" (p. 276). He goes on to comment concerning Heinrich: "der weltfrohe Heinrich lebt in einem Zustand, der dem einer heidnischen Glaubenslosigkeit sehr ähnlich ist." Only when Heinrich leaves it all "an got" (l. 1352; "to God"—p. 33) do things begin to get better for him.

38. Hilda Swinburne, "The Miracle in *Der arme Heinrich*," *German Life and Letters*, 22 (1969), 205, points out in this connection:
> More than eighty lines have intervened since the stopping of the operation, and the talk and actions contained in these lines demand the passage of some time, at least some hours. This not only shows that Sir Henry's decision is permanent; it also makes clear that it is not the case that Sir Henry's change of heart immediately draws from God the reward of the miraculous cure.

39. Peter Wapnewski, "Poor Henry—Poor Job: A Contribution to the Discussion of Hartmann von Aue's so-called Conversion to an Anti-Courtly Attitude," in *The Epic in Medieval Society: Aesthetic and Moral Values*, ed. Harald Scholler (Tübingen: Niemeyer, 1977), p. 215, comments concerning this marriage: "Heinrich's marriage is such that it must appear scandalous to the social consciousness of the feudal era. It is a scandal which Hartmann depicts consciously as such."

40. For comments upon the maiden's status, see Karl Heinz Borck, "'Nû ist si vrî als ich dâ bin': Bemerkungen zu Hartmanns *Armen Heinrich*," in *Medium aevum deutsch: Beiträge zur deutschen Literatur des hohen und späten Mittelalters: Festschrift für Kurt Ruh zum 65. Geburtstag*, ed. Dietrich Huschenbett (Tübingen: Niemeyer, 1979), pp. 37-50.

41. Timothy Buck, "Heinrich's *Metanoia*: Intention and Practice in *Der arme Heinrich*," *Modern Language Review*, 60 (1965), 391, points out that "While the central theme of *Der arme Heinrich* is manifestly the knight's conversion from godlessness to 'eine niuwe güete,' there is disagreement among Hartmann scholars as to whether

this conversion is a gradual or a sudden *metanoia*." Buck's conclusion (p. 394) that "Heinrich's *metanoia*, then, is, in effect, a sudden transformation of his whole being." I agree that there is a suddenness in which Heinrich "sees"; yet, the way for this revelation has been prepared by Heinrich's obvious affection for the maiden.

42. See Mircea Eliade, *The Rites and Symbols of Initiation: The Mysteries of Birth to Rebirth*, Harper Torchbooks, 1236 (New York: Harper, 1 965), p. 125.

43. The case of Chaucer's *Man of Law's Tale* comes to mind, where Constance journeys widely, marries, and produces the heir Rome needs. See S.L. Clark and Julian N. Wasserman, "Constance as Romance and Folk Heroine in Chaucer's *Man of Law's Tale*," *Rice University Studies*, 64 (1978), 13-24.

44. Anderson, pp. 170-1, looks at Heinrich's roller-coaster ride in the eyes of society in terms of the innate capabilities of that society:

> The court, as Hartmann sees it, is a noble society which is the repository of aristocratic ideals. It is, furthermore, passive rather than active: the knight is responsible for living up to its ideals and bears the responsibility for protecting himself from the pitfalls it presents. The court honours Heinrich for his achievements but is unable to warn him of his impending doom. In reaction to his failure to maintain a perfect life, and because he has failed to understand his role in the court, he goes into exile. While living on a peasant's farm, he creates an anti-court for himself—an unintentional inversion of the court he has left. Only when he has re-established himself as a true knight does God's redeeming grace allow him to return to his rightful place in society. This conflict of court and anti-court is the basis for Hartmann's story.

45. Hugo Kuhn, "Hartmann von Aue als Dichter," *Der Deutschunterricht*, 5,ii (1953), 14, stresses Hartmann's didacticism: "Was wollte also Hartmann als Dichter? Offenbar etwas im Grunde Ernstes, fast zu Ernstes: Lehren, belehren und bessern."

46. B. Andersson, p. 338, speaks to the clean lines of the work when he notes: "Der Grundriss *des Armen Heinrich* zeigt im Bau grosse Harmonie. Da ist anfangs das Problem, um dessen Lösung sich die Handlung, ohne Abschweifungen, dreht; am Ende die Lösung, Läuterung des Siechen."

CHAPTER FIVE: IWEIN

1. Roman Polsakiewicz, "Zur Chronologie der epischen Werke Hartmanns von Aue," *Euphorion*, 71 (1977), 91, posits the following chronology: *Büchlein, Erec, Iwein I, Grêgôrius, Der arme Heinrich, Iwein II*.

2. Sacker, p. 25, notes the parallel between "waenlich" (l. 2433; "to be hoped for"—p. 85) and "waenlich" (l. 8148; "[that was] to be expected [here]"—p. 149).

3. Critics have only recently begun to investigate the implications of landscape and topography in Hartmann's works. See Heinrich Siefken, "'Der saelden strâze': Zum Motiv der zwei Wege bei Hartmann von Aue," *Euphorion*, 61 (1967), 1-21; and Joachim Schröder, *Zur Darstellung und Funktion der Schauplätze in den Artusromanen Hartmanns von Aue*, Göppinger Arbeiten zur Germanistik, 61 (Göppingen: Kümmerle, 1972). Siefken's work mostly treats *Grêgôrius*, although it does consider the choice of paths in *Iwein* (p. 13), and Schröder's study catalogs *topoi* and settings in both *Erec* and *Iwein*.

4. For a numerically structured analysis of *Iwein*, see Joachim Berger, "Der Aufbau von Hartmanns *Iwein*," *Amsterdamer Beiträge zur älteren Germanistik*, 8 (1975), 33-57. Superfluity in composition is out of the question not only on thematic but also on structural grounds, as Berger impressively demonstrates.

5. Robert E. Lewis, *Symbolism in Hartmann's Iwein*, Göppinger Arbeiten zur Germanistik, 154 (Göppingen: Kümmerle, 1975), p. 47, states:
> Since battles do occur throughout the work, it is possible to see them as natural symbols. In each case the physical opponents would symbolize the cause for which they are fighting . . . . Although the resolution of conflicts in is consistently decided in favor of one of the two parties, this resolution is not always found in combat itself. The Iwein-Gawein battle is unresolved, but Artus decides the conflict between the two sisters.

6. See S.L. Clark and Julian N. Wasserman, "Conflict and Resolution: Implications of Enclosure in Chrétien's *Yvain*," *Essays in Literature*, 8 (1981), 63-72.

7. An excellent source-book for the concept of enclosure is: Roberta D. Cornelius, *The Figurative Castle: A Study in the Medieval Allegory of the Edifice with Especial Reference to Religious Writings*, diss., Bryn Mawr, 1930. See, especially, pp. 1-13.

8. L. Pearce, "Relationships in Hartmann's *Iwein*," *Seminar*, 6 (1970), 19, considers the castle "as womb symbol, and penetrating into its interior is an image for sexual conquest." Cornelius, pp. 14ff., discusses the body as vessel and, in pp. 10-3, treats the castle as an allegorical edifice.

9. Fritz Peter Knapp, "Hartmann von Aue und die Tradition der platonischen Anthropologie im Mittelalter," *Deutsche*

Vierteljahrsschrift für Literaturwisssenschaft und Geistesgeschichte, 46 (1972), 234ff., considers the heart/body topos in depth.

10. Cornelius, pp. 20ff., discusses the traditional role of "the body as a house or castle with the five senses as the wardens of the soul" (p. 20). One should also note in this connection that Hartmann sets up a telling relationship between Iwein's body and his eyes that closely mirrors the relationship between the room in which Iwein is confined and the windows that allow him to see Laudîne. In the patristic tradition, Artin, p. 187, notes that "the windows of Ambrose's figure are the eyes."

11. Sacker, p. 5, makes a convincing point concerning the description of the Arthurian court:
> If one took as a criterion the actions of the various members of the Round Table (and not the statements made about them), one might well conclude that this company consisted of a weak and passive king, a number of well-intentioned but quite useless knights— whose seneschal Keii is not even well-intentioned— and Gawein: a hero whose great abilities are perpetually misdirected.

12. Hartmann is quite given to these homely nature allusions, of which Enîte's transplanted tree is one and *Die Klage*'s "driu krut" ("three herbs") and nut under the shell are others. While Kâlogrenant's *mist* ("dung"/"manure") and *hornûz* ("hornet") examples are more pointed, the others are softer and work at times in an almost endearing fashion.

13. J.M. Clifton-Everest, "Christian Allegory in Hartmann's *Iwein*," *Germanic Review*, 48 (1973), 251, comments concerning this tale:
> The tale of Kalogrenant has proved something of a stumbling-block for critics in the past; its only apparent connection with Iwein's story was to provide him with a mixed and rather confused motivation for his own visit to the fountain.

14. Artin, pp. 31-54, offers an illuminating discussion on the function of parabolic utterance in Hartmann's source. H.B. Willson, "Kalogrenant's Curiosity in Hartman's *Iwein*," *German Life and Letters*, 21 (1968), 295, also subscribes to an admonitory but not necessarily a parabolic reading of Kâlogrenant's story:
> In a wider sense, Hartmann, in the story told by Kalogrenant, is giving a warning to the whole company of knighthood, of which a small cross-section is actually present listening to it, a warning addressed in particular to the young knight eager to gain fame and honour among his peers and in the estimation of the ladies. It is simply that knighthood consists of much more than mere swordplay and victory over other knights in combat.

15. An excellent introduction to an understanding of the function of parables can be found in: C.H. Dodd, *The Parables of the Kingdom* (New York, 1961). See also the documentation provided by T.D. Kelly and John Irwin, "The Meaning of *Cleanness*: Parable as Effective Sign," *Mediaeval Studies*, 35 (1973), 232-60. Artin, p. 34, points out:

> The nature of parables is as though an esoteric secret were hidden from those not intended to know it, lest knowing, they should profit by it. But that expression is a likeness, not a literal statement, since parables hide the truth only to reveal it.

16. See Robertson, pp. 54-8, who discusses the medieval practice of cloaking moral meaning in pleasant narrative.

17. With respect to the several repetitions of the storm-making spring adventure, one might well consult: Günther Schweikle, "Zum *Iwein* Hartmanns von Aue: Strukturale Korrespondenzen und Oppositionen," in *Problem des Erzählers in der Weltliteratur: Festschrift für Käte Hamburger zum 75. Geburtstag am 21. September 1971*, ed. Fritz Martini (Stuttgart: Ernst Klett, 1971), pp. 1-21. Of particular note in this respect is his comment on p. 13:

> Die programmatische Funktion des Kâlogrenant-Abenteuers als Interpretationsbasis und Ausgangspunkt für die *Iwein*-Handlung wird dadurch unterstrichen. Zwar ist die dreimalige Wiedergabe des Brunnenabenteuers bei Chrestien vorgebildet, aber Hartmann prägt diese wiederum auf seine Weise um
> .... Bei Hartmann memoriert Iwein selbst die Stationen der Fahrt, wie um sich den Weg einzuprägen.... Er [hat] von der *lêre* der Kâlogrenant-Erzählung nichts erfasst.

Also of note is the following study: Peter Kern, "Interpretation der Erzählung durch Erzählung: Zur Bedeutung von Wiederholung, Variation und Umkehrung in Hartmanns 'Iwein'," *Zeitschrift für deutsche Philologie*, 92 (1973), 338-59. Leon J. Gilbert, "Symmetrical Composition in Hartmann's 'froun Lûneten rât,'" *Modern Language Notes*, 83 (1968), 430-4, considers the repetition of the "brunnen" sequence along the lines of numerical composition.

18. Hartmann is not content merely to let the physical terrain and its inhabitants occupy the hero's mind and the thoughts that shape and people it, but also demonstrates that the mind actively molds the outer world that it perceives. The relationship of thought and action will operate both from commission of an action to recollection of that action, and from contemplation of an action to its actual commission.

19. Thomas Cramer, "*Saelde* und *êre* in Hartmanns *Iwein*," *Euphorion*, 60 (1966), 34, notes that Iwein's adventure is no real *âventiure*, since he seeks it out; it does not, significantly, befall him in the traditional medieval sense that adventures are to come to one.

20. For a discussion of this figure, see Paul Salmon, "The Wild Man in *Iwein* and Medieval Descriptive Technique," *Modern Language Review*, 56 (1961), 520-8.

21. Schweikle, p. 8, offers the following incisive commentary:
> Die Komik, die Chrestien bei der Unkenntnis des Waldmenschen ausspielt, wird bei Hartmann anders pointiert. Bei ihm wirkt weniger der unwissende Waldmensch komisch also vielmehr Kâlogrenants simple *aventiure* Definition.

22. Sacker, p. 8, goes so far as to describe this definition of knighthood as defining a "primitive and brutish code of behavior."

23. This would seem to hold true for Laudîne as well, since her initial concern that the fountain have a strong protector gives way to her later anguish at losing Iwein in particular. She speaks of Ascalôn in terms of his "'kraft'" and "'manheit'" (ll. 1386; "'strength and courage'"—p. 71), and he is said to be "'der aller tiureste man'" (l.1455; "'the bravest and most generous knight who ever lived'"—p. 72; I would add here that "the rarest male prize" might be a more accurate translation), as well as "'der beste'" (l. 1475; "'the best [of men]'"—p. 72). Both of the latter appelations must be colored by other references in the work, for one recalls that Lûnete convinces Laudîne to take Iwein on the reasoning that the victor is "'tiurre'" ("'more worthy'") than the defeated, and that there is an extended play on words made by Queen Guinevere at the outset of the romance that characterizes Keiî as the one who holds the "'boeste'" ("'basest'") to be the "'beste'" ("'best, most worthy'"), and vice versa, which proves significant indeed in that Keiî and Ascalôn are bested by Iwein. Laudîne applies these laudatory terms to her former protector, but her superlatives are shown in their testing to be only comparatives. She has not only misjudged Iwein's martial abilities, but also on accepting him as her spouse, on marital grounds, she is also unaware of the nature of the love that she could come to share with him.

24. This is but one of many examples of Hartmann's use of an axiomatic statement. Salmon, p. 814, calls attention to Hartmann's "use of the axiom."

25. It should be noted that Erec recalls his shame at the treatment of the dwarf (l. 931; p. 41), and this is not unlike Iwein's mind returning to Keiî, the motivating force for his adventure.

26. Accordingly, Hartmann allows Iwein to think about her, and the verbs bear out the fact that she has entered his mind: "er gedâhte: 'wie gesihe ich sî'" (l. 1425; "'How can I get to see her?'"—p. 23) and "er gedâhte in sînem muote" (l. 1609; "He thought to himself"—p. 74).

27. Pearce, p. 19, notes:
> In Laudîne's terms, any male who succeeds in forcing his way into the castle is regarded automatically as a hostile and dangerous violator of her self-inflicted

seclusion, a foreign body who must be expelled as soon as possible, and she turns on him in a rage.

28. My former graduate student, Lois Pressler Duewall, first called my attention to Hartmann's use of descriptive attributes, a phenomenon noted in passing by Cramer, p. 44. Both Iwein and Laudîne possess *geburt, jugent, tugent* ("high birth, youth, and virtue"), etc., and this is one indication that they are well suited, since they share so many qualities.

29. Willson, "*Inordinatio* in *Iwein*," p. 245, comments upon women: "*unstaete* they most certainly are, but, strange and paradoxical as it may seem, this *unstaete* is a sign of their fundamental goodness, of their *triuwe*."

30. A fascinating study could be done on Hartmann's use of sex and age stereotypes not only in Iwein but also in the other four long narrative works. What is considered *manlîch* ("manly") or *wîplîch* ("feminine") or *kintlîch* ("childish, childlike") is not always internally consistent, and Hartmann, as is elsewhere the case, reveals a sophistication that recent criticism is coming to recognize.

31. Lunête laments to Iwein: "'wan ich bin leider ein wîp'" (l. 4072; "'I am only a woman'"—p. 103); and the wronged younger sister cries out in frustration to the older sister, "'ichn vihte nit, ich bin ein wîp'" (l. 5649; "'Since I am a woman, I can't fight myself'"—p. 122).

32. The actual physical battles are waged by men whose "manliness"/"bravery" is continually extolled (see particularly ll. 5725, 5834, 6374, 6731, 6944, 7101, 7104, 7236, and 7389; pp. 122ff.), yet there is reason to believe that Hartmann may hold knightly strife to be foolish and nonproductive (see the consummate *âventiure*—ll. 530-7; p. 61) and possibly even wrong: "her Iwein jaget in âne zuht" (l. 1056; "forgetting his courtly manners"—p. 67). Paul Salmon, "'Ane zuht': Hartmann von Aue's Criticism of Iwein," *Modern Language Review*, 69 (1974), 556-61, does not view the phrase *âne zuht* as negatively as many critics have, for he sees it as a logical rhyme for *fluht*. Also interesting in this respect is the discussion of manslaughter in Christian J. Gellinek, "Iwein's Duel and Laudine's Marriage," in *The Epic in Medieval Society: Aesthetic and Moral Values*, ed. Harald Scholler (Tübingen: Niemeyer, 1977), pp. 226-39.

33. The spokespersons of the Arthurian court are generally male: Gâwein, Arthur himself. Both men are shown in the work as either making foolish decisions or convincing others to make them.

34. See Renate Schusky, "Lûnete--eine 'kupplerische Dienerin'?" *Euphorion*, 71 (1977), 23, 25. Lewis, p. 23, calls her "a marriage broker and a schemer," and Dittmann, p. 159, sees her as "die komödiantisch-intrigenreiche Kammerzofe." For a study that presents many worthwhile insights into her role, see Anne-Marie Tar, *Die Funktion der Hauptzofen in Yvain, Iwein, und Tristan*, M.A. Rice, 1982.

35. Ernst von Reusner, "Iwein," *Deutsche Vierteljahrsschrift für Literatur und Geisteswissenschaft*, 46 (1972), 500-1, also calls attention to the identification of Laudîne with the fountain. What proves additionally of interest is that Laudîne sees the man bound up in the land as well (see ll. 2319-20; p. "[she must] quickly choose a husband or lose the land"—p. 83). Lewis, p. 68, concludes: "The *brunne* thus comes to symbolize not only Laudîne herself, but also her vulnerability to the outside world."

36. Tar argues convincingly that Lûnete represents reason, which tempers the rashness that Iwein exhibits and Laudîne displays.

37. Sacker, p. 13, shows considerable insight in noting:
> If he had his way, marriage would involve him in no responsibilities at all, but his wife would just be one more trophy of his buccaneering career, taken down from the shelf occasionally to be dusted and shown to his friends. Laudine's one great contribution to their mutual development is her refusal of this solution.

38. I first recall hearing this formulation in a classroom lecture given during the fall of 1970 by W.T.H. Jackson in his Medieval Literature Graduate Seminar in Germanics at Rutgers University.

39. See Willson, "Kâlogrenant's Curiosity," p. 294: "[Iwein] has no more concern for the feelings of others than had Kâlogrenant. Like him, he has only the overriding urge to gain fame and honour for himself."

40. To remember the fountain and Laudîne is, in effect, to return to them.

41. Von Ertzdorff, p. 143, notes concerning this omission: "Iwein had ein Eid gebrochen, der in an die Rückkehr spätestens nach Jahresfrist band. Dieses und nichts anderes ist die Schuld Iweins nach der Darstellung beider Dichter."

42. Nor does he think of his love. Thought's role in love is emphasized in these lines from Hartmann's lyric works:
> Niemen ist ein saelic man
> ze dirre werlte wan der eine
> der nie liebes teil gewan
> und ouch dar nâch gedenket kleine
>
> (ll. MF 214, 12-5; "No one is blessed in this world except one who never experienced love and also doesn't think about it very much").

Not having success at love and thinking very little about it are linked: they bring happiness rather than experience and mental activity. It is a rather bitter statement that Hartmann makes in these lines, and he advocates its opposite in *Iwein*, where thinking and loving are linked.

43. It should be noted in connection with Grêgôrius, Hartmann makes much of the verb *vergezzen* ("to forget"). In *Iwein*, the line

"daz er sîn selbes vergaz" (l. 3091; "he forgot where he was"--p. 92) comes when the hero remembers Laudîne, and it is appropriate that his reaction at first seeing her, when he is trapped between the portcullises, is virtually identical: "daz er sîn selbes gar vergaz" (l. 1337; "[love] robbed him of reason"—p. 71).

44. Hartmann also notes: "in hâte sîn selbes swert erslagen" (l. 3224; "he had been struck down by his own sword"—p. 94), and Seiffert, p. 9, notes the linkage between this line and *MF* 206,9 in "mîn selbes swert" ("my own sword").

45. See Batts, p. 44:
> By tearing off his clothes, however, he has stripped off the skin, as it were, of his former self, and his rebirth is thus possible as a man now untrammeled by social obligations from his past life. This rebirth is signified by his being anointed from head to foot and his donning new garments.

Humphrey Milnes, "The Play of Opposites in *Iwein*," *German Life and Letters*, 14 (1960), 241, comments: "When Iwein later goes out of his mind, the visual attributes of knighthood fall from him before our very eyes."

46. Jutta Goheen, "'Bistuz Iwein, oder wer?' Hartmanns letztes Epos als Spätwerk," *Amsterdamer Beiträge zur älteren Germanistik*, 7 (1974), 67, comments concerning this monologue: "Iwein begegnet im Monolog sich selbst, nicht einem nach Aussen verlegten Abbild, wie es die Suche nach dem Vater, die Begegnung mit dem Freund verkörpern."

47. It should be noted that this recollection is not without the strife so characteristic in Hartmann's use of landscape, and Iwein's exclamation, "'ez turniert al mîn sin'" (l. 3574; "my mind is full of jousting'"—p. 98) is brilliantly appropriate. Incidentally, it echoes with a slight variation Grêgôrius' outburst when he announces that he has read so much of knighthood "'ze den buochen'" (l. 1583; "[in] books"—p. 111) that "'sô turnierte ie mîn gedanc'" (l. 1584; "'I always jousted in my mind'"—p. 111).

48. Wolfgang Mohr, "Iwein's Wahnsinn: Die Aventiure und ihr 'Sinn,'" *Zeitschrift für deutsches Altertum*, 100 (1971), 74-5, states: "Das Wort *panser* (und *pansif*) gehört vor allem in die Terminologie der damals modernen Minnepsychologie. Im Mittelhochdeutschen entspricht *gedenken, sich verdenken, verdaht, gedanc*." Hartmann is no doubt aware that his use of "thought-terms" belongs to the tradition, but it is my contention that he uses this as a basis for his *Iwein*, in which the theme of mind plays such a large role. Through "thought-terms" Hartmann can link mental strife and the considerations that arise with respect to physical battles.

49. To substantiate this, consider the sudden appearance of terms of mind at this point in the narrative: "er gedâhte: 'ich bedarf wol meisterschaft'" (l. 4870; "'I really need wisdom to decide [what would be better]'")—p. 112); "Dar under gedâhter iedoch" (l. 6555; "[in the midst of this rejoicing] he nevertheless paid mind"—

my translation); and "dar er dâ vor gedâhte" (l. 6870; "as he had earlier planned"—my translation").

50. See George T. Gillespie, *A Catalogue of Persons Named in Germanic Heroic Literature (700-1600) Including Named Animals and Objects and Ethnic Names* (Oxford: Oxford University Press, 1973), p. 87, who lists an "Iwân von Tuscân."

51. Poor Lûnete has come into disfavor because her skill in advising no longer earns plaudits; those who have accepted, encouraged, and even begged for her advice are too short-sighted to see any but immediate benefits of it.

52. One should also note here that the time/choice sequence is altered, because Iwein does not have to choose whom to save and when, as he had to do previously when he had to choose between the lion and the dragon. Now events flow smoothly, and Iwein can dispatch giants as well as Lûnete's tormentors in the short space of one morning. Artin, p. 25, adds another point concerning the fluidity (the expandability and compressibility) of time in medieval romance:

> We can explain the unreality of time in Arthurian romance in similar terms: events are related spiritually; time, though it has great symbolic significance, has no convincing reality as causal or sequential order among events.

53. Thomas Elwood Hart, "The Structure of *Iwein* and Tectonic Research: What Evidence, Which Methods?" *Colloquia Germanica*, 10 (1976-77), 109-10, points out in this connection:

> Kalogrenant's obvious superficial understanding of the concept [of *âventiure*] provides a foil for the deeper meaning exemplified by Iwein's experiences in the remainder of the poem. For although Kalogrenant's adventure furnishes the initial impulse for all that follows, and is in fact repeated by Iwein step for step up to the magic fountain, whatever adventure is sought for its own sake, that is, in Kalogrenant's sense of the word, the immediate consequences are negative. And ultimately it is only his insight which leads to Iwein's return home and forgveness. In other words, just as it is with the *wilder man* of Kalogrenant's tale whose questions reveal the superficiality of Kalogrenant's concept of *aventiure*, so too it is only Iwein's ostracism and life as a *wilder man* that reveal to him the deeper ethical responsibilities which should inform a knight's behavior.

54. Lewis, pp. 97-8, analyzes Laudîne's "inability to recognize" Iwein. "Her mind is so closed to the possibility of Iwein changing that she does not for a moment consider that the stranger before her could be Iwein."

55. This is, in fact, the attitude of the giant whom he defeats, and it is an attitude widespread in medieval romance. One recalls that Herzeloyde in Wolfram's *Parzival* is insistent that she be claimed by the knight who has defeated all others.

56. H.B. Willson, "Love and Charity in Hartmann's *Iwein*," *Modern Language Review*, 57 (1962), 224, comments:
> There is no more significant episode in the whole poem than this drawn battle . . . . plurality gives place to unity, two become one in friendship once more, a reunion which leads to a reconciliation between the two sisters, however reluctant the one may be.

Gertrud Jaron Lewis, "*Daz häzliche spil* im *Iwein*: Ein Beispiel der Erzählkunst Hartmanns von Aue," *Seminar*, 9 (1973), 97-108, treats the rhetorical devices, metaphors, and ornate style of the fight between Iwein and Gâwein.

57. Harms, p. 127, correctly points out that "Im Kampf gegen Gawein ist Iwein angesichts des ganzen Artushofes der Vertreter des Rechts, das der Artushof zu schützen nicht imstande ist."

58. The *vaz/haz* ("vessel"/"enmity") linkage has surfaced as well in *Die Klage* (ll. 1321-2).

59. In keeping with Hartmann's use of words with double meanings, *unkünde* proves significant, for Lexer documents meanings that touch physical as well as spiritual bases: "Unkenntnis, Unbekanntschaft, fremdes Land."

60. Harms, pp. 122f. also calls special attention to Erec's non-recognition of his friend, Guivreiz, in Erec.

61. As noted earlier, the lion, clearly a representation of Iwein's perceptual and mental faculties as well as of physical courage, is able to break through a wall to save a life, just as Heinrich is able to see through a wall in time to stop a sacrifice. In the final analysis, Hartmann demonstrates that walls can be penetrated.

62. For Laudîne, too, Iwein's final return to the spring will have important implications. The return and reconciliation signal that Laudîne's mind is firmly disposed toward Iwein. He is ensconced in her mind, despite obvious reservations and regrets that she has voiced; the immediate conflict has been resolved, but that does not mean that all doubt has been removed or that complete trust has been restored. Rather, doubt's role and also love's role in smoothing doubt have been recognized. The arena of the mind that has seen inner debate now witnesses resolution. The changing of Laudîne's mine, which results in her decision to take Iwein back, has not been without difficulties and setbacks, but Hartmann assures the reader that right change is for the best. For this reason he takes pains to defend woman's so-called changeable mind (ll. 1883ff.; p. 77) and to show that men like Iwein, who are held to be "unwandelbaere" (l. 5352; "steadfast"—p. 94) ought to question their obdurate stance.

63. Hartwig Mayer, "*Topoi* des Verschweigens und der Kürzung im höfischen Epos," in *Getempert und gemischet: Festschrift Wolfgang Mohr* (Göppingen: Kümmerle, 1972), p. 231, notes Hartmann's employment of "der Unsagbarkeitstopos" and, on p. 235, his use of "der Unwissenheitstopos." Related to these *topoi* are statements of authorial inability to do justice to a certain situation or emotion. A representative example of Hartmann's profession of authorial inadequacy occurs in *Grêgôrius*, ll. 2635 (p. 169).

64. Von Ertzdorff, p. 156, would disagree with this statement, for she contends that "Iwein—und Laudine—reifen in der Prüfung zur *rehten güete* und finden *saelde und ere* wieder. Beide sind in ihrer neuen Vollkommenheit weiser, gelassener, und wissender geworden." I can agree with her qualifications that both have matured, but I sense a hesitancy on Hartmann's part that Jackson, p. 79, also notes. If the narrator

> remains always at some distance from the action (though the distance varies more sharply than it does in *Erec* from phase to phase in the work), it is because he is less confident than the narrator of *Erec* that he has all the relevant information, and also less convinced, when he comes to look back on the entire story, of its exemplary truth.